MR. JEFFERSON'S LOST CAUSE

How much better to have every 160 acres settled by an able-bodied militia man, than by purchasers with their hordes of Negroes, to add weakness instead of strength.

—Thomas Jefferson to Albert Gallatin,
December 24, 1807

MR. JEFFERSON'S
LOST CAUSE

*Land, Farmers, Slavery,
and the Louisiana Purchase*

ROGER G. KENNEDY

OXFORD
UNIVERSITY PRESS

2003

OXFORD
UNIVERSITY PRESS

Oxford   New York
Auckland   Bangkok   Buenos Aires   Cape Town   Chennai
Dar es Salaam   Delhi   Hong Kong   Istanbul   Karachi   Kolkata
Kuala Lumpur   Madrid   Melbourne   Mexico City   Mumbai   Nairobi
São Paulo   Shanghai   Taipei   Tokyo   Toronto

Published by Oxford University Press, Inc.
198 Madison Avenue, New York, New York 10016

www.oup.com

Oxford is a registered trademark of Oxford University Press

Library of Congress Cataloging-in-Publication Data
Kennedy, Roger G.
Mr. Jefferson's lost cause : land, farmers, slavery, and
the Louisiana Purchase / Roger G. Kennedy
p. cm.
Includes bibliographical references and index.
ISBN 0-19-515347-2
1. Louisiana Purchase.
2. Jefferson, Thomas, 1743–1826—Views on slavery.
3. Jefferson, Thomas, 1743–1826—Influence.
4. United States—Territorial expansion.
5. United States—Politics and government—1775–1783.
6. United States—Politics and government—1783–1865.
7. Slavery—United States—Extension to the territories.
8. Plantation owners—United States—Political activity—History.
9. Family farms—United States—History.
10. Land settlement—Political aspects—United States—History.
I. Title.
E333 .K46   2003   973.4'6'092—dc21   2002027402

1 3 5 7 9 8 6 4 2
Printed in the United States of America
on acid-free paper

Once again, for Frances

Contents

CONTENTS

CONTENTS

CONTENTS

Acknowledgments

Because I have been at this work for half a century, and at this book in particular for a decade, I despair of being able to recall everyone who has helped along the way, though I think especially of Henry Ammon, Gary Anderson, Randolph Campbell, Edward Cashin, William Coker, William Cronon, Douglas Egerton, Jack Elliott, Philip Deloria, Douglas Erwin, Daniel Feller, Daniel Gelo, Woody Holton, Jim and Lois Horton, Charles Hudson, Peter Kastor, Kenneth Lockridge, Archie McDonald, D. W. Meinig, Mimi Miller, Peter Onuf, Barbara Oberg, Susan Stein, Daniel Schaefer, Terry Sharrar, John Stagg, Richard White, Patty Limerick, Ann Fiddler, Andrew Cayton, Gavin Wright, Daniel Usner, Anthony Wallace, E. O. Wilson, Pete Daniel, and Michael Zuckerman. My wife, Frances Kennedy, is a good historian on her own and has made every part of this process possible by kindly criticism and by keeping me both alive and happy. Thomas LeBien began looking at this material some years ago when at the Oxford University Press, and his suggestions nucleated the beginnings of a book out of a morass of ideas and passages. Susan Ferber at Oxford has done both the heavy work of editing it and the heavier work of convincing me to dispose of great chunks that did not fit. She is an excellent critic. Without her there would be no book before you. Once again, India Cooper demonstrated that copy editors may have minds of their own—fine minds, richly furnished with learning. I am indebted to librarians at the Library of Congress, the New York Public Library, the Laboratory of Anthropology, the University of Virginia, Louisiana State University, and Harvard University.

Chronology

1803 Louisiana Purchase.

Jefferson enters alliance with Spanish authorities to have Bowles eliminated; Bowles kidnapped in June, to die in prison in 1805.

1804 Vice President Aaron Burr kills Alexander Hamilton in a duel and makes a reconnaissance of East Florida.

Dunbar and Hunter probe of the Ouachita Valley.

The Kempers assert the first Republic of West Florida.

1805 Panton, Leslie, and Forbes ("The Firm," to include their successors as partners) arrange Cherokee and Choctaw cessions to the United States.

Wilkinson's soldiers make first probe at Spanish posts on the Sabine.

September: Kemper Outrage.

1806 The Firm arranges Chickasaw cession to the United States.

July: Freeman and Custis withdraw down the Red River after confrontation with the Spanish army.

October 29 to November 4: Wilkinson negotiates Sabine Convention and turns on Aaron Burr.

1808 Jefferson's Embargo Act.

Joseph Bonaparte set upon the Spanish throne.

James Madison elected President.

1810 September 16: Father Hidalgo proclaims Mexican independence.

September 23: West Florida rebels take Baton Rouge.

October 27: President Madison issues order putting down West Florida Rebellion and acquiring Baton Rouge District.

1811 The *Cortes* in Cadiz announces intention to abolish slavery in the Spanish possessions.

December: American armed forces occupy the Gulf Coast of the present states of Louisiana and Mississippi. Governor Claiborne claims all Gulf Coast of present Alabama except town of Mobile (claim repeated by Governor Holmes in 1812).

1812 January: Invasion of East Florida begins, but in May Monroe disavows George Mathews and the East Florida "Patriots."

June: American declaration of war against Great Britain.

"The Firm" turns finally to the Americans.

1813 April: Wilkinson occupies Mobile.

1814 Andrew Jackson completes his Creek War and makes his first invasion of East Florida.

1816   Gaines's attack on Negro Fort.

            James Monroe elected President.

1817   June: Gregor MacGregor captures Amelia Island.

1818   Aury replaces MacGregor; Gaines orders Bankhead to seize Amelia Island.

            Andrew Jackson invades Florida.

1819   Adams-Onis Treaty solemnizes Jackson's conquest of Florida.

1824   John Quincy Adams elected President.

1828   Andrew Jackson elected President.

1836   Texas declares its independence from Mexico.

1845   Texas merged into the United States. Florida also admitted as a slave state.

1861   The South, including Florida and Texas, seeks to secede from the Union.

MR. JEFFERSON'S LOST CAUSE

PART ONE
The Land and Mr. Jefferson

The land is where we live and where the consequences of our presence accumulate, determining what else we can do, and what we can no longer do. The land is thus the book of our lives. Each day we write upon it new pages, some splendid, some sordid, informing our progeny of the truth about us whatever we may write elsewhere.

The book of printed pages you hold calls attention to a chapter in the book of the American land, written between 1776 and 1826. Choices were made by those controlling the government of the United States, and the governments of its territories and states, determining whether or not slavery would be permitted within their boundaries. In 1803, the Louisiana Purchase doubled the extent of the territory conceded by the European powers to lie within the United States; through arrangements made as part of that acquisition, slavery was given fresh encouragement in Louisiana and permitted to expand up the Mississippi Valley. A momentum of events began, eventuating in 1861 in an attempted division of the Union by slave owners, slave sellers, and those they could convince to follow their lead. They so detested the prospect of restriction upon the continued spread of their system of forced labor that they sought to take the states they controlled out of the United States.

They had been threatening to do so since the 1780s. They had raised the specter of disunion to have their way when the nation was placed under constitutional government in 1787, when the Southwest Territories were chartered in 1787–89, when Kentucky adopted its constitution in 1792, and when Mississippi Territory was organized in 1802.*

*No real effort was made to press plantations into the Northwest Territories, as we shall see.

I

From 1784 through 1804, as each new area was opened to slavery, eloquent men and women argued that keeping people in bondage was inconsistent with the nation's founding documents. In 1805, the necessity to organize the domain purchased in 1803 from Napoleon detonated a two-year debate as to how land-use and labor-use might also determine civil society. The contention increased in ferocity as portions of the Purchase became the slave states of Louisiana, Arkansas, and Missouri. Their admission took place before the death of Jefferson in 1826.

Until then he had remained the predominant political figure in the nation. In a series of great papers written before 1784, he had expressed in radiant language his aversion to slavery and his preference for a republic of free and independent farmers, offering proposals whereby a virtuous republic might wisely dispose of its public lands and encourage a benign labor system on those lands. In his later years he was fully informed of the choices being made but interposed no public objection as his edifice of dreams was systematically reduced to rubble. He could not escape full knowledge of the consequences for the land itself of each decision. During his own presidency (1801–9) great plantations worked by slaves engrossed more and more of the choicest portions of a quarter of a continent. He was aware of that outcome. Therefore this is a tragic story.

The tragedy was, of course, larger than the disappointment of a single man. It was a national one: the nation as a whole had it within its power, over and over again, to stop its decline into civil war.

Though responsibility for these outcomes lay with the entire nation, it fell most heavily upon the planters of Virginia led by Jefferson. They held the predominant power in the nation. Virginia was the most populous and the most extensive of all the states. George Washington, Jefferson, James Madison, and James Monroe, all drawn from Virginia's planter class, held the presidency from 1789 until 1825, except for the single term of John Adams. As new domains were acquired by purchases and wars from the Indian nations, from France, and from Spain, the preferences most affecting the allocation of that land were those of owners of large plantations worked by many slaves. The great planters saw to it that the choicest property went into the hands of people such as themselves rather than to family farmers.

These were all political decisions made by narrow majorities. Each could have been tipped to another outcome. None was inevitable. Few political choices are when great moral questions are manifestly at stake. When in these pages there is discussion of economic trends and objectives, illustrated by schedules of statistics, and when climate, soil, wind, and rain come into our discourse, they are offered to show why some decisions were easier than others, not that any were foreordained.

Here in brief are the themes of this work: none of the choices to expand the domain of slavery went uncontested within the councils of government and on the ground itself. As these decisions were made, the contestants on both sides understood that the alternative labor system to slavery was family farming. And each of the choices between planters and family farmers left effects upon the land itself, ordaining its future and that of the people of the South.

The Louisiana Purchase is the central event in this story. Thomas Jefferson is its central character.

Choices and Consequences

Thomas Jefferson was a greatly gifted teacher, but he failed to bring about the social transformation he laid before his nation of students as their great opportunity. He proclaimed two revolutions, one political and the other social. He had little to do with achieving the first and drew back from the second. He could start things but had difficulty finishing them.

He lived in a real place, in a real time, amid real people. He was not completely free to do what he liked. It is possible to determine how much freedom of action he had, and at the same time to begin assessing the effects of his action and inaction, by taking him home to Monticello. We know a great deal about the daily realities of his situation from his notebooks, and more from the accounts of a parade of visitors. Mrs. Anna Maria Thornton was one of the most acute of those observers. Coming to the scene with eyes trained as the wife of an architect and plantation owner, she was conscious of both house and land. As Jefferson's friend, she knew that when he was at home he was amid circumstances he could manage, unlike the ebullient and contentious nation he sought to lead.

The house at Monticello was his own creation, and so, to a remarkable extent, was its setting. He had shaped the mountaintop on which he situated it. In the next few pages we will follow the account in Mrs. Thornton's diary of a visit in 1802, seeking to get as close as we can to the man and the ground— in the rain. Rain is important in this story.

September is a hot month in Charlottesville, though the grip of the summer heat is being loosened by afternoon rains, some of them ferocious. When an especially severe storm is gathering power, giant clouds rear up on the horizon, sending forth red-gold flashes of lightning. The atmosphere becomes thicker and heavier, as if an invisible advance guard of those giants were stalking about pressing down their hands on human shoulders.

On one such afternoon in September 1802, Mrs. Dolley Madison, the wife of Secretary of State James Madison, and Dr. and Mrs. William Thornton drove from Mrs. Madison's plantation at Montpelier to visit President

Thomas Jefferson on his mountain at Monticello. It too was a plantation head-quarters, though the mountain itself was reserved for gardens, buildings, and parklands, not for growing staple crops. They traveled at a leisurely pace. They had good reasons to be interested not only in the President's plans for Monticello but also in the condition of Virginia's plantation economy. They were planting families, who were traveling through a countryside that had been heavily forested less than a century earlier but was now, after heavy cultivation, showing signs of erosion and exhaustion.

Dolley Madison and Anna Maria Thornton had eyes trained to detect those signs. Though city ladies, they had married into the plantation aristoc-racy—the Madison plantations lay in Virginia, Thornton's in the West Indies. Both women knew Jefferson of old. In the salons of Philadelphia they had heard him discourse on government and agriculture. Now they could see him amid the latest works of his own carpenters and gardeners. (Most of his field hands were distributed through his holdings around the county and in Bedford County, to the southwest).[1]

Despite the approaching thunder and lightning, they left their carriages and walked uphill, reaching the house and a litter of debris arising from the inchoate enthusiasms of their host. Over twenty-seven years of construction and deconstruction, of putting up and tearing down, Jefferson had demon-strated how full of invention he was for systems and designs, and how irreso-lute in execution. His house was not yet done.[2]

From the beginning he had set out to do more than provide himself an ideal habitation. He was making symbolic and pedagogic architecture, to be set upon the flattened space presented as his slaves carted away the top of the hill. They created for him a presentation-platform. This was what the Greeks had done. They too planed off topographic irregularities to offer, uncluttered, a platform like that of the Acropolis at Athens, a *temenos*. So presented, a building could teach. For the Greeks a *temenos* set before the citizenry the statue of a god, to suggest what that god might require of men. For Jefferson the humanist, such a space gave clarity to his statements of humane ideals. Monticello was not one man's monument but one man's evocation of a set of ideals for a good society. Jefferson never built without intending to teach something.[3]

As the Thorntons and Mrs. Madison came over the top of the hill onto the *temenos*, they found the columns for the contemplated portico lying upon the ground. When the doors were opened to them by Mr. Jefferson's slaves, they entered what was to become a balconied entrance hall but was still a husk of raw brick. The rain beat on the boards covering the spaces reserved for windows. A single lamp showed a ceiling still unplastered and a floor still made of planks not yet nailed in place. Though she was prepared for the house to be a little "unfinished," Mrs. Thornton later wrote in her diary, "the general gloom" unsettled her. There was, however, consolation: tea was laid in the parlor. Soon the President was presiding. He often started a discussion by referring to the portraits of philosophers and statesmen on the parlor wall.[4]

Mr. Jefferson "has altered his plan so frequently," Mrs. Thornton observed—his habit in many circumstances—having "pulled down and built, that in many parts . . . [his villa] looks like a house going to decay from the length of time it has been created." After she had left Monticello she thought back on her experience of that stormy night, of the plans-perpetually-in-progress in the midst of a ravaged countryside, and concluded that "there is something rather grand and awful, than agreeable or convenient in the whole place." There was, and continued to be, as after twenty more years the house became better and the land below worse.[5]

Rain in Virginia and Its Results

Jefferson wrote that after a storm he was wont to gaze eastward from his portico upon "mountains, forests, rocks, rivers" as the clouds parted before the sun. There on the mountaintop "we ride above the storms! How sublime to look down into the workhouse of nature." Yet in that workhouse of nature, the rainwater was still coursing down plowed ruts running up and down the tobacco-planted hillsides—that was the way the slaves plowed. Each rain widened the plow-scratches into gullies, and the next rain made the gullies into trenches.

A century earlier, when the hillsides were forested, the leaves of the trees had broken the impact of rainfall, so that it reached the ground diffused and found there a resilient and spongy mat of roots and humus. But in order to have fields to plow and plant, the planters had sent forth their crews of slaves to girdle and fell the trees and to rip away the matting with their plows. The hills were scalped and then sliced. There was not much topsoil to begin with; one planter said his had been "about as thick over the clay as the hide of an ox" and much easier to tear away. Thomas Mann Randolph, Jefferson's kinsman, was already urging contour plowing, and both Jefferson and George Washington were experimenting with heavier plows that might cut into the hardpan below the topsoil and hold a contour more firmly, yet because Virginia is a land of downpours, not of drizzles, shallow contours proved to be of small greater defensive value. After each little ridge filled to bursting, the impounded water rushed even more fiercely downhill. The streams of the Piedmont became tobacco-colored, and when they reached the Chesapeake Bay full of silt they filled the little harbors of tobacco ports such as Dumfries and Port Tobacco, while upstream "thousands of acres . . . [were left] derelict."[6]

The countryside through which the Thorntons drove toward Monticello was a "broad plain-like surface with rolling uplands everywhere cut by narrow river valleys—a lay of the land that is particularly subjected to destructive washing even under moderate rainfall." This was the "red and hilly" country Jefferson described to his French friends as "like much of the country of Champagne and Burgundy, on the route of Sens, . . . Dijon, and along the Côte to Chagny, excellently adapted to wheat, maize, and clover." But by 1790 it was no longer excellent. Much of it had washed downstream, and more was to go.[7]

The rainfall was not "moderate"; this was not France. Though only fifty to seventy inches a year might fall upon Monticello, it came in such violent bursts that it rushed to the rivers. We have no precise statistics of the volume of silt it carried in the eighteenth century, but it is likely that it was even greater than it was in the mid-twentieth, when, after much reforestation, the Potomac flooded down from such a bare watershed that half the rain falling upon it was not absorbed—and still is not. Down it goes into Chesapeake Bay, at 220,000 feet per second in spring flood (the low-water rate is about a thousand), carrying "a total of over 400 pounds of soil from every acre in its drainage basin." In 1950, the Shenandoah ranged from 380 feet per second in quiet times to 140,000 in flood; the James, from 600 feet to 97,800. When the water is high they flow as conduits of silt.[8]

The view from Monticello which seemed to be so splendid to Jefferson extends across uplands drained by the headwaters of the James, which "at a ten-foot flood crest," it was reported in 1950, "removes from 275,000 to 300,000 cubic yards of solid material during each twenty-four hours, and annually carries away between three and four million tons of material." The great storms of 1667, 1685, and 1771 caused the river to rise forty feet, conveying the topsoil of several counties into the bay. Nothing worse seemed possible. In 1790, however, Jefferson wrote of "such rains as never came . . . since Noah's flood." The relentless planting of tobacco in a wasteful system had produced great fortunes for the planters, but Jefferson now despaired that years of "clear profits will not repay the damage done to the lands." His home county was described that year as "a scene of desolation . . . farm after farm worn out, washed and gullied, so that scarcely an acre could be found in a place fit for cultivation."[9]

Lessons for Yeomen

Jefferson managed to support his old age by selling slaves to the West, after, in the words of Donald Meinig, the great political geographer of our own time, "the relentless cropping of the rolling red hills . . . brought ruin to the older districts of the Piedmont." The two counties, Albemarle and Bedford, in which he owned plantations were so thin-soiled, so roughly treated, and so frequently stricken by "heavy summer downpours" that by the time of his death they had become "a perfect waste . . . washed into gullies . . . 3 or 4 feet deep." A century later, in the Depression years of the twentieth century, they were two of the five counties in Virginia designated as most needy of restoration by the federal government. Meinig was born in those Depression years and described the Piedmont as having suffered from "the common attitude toward soils [, which] was the same as that toward the great forests and the vast flocks and herds of wildlife: they were nature's riches to be plundered by those lucky enough to get there first. When they were exhausted or unbalanced, the most common American response . . . was to pack up and move on to fresh ground in the West."[10]

The "fresh ground" was there, and still fresh because those who had actually gotten there first had left it *unexhausted* and *balanced*, and they could be dispossessed of it. We will come to how that was done, but before we wave them away we owe them a pause to recall that they had been farming thin soils under heavy rains for a long time. They had domesticated wild plants on what a thousand years later seemed to be "fresh ground." They knew how to sustain its yields without dismantling villages and moving along at anything approaching a tenth of the rate common among the planters of the nineteenth century. They treated land as if it were not cheap. They had to do the work of sustaining it themselves. In economic terms, they had many of the same disincentives to waste that were felt by yeomen farmers. That too is a point to be amplified later. We are here distinguishing the land uses characteristic of various classes among the successors to the Indians, taking note that yeomen among the European-Americans adopted more salutary conservation practices from Indians than did planters because yeomen and Indians had more in common than planters and Indians.

Rains came, whatever humans might do. If crops were to be grown, it would fall upon ground from which the shelter of trees had been removed (to some extent) and from which the sod and compost had also been removed (to some extent). Indians, and many yeomen, were tacticians rather than strategists; they dealt with the little picture. They did not have to apply general rules to vast stretches of territory so that crews of slaves could march across the scene with minimum instruction. They often farmed as if the plot before them was the last they could expect to obtain. So they left some trees in place, the largest and shadiest, the hardest to girdle and fell. Yeomen obtained metal plows as planters did, but because plows were expensive they often followed Indian example where they could, poking the earth and planting messily amid stumpage, thus doing less damage to the poultice of leaves and roots and exposing the soil beneath less perilously to erosion. Like Indians, many yeomen planted in little hillocks, amid the trees, rather than in rows stretching across denuded fields.

Pasteur, Wilson, and the Three Sisters

They might have done so two centuries later out of scientific sophistication, but folk wisdom had anticipated science. Eighteenth-century people knew that erosion washed away nutritive soil in suspension and also washed away nutrients in solution. Since the gap between what they knew and what we think we know now has been filled in stages, for a time that statement could be made without calling to the imagination little victims of erosion struggling to escape the fatal waters. In recent years, however, biological science has animated the scene of flood. We no longer talk of "nutrients" as if they were inert chemicals. There are living organisms among those nutrients, and the practices of Indians and yeomen were kinder to them—unintentionally but effectively—than those of great planters.

White subsistence farmers occupied an intermediate region still often called a frontier, though lacking the precision of a "line of occupation" or boundary. It was not continuous, and great areas of mixed populations remained well behind the farthest advances of the plantation system, in what planters regarded as less desirable land. There agriculture was conducted by people without much capital and (generally speaking) with their own labor, adapting to the demonstrable advantages of the practices of Indians similarly situated. In an intermediate culture they operated their farms otherwise than would overseers managing plantations, who worked slaves to exploit the land rapidly to produce staple crops for international markets.

Indians did not move unless they had to. They learned over millennia that they could stay put longer if they avoided planting a single crop alone or for many planting seasons. They made a practice of combining plants, such as corn, beans, and squash, letting the broad leaves of squash shelter corn roots from the sun and setting beans to grow up corn stalks. Nations as diverse as the Navajo and the Iroquois had stories about these Three Sisters and other associative and symbiotic plants. Observation—the basis of science—showed that corn, beans, and squash reinforced each other's nutritive value in the pot and also enhanced each other's growth in the field.

But each plant had to be set separately, and symbiotically. Few planters and overseers trusted slaves to do such complex tasks, and, besides, they could afford to abandon what they impoverished. However, the Three Sisters were welcome on the family farm. Why was this such a good strategy? Because it anticipated the research of Louis Pasteur and E. O. Wilson. Pasteur was three years old in the year of Jefferson's death. Before he himself died at the onset of the twentieth century, he had taught mankind about little organisms. We associate Pasteur with pasteurized milk, antibacterials, and germs, but agriculture owes a lot to him, to his microscope, and to Wilson's world of tiny living things. Wilson has taught us about the vitality and complexity of each handful of soil. Each is an ecosystem, wriggling and throbbing with lives—little lives, but lives.

A farm, whether cultivated by an Indian or a yeoman or a planter's slaves, is a congeries of microscopic jungles. Each may remain in productive balance until humans introduce exotics into it—such as a corn plant. If many corn plants are introduced, and favored by the farmer season after season, corn-loving organisms will proliferate at the expense of others. The jungle will grow sick. Cotton, tobacco, corn (or beans, or squash) set out alone year after year will "deplete" the soil of some nutrients—those that plant consumes most voraciously—and will also stimulate the crowding out of a diversity of organisms by that set which thrives with the dominant plant. Rebalancing will then require adding back lost nutrients and inserting other organisms, some as small as the inhabitants of manure and some as large as other plants. Thus rotation and restoration are different yet complementary. A preference for staying put—which anthropologists call "sedentism"—may arise from necessity or from love of the land. In either case the consequences will be governed by the laws of Dr. Wilson's jungle.

Indians moved too, when trees or game or soil was exhausted. There are no comprehensive comparable statistics, but it is a good guess that their villages in the Southeast shifted location less frequently than did slave-worked plantations, because Indian agriculture was less intrusive and destructive. So was that of white yeomen. One reason why human responses to soil depletion and sickness accelerated in the plantation system is that fire, used as a tool by all these cultures, had more profoundly deleterious effects in the hands of the planters. When fire was used together with row crops, sod-busting plows, staple crops grown without siblings, and a refusal to rest the land by rotation, it did less good and more harm. Fire lays upon the surface nutrients such as phosphorous and calcium previously stored in tree trunks, branches, leaves, and roots, as if they had been pumped there. When the soil is deep and has many nutrients to pump up, or is restored with new nutrients, it may produce crops for a long time, and fire can be brought back to do its pumping repeatedly. But that will not work if the land has been deeply depleted and eroded. As it was, fire was a sign of the advance of planters moving successively through the forests, scarcely pausing in the process—slash, burn, grow, move, slash again, burn again, grow again, move again.[11]

Yeomen, Planters, and the Land

The observation that yeomen were gentler to the land than planters is simple reporting, as supported by economic analysis. It has no moral overtones as to the preferences of yeomen, though, of course, it leads to moral conclusions as to what the welfare of the land may require of public policy. One can reach those conclusions without any commitment to the view that "those who labor in the earth are the chosen people of God, if ever he had a chosen people." Not only can we rely upon a multitude of contemporary testimonials, but we can confirm those by expectations grounded in economic analysis, without requiring "peculiar . . . virtue . . . [in] those, who . . . [worked] their own soil."[12]

The great planters won the West at second hand, appearing on the scene only after armies had swept it of its Indian defenders. Small farmers had no armies to deploy; they did their own fighting, as they did their own clearing and farm work. A yeoman would, therefore, naturally make a calculation differing from that of a planter with friends in the government, assessing in his own way the costs and benefits of staying and replenishing, as against ripping through a piece of property and moving on. A planter might never go near the frontier—Jefferson did not, nor Madison. The man who could afford to buy land in bulk and place upon it a labor force of slaves made a calculus of staying or moving different from that of a farmer for whom moving might bring death either by Indians or by a tree falling in the wrong direction when he set an axe to it.[13]

A second difference between these two sets of calculations emerged from the stock pen. A yeoman could add organic fertilizer to his fields because he had plenty of manure conveniently at hand, having collected it from the small enclosures where cows were kept to be milked or to provide beef for the family. The family farmer might grow crops for the market, but first he had "to provide food for the family and feed for the milk cow and his work stock." Thus a larger portion of his property, acre for acre, was set aside for the family garden and for stock—and more was replenished by manure—than was the case on a plantation. The family farmer, by manuring, returned more to the earth than the plantation owner, who devoted every acre he could to his cash crop and turned out the cattle to range where the staple would not grow. The family farmer grew his own food when he could, while the planter, intent on getting crops to market, would supplement food grown domestically with purchases necessary to keep slaves or mules or cattle working.[14]

The planter had money to buy new land. He also sought to get maximum return from his capital investment in slaves. So, unlike the yeoman, who lacked cash and had no slaves to keep busy, the planter bought the cheap land and kept his corps of slaves working in off-seasons. Their winter work was clearing the next summer's cropland. It might have been restoring the old, but, as Jefferson wrote, "we can buy an acre of new land cheaper than we can manure an old one."[15]

That had been true in Virginia in the 1790s and was still true a half century later in Mississippi. Land was still cheap, and slaves were still ambulatory wasting assets:

Slaves were sent out from the headquarters plantation during slack periods of the year to clear land, build cabins, and to make the general preparations necessary for a gradual transfer of farming operations from the old place to the new. . . while they were squeezing the last vestiges of profit from their capital investments in older tracts. . . . With seemingly limitless tracts of fertile land available at low prices elsewhere in Mississippi, Louisiana, Arkansas and the Texas Republic, Mississippi cotton growers had but small incentive to devote time, labor or money to soil conservation.[16]

There were additional reasons why a crew of slaves was more dangerous to the land than an equal number of yeomen farming their own land. Why were they given light plows even when it became more widely known that some contour plowing might help retain rainfall and that heavier plows would make more effective contours? Because they had no reason to be solicitous of their owners' soil or machinery. A yeoman might become attached to land he had cleared and planted, where he had chosen to live, where his children had been born and his wife had toiled beside him.

If a yeoman happened to become prosperous enough to get a new piece of equipment, such as a fancy new heavy plow, he could be trusted to care for it. Why should a slave care? And from the planter's vantage point, why give him a chance to show how little he cared? One plantation owner complained that "complicated tools, implements, or machines" not destroyed deliberately by his "hands" would be wrecked out of indifference. Scientific farming "required a higher degree of supervision than . . . planters were willing or able to provide. For similar reasons, the care of livestock and the maintenance of plantation roads, fences, buildings, and farming equipment were neglected on most plantations to an extent that would be shocking to farmers of a later age."[17]

As suggested a moment ago, small farmers took better care of their own equipment and their own land because they were without the planters' means to replace it. Being poorer, they and their families did their own work, or most of it, whereas planters could hire overseers to drive their slaves for them. A class of overseers arose to permit the plantation owners to engage in more pleasant tasks and also because many planters held many scattered properties. The Hamptons, for example, farmed properties situated in county-sized units from upcountry South Carolina through Georgia, Alabama, and Mississippi into Louisiana. Their overseers were compensated on the basis of crops produced and were likely to move their crews off one holding onto the next as soon as they had harvested the first large crops. They had little incentive to take a long view by investing in an old ravaged place. John Taylor of Carolina said of the typical overseer that "he is bribed . . . to impoverish the land. . . . The . . . lands suffer a thousand times more than tenant farmers would have done."[18]

As we go along, we will come to other reasons that explain why yeomen were kinder to the land than planters. We will also observe Jefferson's deepening silence on the matter.

Cheap Land and Slave Labor

Migration was *driven* by soil loss and soil sickening and *drawn* by cheap land. In the West, land was cheap because the cost of acquiring it was low. The Indians, lacking equivalent military technology to that possessed by those who came westward against them, and weakened by disease, were swept aside before they could develop prolonged coalitions or campaigns.

In the 1780s, European competition fell away as well. After two centuries, the French, British, Dutch, and Spaniards ceased to devote much energy to building empires in America. From 1720 onward they were engaged elsewhere, fighting nearly continuous world wars against each other until Napoleon was vanquished in 1815. By the end of the eighteenth century, Britain, the most dangerous among these offshore powers, was becoming more committed to trade than to conquest (except when conquest came very easily, as it did in Africa and the islands of the Pacific). Its American policy after 1783 was to develop a profitable exchange with the planters, leaving to them the costs of conquest and burdens of managing slaves. There was only one interruption of this policy, arising from the peculiar cobelligerency of the Americans with Napoleon during the War of 1812.

International demand for land no longer, therefore, much affected the overall pricing—including the maintenance of fleets and armies—of the vast domains acquired by the United States. The resulting cheapness of the price of that land had, however, immense consequences for the society that emerged within the area from which the Great Powers withdrew. The great historian of progressivism, Frederick Jackson Turner, assessed the availability of cheap land to be the defining blessing of American history. Blessing for whom? For Indians? For slaves? For the land itself? Cheap land was treated as disposable. Cheap things usually are. The descendants of free farmers who emigrated from Vermont or Pennsylvania to Iowa or Wisconsin naturally enough rejoice in the positive influence of cheap land on the frontier in American history. The slaves, however, had little to celebrate as they slogged westward. Nor did the Indians. In the presence of slavery, the frontier induced a migrant agricultural capitalism with results deadly both to humans and to the land itself.

The saga of the South was one of repulsion as well as of attraction. A widening expanse of exhausted soil—the shadow of the frontier—drove people westward while new lands drew them on. A thesis complementary to Turner's might be entitled "The Influence of What Followed the Frontier upon American History." The shadow had been there since the English colonists of Virginia planted tobacco in their parade ground and in the areas laid out for streets. Having sickened the arable soil within their stockade, they invaded the Indian fields outside. The Indians counterattacked, but English weapons and English diseases reduced their numbers, and within thirteen years the

English were able to buy slaves to do their work for them. Thereafter the shadow widened rapidly, as the slaves wasted the land. This disagreeable story, in which the responsibility lies with the colonists, was not that told by Jefferson in his *Notes on Virginia* and his draft of the Preamble to the Declaration of Independence.

Jefferson's version of events was that Virginia enjoyed nearly a half century of yeoman pioneering before slavery came to define the lifestyle of the planters. Jamestown was settled by the English in 1607. In his *Notes*, Jefferson wrote that he had "found no mention of Negroes in the colony until about 1650," and writers following his lead added that "scouring tillage" emerged when black slaves became available to do the scouring. In fact, however, the slaves were there by 1620 and were instructed in the tillage their masters wanted. In his draft of the Preamble, Jefferson placed the blame for their presence upon the intervention of slave sellers managed from London with the personal complicity of the King of England. What if all this had been true? What then would have been possible after independence? Relieved of the intrusive British, freed of the incrustations left upon them by kings, clergy, and commercial corruption, the planters might more easily have restored the old order, a yeoman's Virginia. And they might also have removed the slaves. But as it was, that task, to which some of them aspired, was too much for them.[19]

Scouring tillage expanded the shadow of the frontier, leaving behind it an unstable Virginia, though that is not a topic much discussed, and the impressions in the Tidewater are all to the contrary. As is often the case, the architecture put in place by people who are insecure seeks to impart the impression of long tenure and tranquility, and much is said of old families, of first families, of family houses. A title search of most of the great plantation headquarters tells another story, one calling for compassion even for plantation owners.

Architectural historians have written much in recent decades of the "impermanent housing" characteristic of the poor farmers of the Chesapeake colonies. This had to do not necessarily with their moving a lot but, instead, with their being so poor that they built fragile structures. We do not know much about comparative sedentism among the classes in the Chesapeake, but it is useful to set aside some confusing architectural symbolism and note that impermanence was not confined to the lower classes, if we are to judge by how briefly the first families of Virginia occupied their famous plantation headquarters along the York and James rivers. Many a Virginian can recite the names associated with these red-brick, beautifully proportioned mansions, yet their builders' names did not remain very long on the mailboxes—so to speak. They were a peripatetic lot, however much their hierarchic orderings of buildings—big brick central mass descending through flankers to ever smaller outbuildings—bespoke order and repose.

Many if not most tobacco-planting families ran through the fertility of their Tidewater holdings by the end of the eighteenth century, to face bankruptcy at worst and migrancy at best—unless they had speculated successfully in western lands, reverted to mercantile life, or married a scion to a merchant's daughter. Westover was built in 1730 and sold out of the Byrd family in 1814, after several decades in which it could only be retained by transfusions of cash from Mrs. Byrd's mercantile father in Philadelphia. Carter's Grove was completed about 1753 and sold less than forty years later, as was its contemporary, Betty Washington Lewis's Kenmore. The other Lewis mansion, Woodlawn, was completed in 1802, but "by 1845," we are told by the Garden Club of Virginia, it "was neglected—no white man lived there—fences were gone— patches of barely cultivated land existed—rickety cabins housed a few slaves." Stratford, completed about 1725, bade farewell to its last Lee five years before Monticello was lost to the Jeffersons.

The expansion of the plantation system into the Piedmont repeated the Tidewater sequence. The family farmers were forced out, the land was mined out, and then the planters—many of them, at any rate—moved out to face the perils of the frontier. That was better for the independent-minded than falling into dependent status where they were. Yeoman farms were first "enlarged into plantations as numerous small farmers sold their holdings at better prices than they expected to obtain and sought homesteads in frontier states or territories. . . . [T]he result was that [during] the first quarter of the nineteenth century, many counties and parishes of the upper Tidewater and Piedmont were transformed into communities with larger average land holdings, more slaves, and fewer free persons." Then that land, too, sickened, and those planters who had squeezed enough profit out of their land to buy more in the West drove their slaves ahead of them across the Appalachians or down into the upland Carolinas and Georgia.[20]

2

Washington, Jefferson, Three Worthies, and Plantation Migrancy

In the 1790s, Arthur Young, the English agronomist, began corresponding with George Washington and Thomas Jefferson, the two most celebrated American planters. Young was bold enough to ask how they explained the apparent indifference of their peers to the obvious deterioration of Virginia's capital base in land. Jefferson's response was, "We can buy an acre of new land cheaper than we can manure an old one." Washington was rueful but equally blunt: plantation management, he told Young, had become a business of seeing to it that "a piece of land is cut down," meaning stripped of its timber, and then "kept under constant cultivation, first in tobacco and then in Indian corn (two very exhausting plants), until it will yield scarcely anything" at all.[1]

That was how things had gone at Mount Vernon. Washington had done all he could to reinvigorate its yellowish soil with manure, compost, and chemical fertilizers but after a time reached the conclusion that nothing would be sufficient within the slave labor system. Three years before his death in 1799, he assessed the condition of the land and the people given into his charge and proposed that his estates both in the Tidewater and in the West be turned over to family farmers. He announced that he would be willing to parcel out his property into small holdings to be worked by yeomen—he called them "*real* farmers"—and expressed a preference that they work without slaves. Anticipating the great debate of the next century, Washington wrote that "to exclude them [slaves] . . . is not among the least inducements for dividing the farms into small lots."[2]

Washington did not use the term "yeomen," redolent of Olde England, for he had no romantic illusions about the man who labors on the land. But he had observed that "real farmers" treated their farms better than slaves treated plantations. It is arresting to note that the treatment of land mattered so much to Washington. He was early in that, as in many other things. When he died, he left provision that his slaves should be freed and sustained thereafter in

17

their old age. That was unusual, but well within the range of possibilities open to rich, influential, and powerful men of his day—Jefferson's day.

Washington and Jefferson were not abstractions or prototypes for Arthur Young or for their slaves, exemplary though each was in his way. They were men, struggling to live moral lives. They had much in common, so much that when we set these commonalities in place we can more clearly see how they differed. They were tall, two or three inches above six feet, in their prime. They were sandy-to-red-haired, though they both grew gray. They were blue-eyed, and their skin was fair: Washington's was "clear though rather colorless pale . . . and burning red in the sun"; Jefferson's was "very clear and pure" and freckled as well as reddening. It is likely that Jefferson weighed only a little less than Washington—175 pounds in mid-life, though "his slim form and delicate fibres" probably did not gain the additional twenty-five pounds gained by Washington in old age. That poundage accumulated over the plates of massive muscles felt under his uniform by those few who dared put an arm around his shoulders. (Gouverneur Morris once took a wager to do so and regretted his affront for the rest of his life.)[3]

Jefferson and Washington were the sons of two famous athletes, even larger men than they. Augustus Washington was known as "a blond giant"; Peter Jefferson was said to be able to lift a hogshead of tobacco waist high with each hand. Those fathers died when the sons were young: Jefferson was eleven, Washington fourteen. Jefferson was not fitted for the military life and avoided it; it was not to be his route to eminence. He was often reminded that he stayed so far from the fray that he was not even Odysseus to Washington's Achilles, and in response permitted himself occasional disparaging comments upon Washington's failures in the world of the salon.

> His temper was naturally irritable and high-toned. . . . His heart was not warm in its affections. . . . [H]is colloquial talents were not above mediocrity, possessing neither copiousness of ideas or fluency of words. . . . His mind was great and powerful, without being of the very first order; his penetration strong, though not as acute as that of a Newton, Bacon, or Locke, and as far as he saw, no judgement was ever sounder. He was slow in operation, being little aided by invention or imagination.[4]

There was a portrait of Washington in Jefferson's parlor, along with Newton, Bacon, and Locke—but well below them on the wall.

Jefferson's military service was limited to logistical functions as a colonel in the Virginia militia and as a wartime governor. Washington permitted himself an occasional outburst against Jefferson's refusal to be more venturesome: "Where is Jefferson?" he asked when his troops were freezing at Valley Forge and Jefferson was snug at Monticello. Yet most of the time, apparently, Washington expected no more of the philosopher-statesman than did John Quincy Adams, who said of him that he "had not the spirit of martyrdom." Adams was not referring to Jefferson's failure to risk military exposure during the Revolution. Instead, he was commenting upon his refusal to persist in action against slavery after early rebuffs, though "he saw the gross inconsistency between the principles of the Declaration of Independence and the fact of Negro slavery . . . which from his soul he abhorred."[5]

Jefferson was a fine horseman and lived much in the open, but he did not compose his body, his clothing, and his horsemanship to provide an easy field of projection for those who might have sought in him a leader of Washington's stamp. Jefferson was, instead, an intellectual statesman. He dressed, looked, and walked like one. The portraits each had painted as a young man show Jefferson to be a fashionable fellow fit for a parlor, while Washington saw to it that he was depicted as an English officer complete with the insignia of rank in the field. Washington wanted command and knew what was required in a military age to radiate authority. Though he was "wide shouldered," his tailor ensured that there was ample space about his thin chest so that his trunk was shown as bulky all the way to his wide hips. His most arresting physical attributes were his very large nose, hands, and feet. The marquis de Lafayette said that Washington had the largest hands he had ever seen—no manufactured gloves would fit them. His shoes were bateaux.[6]

Jefferson, Secretary of State in Washington's first administration, and Alexander Hamilton, Secretary of the Treasury, contended—it is often said—like siblings for the affection of Washington. That implies that the Father of His Country was old enough to be their father. He was not. Jefferson and Washington were closer in age than Jefferson and Hamilton. (Aaron Burr was Hamilton's age: they were both born in 1756 or 1757, Hamilton's date of birth is not certainly known.) Washington was born in 1732 and Jefferson in 1743. They never treated each other as father and son, as did Hamilton and Washington.

Philosophers in the Parlor and Lessons on the Land

What might Jefferson have meant by suggesting that Washington was not as "acute" as Newton, Locke, and Bacon, "my trinity of the three greatest men the world had ever produced"? What can we learn from them, as they look down upon us from the places of greatest honor in the room of greatest honor in a house Jefferson intended as instructional? Their portraits hang above all others on the unpainted plaster wall, as icons of Jeffersonian humanism. Framing them from the top was a frieze based upon a French illustration of a Roman temple, and below them, where they might in the right light be reflected, was a floor of polished beech and cherry wood.

Isaac Newton (1642–1747) sprang from a farming family but resisted all pressure to stay down on the farm, preferring instead the library and laboratory. He was severely nonpolitical, unlike his near contemporary John Locke (1632–1704). Locke, like Jefferson, was an agrarian theorist, affirming the superior qualities of working the land over all professions except, of course, those of the library and laboratory. Lockean doctrine held that the origin of all private property lay in the preemption of parcels by individual owners by working them—or, one might say, using them.[7]

If one turns from contemplating Locke's portrait to look through the windows of Jefferson's parlor to the landscape beyond, the Lockean lesson of preemption was expressed in the flattened mountaintop, the rearrangement of some native trees and flowers, and the replacement of others by a multitude of exotic plants. It was very handsome, this benign, gardening aspect of preemption. Its less presentable aspect lay below, in the "workhouse of nature."

Preemptive humanism was a Renaissance reassertion of the assertive impulses of Adam and Eve after they left Eden. It was a natural garden, in which they had been mere visitors, not proprietors. Once outside, wrote Locke, they were set to make the best use they could of a world God "hath given . . . to men in common . . . to make use of it to the best advantage of life and convenience . . . to appropriate . . . some way or other." His biblical citation was the psalm "The heavens, even the heavens, are the Lord's, but the earth hath he given to the children of men." Jefferson agreed: "The earth is given as a common stock for man to labor and live on." When things went well, the plantations could finance the gardens.[8]

Bacon, it happens, had cautionary words to say about all this, words not quoted widely in the plantation South. He knew farming at home and in the plantations, for he was a farming squire's younger son and an expert on plantation management in Ireland. He left the farm to thrust himself toward a peerage—he became a viscount—by providing legal services to his uncle Lord Burghley and to Queen Elizabeth and by espousing schemes for the harsh pacification of Scotland. He was, like Jefferson, an ambitious politician and scholar with a bent for science: he died from a rheumatic illness caused by experimenting in the preservation of flesh through stuffing a fowl with ice.

Bacon preceded both Newton and Jefferson in urging an experimental approach to statecraft and science and was well ahead of them in discerning the effects upon the land of a plantation system. Observing Britain's first plantation system at work in Ireland, Bacon warned:

> Take it from me, that the bane of a plantation is when the undertakers or planters make such haste to a little presentable present profit as disturbeth the whole frame and nobleness of the work for times to come.[9]

With that in mind, let us head westward.[10]

Westward Sweeps the Course of Desolation

It is positively bad economy for the Virginia planter to undertake the improvement of his estate . . . [I]t is a more profitable operation to emigrate with . . . [his] slaves to Mississippi and Louisiana, and there to employ their labor in raising cotton and *killing* land, than to attempt the improvement of the worn outlands at home.

> (An anonymous mid-nineteenth-century Southern
> agronomist, quoted by Lewis Cecil Gray,
> *History of Agriculture in the Southern
> United States to 1860*, p. 913.)

Tobacco and cotton reversed their status in American agriculture after the Revolution. In the 1770s, tobacco exports of the thirteen colonies were five hundred times more important than those of cotton, but after the development of mechanical ginning in the 1790s cotton rose in relative importance while tobacco declined. By the 1850s, tobacco exports from the United States brought only a ninth as much money as those of cotton.[11]

Though the uses of the two crops differed, the means by which they were cultivated were equally destructive to the land. Cotton culture was restricted to the Tidewater and Piedmont, where the soils were not rich and robust enough to sustain it as a crop for more than a few growing seasons without sickening. An acre of cotton consumed in a hundred days as much mineral matter as an acre growing yellow pines in twenty years and radically altered the family relationships among microorganisms that were reasonably harmonious when growing pines.[12]

The Virginians turned to upland cotton very early. In 1768, they exported fourteen times more cotton than South Carolina and one hundred forty times more than Georgia. It was soon apparent, however, that only the southernmost counties of the Piedmont would yield much cotton, so many Virginia planters migrated southwestward into the Carolinas and Georgia, the Hampton clan being the most famous to do so. They were joined by Carolinians trained in the Barbadian tradition, as pulses of migration answered every increase in cotton prices. There were 9,000 whites and blacks in Alabama in 1810, 128,000 in 1820. Mississippi had 75,000 in 1820 and nearly double that number before 1830, when there were 310,000 in Alabama. In 1840, 591,000 people lived in Alabama and 376,000 in Mississippi; in 1850, 772,000 in Alabama and 607,000 in Mississippi, only a few thousand of whom were Indians.

The evidence of local records in Georgia, Alabama, and Mississippi indicates that the average planter family moved at least twice in a generation, each time setting a few flowers at the doorstep, each time learning how to find a church, a store, a compatible neighbor. As the practice of working soil to death and slaves to exhaustion was repeated over and over again, the desolating army of King Cotton moved on a broad front across the South, drawing people away from home and leaving blighted hopes behind. By 1847, the first cotton lands planted in Georgia were already exhausted; the number of white farmers in Wilkes County fell by half in twenty years.[13]

As the environmental historian Albert Cowdrey has instructed us, cotton should not bear all the blame. It is not any more destructive than corn, its companion. The slaves had to feed themselves, and they did so by raising corn. Since they had little reason to expect to have to raise it long in the same place, they were no more solicitous of the land they put under rows of corn than of that they put under rows of cotton. In combination, cotton and corn left "worn-out, sad, exhausted plantations" everywhere. Between Savannah and Augusta, Eli Baxter saw by the 1850s "barrenness . . . exhaustion [and] . . . dreary desolation." One Southern lady wrote that soil-destroying crops sucked away the natural nutritives and then the frontier sucked away the talent, leaving "deserted plantations where slaves had cultivated the soil as long as it will produce anything, then left for another to be used in the same way." Adam Hodgeson moved west out of Georgia amid "many gangs of slaves whom their masters were transporting, to Alabama and Mississippi. . . . Often a light carriage, of a sallow planter and his lady, would bring up the rear of a long cavalcade, and indicate the removal of a family of some wealth, who, allured by the rich lands of Alabama . . . had bidden adieu to the scenes of their youth and undertaken a long and painful pilgrimage through the wilderness."[14]

One of the many westering Georgia Lamars wrote in 1847 to his cousin Howell Cobb: "Lord, Lord, Howell, you and I have been too used to poor land to know what crops people are making in the rich lands of the new counties. I am just getting my eyes open to the golden view. . . . Buy we must." A kinsman who became an Alabama senator complained in 1855 that the small planters of his state "after taking the cream off their land . . . are going farther west and south, in search of other virgin lands, which they may and will despoil and impoverish in like manner."[15]

By the 1850s, the Black Prairie of Alabama, once a luxurious landscape, was showing the cost of cotton culture. This crescent of broad, deep, and fairly flattish soil had over the millennia grown so richly dark with the gifts of composted vegetation that Europeans referred to it as a "Black Belt" girdling the lower hills of the Appalachians. When aerated by a plow, it could grow upland cotton as well as any other soil in the world—for a time. But it could be sickened, as well, by a failure to provide for its recovery from any single crop.[16]

Finally a distempered landscape extended from Georgia through the Black Prairie westward toward the Mississippi through places once farmed by the Cherokees and Choctaws. By the 1850s, within the great bend of the Tennessee River lay "fields once fertile, now unfenced, abandoned and covered with . . . foxtail and broomsedge. . . . [A] country in its infancy, where, fifty years ago, scarce a forest tree had been felled by the axe of the pioneer, is already exhibiting the painful signs of senility and decay, apparent in Virginia and the Carolinas."[17]

Moving westward, the planters came to Mississippi, where John Hebron Moore—the magisterial agricultural historian of the state—reported that "inherited farming methods from the tobacco era were applied to each new parcel of land . . . [and that] little or no attention [was given] to developing methods of farming that would increase the yield per acre." By 1860, the alkaline uplands of Mississippi and Alabama were showing their bones. The cheerless and sterile white of Selma chalk lay exposed to a furious sun, while from the clefts in the chalk emerged only a few cedars, the scavenging species of the woodlands. Disconsolate weeds commenced the next million years of composting.[18]

Farther west, along the Mississippi, wrote Moore, "both land erosion and soil exhaustion had been characteristic of corn and tobacco culture." In the Natchez District, swidden cultivation upon loess soil was even more pernicious than upon the clayey landscape of the Piedmont. The Mississippi River had for millennia conveyed in suspension mineral-rich dirt downstream from the glaciated Midwest, depositing it along the Arkansas side, in banks of rich, soft, light, granular soil. Westerly winds picked up these grains in soil-storms and drove them against the Natchez escarpment on the east bank, forming loam-dunes. These moist and fertile hills acquired a deepening covering of matted roots of trees, vines, and shrubs. But when those trees were girdled, felled, and burnt, that poultice was singed as well, and exposed to the cruel plows that tore it away, opening the surface to local rains as fierce as those of Virginia. Though the planters of Natchez enjoyed a decade or so of delightful cotton crops, the loess was soon so battered that the planters ceased attempting to plow it. Then their cattle were turned loose upon it, gullying it further.

Leaving the loess hills behind, the planters pressed onward onto "new timber or cane land . . . [to be] cleared and brought under the plow." The frontier drew them on. They could "anticipate the exhaustion of their soils well in advance . . . [by] investing part of their profits in tracts of land in newly opened areas or in adjoining states. . . . [T]his unending process of clearing, cultivating, and destroying the fertility of the soil . . . resembled nothing so much as a cancerous growth spreading death and desolation across the face of the earth."[19]

The Gospel of Garland Harmon

The rush went on toward the West. Migrancy remained a way of life until, under circumstances of immense importance to the South's view of itself, there began to appear among its people a truly "deep and abiding love for the land." It glimmered in the lament of a Putnam County, Georgia, farmer of the 1830s that he and his colleagues had "not yet learned to redeem land" though they were thinking harder about the "careless, slovenly, *skimming*, habit of farming" that had "nearly worn out one of the prettiest and most pleasant counties in the world." Then they began to hear an unexpected voice for reform from a professional overseer for absentee planters. He was Garland D. Harmon, of Floyd County, Georgia, who became an evangelist of soil renewal and staying put. Otherwise, he told his clients, the "tide of emigration" would rush on "until the South becomes a desert waste."[20]

> Thousands of plantations have been brought from the woods into cultivation within the last fifty years, and worn out, and. . . [their owners] forced to leave or starve. . . . Let us quit moving. Let the planters of the old cotton-growing districts . . . feel themselves at home. Let them fill up the old gullies—improve the old red hills—prune the old orchard—improve the old homestead—enjoy the society of old friends—visit the moss-covered church, in whose yard slumbers the remains of long-departed friends. Then . . . will the South begin to grow stronger and her institutions [be] placed upon an immovable basis.[21]

Mesmerizing "visions . . . of the fruitfulness of Alabama, Mississippi, and even Texas" must cease to distract his fellow Georgians, wrote Harmon, from "nativity, friendship, kindred and comfort . . . [upon] the soil of . . . [their] ancestry." Breaking the Western addiction, and cutting Georgia loose from British domination of the international market for cotton, would not be easy. It would require revitalizing that soil and following the Northern lead toward developing a domestic interchange of farming with urbanization and industry. Such a radical redirection was too much to expect of the planters when cotton prices rose in the 1850s.[22]

Most Southerners seemed to prefer to "be seen with an axe on . . . [their] shoulders than perched on top of a manure pile," but a few began "the great work of renovating Southern lands." In the older provinces of King Cotton, more of them sought to diversify their crops and to revitalize their land. One of them wrote: "Others may skin the earth and roam like savages from one wild to another, but for me and my offspring, here is my home." Among those who felt that way was Garland Harmon.[23]

At the end of his career and on the brink of the Civil War, Harmon returned to Georgia from Mississippi and Louisiana. He had become certain that "a worn out place may be improved at less expense than one can be taken from the woods." When he saw one such "worn out place," he walked across its gullies and barrens and, in his imagination, "horizontalized it, composted it, sub-soiled it, laid off my grass lots and clover lots, arranged my buildings, planted an orchard, set out shade trees, employed a landscape gardener, plotted off my vegetable garden, and then, when all was accomplished entertained my friends. . . . Oh! How near Paradise it might become."[24]

Garland Harmon was well in advance of most planters and all but a handful of overseers. His gospel of land-loyalty was not much heeded in the antebellum period. The severe verdict of John Hebron Moore upon his fellow Mississippians was that they "were almost unique in history . . . farmers largely devoid of that deep and abiding love for the land characteristic of agricultural peoples everywhere." After 1865, however, white Southerners were forced to consider what might be done with what was, still, a very desirable million square miles of property. Amid civil carnage a new world had been discerned; slavery, the scourge of the land, was abolished. A defeated people and a liberated people began to accommodate each other, and across the ravaged land came a new birth of land-loyalty, bringing new hope for the land itself.[25]

As if in reaction against profligacy, haste, and migrancy, postbellum Southern writers developed a land-affectionate prose reaching the level of genius in the twentieth-century work of Eudora Welty and William Faulkner. It took a while for former slaves to develop an equal fervor, but they did, once they became accustomed to freedom from being herded from one master's land to another. Even then, though, like Miss Welty many of them were emphatic that they were not just Southern writers and that all places, well understood, imparted "recognition, memory, history, valor, love, all the instincts of poetry and praise, worship and endeavor." Yet prose like hers and Faulkner's, especially when heard in their own voices, encourages the thought that Southerners *have* become, in her words, *especially* "bound up in place": a place where, as Albert Cowdrey put it, "life . . . is lived . . . linked beyond separation to a certain ridge, a certain river, a certain quality of days in summer. . . . [S]outherners . . . know in their bones—there is no life apart from place, and no place is exactly like any other anywhere . . . [An] intense, almost physical bond . . . ties the southerner to his place. . . . [F]rom wiry grass and pine thickets, from sun-struck spiderwebs or a misty day in autumn, what a wealth of declamation has been drawn."[26]

3

The Way Not Taken

After 1783, France and Britain withdrew from all but sporadic interventions into the politics of the Southland, and Spain barely summoned the energy to cling to its possessions along the Gulf of Mexico. In the space thus created, the government of the United States controlled by the owners of great plantations and of many slaves became free to eliminate Indian competition. Thereafter it was able to decide how an empire of cheap land acquired from them might be allocated. In this open scene, the planters could make decisions without inhibition, arranging the society they wanted and the disposition of land that would best serve their interests. It is difficult to think of another group of people in human history who have enjoyed so luxurious an occasion to turn theoretical preferences into desired outcomes.

The most articulate among the Founders in setting forth how they should best make use of this immense opportunity was Thomas Jefferson. He was also the most powerful man among them as they swept aside the subsistence economy of the American Indians of the South, sustained the trans-Atlantic shipment of labor from Africa, and filled the Southland with African slaves while its independent farmers were thrust to the sidelines. These were not the outcomes advocated by Jefferson in his writings of the 1770s and the early 1780s. He had urged a contrary model for civil society and another use of the land in the famous words:[1]

> Those who labor in the earth are the chosen people of God, if ever he had a chosen people, whose breasts he has made his peculiar deposit for substantial and genuine virtue. . . . Corruption of morals in the mass of cultivators is a phenomenon of which no age nor nation has furnished an example. It is the mark set on those, who not looking up to heaven, to their own soil and industry, as does the husbandman, for their subsistence, depend for it on the casualties and caprice of customers. Dependence begets subservience and suffocates the germ of virtue, and prepares fit tools for the designs of ambition.[2]

The implications were obvious: public land should be allocated to encourage family farming, free of "dependence" and thus free of subservience. There was plenty of land available. In 1776, thirteen of the fifteen British colonies of North America declared themselves an independent nation. In 1783, the Europeans—though not the Indians—conceded to them an area of 890 million square miles. Jefferson's Louisiana Purchase brought 828 million more, though again the Indians were not consulted and in a variety of ways expressed their dissent. The native people living in most of these areas were removed by policies commenced during Jefferson's presidency from 1801 to 1809 and continued through a series of forced emigrations in the 1830s. The acquisition of the claims of the King of Spain to Florida occurred in 1819, though the Florida Indians resisted until the 1850s. Texas and Oregon Territory were annexed in the 1840s, and the defeat of Mexico added to the United States 919 million additional square miles.

The Makers of a New Order

Such enlargement and quantitative improvement was impressive to the world and useful to its beneficiaries. Yet it must be admitted that qualitative improvement did not keep pace with engorgement. The American nation became bigger but not necessarily better, from the point of view of those of us who admire the aspirations of the Founding Fathers. For us, the brightest pages of American history are those written in the Revolutionary years between 1776 and 1783, when Thomas Jefferson and other great men aspired to create a nation conceived in liberty and dedicated to the proposition that all men are created equal. They did more than aspire; they had the courage to make a rebellion to make things new. The land was ready for them. Some of their descendants have of late fallen into asserting them to be "men of their time," as if embarrassed by their boldness. They need no deprecatory help of that sort; they did not wish to be so confined. Yes, they were only "respectable lawyers, doctors, merchants, and landowners," in the faintly condescending description of Winston Churchill. Yes, they may have seemed at the outset "nervous at the onrush of events." How could such a group, Churchill wondered, hope to achieve such exalted aspirations with "no common national tradition except that against which they were revolting, no organization, no industries, no treasury, no supplies, no army?" Yet in their dun-colored bourgeois clothing, drab as they might have appeared to sovereigns and to gorgeous courtiers, they were determined to transform the world they found and to make their own traditions.[3]

As Jefferson wrote Joseph Priestley, "We can no longer say there is nothing new under the sun. For this whole chapter in the history of man is new." In his old age, Jefferson reminded his colleagues of that glorious explosion of possibilities when "our Revolution . . . presented us an album on which we were free to write what we pleased." They proclaimed in their Great Seal, now emblazoned upon our dollar bill, that they intended to transcend their time. They would establish a "Novus Ordo Seclorum."* The phrase had two possible translations. The first, "A New Order in the Universe," situated their endeavor in space, as the second placed it in time as "A New Order Among the Ages." Thus the Founders blazoned upon their Seal and their currency, as if upon their shields, an intention to initiate an *epoch*, morally and intellectually, within a *place in geography* in which a new kind of human might be nurtured. Their Declaration signaled both the starting of a clock and the staking of a claim.[4]

After their victory in an eight-year war, the energies of the republic they founded went into geographic expansion as much as into reconfiguring their civil society within its original bounds. Their sense of making a new beginning in time as well as space was expressed not only in the words of the great ones among them but also by the ordinary people who moved out of old places and established themselves anew, "free from clutter," on the land. With confidence equal to Jefferson's, the arch-Federalist Yankee Manasseh Cutler told a corps of Revolutionary veterans commencing a Western settlement at Marietta, Ohio, in 1788 that their venture was "a new thing under the sun."[5]

That sun was soon hidden by clouds, as many of the hopes of the Founders were disappointed. This is a book about that descent—by no means inevitable—from light to dark. The plantation system might have been constrained before it became so proud and powerful as to lead its leaders to sunder the Union. That is our theme: had different outcomes been achieved in a score of narrow contests between 1802 and 1820, chief among them those provoked by the Louisiana Purchase, the war of 1861–65 might have been prevented. Jefferson had no way of knowing the ending. He did, however, fully understand how matters stood halfway down the descent.

Jefferson's Epitaph

Jefferson took office as President of the United States in 1801, having ascended to the supreme magistracy of his country after an apprenticeship in the Virginia legislature, a glorious moment as draftsman of the Declaration of Independence, a less glorious tenure as governor of Virginia, a recovery as a successful special ambassador to Europe and minister to France, and mixed reviews as Secretary of State and Vice President. His first presidential term reached its apex with the Louisiana Purchase. His second was not triumphant, ending, as it did, with a trade embargo amid a general depression and leaving

*That is the way the Latin term is spelled on the dollar bill. Not "secularum."

as its legacy infirm national armed forces to face the British threat that matured into the War of 1812. But he had been so successful in eliminating all serious rivals that he faced no serious challengers. After stepping down, Jefferson remained a force in the nation's affairs, offering frequent advice to two Virginian successors, James Madison and James Monroe.

When Jefferson set forth his epitaph, upon the obelisk marking his grave at Monticello, he insisted that it carry "not a word more" than these:

> Here was buried
> Thomas Jefferson
> Author of the Declaration of American Independence
> Of the Statute of Virginia for Religious Freedom
> And Father of the University of Virginia

The Declaration was issued in 1776. The Statute was enacted in 1786. "Not a word," Jefferson stipulated, should be set upon his tomb of the events of his career until the paternity of the University in 1817. He said he wished "most to be remembered" by the Declaration, the Statute, and the University, and not by any of the achievements of the three intervening busy decades.[6]

In another mood, the elderly Jefferson had spoken to posterity not of what he wished to recall but of what he could not ignore:

> I regret that I am now to die in the belief, that the useless sacrifice of themselves by the generation of 1776, to acquire self-government and happiness to their country, is to be thrown away by the unwise and unworthy passions of their sons, and that my only consolation is to be, that I live not to weep over it.[7]

Did a great man ever write so sad a summary of the condition of a country over which he had been the preeminent statesman for a quarter century? Jefferson had been justly proud of his draftsmanship of declarations and statutes. His tragedy lay in his unwillingness to make full use of his talent for persuasion to tip the balance when, on a series of occasions, choices were made to permit, and sometimes to encourage, the spread of slavery. Had he exerted himself, the Southern land might have become a seed-bed for family farmers. Instead, time after time, he recoiled from opposing the pursuit of a way of life dominated by great plantations and a reliance upon both slavery and world markets.

Why was he so diffident? Jefferson had his personal economic interests to protect and political ambitions to advance. His political base was among those who were deriving the chief benefits of that way of life. He admitted as much when he was recruited by a group of French abolitionists calling themselves *les Amis des Noirs*—Friends of the Blacks. They had been encouraged by his anti-slavery language in the French edition of his *Notes on Virginia*.

The offer was no kindness to him, for it crowded him into a choice between liberal French opinion and that of his Virginia constituents. He declined the invitation, giving as his reasons that "those whom I serve have never been in a position to lift up their voices against slavery. . . . I am an American and a Virginian and, though I esteem your aims, I cannot affiliate myself with your association."[8]

This was only one of many such decisions on Jefferson's part demonstrating something more profound and subtle in him than any simple desire to achieve office with the support of the powerful men of Virginia. Jefferson was driven by an insatiable hunger for the approval of his fellow planters. Such a need for the affirmation of peers is common among political persons. In Jefferson's case it was so intense as to overwhelm his commitment to concepts distasteful either to his contemporaries among the planter class or thereafter to their sons. He sought brothers while attacking the authority of fathers.

Disestablishing the Grandees

In 1769, young Squire Jefferson was welcomed into the Virginia legislature. He was a great figure in his locality. The other planters and merchants would have made a place of sorts for any scion of a respected counselor to the Royal Governor and of a mother whose lineage was ancient by Virginia standards, but Jefferson was so brilliant that he rapidly moved upward from his allotted junior position. As the chairman of important committees he commenced assaults upon the power of those institutions of continuity and authority identified at the time by Edmund Burke as the means of holding together an orderly society across generations. Chief among these is the proprietorship of land.

In Britain as in its colonies, land was more than a place to grow crops and settle retainers. As both Burke and Jefferson were aware, it was a political device. Until the coming of the Normans, kingship in Britain was not fixedly hereditary, nor did a chieftainship necessarily entail even the temporary, personal possession of land. Service to the king or leadership of a clan only later assured enfiefment—the giving by the sovereign of land to be held and passed to one's children. Hereditary kingship and the inheritance of land allotted by kings to their followers were institutions of the Middle Ages intended to provide stability—even at the cost of rewarding unworthy heirs. For the same reason, kings and barons were willing to grant land to monasteries, bishops, and parish clergy. The church was an adhesive force across society and across time. In Virginia, the established church held land, and a hereditary aristocracy had been encouraged by officers of the Crown who granted land to useful friends.[9]

Thomas Jefferson acted as if continuity were an annoyance. A landholding church and a landholding aristocracy were anathema to him. He commenced his own small revolution against them well before the first Continental Congress was convened in the mid-1770s. There were no great monasteries inviting his dissolution, but in 1769, as soon as he entered the legislature of Virginia, he assaulted the church as landholder and as the recipient of tax support. In 1779, he was able to secure passage of that law disestablishing the Anglican Church of Virginia to which he referred as the Statute of Virginia for Religious Freedom. Its chief effects were that the general revenues of the Commonwealth would no longer support the buildings, deacons, or priests of the Church of England.

The great planters of Virginia had been the partners of the church, receiving tracts of land from the same royal largesse. By inheritance, Jefferson was himself one of their number. Without cavil from him, most of them skillfully adapted to the Revolution, escaping the fate of the great Tory families of New York and Pennsylvania. There, the Penns, Allens, and DeLanceys lost their power, their lands, and their country. Though Attorney General John Randolph, William Byrd III, and Byrd's son Thomas Taylor Byrd were so loyal to the Crown as to go into exile, most of the Tidewater aristocracy and nearly all the newer Piedmont oligarchy stayed in the saddle and cantered easily into the post-Revolutionary world.

Within dextrously constrained limits, Jefferson led the new men against the old. His tightly focused efforts at reform never threatened the sacred institution of landed property itself and only brushed slightly its subinstitution, property in slaves. He assaulted only primogeniture and entail, devices lingering from the Middle Ages inhibiting the ways a man—and a very occasional woman—could dispose of land or slaves. Primogeniture was a legal presumption that when a man died without making a will he intended to leave his estate in land and slaves to his eldest son. Entail kept such an estate as a unit. Most estates in Virginia were not entailed, and primogeniture applied only in the absence of a will, so the Old Dominion had no more difficulty in abolishing primogeniture and entail than did all the other states. Few of Jefferson's generation disagreed with Alexander Hamilton's declaration that "an hereditary succession by right of primogeniture, is liable to this objection—that it refers to birth what ought to belong to merit only." Jefferson had only to bring Virginia along with others.[10]

In this instance as in so many others, his language in doing something was more radical than what he did. His diction tells us how his mind worked. His action tells us what he found to be possible. Primogeniture and entail were to be shaken off as a crustacean shakes off a shell or a snake its skin. These devices were like an established church—carapaces to be shed physically, by moving out of them. Movement brought freedom. So it was, he said, with "our emigration from England to this country." That mass movement "gave her [Britain] no more rights over us than the emigration of the Danes and Saxons gave to the present authorities of the mother country [North

Germany and Denmark] over England." In his symbolic imagination Jefferson was a pioneer. New land, like a new generation, should provide that freedom that brought "happiness." One way to escape the burden of the fathers was to move away from them.[11]

It is not easy to assess the consequences to the land of the abolition of primogeniture and entail. In the 1930s, the authors of the U.S. Department of Agriculture's famous compendium, *Soils and Men*, mentioned only the adverse effects of "the philosophy of distributing . . . property equally among the several heirs. . . . [It] has resulted in subdivision into uneconomic-sized units . . . particularly . . . in the southern Appalachian highlands . . . until the farms are entirely too small and the land is used for purposes to which it is not adapted." In the New Deal years, amid a leached and gullied desolation, the writers of *Soils and Men* could observe the cribs and cabins of "poor people who can neither buy nor move away." The richer planters had long before bought and moved.[12]

The benign effects of the reforms of the 1770s become easier to discern as one descends from the highlands into the Piedmont and out upon the more resilient, slow-sloping alluvia of the Tidewater, where some parcels were excised from great estates to become smaller units. Critics of land reform are wont to point to the tiny holdings provided the peasantry of France by its more revolutionary laws. Jefferson's did nothing so radical, for good or ill.

The Brotherhood

The small farmers apparently thought Jefferson to be a friend to their interests, for they flocked to support his political ambitions when he returned to Virginia in the 1790s. He had survived his failed governorship of Virginia during the Revolution but had renewed his intellectual and political capital by his successful tenure as the American representative in Paris and then had become Secretary of State in the administration of George Washington. The further restoration of his political fortunes required that he cobble together a coalition to support his ambitions. That would have been impossible had there been a hollow core among his peers of the planter class of Virginia. That was the public side of the matter. More intimately, he sought to support his reemergent self-esteem by assembling in his neighborhood a brotherhood composed of people of intellect and taste. They would live closely enough to his teaching-station at Monticello to constitute an extended, personal "academical village," anticipating that of the University of Virginia.

Jefferson began by writing his friend Madison of the need for "agreeable society . . . the first essential to the happiness . . . of our existence. . . . I view the prospect of this society as inestimable. . . . Monroe is buying land almost adjoining me. [William] Short [his secretary in Paris] will do the same. What would I not give if you could fall into the circle. With such a society I could once more venture home and lay myself up for the residue of life. . . . Think of it. To render it practicable only requires you to think so. Life is of no value but as it brings us gratifications. Among the most valuable of these is rational society."[13]

Madison was Jefferson's true brother of the spirit, Monroe less so, and Short more a son than brother. Beyond these intimates he sought out the approval of others of the planter class, especially among the "new men" of the Piedmont.[14]

Jefferson's perpetual revolt against the fathers left him very much in need of brothers—brothers of the soul. They should be, we are told by an acute observer (and elegant stylist) of our own time, "graceful without foppishness, polite without arrogance, tasteful without pretension, virtuous without affectation, independently wealthy without ostentation, and natural without vulgarity," and he selected them with care. Not just anyone would do. A cool reception greeted a stranger who wandered into the circle without invitation. Toward those who had no claim upon his attention, no kinship of class or blood or intellect, Jefferson was no more effusive than would be any other gentleman of his breeding and experience. Despite his democratic rhetoric, the Squire of Monticello was very selective in his companions.

He was, in fact, without illusions about what might be expected even of his fellow planters. When writing his French friends, Jefferson often lamented the absence in Virginia of the urbanity of Paris. His local "society . . . [was] much better than is common in country situations . . . [yet] perhaps there is not a better *country* [his emphasis] society in the United States. But do not imagine this a Parisian or an academical society. It consists of plain, honest, and rational neighbors, some of them well informed and men of reading, all superintending their farms, hospitable and friendly."[15]

These were the people whose necessities mattered most to him and whose opinions worked their way through him into the disposition of the American public land. Jefferson's receiving-set was always tuned to them. He admitted to Madison in 1793 that "the esteem of the world" had been "of higher value in my eye than everything in it," putting the affliction in the past tense. Madison knew his friend well enough to smile at the implication that he had taken a cure for the disease. Jefferson solicited fraternal affirmation with as much energy as he resisted "every form" of paternal tyranny.[16]

Jefferson reached the apogee of his public career in the first year of his presidency, rejoicing to his grandchildren how "charming" it was "to be loved by everybody." No politician was ever loved by everybody very long, however, and at the end of his final term, Jefferson's mood was much altered. When he returned to his Albemarle neighbors, he asked, "In the face of the world, 'whose ox have I taken, or whom have I defrauded? Whom have I oppressed, or of whose hand have I received a bribe to blind my eyes therewith?' On your verdict I rest with conscious security." Fifty years later, Henry Adams added another kind of verdict. Jefferson, he wrote, "left office as strongly and almost as generally disliked as the least popular President who preceded or followed him. . . . Loss of popularity was his bitterest trial. He who longed like a sensitive child for sympathy and love." In his subsequent career, Thomas Jefferson did not suffer the loss of much popularity among his fellow planters.[17]

Their approval came at a price, however. As the outcomes he asserted to be his desires are set alongside those that occurred in his beloved Southland, a significant portion of the gap between the two may be explained by his willingness to pay that price.

The Unpropitiated Son

"He who longed like a sensitive child for sympathy and love." Whose love? Though this is a work of political and environmental history, not an exploration of Jefferson's romantic life, we must give some attention to his young manhood, because the emotions arising from it were projected into his later public behavior, and ultimately upon the land itself. His character emerged in the triangle among a father, a mother, and siblings—siblings of the blood or the heart.

After the death of Jefferson's father, his son achieved manhood without paternal mediation. Thomas and his younger brother were left within a household dominated by their five sisters and by the widow, to whom his father's will had passed all the patriarchal as well as matriarchal prerogatives of a traditional English family. After the son was able to take as his own the property his mother held in trust for him, his behavior continued to show the characteristics of that personality psychoanalysts denote as the "uninitiated man." A young man deserted by his father, either by departure or by death, at the crucial occasion of coming of age may erupt in spasms of rebellious boldness but may not be expected to be persistent in the face of disapproval.

When such a young man is placed in subordination to a woman, especially an assertive woman supported by other assertive women, he often fuses his anger at his father's desertion into resentment against her inhibition of his assertions of manhood. However sweet she may be—and Jefferson's mother was not famously sweet—he will turn upon her the concentrated insubordination he might have diffused between her and her husband.[18]

The antipathies characteristic of an uninitiated young man pervade Jefferson's "Commonplace Book," an anthology of quotations derogatory toward women. Kenneth Lockridge, a modern scholar, has dissected Jefferson's and two other similar works composed in eighteenth-century Virginia. In Jefferson's case, rage against the matriarchate blazed like a forest fire across a mountain divide to engulf the patriarchate as well, and intergenerational authority in general. Is it any wonder that as Jefferson was engaging in such incendiary activity he sought sympathy and love from a band of brothers? His aversion to authority was rage doubly wrathful—and doubly needful. He *did* long like a sensitive child for sympathy and love, longed to set himself free from the feminine yoke and to secure revenge upon all fathers. No wonder he turned for support to his brothers—not to all mankind, certainly not to blacks or Indians or peasantry, but to his brothers of the comforting and familiar class of upcountry planters. And no wonder he became disinclined to risk failure in their eyes. Unless their approval came quickly, his actions became as timid as his ideas were bold. A man of greater commitment to reform and with a steelier disposition might have persisted even in the face of disapproval in many of the causes he espoused but then abandoned. For someone as indisposed to risk as Jefferson, however, impediments set by his peers in the path of the achievement of his stated ideals became adamant. As he said of himself, "I do not love difficulties. I am fond of quiet, but irritable by slander and apt to be forced to abandon my post." Jefferson was not a man for long sieges.[19]

Though much celebrated in his old age, Jefferson had three times withdrawn, bruised, from public life: in 1781, after his failed governorship; in 1793, when he retreated from his service in the Cabinet of President George Washington; and in 1809, after his presidency ended in the midst of economic disaster. According to his friends, he suffered the disapprobation of his peers most painfully after he abandoned his post as wartime governor of Virginia. Though a colonel in the militia, he had remained away from the fighting throughout five years of revolution. Then the British cavalry came against him and drove him from Monticello without a fight. Though he rightly asserted that resistance would have been quixotic, the Virginia legislature investigated his performance, the charge being, in his own words, "treason of the heart and . . . weakness of the head." It was a dreadful time for him. "The affection of my countrymen . . . was the only reward I ever asked or could have felt," and for a while it seemed that he had "even lost the small estimation I before possessed." Returning to Monticello, he pronounced himself "thoroughly cured of political ambition . . . [after] thirteen years engaged in public service."[20]

The legislature cleared him, but, beset by the loss of his wife, as well as his shattered self-esteem, Jefferson did not recover quickly. He declined service in the Congress and then refused to represent "the United States in general . . . [and] the state of Virginia in particular" in Europe. A year passed. Finally his colleague James Madison admitted: "Great as is my partiality to Mr. Jefferson, the mode in which he seems determined to revenge the wrong received from his country does not appear to me to be dictated either by philosophy or patriotism. . . . It argues, indeed, a keen sensibility and a strong consciousness of rectitude."[21]

Madison's judgment was severe, but Jefferson's other qualities were so great that this unhappy period was put behind them both. Neither was "thoroughly cured of political ambition," as they demonstrated by joining in an alliance bringing each of them in turn to the presidency. That alliance did not require them to propose measures contrary to the fundamental interests of their class and section. They were, therefore, rewarded with the "sympathy and love" of the greatest portion of that class.

The effects upon the land of the gratification of the desires of the planters could not at once be contrasted to those emerging north of the Ohio River. Nor does it appear that Jefferson gave much thought to the ecological consequences to the South of his abandonment of the professed tenets of his revolutionary Lost Cause and his subsequent support of the militant expansion of slave-driven plantations. He may have loved "quiet." He may truly have been "of a pacific disposition." But the planters were not. When war would provide new plantation land on the cheap, they demanded military action to secure it from the government led by Jefferson and then by Madison, and they got it. Jefferson supported their advocacy of wars to seize Spanish territory in 1790, 1792, 1793, 1795, and 1802. In his annual message of 1805, he was at it once again: "The spirit and honor of our country require that force be interposed to a certain degree." In 1806, he wrote Dupont de Nemours that force might be required to "take or obtain our just limits," and in 1807 he rejoiced that "our southern defensive force can take the Floridas, [and] volunteers for a Mexican army will flock to our standard. . . . Probably Cuba would also add itself to our confederation."[22]

Jefferson may have abhorred slavery, but under his aegis the government of the United States assisted planters to follow close upon the progress of its armies to deploy their own battalions of slaves. As the plantation system expanded, the "boisterous emotions" that Jefferson observed among his fellow slave owners in their relations with their own slaves were expressed in the large in the conduct of American foreign policy. The planters had economic interests to serve, but they also had guilt to expiate. Their militancy had a ferocity that may best be explained by the infusion of interest with passion. Thus in two ways the foreign policy of the United States during its expansionary epoch was plantation policy.[23]

Like many others of his class, Jefferson referred to the inhabitants of his slave quarters as "family" and assumed toward them the role of patriarch. When they asserted themselves, they could be treated as ungrateful children, yet punished without the restraints of kinship or even of racial identity. The perverse consequence was that release through violence was more to be expected among those who felt guilt in owning slaves than among those who did not. Self-loathing was accumulating; the planters as a class were confronted by increasing antislavery sentiment throughout the North Atlantic world. Much cruelty has been wrought by people expiating self-loathing who seek to convince themselves that they have been provoked. In its quiet periods, their anger appeared as indifference to the suffering of the ungrateful. An aspect of this was indifference to what those ingrates did, in their folly, to the land.

These are general propositions grounded in experience but not subject to statistical demonstration. They may be grounded somewhat, however, in specific lives, such as that of Thomas Jefferson. The foregoing paragraphs suggest why a man who thought of himself as a patriarch among his slaves might not be much inhibited from doing them injury in public policy and might, in fact, express in that policy boisterous emotions arising from a guilty recognition of the gap between his professed ideals and his political necessities. The slaves were one class of persons who languished in that gap. The yeomen were the other. Let us look more closely at Jefferson's commitment to them. How hard would it be for him to heed his planter-peers at the expense of a felt affinity for the yeomanry? How democratic was Jefferson?

Monticello Again

There is a boardwalk stretching from Thomas Jefferson's bedroom-study at Monticello along the top of a series of half-buried storage rooms to a little structure at the southwestern extremity of one of the wings of his villa. That traversal, which looked out across his slave quarters, was a walk backward through his biography.

Monticello stands today in glory, with all doubts resolved, inspiriting us to strive after the ideals Jefferson professed and to seek to understand why he found it so difficult to live up to them. Since we know that his house expresses an ideal, and since much in life is not so consummate, the villa in all its parts invites us to seek after the man who never quite brought it to such a state.

Like all men and women, Jefferson himself was forever unfinished, forever changing over time. His first house on the site was that little building at the end of the southwestern wing. It was his yeoman's cabin, constructed in the 1770s. In the 1780s, at the center, he had begun a Palladian mansion fronted by a double, over-and-under portico, but completed it only up to the level of the top of the first-floor windows. Then he went off to France and Holland, where he saw how such things had been done in marble and on an overwhelming scale. He returned to start all over—except that he retained the parlor, at the core of his house, as his symbolic classroom.

The young Thomas Jefferson of history is not to be found in that parlor. To find him, we must make our way to his first cabin, relegated to the status of an "office" in 1802, when the Thorntons and Mrs. Madison came to visit. It had been more than that to Jefferson. It had been his honeymoon cottage— and before that a declaration of a more modest social affinity than those implied by either of his rotundas. His first invocation of Roman grandeur was the dome of the present, finally finished Monticello. The second was the central building of Mr. Jefferson's University down below.

Jefferson was an artist of the language of architecture, as he was of words. The houses he built, tore down, and rebuilt upon the presentation-platform of his truncated mountain were like revised texts of self-definition. They were personae-in-progress, a succession of speaking-masks like those worn by actors in Greek drama. He used shape, color, and the placement of his buildings to impart lessons to his fellow citizens, lessons about himself, about the placement of humans in land, and even about the placement of leaders amid classes of persons.[24]

After his retirement from the presidency, Jefferson caused two sets of neo-Palladian pavilions to be placed facing each other across the Lawn at the University of Virginia. They flanked a larger rotunda than that at Monticello, this new one explicitly a teaching-place. The domestic version had housed the parlor and its iconostasis of instructive portraits. That great dome, around which the University pivoted, housed classrooms and the library. However, as Jefferson insisted, the entire "academical village" was to be exemplary, not just its faculty. The pavilions were templates—which might be snipped apart like paper-dolls—to be followed by builders across the South as expressions of the plantation system in its triumphant phase. Their effects can be seen to this day all the way to Austin, Texas. They are at their most flamboyant in Middle Tennessee, where deep soils and diversified agriculture permitted that system both unusual prosperity and unusual longevity.

Jefferson had addressed the world with quite another message in his young manhood. His first completed essay in architecture was the cabin at Monticello, with a steep-pitched gable roof, to which he brought his bride in a snowstorm in 1772. It was eighteen feet square, set over a traditional hill-country half basement. These dimensions were themselves already traditional among the yeoman of the uplands. As Jefferson grew to eminence and greater affluence, he retained this little yeoman's house as the "south outchamber" of the plantation complex at Monticello, as if to remind himself of the ideals of his youth. This yeoman's cabin was the symbol of his Lost Cause.[25]

Near the end of his life, Jefferson wrote Madison that a "long succession of stunted crops," and the "general prostration" of the land and of farming upon it, were forcing him to consider selling off Monticello and repairing to a cabin in Bedford County. His mortgage debt was still lying heavily upon him, and though he was able to satisfy his creditors' demands for interest payments by selling slaves, the land he had mortgaged was so stripped and gullied that it could not be sold to make principal payments even if offered at "reduced prices." It did not quite come to that, however; he kept the dogs of finance at bay until his death and was never reduced to completing the great cycle of life once again in a log cabin.[26]

Yet even in the symbolic statement of his first log cabin, there was nothing simple about Jefferson. Though it appeared to be Virginian, his visitors who came bearing knowledge of architectural theory as it was then being taught would instantly perceive that it was a little temple, constructed of natural materials in natural shapes, according to the prescription of Vitruvius, the Roman architectural theorist, as revived by French and British theorists of Jefferson's day. Though it may have comported with American backwoods practice, Jefferson was unlikely to settle for mere emulation. He was a teacher. He achieved a telling amalgam of the Arcadian and the Appalachian by lamplight, while the spirit of Vitruvius stood at one elbow and those of Jean-Jacques Rousseau and the architectural theoretician Jean-Nicolas-Louis Durand, Jefferson's contemporary, stood at the other.

Jefferson was making use of Durand's "architecture that speaks" to situate himself among the yeomen, according to principles—both architectural and social—widely shared among intellectuals of the Revolutionary epoch. They were most clearly set forth by Durand in his lectures delivered in the year of the Thorntons' visit to Monticello, calling for a residential architecture of "natural and national" forms to enhance that "happiness and the preservation of individuals and society" that came from working the land itself. Jefferson missed that lecture but gave as good a one himself, in the ground, demonstrating that simplicity of form and of life advocated by the trans-Atlantic aristocracy of which he was so splendid an ornament. At the same time, he expressed an affinity for people he felt worthy of his leadership by borrowing from them the form of their characteristic habitation. His cabin expresses the kind of society he wanted to encourage for his country once its independence had been achieved.[27]

Jefferson was a wealthy man and soon was done with cabins. As he put some things up and tore some things down, he kept his cabin, to be reached by that pleasant walk looking down upon his slave quarters. As the architecture speaks to us, we are induced to inquire: why did things turn out this way? Surely the answer lies not only in his love of physical comfort but in his need for psychological comfort as well, as he withdrew from a romantic association with yeomen to situate himself amid his planter neighbors.

Jefferson and Democracy

Jefferson could accommodate his fellow planters and take few risks to advance the interests of yeomen or slaves because he was not disposed to welcome resentment on the part of slaves and took no exalted view of the actual yeomen of his acquaintance. The slaves seemed ungrateful and the yeomen unworthy. Jefferson's willingness to go to war for more plantation land, and to expose the land of the South to the depredations of the plantation system, can, therefore, be partly explained by his taking little emotional satisfaction in setting free people he disdained or in securing a republic favoring those from whom he expected little.

Jefferson was not a democrat and never said he was. Though he never endorsed in public Alexander Hamilton's celebrated dictum that the public was "a great beast," their views in the matter were not altogether different. Andrew Cayton has rightly written that the Federalists sought "an Empire of System" that might be thought to be contrasted to "the much discussed Jeffersonian 'Empire of Liberty,'" yet the two were grounded in similarly skeptical views of human nature. As Cayton points out, Jefferson was not enthusiastic about permitting settlement willy-nilly in the West. Though he was willing to provide Lockean justification for hardy pioneers who took land from Indians, they were not immediately to be given the franchise. Like his Federalist counterparts, Jefferson advocated placing the frontiersmen in purgatorial suspension "til their governments *become* [Jefferson's emphasis] settled and wise." Only when tamed could the yeomen be expected to become "a precious part of our strength and of our virtue."[28]

Jefferson did not go on the stump with that proposition. Such "condescension," however "mild," would be resented among the constituency he was building. But no one who has read much in his correspondence argues that he was an advocate of "broadly popular suffrage" as that term is defined today. When writing of direct popular election of the upper house of a Virginia legislature, Jefferson observed to his friend Edmund Pendleton that he had "ever observed that a choice by the people themselves is not generally distinguished for its wisdom."[29]

Jefferson might assert a "cherishment of the people," but only as a shepherd cherishes his sheep. Charles Beard was no doubt correct in saying that "neither he nor his party regarded universal manhood suffrage as an essential element of Republican faith. Among the very last states to surrender the domination of the landed class, based upon freehold property qualifications on the suffrage, were Virginia and the neighboring commonwealth of North Carolina."[30]

When in a sardonic turn of mind, Jefferson admitted to his friends that their humbler fellow citizens could not be trusted to honor the sacrifices of the Revolution, writing that common people were so easily duped that the best hope of free government lay in the absence in America of any rogue so rich as to bribe them *all*.

Even before the Revolution had been won, Jefferson had warned his French friends:

> From the conclusion of this war we shall be going downhill. . . . [T]he people
> . . . will forget themselves but in the sole faculty of making money, and will
> never think of uniting to effect a due respect for their rights. The shackles,

therefore, which shall not be knocked off at the conclusion of this war will remain on us for long, will be made heavier and heavier, till our rights shall revive or expire in a convulsion.[31]

His presidency did little to increase Jefferson's faith in democracy. In his postpresidential years the enlivening principles of the Revolutionary years withered, and he became nearly as sour as his old allies John Taylor and Nathaniel Macon. Macon was heard to scoff at those who took seriously the notion that all men were created equal, or should be treated as if they were. The most these Old Republicans were willing to offer on the altar of democracy was a bouquet of nostalgia for the world of their youth, in which the small planter stood beside the great planter to keep the slaves down.[32]

The mature Jefferson expected little from yeomen even when, in Madison's words, they "had the complexion of the serfs in the north of Europe, or of the villeins, formerly in England." And what good could be expected of husbandmen whose skin color was dark? Those "of our complexion" might, under the proper guidance, become freeholders and voters, but neither Madison nor Jefferson anticipated virtuous behavior from manumitted blacks, describing them "as incapable as children of taking care of themselves . . . pests in society by their idleness."[33]

Jefferson and the Family Farmer

Though Jefferson was a master of political prose, he never set forth his political creed in systematic works like those of the great French and British theoretical politicians of his time such as Edmund Burke. He was a fragmentarian, offering bits of theory in letters and in pages and paragraphs within his public papers such as the Declaration of Independence. His largest work, the *Notes on Virginia*, is not a treatise but a collation, and in some ways an anthology, from which theory erupts into the statistical, anthropological, economic, and natural-historical answers he offered to a series of questions propounded by French friends. Jefferson left to posterity the task of collating these beautifully written mini-essays into a comprehensive view of the circumstances for which statesmen should strive: a society in which life, liberty, and the pursuit of happiness might best be sustained, by independent yeomen working their own soil.[34]

Jefferson—at least the young Jefferson—advocated a therapeutic view of land. It was not merely a commodity, but an agency, a crucible nurturing good citizens *in vitro*. According to the Enlightenment belief that human nature is plastic and subject to benign manipulation by nature itself, the allocation of land to yeoman farmers would be at once moral and artistic. The earth itself could act sculpturally, as a mold for character. As a man or woman worked the soil, the soil, as an instrumentality of moral economy and social policy, would work upon him or her. For that to occur, social policy must arrange first that land be allocated to family farmers. Thus the health of the society as a whole would be enhanced by increasing within it the number of morally healthy individuals. The farmer labored for his own good. But because he would be a good steward admixing his work with the land itself, he labored for the good of that land, as well. The land would return the favor. Both the soil and the yeoman were to be moral agents.[35]

George Washington may be the father of our country, but Jefferson was the father of the family farm, bestowing upon his nation at its birth the concept that there are not only "powers of the earth," such as kings and nations, but powers *in* the earth—inherent in land itself. Some cynics have responded to his theorizing by noting a hole in the argument through which the Piedmont planters might fall: they could receive few therapeutic effects from immediate contact with the land. Most of them followed George Fitzhugh's admonition "to avoid and escape from" manual exertion; most of Jefferson's peers pursued "less laborious, more respectable, and more lucrative employments . . . [for] none work in the field who can help it." But the cynics missed the point. After the planters were gone, the farmers remained.[36]

Jefferson could "help it," and did. According to his overseer, Edmund Bacon, he had "but little taste or care for agricultural pursuits." After pointing out how "misguided" it would be "to imagine Jefferson walking behind a plow," Joseph Ellis has concluded that despite the genuine fervor of Jefferson's "inspirational hymn to the virtuous farmer . . . the truth was that farming bored him." Jefferson himself wrote "of the proprietors of slaves . . . [that] a very small proportion indeed are ever seen to labor." The hole in the ranks of the virtuous, if it was a hole, was bigger than Virginia, for verily few of the Founding Fathers themselves were family farmers. "Those who labor in the earth[,] . . . the chosen people of God, if ever he had a chosen people," were not well represented among those attending the Constitutional Convention of 1787. Only Jacob Broom of Delaware, "perhaps the most obscure of the Framers," qualified by profession as having received the Almighty's "peculiar deposit for substantial and genuine virtue." The others were: thirteen planters, whose labor in the earth was done by slaves; sixteen lawyers (some planters were also lawyers); eight merchants; thirteen gentlemen drawing income from governmental positions, parishioners, and investments (including Mr. Witherspoon); three physicians; and Benjamin Franklin, retired printer. Jefferson and the others would have seen no anomaly in this, for they intended to lead the virtuous husbandmen, not to be led by them.[37]

Independence

Dependence begets subservience and suffocates the germ of virtue, and prepares fit tools for the designs of ambition.

(Jefferson in *Notes on Virginia*, in *Writings*, Lib. of Am. Ed., p. 289 ff.)

How independent were the planters? How independent was Jefferson? He was reared in affluent dependence. His mother left him thousands of acres and many slaves, and his wife brought him more, yet they also bestowed upon him heavy debts to British and Scottish creditors, who might at any time call his loans. He depended upon their sufferance. His comfortable style of living, his status in the society of planters, and his political base were built upon credit. Furthermore, as a grower of tobacco, he was as dependent as were his cotton-growing colleagues on prices set by the masters of British, Scottish, and Dutch finance. So he was dependent upon credit supplied by others, a market controlled by others, and, of course, the labor of others.

Independence may be defined as freedom to make one's own way and to pursue happiness according to one's own bent. Who had the greatest range of options of that sort in early nineteenth-century America? The best demonstrations of independent yeomanry were not to be found in the planters' domain but, instead, among the subsistence farmers of the Southern hills and pine plains and the interdependent farmers across the Ohio. In the free Northwest, a sophisticated symbiosis was emerging in which the growers of crops were providing foodstuffs and building materials to nearby towns while drawing their manufactured goods from their urban neighbors. This was independence through interdependence. The only truly free and independent yeoman of the South was a subsistence farmer of the hills, and this kind of freedom—however much it may have been touted in theory—came at the price of poverty.

This chapter tells of the two Virginias visible to Thomas Jefferson from a favorite vantage point, upon a "very high point of land" atop the Blue Ridge Mountains. Though he could not see all the way across the Ohio River, in the

43

middle distance to the west lay the highland farmlets and apple orchards, and beyond them ridge after ridge of wild country. He never penetrated the Appalachian near-West, but it was a scene so familiar to his imagination that when he returned to his study at Monticello to compose his *Notes on Virginia* he was able to describe it in detail to his readers:

> The passage of the Potomac through the Blue Ridge is one of the most stupendous scenes in nature. . . . On your right comes up the Shenandoah, having ranged along the foot of the mountain a hundred miles to seek a vent. On your left approaches the Potomac, in quest of a passage also. In the moment of their juncture they rush together against the mountain, rend it asunder, and pass off to the sea.[1]

Beyond the "piles of rock on each hand, . . . [composing] the evident marks of their disrupture and avulsion from their beds by the most powerful agents of nature," lay the perilous but immensely valuable unknown. As Jefferson turned to face eastward, his gaze was gladdened by his own plantation country,

> as placid and delightful as that [the West] is wild and tremendous. For the mountain, being cloven asunder, she presents to your eye, through the cleft, a small catch of smooth blue horizon, at an infinite distance in the plain country, inviting you, as it were, . . . to pass through the breach and . . . [into] the calm below."[2]

Jefferson was a man of the "plain country"—plain topographically but refined socially. The "wild and tremendous" West was an object for study, a potential source of profit from the sale of land, and a place for experiment in new ways to organize society. His home, however, and the home of his friends, was the narrow Piedmont, a shelf of land midway between Appalachia and the Tidewater, and also a middle ground between the intellectuals of Western Europe and the rough pioneers of the West. The Atlantic world came close to the trans-Appalachian West at Harpers Ferry. On a single spring day, Jefferson might travel on a good horse the less than sixty miles between that point and the saline Potomac below Great Falls, traversing a gentle countryside that, he assured the French, looked as though it were just on the other side of a river from their own familiar fields, rather than an ocean. This was the land he had said was "like much of the country of Champagne and Burgundy."[3]

Between 1776 and 1800, a great gulf opened politically between the Virginia Piedmont and "the country of Champagne and Burgundy." France and the United States passed through very different revolutions. Some great estates remained intact in France, but much of its land was distributed to peasant proprietors. No such land reforms occurred in Virginia. The Old Dominion remained relatively "placid" and "calm" under the control of Jefferson and his planter colleagues. A recent scholar, Allan Kulikoff, has described them as "capitalist farmers" and "agrarian realists" who were able to sustain their dominance over the yeomen who had supported them in the Revolution while perfecting "new, capital-intensive techniques, making older strategies of communal self-sufficiency in food difficult, if not impossible."[4]

A Dependent Arcadia

Some self-sufficient farmers remained, mostly in the hills. Those who were able to follow the example of the great ones did so, sweating in the fields just long enough to acquire a Negro or two, thereby becoming, by their definition, planters. Though they and their mentors might assert in theory that "the best possible society was one dominated by small, independent producers," all of them, grand and not so grand, linked "small-scale farming to agricultural participation in the market. . . . Unlike yeomen, agrarian realists were committed to the search for foreign markets," and by 1800 these realists included "nearly every farmer" selling tobacco. Though they sacrificed self-sufficiency—independence—as they became dependent upon the labor of others and upon distant markets, it was a profitable dependency. Thanks to those markets and to the labor of their slaves, three out of five white heads of families in Virginia's plantation country owned land in 1775. Some owned much property; some owned only a little and worked it themselves. Many owned a middling acreage and a middling number of slaves. Yet even those who relied neither upon the labor of others nor upon foreign markets lacked the ferocious independence of peasants. Instead, in the South, they were being trained to take their cues from the planters.[5]

A contrast between American submissiveness and European independence among the small holders of land does not sit well in our national self-definitions, nor does another truth about the antebellum South: the febrile susceptibility of the planters—the "agrarian realists"—to signals sent them by British bankers and industrialists, and their willing acceptance of subservience to the pricing of their products, and of the money they borrowed, by others. Why were they and their successors of the cotton kingdom so easily recolonialized? Did they not have opportunities equal to those beckoning the farmers of the North toward national independence grounded in regional interdependence?

Between 1776 and 1783, the Virginia planters led a revolt against the devices of colonialism, and in wartime they became perforce largely independent economically. Peace brought political independence and the opportunity to reorder their economy to sustain some of that freedom of action enjoyed during the Revolution. But the planters had neither the will nor the energy to break their previous habits of dependence upon international markets and their reliance upon enslaved labor. They remained reluctant to diversify their economic base toward domestic industry and urbanization and instead reenthralled themselves while continuing to enthrall their labor force. Thus they sentenced the Southern land to the continuing degradation inherent in a slave-and-staple system.

Perhaps Mr. Jefferson's Lost Cause never had a fair trial. One could argue that he had no sooner sketched it out than it was overwhelmed by the predilections of his fellow planters for quick returns on their investments in land and slaves, by the blandishments of British credit, and by the immense hydraulic suction of British demand for raw cotton. That is not the view taken in this book, however. Though these forces worked powerfully against his cause, a series of occasions were presented to him and others when the outcome was not predetermined. From each of these turning points, another trajectory of events might have commenced.

That drama has been bleached of much of its color by Jefferson's version of Virginia's circumstances before these choices were made. He presented a picture composed of his personal preferences among multiple truths, drawing those preferences from the pastoral self-portraits of earlier planters such as William Byrd II. After Jefferson's death, its contours were underlined and sharpened by the finest stylists among the historians of the nineteenth century to provide impressions of Jefferson's Virginia compatible with his. The two most convincing of these, Henry Adams and Francis Parkman, had their own somewhat perverse Yankee reasons (discussed in the note introducing the bibliography) for preferring to imagine a simple, sentimentalized, Arcadian Virginia rather than the more complex reality, which was considerably more robust and more capable of adopting other courses of action.

For Byrd, Jefferson, Adams, and Parkman, Southern agrarianism was, from the outset of European settlement, so unlike that of the North as to make it seem impossible for it to adjust similarly to an urbanizing and industrializing, and therefore, diversifying, age. From his crag at Harpers Ferry, Jefferson told us of plantation country basking in Arcadian simplicity, "placid," "delightful," "plain country, inviting you . . . [into] the calm below." This was the "silent country" evoked fifty years earlier by Byrd's assertion that he lived "in a kind of independence of everyone but Providence." Both Adams and Parkman agreed, telling their readers of the "idyllic conservatism" and "simple and isolated lives" of the planter-patriarchs.

Simple, independent, isolated, calm, placid? Was this Jefferson's Virginia and Byrd's? Did they repose in an Arcadian scene so serene that they had no occasion to consider the desirability of such exotic phenomena as cities or commerce—let alone manufacturing? Was slavery uncontested by slaves or by conscientious masters, so that the tranquility of the shores of the Chesapeake was unbroken? Were there were no disruptions, no alternative subcultures wherein other choices were made? And was the patriarch's pastoral regime so beneficent that they did not even overgraze?

No, of course not. Virginia was not so tranquil, nor so simple.

The Virtues of Diversification

Let us start where the planters did, on the ground, and from time to time make a trip to town. The institution of slavery was not entirely a rural phenomenon along the Chesapeake. As in other cultures, slaves worked in town and in industry. Still, despite experimental deployments of slaves to do more factory work, the recolonialized South after 1800 kept its eyes downcast upon rows of cotton and tobacco plants. Slavery and this fixation on staple-crop agriculture distorted the society of the Chesapeake in two ways. It developed cities having strangely negative effects upon diversification of economic risk and also an elite whose self-perceptions evolved away from their commercial origins. These two phenomena acted together to reinforce a downward spiral into dependent agrarianism amid a deteriorating landscape.

When land is deeply and persistently damaged it loses its capacity to support the full range of its original capabilities. As diversification becomes more difficult and less likely, risk increases. Such a shriveled culture must rely upon the success of the limited number of crops or industries a crippled land can support and its ruling class understands. That is what happened to Virginia, despite its origin as a community possessing both towns and farms and managed by an elite well trained in commerce.

As noted in the first chapter, the planters' reliance upon slavery forbade their improving agricultural practice by putting expensive tools in the hands of the labor force. So disabled, they saw no choice but to continue their hasty, wasteful production of row-crop staples. In the short and medium term, their incapacity to risk modernization of agricultural technique and technology left them at the mercy of the violent oscillations of the price of tobacco. In the long term, they and their descendants were deprived of the greater resilience that comes from land that has grown a variety of plants.

The planters of the Chesapeake did not reach the decisions sentencing them to these outcomes on their own. They were subjected to persuasion. During the colonial period, their British overlords repressed their every effort to achieve diversification, and with it economic independence. After the Revolution, British—and, later, Northern—bankers and millers cast a web of incentives and disincentives reinforcing by subtle persuasion the planters' prejudices and their economic myopia. Year by year, the plantation system, renewing habits derived from colonial status, visited its ill effects upon the land and deepened the dependency and risk-exposure of the planters.

The colony of Virginia was established in 1607 at Jamestown, where, among their rows of tobacco plants, these settlers managed to provide space for a diversified economy. They were townspeople by force of circumstance—they lived within a stockade. They were also, in a modest way, industrial. By 1630, they were manufacturing nets, seines, root beer from sassafras, building supplies, pitch, tar, glass, and soap. And they had a supply of artisans: their leader, Captain John Smith, had issued a requisition for "carpenters, husbandmen, gardeners, fishermen, blacksmiths, masons, and diggers of trees [and] roots"; some of the forty Sussex ironworkers who answered that call became the Founding Fathers of great Virginia families.[6]

Before the end of the seventeenth century, Virginia's mills were producing flour, fulling, textiles, and grist, and Governor Alexander Spotswood's foundry at Germanna gave encouragement to a search for bog iron by two generations of Washingtons. William Byrd, the son of a London goldsmith, went into the Indian trade with pots and weapons, while the Lees, Steggs, Carters, and Harrisons remained retailers throughout the colonial period. John Berkeley, John Carter, and William Fitzhugh were trained respectively to be an ironmaster, a vintner, and a woolen draper, as respectable in their ways as the Skipwiths and Randolphs who came to Virginia as merchants and lawyers.

Tobacco was, however, so profitable that it drew these mercantile gentlemen away from their trades. Besides, they brought more than artisanship from England: they carried prejudices from a home country where a man was not fully a gentleman without a country seat. When their Indian trade and their field slaves provided surplus value to build their own country seats, they began to think of themselves as gentlemen, despite their frequent trips to the countinghouse. A disjunction appeared between who they were and who they wished to be thought to be. Every great Virginia planting family had a mercantile branch. Every squire had a cousin who was a ship master or merchant who might come to call at the plantation dock. Sometimes more than a dock—the Harrisons owned a shipyard. In the 1760s, more seagoing vessels were built in the cities of the Chesapeake than by the combined efforts of New York, Pennsylvania, and New Jersey. Norfolk and Portsmouth had an ocean at their front and the Chesapeake's sheltered harbors at their sides. At their back, the Great Dismal Swamp was a paradise for lumbermen, shingle slicers, fur trappers, escaped convicts and slaves, and duck hunters. Norfolk began to ship to the West Indies the wheat of Southside Virginia, challenging Baltimore as an exporting center while retaining the refitting business that had given employment to carpenters, ironworkers, glazers, and sail and block makers.[7]

The Washingtons, Carters, Byrds, Custises, and Braxtons did mercantile business on the Virginia side of the Potomac, while their kinfolk, the Dulanys, Taskers, Chews, Galloways, Ringgolds, Carrolls, and Ridgelys, owned ships and trading stations in Maryland. This was not Arcadia even within the demesne of Nomini Hall, seat of Robert Carter, often the subject of essays as an exemplary planter. Like Augustine Washington, Carter was an ironmonger, operating forges and mills, and a merchant, maintaining schooners and sloops to serve his own needs and those of others dealing in tobacco, lumber, and grain. Though Carter was very rich, and though some of the Maryland "planters" were as well, they prudently employed the device of joint stock partnership to finance ventures such as the Patapsco Company to build and operate ships larger than those any one of them wished to put at risk.

While emphasizing how mercantile these planters were, we must also be sure to attend to the junction-box where their commercial connections brought to them signals inducing them to think of themselves as noncommercial. It was in the interest of their associates in England and Scotland to beguile them by treating them as if they were really country gentlemen, or else they might heed the exhortations of Benjamin Franklin and Alexander Hamilton to join in the liberation of their fortunes through building a diversified economy. They were accustomed to listening carefully to messages received from London and Liverpool. Their receptors for mercantile information were wide open and brought into their consideration a set of ideas schooling them in indifference to long-term losses. As a class, the more they settled into agrarianism without diversification the worse became the potential of the land they managed to permit future generations to diversify—if for no other reason than because diversification is expensive and the land became poorer. Those planters who left Virginia for the West taking capital and slaves with them, including several sets of Randolphs and Skipwiths, left desolated land behind. They had treated it as a commodity fungible with any other piece of land. Many of those who remained, drawing income from Western speculations, took the same view of their slaves. They were also fungible assets and could be sold off to the West with few compunctions.

Some planters, of course, never lost their commercial touch. From the windows of their town houses in Alexandria, or from their docks and warehouses on the shore below the lawns of their plantations, the Carters and Beverleys kept an eye on business. But even among them the desire not to be thought to be mere tradesmen grew over time to include such a resourceful, sophisticated merchant-planter as William Byrd II. A letter Byrd wrote a friend in England shows that he could push his ledgers to the side of his writing-table and think of himself as living a simple, placid, detached, agrarian life, "like one of the Patriarchs . . . [amid] flocks and . . . herds," with his every need supplied by his "bond-men and bond-women, and every sort of trade [skill available] among . . . [his] own servants, so that [he might] . . . live in a kind of independence of everyone but Providence." Byrd admitted that it was disagreeable to have to apply the whip to his "bond-men and bond-women" in order to "keep all my people to their duty, but then 'tis an amusement in this silent country." Fortunately for those "people," he could also find amusement in "a library, a garden, a grove, and a purling stream[, . . .] the innocent scenes that divert our leisure."[8]

Commercial Squires and Ungovernable Governors

Silent it may have been after nightfall, but the Westover estate was neither innocent nor hermetically sealed. Byrd studied the wage rates of the serfs of Livonia at the far end of the Baltic, who were producing grain in competition with his. He followed every change in British "imperial preference" to find out how he might benefit from the subsidies British imperialism distributed, and he knew precisely how French tax policy affected the pricing of his tobacco. His ear was constantly cocked for the instructions of the market. Though planters drew words like "patriarch" from myths of the pastoral simplicity and wrote of "silent" countrysides, a slave owner had to be a special kind of patriarch, as we have noted in Jefferson's case, though he, too, described himself as "blessed as the most fortunate of patriarchs."[9]

An Arcadian or even an English country ideal does not square with a dependent, nervous, and unstable plantation culture. The great landowner of the Chesapeake may have disdained "commercial gentlemen" after he himself had risen away from commerce, but he had "more incentive to enterprise" and was "less fearful of soiling his hands[,] . . . more capitalistic in his frame of mind, had a sharper eye for the cash-balance sheet, and was more versatile in his intellectual interests" than any idealized backwoods squire. "The spirit of business enterprise was kept alive in Virginia even among the congealing aristocracy. Leading Virginia families like the Ludwells, Spencers, Steggs, Byrds, Carys, and Chews . . . were but recently descended from merchants. For several reasons, a successful planter might remain something of a merchant."[10]

Jefferson was not a successful planter in part because of his refusal to be "much of a merchant." Indeed, despite the past of the Chesapeake planters and the imperatives of any prosperous future, he discouraged others from being so. He expressed contempt even for those merchants—such as William Panton—who played essential roles in his geopolitics. His self-perception and his selection of close colleagues did not include a role in commerce. The consequence was that his opposition to the industrial and commercial trends of his time became precisely what the British neocolonizers desired. Jefferson's disavowal of the commercial nature of his class was expressed not only in his statements of abhorrence for merchants and manufacturers but also in his insistence that the "cultivators of the earth are the most valuable citizens . . . the most vigorous, the most independent, the most virtuous." To avoid contaminating them, he exhorted his country to avoid diversifying its economy. In the face of British neocolonialism, he wrote that "as long therefore as they [the farmers] can find employment in [agriculture] . . . I would not convert them into mariners, artisans or anything else." Only if the public domain of land were exhausted would he "perhaps wish to turn them to sea in preference to manufactures, because comparing the characters of the two classes I find the former the most valuable citizens. I consider the class of artificers as the panders of vice and the instruments by which the liberties of the country are generally overturned."[11]

His neighbors of the Chesapeake were already at sea, and Virginia was already manufacturing. The power of Jefferson's ideology was exerted in keeping them from further exposure to commerce and, with a few exceptions when his tinkering instincts were aroused, in preventing further capital commitments to urban manufacturing. In effect, he was siding with the British Board of Trade as it renewed its efforts to keep the South dependent—more subtly now, and with new weapons.

The mercantilists in charge of policy in London were accustomed to contending against the leaders of Virginia even while it was a colony and the primary advocates of the colonials' interests against them were—surprisingly enough—Royal Governors. Despite the harsh things said of him by Virginians of Jefferson's day, Sir William Berkeley encouraged their forefathers of the 1660s to undertake mining, smelting, manufacturing wool and linen, and shipbuilding: "Berkeley was ready to try the Yankees' game, and with a fair chance of winning it." Yet his far-sighted policy found no more support among the planters of the seventeenth century than James Madison's later efforts along the same line among his contemporaries. Tobacco was still king; the planters were becoming conditioned to a lucrative dependency. In 1679, an effort by some of them in the Assembly to carry forward Berkeley's program was "brought to nothing" by the combination of lassitude among their colleagues and British intrigue. In 1695, Sir Edmund Andros attempted to interest the colonists in cotton as a diversifying crop away from tobacco, but the planter-historian Robert Beverley lamented a decade later that they were still not listening, as their retrograde habits were reinforced by "the opposition of the merchants of London." After Berkeley and Andros came Governor Alexander Spotswood, himself the proprietor of mines and smelters. Spotswood had some success in inducing "manufactures of cotton, flax, and hemp" when tobacco prices were in decline, but as soon as they ascended again the planters abandoned all else. In 1713, a group of them admitted that their habits were already so battened upon the planters that "they would never have thought of 'other ways of living' had tobacco but yielded them a living price."[12]

Those merchants of London knew what they were about. For *themselves*, they had adopted the counsel of Isaac Newton's prose hymn to the virtues of diversification—another piece of advice insufficiently heeded by Jefferson. As literary gentlemen, they were aware as well of the smug verse of Antonio, one of Shakespeare's merchants of Venice:

> My ventures are not in one bottom trusted,
> Not to one place; nor is my whole estate
> Upon the fortune of this present year;
> Therefore, my merchandise makes me not sad.[13]

That sound policy was not to be permitted to colonials. They were to do as they were told by Orders in Council, and less candidly by the subliminal instructions of pricing. When tobacco prices slumped, the price of "merchandise" made the colonials worse than sad—they were desolate, but still could not break their "sot weed" habit. As early as 1697, it was said that "tobacco swallows all others." When caught in a little diversification in the 1730s, a cringing Virginia Council thought it best "to quiet the fears of the British authorities," averring that there would be no further experiments of that sort. Though "the shift to manufacturing had happened several times before," they said, "so soon as tobacco prices rose again all these 'newfangled manufactures' would vanish." And so they would, unless cities were built and industry grown. That would not please the Commissioners of Customs, however, who gave it as their view that city-building in the colonies would be "detrimental by drawing the inhabitants off from their planting tobacco in the country to . . . setting up handicraft trades."[14]

On occasion, from the closing decades of the seventeenth century onward, the cannonades of the French fleet did blast apertures into this cozy system. When tobacco shipments to England or Scotland were sufficiently harassed by the French, the planters were driven, "half against their will, to industrial pursuits. By 1695 several cotton culling machines of a primitive sort had been set up in Virginia, one of them at Jamestown, and legislation enacted to encourage fulling mills . . . and by 1711 one Virginia county annually produced 40,000 yards of woolen cloth, cotton, and linen cloth. . . . The depression in the tobacco trade late in the 1720s produced another flurry of industrial activity, much of it . . . transitory."[15]

The Board of Trade continued to do all it could to discourage the Americans from manufacturing, causing a Pennsylvania statute to be vetoed lest it give "encouragement . . . by law to making . . . manufactures [products] made in England." Such a measure must be quashed, whatever good it might do the colonials, "it being against the advantage of England." William Pitt told the House of Commons that "if the Americans should manufacture a lock of wool or a horse shoe, he would fill their ports with ships and their towns with troops."[16]

As soon as the Revolution had been won on the battlefield, and political independence achieved in the Treaty of Paris, Hamilton moved to the next battle line, leading a fight for economic independence through diversification of the economy. Jefferson did not join him in that second struggle. He remained once again a civilian, so to speak, as Hamilton strove to increase the capacity of the new American Republic to resist reincorporation into the British Empire, this time its invisible economic empire.

Hamilton succeeded in the North. Though Jefferson's resistance prevailed in the South, there was no more inevitability in that outcome than in the triumph of the plantation system. Southerners had the capital and the mechanical skills to do otherwise. Eighteenth-century Richmond and Charleston took pride that their remarkable mechanics showed greater capacity to produce patentable inventions than their counterparts in Boston or New York. In 1800, the South had at its disposal more minted gold than the North, larger silver deposits, and, unlike New England and New York, large deposits of coal and iron. Its sources of water power were equal to those of the North, and it had easier and shorter access to the West. Yet it remained tepid technologically. Not until the twentieth century did it develop a balanced economy.

Diversification, the Pursuit of Happiness, and Cities

As the South between Baltimore and New Orleans settled into an agrarianism bound by tradition, habit, and agrarian mythology, the rest of the nation was experiencing exuberant urbanization. Boston tripled in size in the eighteenth century, New York grew by a multiple of eight, and Philadelphia went from a village of four thousand five hundred to a thriving city of forty thousand, while Baltimore, Southern but apparently immune from Arcadian mythology and indifferent to British preferences, rose from a cluster of houses harboring two hundred people in 1750 to the thirteen thousand counted by the first federal census.[17]

Jefferson conceded that cities multiply choices; he loved Paris, where his own pursuit of happiness was at its most exuberant. It is odd, therefore, that he never included diversity of opportunity among the inalienable rights of man. An active pursuit of happiness is possible only when one can choose what sort of happiness to pursue. Cities have traditionally provided a wider range of choice than the countryside. Why else would people have escaped to them from the dull, drilled routine of the country? Perhaps Jefferson was inhibited from thinking of cities as places where such an inalienable right might best be exercised by the behavior of the black people of Virginia and Maryland, who had often shown that they had thought of urban sanctuaries in that way. Slavery had reduced fields to outdoor prisons. Those who could escaped to the cities of the region, where urban free black colonies nucleated. One reason for Jefferson's bias against cities in general, and against industrial cites especially, was surely that even in the South cities were places where black artisans congregated.

Artisans in general, he had written, were "panders of vice and the instruments by which the liberties of the country are generally overturned." Black artisans had repeatedly led revolts to overturn slavery. It is small wonder that Jefferson was apprehensive of towns, for in "Baltimore, Richmond, Norfolk, and Petersburg . . . free blacks were relatively numerous. Baltimore [an industrial city] . . . was the one place in the Chesapeake where free blacks formed a majority of the black population in 1810." In the other urban book-end to the

South, New Orleans, the proportion of free blacks had risen even while the total population was itself rising rapidly; by 1806, that proportion was 14 percent, and only 37 percent of the population was white. In Delaware and New Jersey, such an increasing percentage of free blacks had presaged the extinguishment of slavery. The growth of the free black populations of Baltimore and New Orleans might have had the same leavening effect in Maryland and Louisiana.[18]

Jefferson could not be expected to look beyond the convulsions he feared from the presence of free blacks anywhere in the South to envisage a future when a flight of blacks to cities reduced the role of rural slavery and thus not only increased the resilience of yeoman agrarianism but also provided urban markets close by. The benign consequences of increasing tenure in one place, bringing of necessity greater care for the land, could be observed as early as 1810 in the interaction of yeoman Ohio and the cities of Marietta and Cincinnati, both refuges for blacks. Cleveland was slower to grow, but in its hinterland a free and independent yeomanry of blacks and whites prospered by 1830 amid emigrants from the port cities of New England who had become accustomed to living among free blacks and were exhorted by religious people, especially Quakers, to welcome blacks to freedom. In Yankee Cleveland and Quaker Oberlin, blacks soon held elective office, while around Baltimore and Cincinnati, and for a time even near New Orleans, black and white yeomen prospered.[19]

Eastward Toward Civility

Toward the end of his life, Jefferson acknowledged indirectly that there might be virtues to be found in life in towns smaller than Paris—even in Baltimore, Richmond, Norfolk, and Petersburg. In 1824, he wrote that "a philosophic observer" of the United States would find increasing civility as he traveled downhill from the dens of "the savages of the Rocky Mountains" eastward through the "gradual shades of improving man." He would come next to the rude life of "those on our frontiers in the pastoral state [presumably in the Great Plains]. Then would succeed [in the experience of the traveler] our own semi-barbarous citizens, the pioneers of the advance of civilization [in Missouri or Kentucky, perhaps], and, after coming over the Appalachians to traverse the Piedmont," would reach "our seaport towns" where would be found the nation's "as yet, most improved state."[20]

Yet even so, the ports of the Chesapeake were not full-service cities, competitive to those of England or Scotland. As markets where British manufactured goods were exchanged for Southern staples, they served the English and Scottish interest very well. Their lack of sooty diversity commended them to Jefferson, though that virtue was dispelled by their harboring hives of Scots traders and creditors, for whom he had a special antipathy.

Until Richmond became fully industrialized after the Civil War, even it was an agency of neocolonialism rather than an antidote to it. The Chesapeake cities were implements and conduits of British commercial policy, not providers of manufactured goods that might be sold to the planters in competition with the products of Manchester or Liverpool. Though "Virginia and Maryland were not without town life," and though "the maps . . . [were] filled with places that contemporaries considered towns," these little cities were predominantly dedicated to distribution and exchange, not to making things. (Some further reflections on this theme are offered in the Appendix; see "Jefferson, Madison, Adam Smith, and the Chesapeake Cities," p. 245.)[21]

Throughout most of his career, Jefferson was too constrained by prejudice against artisans and multiracial towns to give support to urbanization in the South. There was a revealing exception, that flirtation with Eli Whitney in the interest of "our manufactory of Richmond." Had it been more than an exception his Lost Cause might have prospered more than it did. Family farmers might have been able to work out reciprocal relationships with such manufactories, as they did in the North. As it was, the effect of Jefferson's tugging the South back from urbanization and symbiosis was to shrivel the range of choice available to its citizens, to impede their pursuit of happiness, and to worsen the degradation of the land.

The Thousand-Foot Line

There was another Virginia, partway back along that progression toward civility Jefferson depicted as eventuating in the little towns of the Chesapeake. Beyond a line drawn roughly a thousand feet above them and behind the plantations of the Piedmont, in the mountains where Jefferson had stood at Harpers Ferry, there commences a crinkled plateau of granite ridges. They are all that is left of an Appalachian massif that had once been as tall as the Himalayas are today. After millions of years of erosion, depositing the Tidewater and the Piedmont, some Blue Ridge peaks still stand more than six thousand feet above sea level—and can be very brisk in winter. Mount Mitchell, North Carolina, is fifteen hundred feet higher than Denver. Though no farther from the equator, Mount Rogers, in Virginia, can be considerably colder than Colorado Springs. The increase in frosty nights that accompanies an ascent through the South had immense agricultural and political consequences. Cotton will not grow in mini-climates much colder than those at one thousand feet in altitude.

Seen from Jefferson's vantage point, the Appalachians lie in range after range like the spines of great lizards asleep amid cranberry bogs and early frosts. This is Appalachia—the Bacon South, where European hogs have prowled and rooted since 1539, when scores of them escaped the army of

Hernando de Soto, and an Indian, European, and black population began admixture. In Virginia, the European component of that medley increased after the settling of Jamestown, as soon as people who were not comfortable within stockades—or other inhibitions—went off toward the hills. The Appalachians have nourished free spirits and distilled natural spirits ever since.

One of Thomas Jefferson's skills was an ability to draw support from such people as well as from his colleagues down below in the Tobacco South and the Cotton South. With his unerring symbolic sense he set his headquarters at Monticello within a hundred feet of elevation from the Thousand-Foot Line, for under his orders his slaves flattened his mountain to a level 867 feet above the Chesapeake and set upon it a house that is 44.7 feet tall—getting very close to the thousand-foot elevation of Carter's Mountain across the road.[22]

In slave-and-plantation country, planters raised staple crops such as tobacco, wheat, and cotton, to be bundled or bagged or baled for transport down rivers in vessels of shallow draft for transfer to ships and distant consumers. Above a thousand feet, however, agriculture was not carried on with much attention to world markets, and there was little slavery. As the result, the topographical map of the South was also its political map. The Thousand-Foot Line divided it between counties where the Confederacy recruited easily and those where most males of military age in 1861 took an oath to serve the United States.

The Thousand-Foot Line is a rough indication of the consequences of the finicking requirements of the mallow family of flowers. Among the mallows are hollyhocks, hibiscus, and cotton. None does well in cold, windy, mountainous terrain. In the Western Hemisphere, the wild form of cotton is a perennial plant bearing white or yellowish flowers and seeds, whose fibers, seen under a microscope, are shaped "like a twisted firehose."[23]

There was a cotton belt in Arizona centuries before the arrival of metal-clad Spaniards in the region, and the fibrous mallow was important enough to the Aztecs for them to greet Cortés with a robe of cotton when he first arrived at the city of Tenochtitlán. Twenty years later, Hernando de Soto's Spaniards who died in battle in Alabama may have worn cotton padding under their armor, and as the survivors of de Soto's force struggled through central Texas, they found people wearing cotton tunics there. The absence of the technology of mills, looms, and gins decreed that cotton remain a luxury until the end of the eighteenth century. Then new machines changed the world: cotton began to be employed both in clothing the masses and in creating great fortunes for planters and millers.

Cotton homespun was worn by European settlers before that, but it was only grown as a cash crop on peculiar occasions such as that in the middle of the seventeenth century when a downdraft in tobacco prices caused the planters of the backcountry behind Norfolk, Virginia, to grow it for sale. We have observed cotton's imperial march southwestward and will come shortly to an account of how a refined set of cotton gins made upland varieties usable in great quantities. "Upland cotton," as that term is used among cotton brokers, did not denote a plant growing very far upland—that is to say, above the Thousand-Foot Line. The machines mobilized by King Cotton as his panzer columns were denied a direct route to the West by highlands too cold, bleak, and windy to suit a tropical mallow. Cotton requires at least 150 frost-free days in the year, three or four inches of rain per month falling evenly across the summer, and no appreciable downfall in the autumn. Even when wind, rain, and temperature are salubrious, it will perform its wonders better in some soils, such as the humus of the Black Prairie of Alabama and Mississippi (when terraced properly) and the brown alluvia of the Mississippi delta (when ditched and drained). It will not grow happily in the sandy pine barrens of southern Virginia, northern North Carolina, eastern Mississippi, or southern Alabama or Georgia.

Hogs often do "just fine" where cotton does not. In the Bacon South, agriculture was largely for local consumption, producing food rather than fiber. The bacon trade was not important to Virginians of Jefferson's class. It was a poor people's occupation, sustaining yeomen largely independent of international economic forces. Some salt pork did go abroad on vessels revictualing in Norfolk or New Orleans, but most pork stayed home. Only a third of the South's cattle at the end of the antebellum period were being slaughtered for all markets, domestic and foreign. The rest were butchered for home consumption. The importance of the Bacon South, as computed in the combined value of cattle and hogs, must not be hidden from us by a screen of white columns rearing up from the lowlands: the annual value of Southern livestock slaughtered in 1860 was one and a half times the value of cotton sales. The value of Southern livestock on the hoof was twice that of the cotton crop. During the heyday of the open-range Bacon South, the fifteen years from 1845 until the Civil War, it enjoyed a bigger boom than the fabled Cattle Kingdom of the West chronicled by Walter Prescott Webb in his classic *The Great Plains*—twelve times bigger.[24]

Grazing was immensely important to the hunter-gatherer-farmers in the hills, as hogs and deer offered protein, while the growing of corn, beans, and squash provided a more or less balanced diet, and there was always the possibility of raising more stock than could be eaten at home or swapped for local goods. Then the slaughterhouse beckoned. Writing recently of the importance of swapping, Allan Kulikoff provides the dignified term "the borrowing system." He has also offered scholars of small-scale agriculture a rich range of examples of how European peasants became American yeomen in the middle ground between pure, isolated subsistence and systematic, plantation-scale staple production for offshore markets. Yet, as these new people of pink-and-white complexion found infinitely varied devices to replace the older peoples and older ways, much of the Southern landscape remained as it had been. The hogs and cattle were as new as the Europeans, but until mid-century four fifths of the South remained unfenced and untouched by metal plows.[25]

One of these new yeoman wrote another:

> You may . . . keep as many cows here as you wish, for feed does not cost a penny. Cattle feed itself in the woods, in winter and summer, no cattle here is fed in the barn. Grass grows six to eight feet high in the woods and one person has as much right there as the other. Similarly you can keep as many pigs as you wish, and you need not feed them."[26]

Appalachia was not, however, Arcadia. Though it went for Jefferson in elections, its population was sparse, and he gave it neither an erg more energy than it required nor an ounce more bucolic virtue than it deserved. It is safe to say that when he wrote or thought of yeomen he did not have in mind hillbillies but instead Virginia's subordinate class of small farmers. For these, not for the subsistence farmers and herdsmen, he invoked versifying and chronicling Greeks and Romans. Theocritus, Horace, Cicero, Livy, Cato, Hesiod, and Virgil were summoned to Charlottesville, not to Sperryville. Squire Jefferson, sitting at the close of day in the library of the house on the hill, might turn from his book and easily fuse "the image of the noble husbandman in Virgil's *Georgics*—industrious, virtuous, self-reliant" with the "cultivator" of the Piedmont who last doffed his hat as the squire rode past. He was "the American agricola."[27]

Though the highlander sending the hogs to market may not have qualified for classical raiment in Jefferson's own time, the Sage of Monticello wrought words so mightily that within forty years anybody farming or driving his sheep downhill to the shearing station and thence to the slaughterhouse could believe himself fit for the insignia of yeomanry. In 1832, Charles J. Faulkner of western Virginia drew no derision from his audience in plantation country when he remarked upon the "morality, virtue, frugality, and independence . . . of the Virginia peasantry west of the Blue Ridge," where survived the "native, substantial, independent yeomanry." They, he said, "constitute our pride, efficiency, and strength, they are our defence in war, our ornaments in peace. . . . [N]o population . . . upon the face of the globe, is more distinguished for their elevated love of freedom—for morality, virtue, frugality, and independence, than the Virginia peasantry west of the Blue Ridge."[28]

While some Virginians did remain in the hills, many others did not. Over the antebellum years many of the best lost their lives in adventures which if successful would have made their country more dependent, rather than less. As the planters' frontier expanded, many died for the cause of cotton in Florida swamps and amid Texas grease-bush. As the military and financial power of a government established to increase independence was deployed to expand the boundaries of the United States, enlarging the acreage put under cotton, the unintended consequence was a commensurate increase in dependence upon foreign markets.

That perverse outcome was the more dire because of the failure of the South to generate its own domestic manufacturing. The results could be seen each time a sharp decrease in British buying of cotton caused an economic crisis in the United States. Jefferson's apprehensions about dependence were amply justified, though he could not have foreseen how a doctrine he had drawn from individual psychology might become applicable to an entire class of people—his class of people. Between 1800 and 1860, the South settled ever more deeply into dependence, satisfying the British market at the cost of a future in which its "sons . . . in the far west" looked backward to see "the homes of . . . [their] fathers in the possession of the alien and the stranger," and the bones of their grandfathers "turned up by the plowshare of the foreigner, and their ashes trampled beneath his unhallowed feet."[29]

Powers of the Earth

The rise of the American Republic has coincided with the rise of the modern corporation. Since 1790, power has flowed increasingly into the hands of persons concerting their purposes in corporate entities that by their nature are quite unsentimental about the earth. Corporations may be led by conservationists, but as corporations they are dedicated to the proposition that all land should be used to generate profit. A "decent respect" for the realities of life required the founders of the United States to recognize the growing importance of such "powers of the earth." Thomas Jefferson was no less adept than Alexander Hamilton in making use of them, though for other purposes. Having discerned that corporations and partnerships organized for profit were indifferent to any call to use land as a moral crucible, he became skillful in using them to obtain land for his friends of the plantation system.

Jefferson understood power very well. He was early among his colleagues in giving attention to the rise of both popular majorities and corporations. He did not mention the latter specifically in his draft of the Declaration of Independence, giving pride of place instead to "the opinions of mankind." Such matters would have greater influence, now, he seemed to be saying, though he need not have anticipated any burgeoning "democratic age." The task under his hand only required him to revise a resolution offered by his own Virginia delegation that the United Colonies were "and ought to be" free and independent states, and to construct a litany of complaints against the British Empire. Jefferson took these drab materials and, recasting them into incandescent phrases, set them aglow in the sky, drawing the eyes of his countrymen from their grievances, and inviting them to proclaim universal redemption to the world.[1]

> When in the course of human events it becomes necessary for one people to dissolve the political bands that have connected them with another, and to assume *among the powers of the earth* the separate and equal station to which the laws of nature and nature's God entitle them, *a decent respect to the opinions of mankind* requires that they should declare the causes which impel them to the separation [emphasis added].[2]

There was a new power in the earth—public opinion. People rising to influence were coming to hold certain "truths to be self-evident," among them "that all men are created equal, that they are endowed by their creator with certain inalienable rights; that among these are life, liberty, and the pursuit of happiness." Jefferson contributed to the Revolutionary cause the nucleating power of ideas, summoning a virtual—in the modern sense—convention of like-minded people on both sides of the Atlantic. Yet, as a practical statesman aware that there were "powers of the earth" of a more traditional sort, he made certain that no reader would take him and his fellows to be naive about the realities of world politics.

Those powers most visible to Jefferson and his Revolutionary colleagues were the empires and kingdoms of Europe. As Americans, however, they also had to take account of the native peoples that were still more numerous in the interior space of the continent than Europeans or the descendants of Europeans. Most of these powers were still refusing to take the stations appointed for them in the decrees of European sovereigns, the texts of crusaders, or the laws of the market. Since the 1520s, the unexpected vigor of the Indians had bewildered the Europeans. In their own confusion the Spaniards gave the term *confusión* to all that lay outside their presidios and fortified villages, and William Bradford described New England beyond the stockade at Plymouth as "a hideous and desolate wilderness, full of wild beasts and wild men." These "wild men" were often well organized and were thus "powers" to be taken into consideration, among them the imperial Iroquois and the disciplined and resourceful Cherokees.[3]

By 1776, the routes taken by the ancestors of these Native Americans into North America, tens of thousands of years earlier, were in the hands of a Russian Empire. The Czar had forts at Honolulu, on Kauai, and just north of San Francisco. While he professed friendship to the American rebels, his officers threatened both the northern fringes of New Spain and the westernmost posts of British Canada. By 1790, Spain, Britain, Russia, and the United States were vying for good harbors along the coasts of what are now British Columbia, Washington, and Oregon.[4]

In 1781, Spain exerted more influence over the land mass now occupied by the United States than any other European power. Bernardo de Gálvez had just shown the world that his country could still produce military marvels. While Washington executed his Yorktown campaign, Gálvez swept the British forces from the Mississippi Valley and the Gulf Coast, in the most astounding demonstration of complementary strategies by two great captains since those of Prince Eugene and Marlborough. In the spring of that year of marvels, Washington kept the garrison of New York occupied with trivial alarms while swinging his entire army down to Virginia to contain Lord Cornwallis at Yorktown. Perhaps Washington deserves greater credit than Gálvez for rising to such feats of arms, for his experience as a commander had been limited before 1776 to subordinate duty with tiny forces against the French and Indians. During the five years of revolution, however, he learned to match the prowess of Gálvez, who had been trained in Algeria, in Portugal, and in campaigns against the Apaches.

As we consider the nature of power in this period, especially power transcending nationality, it is well to bear in mind that the Founding Fathers were required to parse out the complexities bristling from such simple terms as "American," "British," and "Spanish." There were more non-Americans fighting for American independence at Yorktown—largely French—than native-born, and only a minority of the opposing troops under the command of Cornwallis were born in England. Though Gálvez happened to be a son of Spain, his predecessor was Hugh O'Connor, representing scores of high-ranking servants of the Spanish crown who were of Irish origin. Gálvez stormed into the Prince of Wales Redoubt at Pensacola with free blacks, Canary Islanders, Spanish grenadiers, French chasseurs, Catholic Germans, Belgians, and Indians of many nations. Those from whom he seized the Red Cliffs included Chickasaws, Creeks, and Choctaws, Protestant Germans from Waldeck, and Loyalists from Pennsylvania and Maryland. Such coalitions demonstrated that while European dynasties could still summon liegemen, so could the Europeans' creedal clusterings—the "Spanish" forces were Catholic forces and Hapsburg or Bourbon forces more than they were national. Though we may write of Indian "nations" we must be careful to take into account the constant recombinations of people moved by tribal, and subtribal, traditions and religious movements. Each of these cultures had its own belief structures. Each had its own habits in regard to the land.

On the ground, at decisive moments, the true "power" was any man who could assemble a fighting force, and among these the most potent were often captains of commerce as well as of the sword. Corporate officers—CEOs, in modern parlance—led armies and navies into battle in Canada, India, and South Africa and along the shores of the Gulf of Mexico. The Hudson's Bay Company alone could bring to the field more troops than most of the principalities of Europe.

Land Companies, Trading Companies, and Triassic Capitalism

Along the south coast of the Gulf of Mexico, the French Company of the Indies had a brief and unsatisfactory fling at establishing a trading empire to match that of the Hudson's Bay Company, but after 1750 corporate power was felt by the American South through the less conspicuous though more resilient entities discussed in Part Four. These were rubble-dwellers, at first, survivors of earlier endeavors on the grand scale, for as Lewis Cecil Gray instructed generations of readers in his thousand-page history of agriculture in the South before 1860, "the plantation system under private initiative evolved out of the wreckage of the quasi public colonization enterprises. . . . [It] had its genesis in the economic organization of the early joint-stock . . . companies." Though Gray wrote of these early joint-stock ventures as "colonizing," they were not so as we will define that term. The most potent of them, the British East India Company, was instead a trading company, not much interested in colonization. It was known across the globe; the ubiquity of its flag was a graphic reminder of its importance. It bore a square of blue set at the upper left-hand corner of a field of alternating white and red stripes—thirteen of them—long before Betsy Ross and her sisterhood produced the Star-Spangled Banner. For many years thereafter, the company flag was better known across the world than the Stars and Stripes.[5]

Though the East India Company's flag was flown by an occasional trading vessel passing the coasts of the southern portion of the United States, the company itself had no role in initiating or sustaining there the plantation system, nor was it, therefore, responsible for the ravages wrought upon the land by that system. That was the moral burden of the smaller trading companies that arranged for the planters to acquire much of that quadrant of the continent. Though neither truly imperial nor truly colonial, these enterprises deployed power on an imperial scale and opened vast provinces of new land to agriculture.

> [In a trans-Atlantic context the] conjunction of slavery, colonialism, and maritime power permitted the more advanced European states to skew the world market to their own advantage . . . by transferring forced laborers to parts of the globe under European control, and favorably situated for supplying European markets with exotic products [such as cotton]. But monopolies decreed from European capitals were of limited efficacy unless they were backed up by a host of independent *merchants and planters* [my emphasis], displaying entrepreneurial qualities. . . . It was the private initiative of merchants and planters that led to successively larger-scale employment of slaves on the plantations of the Atlantic islands, in Brazil, and in the Caribbean in the mid seventeenth century.[6]

These merchants and planters operated in the South during a period we may call the Triassic phase of American capitalism, borrowing a term from the first of three stages in the geological history of the continent during the Mesozoic period. This first of three in the nation's economic ecology over the two centuries after 1770 ended with John Marshall's Dartmouth College decision of 1819. Then the Jurassic began. As a consequence of snares and obstructions placed by the Marshall Court and its successors in the path of efforts of state legislatures to limit the depredations of corporations, that Jurassic age—roughly 1820 to 1900—was enlivened by an immense proliferation and engorgement of business firms. The succeeding Cretaceous is our own progressive and postprogressive period, affected since about 1900 by the countervailing forces of Populists, Progressives, and the New Deal, protecting labor unions and creating a panoply of governmental bodies to regulate business, despite a mildly Jurassic resurgence since the 1980s.

The Triassic period, extending from the mid-eighteenth century to 1820 or so, was Jefferson's world, *before* Marshall and his colleagues set the federal courts in brood upon the nests of the baby corporate dinosaurs just then hatching. Powerful aggregates of capital were being formed, but they were not yet deployed in developing large industrial enterprises. Instead, they put their money to work buying land, slicing up whole river valleys and mountain ranges like loaves of bread, selling off the slices to smaller capitalists and planters, and providing the crumbs to yeomen.

The slicers and sellers were Jefferson's neighbors, peers, and members of his administration. He grew up amid landowners who owned properties to plant and larger ones to sell, both in the Piedmont and in the West. His father and mother bestowed upon him a total of 2,650 acres in the Charlottesville area, an equal number elsewhere, and thirty or more slaves. His marriage brought him more land, together with 135 slaves. By 1782, his holdings had grown to 4,125 acres and nearly two hundred slaves. In that neighborhood, Edward Carter owned 9,700 acres and Robert Carter Nicholas 7,500, with 10,000 more in the next county over, where Jefferson's other kinsmen, the Coles, assembled 15,000 acres into one vast contiguous imperium.

All of them, Jefferson included, planted in the East and speculated in the West. The headquarters of Jefferson's guardian, Squire Thomas Walker of Walkerton, was a spread of 17,000 acres, worked by hundreds of slaves. Walker had been a partner of Jefferson's father in a Western speculation claiming more than 800,000 acres, most of them in Kentucky. Their Greenbrier Company was a satellite of the Loyal Company, claiming 1,350,000 acres. Neither company was required to pledge to settle families or limit the size of the suballotments to others. They could engross and hold huge latifundia against all claims by small holders, while the Ohio and Mississippi Companies were equally ambitious in serving the Washingtons, Lees, Carters, Fitzhughs, and Harrisons.

Statesmen had to work out their economic and political lives under the huge feet of such artificial megafauna. The land companies of the Triassic age of American capitalism were not to be trifled with. They bought and sold legislatures and co-opted Supreme Court justices and Cabinet secretaries. The assets over which they snarled and stabbed were not factories or warehouses but instead that very land the theoretical Jefferson contemplated as a seed-bed for citizenship. These land companies were not interested in such abstractions, though Jefferson, Madison, Hamilton, and Marshall, while doing business with them, sought to formulate theories to accommodate them.[7]

The Great Land Companies and Revolution

Speculation in Western land led many planters into rebellion against a British government that had twice sought to cut them off from the West. On the first occasion, in 1763, the King set a line against further incursions against the Indians, primarily because the French and Indian Wars had demonstrated that it was costly to provide protection to "frontiersmen" intruding upon the native people living in the West. These "frontiersmen" might be individuals operating on their own, or men such as Daniel Boone and George Rogers Clark representing corporations, and since the Crown and the taxpayers of Britain were disinclined to finance further uniformed auxiliaries to the little armies of the corporations and their agents—such as Boone and Clark—the Quebec Act of 1773, a proximate cause of the American Revolution, expressed that lack of enthusiasm.

Though George Washington was himself a major speculator in Western lands, and had been both a critic of the Quebec Act and an avid seeker after means to avoid its provisions, as President after 1789 he was willing to sacrifice his personal interests and stand against the avarice of the speculators and the land-lust of the pioneers. There was a certain symmetry in that, for Washington's entry upon the world stage a generation earlier, during the French and Indian Wars, had come as a militia officer assigned by Governor Robert Dinwiddie to advance the interests of the Ohio Company. Both the governor and Washington were among its shareholders. The events of Fort Necessity and of Braddock's Field had emerged from Dinwiddie's provocation of the French by insisting that they abandon forts built upon land the speculators sought to sell to settlers. There had been resistance at the time from the lower house of the Virginia legislature, which "had no desire to push the interests of a speculative company from which it derived no benefits. . . . If the war were fought over economic causes, it seems to have been really for the economic interest of the very few . . . a rich man's war and a poor man's fight." Other colonies refused to join in the ensuing campaigns, seeing no reasons for "sending men and money to advance the personal business of these speculators."[8]

In 1783, the Federalist-dominated Congress took its cue from Washington, going so far as to issue a proclamation forbidding "all persons from making settlements in land inhabited or claimed by Indians." In opposing these restrictions, Jefferson's friends drew to their side many of the Tidewater planters who still possessed claims on land in the West carried over from the colonial regime. Some were the sons and grandsons of beneficiaries of land grants from Royal Governors. During his campaign against primogeniture and entail in the 1770s, Jefferson had said that these favored persons, who had "procured" such grants by undue influence, were "desirous of founding great families for themselves." According to Frederick Jackson Turner, these favored

65

persons had only to form new corporate entities including shareholders from the rising Revolutionary planters to etch permanently their marks upon the land. Turner offered a somewhat romantic version of "the Kentucky rifleman" as yeoman-antagonist to these "aristocrats" (and employed the term "savages" in a way now embarrassing to anyone who knows much about the relative behavior of pioneers and Indians), but he made his point:[9]

> The lands for which they risked their lives in conflict with the savages, were being seized by speculative purchasers from Virginia, who took advantage of the imperfect titles of the pioneers. One of the most important features of the economic history of the eighteenth century, is the way in which preparations for later aristocracy were being made, by amassing vast estates of wilderness by grant or purchase . . . [that] served as nuclei for the movement of assimilation of the frontier to the southern type when the slave population began its westward march.[10]

One should not take Turner too literally. The speculators did not themselves often deign to remove themselves to take residence in log cabins in the West, there to "nucleate" plantations "of the Southern type." They stayed home, but the system they established did lend itself to the acquisition across the South of large holdings. Battalions of slaves could be poured into such comfortably scaled plantations once the army had been called in to drive out the Indians.

Jefferson and Western Speculation

> Among these speculators were Jefferson and many of his relatives and friends. [They] grew up in an eighteenth-century Virginia feverish with speculation in Indian lands, when ambitious men formed numerous land companies . . . that schemed to acquire title to Virginia's western domains beyond the Appalachian mountains. Their efforts led directly to the French and Indian War, Lord Dunmore's War, and the bloody forty-year struggle between the "Long Knives" of Virginia and the Native Americans of Kentucky and the Northwest Territory, which culminated in the War of 1812.[11]

Only a man impervious to the enthusiasms or blind to the interest of his dearest and most powerful colleagues could have resisted such a fever. Jefferson did not possess the antibodies required, though later insisting that he had avoided contagion, and though some of the most admired of Jefferson scholars have taken him at his word. One of the most scrupulous once contended that "unlike so many of the prominent men of his day he never himself meddled in western lands and seemed to have no connections with speculative interests." That is what Jefferson said, and several times, commencing with a clear denial to James Madison, written from Paris on November 11, 1783, that he had had any role in "land jobbing." He did admit, however, that he had "meddled" on three occasions: in 1757 he had been "one of eight children to whom my father left his share" of the Loyal Company, whose other prime movers were a panoply of the Piedmont gentry, including his guardian, Dr. Walker, his tutor, James Maury, four Lewises and four Meriwethers. The two other instances given to Madison by Jefferson were an agreement in 1777 with J. Harvie and Christopher Clarke to "take up" five thousand acres in Kentucky, a project soon thereafter aborted, and in 1782 a claim purchased which, Anthony F. C. Wallace informs us, "would almost certainly be Cherokee territory, or former Cherokee territory."[12]

Jefferson's financial records show some further speculations. In January 1769, soon after he came into his Western inheritance, he joined Walker in a speculation on his own, near what is now Parkersburg, West Virginia. In the spring of that year, he participated in a petition with Patrick Henry and others for another fifty thousand acres on the Ohio, and in 1771 he and a number of kinsmen sought to acquire unpatented claims along the Greenbrier River. In 1773, he became a partner in a ten-thousand-acre speculation on another tributary to the Ohio, the Little River, with Augustine Claiborne. Yet he wrote again to Madison, on January 30, 1787: "I never had any interest Westward of the Allegheny; and I never will have any." (The Claiborne clan became even more important later to Jefferson's Western activities, as William C. C. Claiborne demonstrated his reliability and devotion to the planters' cause in Tennessee, Mississippi, and Louisiana; see Part Four.)[13]

Did Jefferson feel the incompatibility between his own investment in huge speculative tracts and a commitment to a "republican order . . . bottomed [upon] . . . a mass of small independent farmers"? Possibly. The best of men may catch a fever, especially when susceptible to the enthusiasms of his class. Might his personal investment activity explain his failure to exert himself for his Lost Cause? Again, possibly, though the explanation cannot be so simple. Indeed, if one wanted to find anything simple in Jefferson's behavior, in contrast to that of Washington, it might be that the latter was less susceptible to group enthusiasms or group approval.

As President, Washington was able to free himself from the constrictions of class and sectional or even personal interest to consider the broad necessities of the bankrupt and fragile regime over which he presided. Though his immediate circle of planters hectored him to lavish more of its meager forces upon the removal of the Indians from the land they coveted and to organize the West to suit their ready acquisition, Washington did not bend. Jefferson was more malleable. After 1784, and after asserting contrary intentions, he found it possible to concede to their desires. They got land in the West on their terms, though each concession removed an opportunity for his yeoman republic, with incrementally adverse consequences for the welfare of the land.

Daniel Boorstin once drew his readers' attention to the imperatives driving Virginia's planters to become speculators. They had been using up their estates, and "a prudent planter had to be a land speculator, alert to opportunity, ready to make new purchases." Otherwise they would be disagreeably reduced to "laborlords" of surplus slaves rather than landlords of great estates. Jefferson found himself in that sorry state not because he *abstained* from speculation but because he did not speculate wisely and he chose unwise partners. His final insolvency was deepened by his inability to stand aloof from the Western speculations of Governor Wilson Cary Nicholas, one of his most consistent political allies and his regular colleague in business. In her *Domestic Life of Thomas Jefferson*, Sarah North Randolph attributed the "coup de grace" given Jefferson's personal fortune to an anonymous "one of his warm, personal friends, for whom he endorsed heavily." The endorsee was Nicholas.[14]

Jefferson was, indeed, engaged in "land jobbing," though this was merely one strand of many binding him to his colleagues of the planter-speculator class. For a full generation after Independence, the Founders continued to dispose of the public domain in large blocks, as the British governors had before them, rather than in the small allotments recommended—sporadically—by Jefferson.

Veterans' Benefits

The genius of Alexander Hamilton affected the distribution of public land in ways so subtle that friends of the family farm have given Hamilton insufficient credit for countervailing the overweening power of the speculators and planters. (Hamilton's successful scheme is set forth in the Appendix; see "Debt and Land," p. 251.)

The Constitutional Convention faced twelve million dollars in debts owed foreigners, forty million owed domestic creditors by the United States, and twenty-five million in obligations of the states. Hamilton managed to overcome many Jeffersonians' objections to full funding at federal expense of the debts of the states and of the continental government. His funding scheme first took care of the foreign and domestic debt owed civilians and next of paying off debts due the veterans. In good Roman fashion, the Founders turned to conquered provinces—in their case conquered from Indians—to pay the conquering troops. Hamilton urged large land grants to veterans to tie them to the government and to set them stalwartly side by side with the speculators and settlers, many of whom were constituents of Jefferson's.

Thereafter, two classes of veteran-landsmen appeared in the West, the settlers and the sellers. The most celebrated of those who wished to find homes there were the members of the Order of the Cincinnati. Those portions of Ohio and Indiana settled by these veterans, and the "Firelands" of Ohio allocated and occupied by the victims of the burning of Connecticut towns by the British, manifest to this day the sustained occupancy of many generations of revolutionary families and the fundamental requirement for extended tenure—care of the land.

North of the Ohio River as in Appalachia, small owners were more tightly locked to the soil than the absentee planters who acquired property south of the river and turned it over to overseers and slaves. Hamilton owned land in Ohio, Jefferson in Kentucky, as it happens. When land was worked by veterans, the very soil was thought by their contemporaries to *endorse* their virtue, rather than *create* it. These "enlightened people" brought their enlightenment with them. Thereafter, in their virtue, their farms could impart additional "quiet independence."[15]

Surveying all this shuffling and settling, Benjamin Rush, a friend to both Hamilton and Jefferson, was unwilling to agree that mere occupancy of Western land guaranteed virtue. Veterans might have demonstrated virtue, but Rush denied the therapeutic value of farming. Owning property, he wrote, might only give a settler sprung from the lower classes "high ideas of liberty" because he came to the West with a "tone of mind . . . seldom" sufficiently refined to make him "a good member of civil or religious society." According to Rush, the aggregate of such persons might rise toward the "republican virtue" of persons like himself only if seeded with Cincinnati of "benevolence and public spirit . . . the natural offspring of opulence and independence."[16]

Armed Occupation

This sounds rather snobbish and Federalist, yet it was realistic. The Federalists proposed to deploy trained soldiers as farmers in the Northwest not only to reward them for past service but to keep them ready for future contingencies. Pontiac and Tecumseh had taught the lesson that land policy in the West should also be defense policy. Its purpose should be to gain "security and territorial control by planting garrisons in conquered territory," as well as to relieve the taxpayers, who would otherwise have had to find the cash both to pay the veterans and to pay off past lenders to the war effort. Though classically trained statesmen of that generation evoked Roman precedents and prototypes such as Cincinnatus, they need not have reached so far, for medieval traditions were still at play among them.

Enfiefment—settling soldiers on their own pieces of land—was the defining institution of feudalism, and it was not dead in 1790. The Spanish authorities of New Mexico were even then allocating grants to yeoman-militiamen in accordance with rank. North of Santa Fe as late as 1840, soldiers were "enfiefed" as a baron might have been in eighth-century France, or as a border chieftain might have been given land in return for military service by the

Plantagenet kings of England. In the seventeenth century, along what is now the frontier between Canada and the state of New York, the British, Dutch, and French, in their own peculiar ways, sought to garrison boundaries and to protect trade by "enfiefing" military chieftains. Along Lake Champlain and the Mohawk, French *seigneuries* were put in place opposite Dutch *patroonships*; after the English seized the Dutch colony, they retitled these patroonships "manors." Though medieval, this was not feudalism. Nobody by that time thought seriously of sending armed men into battle led by a diamond merchant, such as the first van Rensselaer, or a clergyman's mercantile son, such as the first Livingston. These entrepreneurs were expected to recruit others to garrison the borders of their holdings.[17]

Individual Roman soldiers had received land grants as well as "scrip" redeemable in land from the empire as well as from individual colonies. In good Roman fashion, British grants were graded in size by rank—generals got more than colonels, colonels more than majors, etc. During the Revolution, some of the same soldiers, now calling themselves Americans, received further allotments for new military services. (For Roman precedents extended through Florida to the Homestead Act, see "The Romans, Armed Occupation, and the Homestead Act" in the Appendix, p. 248.)

The gap between settlers and sellers emerged at this juncture, Many of the states, including Virginia, did not require that their veterans take up occupancy on the lands reserved for them in the West. They need only walk down the street to the local speculator, where they could sell the "scrip" designating each claim for cash. Most of the Revolutionary warrants found their way into the hands of "consolidators" who resold the claims they represented to prospective settlers or to a second round of speculators. The GI Mortgage of the Second World War placed far more veterans in suburban lots than Revolutionary scrip created yeomen farmers.

In his draft of the *Declaration on Taking Up Arms*, of July 6, 1775, Jefferson wrote that the peculiar circumstances of America, "its political institutions and its various soils and climates[,] opened a certain resource to the unfortunate and the enterprising of every country and ensured to them the acquisition and free possession of property." Skeptics have pointed out that the *fortunate* and enterprising would get what they wanted in the meantime unless barred from doing so by a land policy favoring the not so fortunate. Jefferson did *not* advocate "free *acquisition*," though his mentor in many things, John Locke, had come close to doing so.[18]

The nation was perpetually at war with its Indian neighbors, so "making use" of land (Locke's formulation) could not easily occur unless the enemy was deprived of it. So the Proximity Principle gained a corollary, the Armed Occupation Principle. A "natural right" useful to those with superior weapons became, in practice, "tomahawk title" to land seized from the Indians, settling into "corn title" when that land was planted. Armed Occupation was a squatter's right as ordained and organized by the sovereign. Armed men were placed on their own land, at the edge of settlement to confront likely foes. These pickets (in the military rather than the trade union sense) were expected to defend the lands of the entire community. Their fortified homesteads were like armored trains on a siding; they could be put back on the main line when the authorities desired to push the frontier ahead again.

As these little garrisons were set out in old Indian fields, their meaning was as clear as the language directed to the Iroquois at the Treaty of Fort Stanwix in 1784: "You are a subdued people, you have been overcome in war which you entered into with us, not only without provocation, but in violation of most sacred obligations." Sometimes the victors adopted an evangelical tone like that of Theodore Roosevelt a century later:[19]

> The most ultimately [*sic*] righteous of all wars is a war with savages. . . . [I]t is a silly morality which would forbid a course of conquest that has turned whole continents into seats of mighty and flourishing nations. . . . [W]hether the whites won the land by treaty, by armed conquest, or, as was actually the case, by a mixture of both mattered comparatively little so long as the land was won.[20]

Thanks to Roosevelt's hero Alexander Hamilton, only a portion of the conquered land endowing the early American Republic was liquidated to pay Revolutionary war debt, but it was desired by the planters that their taxes be reduced by the amount that was. Since potential buyers were to be found in the North, some of the conquered territories could not be sold if organized with legal protection for slavery. Otherwise tax money would have to substitute for land-sale money.

Thus the Northwest Ordinance was passed with Southern support as a scheme for debt reduction, and thus tax reduction, though it inhibited the spread of slavery. Otherwise, buyers and settlers from New England would have shied away, and New England was where the ready money was. Richard Henry Lee of Virginia told his constituents that the ordinance was "preparatory to the sale" of "4 or 5 millions of acres [of Ohio], in order to lessen the domestic debt." The intended buyers of this tract were Manasseh Cutler and his Marietta associates, who proposed bundling debt reduction, veterans' bonuses, and freedom from slavery.[21]

The Yankees were not required to abandon calculation. Five million acres were cheap at about nine cents an acre. But their social ethics informed their land policy, as they demonstrated when the plantation system threatened to ooze into their neighborhood. As prospective planters began appearing among them with slaves in tow, they responded by crying that this was "flagrant trespass"—not only upon the "rights of humanity" but also against the ordinance. Thereupon Cutler and his colleagues returned to the Congress urging that the national government send in the army to prevent the contamination of Marietta with slavery, to protect the rights of the Indians, and to see to it that until order was restored there be no "further sale of lands there for the discharge of public debt."[22]

Armed Occupation Marches On

When Jefferson became President, in 1801, James Oglethorpe had been dead for sixteen years, having left a number of sound ideas as his legacy. In the 1730s and 1740s, Oglethorpe had sought to create in Georgia a republic of Scots yeomen, divided into holdings of acreage of less than plantation size. Each citizen-soldier was expected to grow his own food and fiber, to abstain from attempts to defraud the neighboring Indians by bribery and alcohol, and to maintain himself without slaves. The founder of Georgia had been reminded of this Roman idea while campaigning against the Turks in the Balkans. In Romania, once Dacia, the grids of Roman garrison towns set the patterns for eighteenth-century villages. As a classical scholar, Oglethorpe learned in Dacia of the Caesars' retirement planning for legionaries: if aging but not decrepit, these soldier-citizens would receive acreage and mules, would keep their armor and weapons polished, and were expected to be ready to spring from the plow and resist an enemy.

Oglethorpe failed to bring Roman Dacia to Georgia in the 1730s. The planters overwhelmed him, though he protested that "if we allow slaves, we act against the very principles by which we associated together." Those principles, he said, were "to relieve the distressed" and to hold the southern flank of the British dominions in North America. In 1776, old Oglethorpe was delighted by the eloquence of Jefferson's reaffirmation of his cause, and he lived to rally many former followers among the Scots of Georgia to American independence as proclaimed in the Declaration of Independence. Though aging as well, they also were not yet decrepit, as they demonstrated during the ensuing war. Oglethorpe lived to call upon John Adams in London, where Adams was serving as the first minister to Great Britain, and his Armed Occupation Principle had a longer life in American land policy than Jefferson's Lost Cause did in the South.[23]

Yet, as George Washington had said in 1796, the division of farm land into small units to be cultivated by "real farmers" was a sound idea even if there were no embattled frontier to be defended near at hand. It might, as Washington noted then, deter reliance upon slave labor. That too would be "among the . . . inducements for dividing the farms into small lots."[24]

6

Jefferson's Opportunities and the Land

The Lost Cause of Thomas Jefferson—a Southland republic of free and independent yeomen—enjoyed three great opportunities for success, three brief "seasons of youth." The first blossomed in Jefferson's home "country," Virginia, during the Revolutionary period from 1775 through 1783, when half the states of the new Union set slavery on the way to abolition. None among the Virginian Founders was of a mind to defend human servitude as a component of a Southern way of life, and more than a few, including George Washington, John Randolph of Roanoke, and Robert Carter, manumitted their slaves, as neither Jefferson nor Madison did. James Wood took a bolder course: after serving as governor of Virginia, in 1801 he became president of its abolition society. He was not shunned for this dereliction, for he continued to serve on the Council of State until his death. These, too, were "men of their time."[1]

Jefferson sought to create the impression among his anti-slavery friends in France, especially the *Amis des Noirs*, that he was a man like Wood—that he had striven conscientiously, consistently, and with some success first to abolish slavery where it was and, failing in that, to prevent its spread. Here his memory failed him again, apparently, as it had in the matters of Western speculation reviewed in the previous chapter. Yet here again his version of events has been taken as gospel by many of his admirers, though he is the sole source for most of his assertions.

It would not have been easy for him to have been so bold, for though the "men of his time" listed above were present in Virginia and did take action against slavery, they were typical neither of Virginia planters nor of the other Southern constituents whose support Jefferson required to reach his national goals. Had he actually taken all the actions he claimed, in the ways he claimed them, that would have required him to be a man of Wood's mettle, and that was not his way to the presidency. Washington was an exception to many rules; many things were permitted a military hero of such massive gravitas. Jefferson was given less slack and did not pull very hard.

In his *Autobiography*, composed when he was an old man, Jefferson asserted that in 1769, nearly a half century earlier, during his first year in the Virginia legislature, he had "made one effort . . . for the permission of the emancipation of slaves [voluntary manumission by planters, not "emancipation" in the Lincolnian sense] which was rejected." This effort in the form of "an amendment" offered the Assembly failed, according to Jefferson's account, because "the public mind would not yet bear the proposition." The legislative record does not disclose evidence that Jefferson did, in fact, offer such an amendment. Perhaps he misremembered an intention as an act—we sometimes do, as we get older.[2]

The elderly Jefferson recalled that he tested the public mind once more in 1776, inserting a provision for the abolition of slavery in a *draft* constitution for Virginia. In confirmation of that assertion he included such a draft in his *Notes on Virginia*. There is no other documentation, and despite the much broader effect claimed for it in many an account, the draft in the *Notes*, if submitted, did not cover Virginia itself. It would have freed only persons "hereafter coming into . . . [the] territories . . . laid off westward of the Allegheny Mountains." Such a ban, if proposed, would have been inconvenient to the Piedmont speculators with whom he was associated. They anticipated sales of land in tracts of a size to be efficiently worked by slaves. If in this instance Jefferson did perform upon an intention, this was, or would have been, a bold proposition despite its exemption of those currently enslaved in Virginia itself.

Leaving aside the mysteries of what Jefferson may or may not actually have ventured in his early middle age, the influence of his antislavery rhetoric was strong upon several of his young protégés, such as Edward Coles and Thomas Worthington. Moved by his eloquence, they acted. After manumitting their own slaves they betook themselves to the free soil of the Northwest Territory to live among yeomen—some of whom were darkly complected. Worthington became an antislavery governor of Ohio, and Coles an antislavery governor of Illinois.

Sometime in the 1780s Jefferson apparently floated a suggestion that might have set in motion a drift in Virginia itself toward the yeomanry. In a letter to Madison he proposed that the General Assembly of Virginia *might* consider legislation that after 1800 "all persons born" in the Old Dominion might be "declared free." Though the mere opening of such a *possibility* of *future* action to take another *future* action might not seem revolutionary, Jefferson was unwilling to be its sponsor. He sent his suggestion to Madison as if it were a box of explosives, urging his friend not to disclose it to anyone else. Madison was to open the box only "to serve as a basis for your amendment, or . . . suggest amendments to a better groundwork." When nothing happened, some French writers, to whom he had implied that the thought had been a deed, criticized him for not following through. He responded by asserting that "the moment of doing it with success was not yet arrived, and that an unsuccessful

74

effort, as too often happens, would only rivet still closer the chains of bond-age, and retard the moment of delivery."[3]

As his prospects for the presidency improved, Jefferson wrote the Mar-quis de Chastellux in Paris that he did not want those portions of the *Notes* which he referred to as the "strictures on slavery" to be published in the form in which they might be read at home.[4]

> They are the parts which I do not wish to have made public, at least, til I know whether their publication would do most harm or good. It is possible that in my own country, these strictures might produce an irritation, which would indispose the people towards the two great objects I have in view, that is the emancipation of their slaves, and the settlement of their constitu-tion on a firmer and more permanent basis.[5]

These apprehensions were reiterated to his acolyte, James Monroe: "The terms in which I speak of slavery and of our constitution may produce an irritation which will revolt the minds of our countrymen against reformation. . . . I have asked of Mr. Madison to sound this matter as far as he can." Before Madison could gather feedback from focus groups, as the expression now goes, unau-thorized publications of the *Notes* forced Jefferson's hand. The ensuing cho-rus of disapproval from the Carolinians and Georgians excited from him reassurance that he had no intention of acting upon such principles in any way that would threaten their interests.[6]

1784—The Second Opportunity—
The Trans-Appalachian West

In 1784–85, a second occasion was offered Jefferson to prove his commit-ment to his Lost Cause. His great biographer Merrill Peterson has assured us that—so late as that—the elimination of slavery remained "in his mind a mat-ter of fundamental national importance overriding questions of local au-tonomy." Peterson knows his subject's mind intimately. However, the abolition of slavery was not so important as to lead Jefferson to use his influence in Kentucky at the time, where the outcome of the struggle was still in question. Kentucky, the only Western territory where a substantial number of slaves already resided, was also the home of a group of influential and vocal oppo-nents to slavery. (The relationship of Jefferson to the Ordinances of 1784 and 1787 is exceedingly complex. I have done my best to describe its course in "Jefferson and the Ordinances" in the Appendix, p. 249.)

Jefferson was Virginia's most influential delegate to the Confederation Congress, bringing forward as his deputy James Monroe. Monroe on this occasion, and on another, more crucial one at the time of the Louisiana Pur-chase, had immensely important though uncelebrated effects upon the future of slavery in the Mississippi Valley. In 1784, he was Jefferson's junior colleague on the committee of the Congress deliberating upon the proper organization of the territories ceded to the nation by Virginia and by other Eastern states. Monroe owned or would soon own claims upon more than a hundred thousand acres of potential plantation land in Kentucky, where Jefferson and his immediate circle had even larger holdings.[7]

The "local autonomy" of Kentucky was like the "local authority" to be sought out in Florida later (see Part Four). It was comprised of planters, and truly it might have been offended by a proposal to keep slavery out of the entire trans-Appalachian West. There is no dispute as to what Jefferson did: he seconded a proposal offered by Timothy Pickering of Massachusetts that north of the Ohio (and south of Kentucky) "after the year 1800 . . . there shall be neither slavery nor involuntary servitude in any of the . . . states [to be formed], otherwise than in punishment for crimes, whereof the party shall have been convicted to have been personally guilty." This draft language never made its way into legislation. In his account of the demise of Pickering's proposal, Jefferson told Madison—and, by copy, posterity:

> [The proposal] was lost by an individual vote only. Ten states were present. The four eastern states [Massachusetts, Rhode Island, Connecticut, and New Hampshire], New York and Pennsylvania were for the clause. Jersey would have been for it, but there were two members, one of whom was sick in his chambers. South Carolina, Maryland, and ! Virginia ! voted against it. North Carolina was divided, as would have been Virginia, had not one of its delegates been sick in bed.[8]

Jefferson was an experienced politician of forty-one. He was in command of his delegation. Monroe, an ambitious young lawyer-planter-speculator of twenty-five, was serving in his first national office. What was Monroe's position on Pickering's Land Ordinance? Neither he nor Jefferson told us. We do know, however, that when Jefferson went off shortly afterward to his ministry to France in 1784, Monroe assumed some of his chairmanships, including that concerned with territorial organization. As Jefferson wrote Madison, "the fate of millions unborn" did indeed hang "on the tongue of one man, and heaven was silent at that awful moment." The tongue thereafter was Monroe's. He might have spoken lines composed by his just departed leader, had Jefferson felt as intensely as Peterson suggests.[9]

Jefferson went his way to France but remained in close touch with his circle of supporters. We have no way of knowing how he and Monroe left the matter, but when, in 1786, Monroe was made chairman of a committee to take up again the ordinance of 1784, he did nothing to restore the language of Pinckney and Jefferson. We are told by Monroe's biographer Dr. Henry Ammon that the committee produced "a report adhering closely to his [Monroe's] views . . . [yet] the provision excluding slavery, struck out in 1784, was not restored. . . . Jefferson made no comment about the omission. . . . Monroe never explained why he did not incorporate this provision, to which Jefferson attached so much importance." Nor did Jefferson.[10]

After 1785, while Jefferson was in Paris, Monroe fully succeeded to his role in such matters. When the Northwest Ordinance was finally passed, the West was divided between the two societies. That north of the Ohio moved toward diversification among free farms and manufacturing towns, while the South sank into a plantation culture. Though the ordinance required that slaves seeking sanctuary in the Northwest be returned to their owners, that might not have been so important if Kentucky, bordering the Northwest Territory on the south, were a free state. But after Jefferson's return, it was organized as a slave state on the Virginia model.

The Kentucky constitutional convention of 1792 showed that the contest between the two sides was still unsettled—a little weight on the antislavery side, in the interest of the Lost Cause, might have swung things the other way. Six militantly antislavery clergymen led by the organizer of Presbyterianism in Kentucky, the Reverend David Rice, were joined by five prominent Baptist and Methodist laymen and five other delegates against the twenty-six planters who dominated the convention. As the sectarian affiliations of the antislavery forces indicate, the West was ripe for the politics of conscience and hungry for leadership. The planters prevailed, however. Their ranks were impervious to the spirit of reform among the evangelical frontiersmen and unbroken by any dissents on behalf of Jefferson's Lost Cause. Not a murmur was heard from Jefferson.[11]

Though Rice and his allies failed to incorporate Kentucky as a free territory, they managed to bury a pleasant implication in its constitution that "all free male citizens of the age of twenty-one" could vote. That could have meant free male Negro citizens. Lest such a dire possibility be left open, a later constitutional convention felt it necessary to expunge the language. The association of land use and manumission was not yet a dead issue, however. In 1816, the Kentucky Abolition Society proposed that Congress set aside "vast tracts of unappropriated lands . . . [as] suitable territory . . . to be laid off as an asylum for all those Negroes and Mulattoes who have been, or those who may hereafter be, emancipated within the United States." That would have meant accepting manumission without forced exportation, an outcome Jefferson was never willing to consider. Free blacks had no place in his ideal republic. His kinsman George Nicholas drafted the final version of the Kentucky constitution of the 1790s, accepting most of its provisions from that of Pennsylvania, rather than that of his native Virginia, but breaking away short of Pennsylvania's lead in banning slavery.[12]

In 1796, the planters of Middle Tennessee triumphed over the yeomen of the highlands, and that state, too, came into the Union with a slave owners' constitution. Two years later, Mississippi Territory was organized as the

Northwest Territory had been, but with one exception. The provision of the Northwest Ordinance forbidding slavery was omitted. It is often written that opposition to slavery in the West languished from 1789 until the Missouri debates of 1819–21, and that therefore Jefferson's silence on the matter was of little importance. In fact, however, the struggle for Kentucky in 1792 was extended into a lively debate over the admission of Mississippi as a territory containing slaves. In 1798, George Thacher of Massachusetts gained considerable support in the Congress for a proposal that instead Mississippi come in as the Northwest Territories had—as free soil. In Mississippi itself a law was passed by the lower house of the territorial legislature forbidding further imports of male slaves. "By 1802," however, "cotton was becoming so important that . . . [it] was rejected by the council."[13]

Nonetheless, historians who have studied events in Mississippi—surely by then a more difficult setting for resistance against slavery or to situate a yeoman's republic than Virginia—seem agreed that during Jefferson's lifetime "most Mississippians had been apologetic about the institution, viewing it as a necessary evil." We are informed by one such chronicler that as late as 1828

> [the great planter Gerard C. Brandon] characterized slavery as "an evil at best," and such prominent figures as William Dunbar, George Poindexter, W.C.C. Claiborne, and Seargent S. Prentiss voiced similar opinions during the early decades of the century. . . . Just six months before the attack on [Fort] Sumter, the fiery Virginia secessionist, Edmund Ruffin, was astonished to encounter a wealthy Mississippi planter who not only preferred submission to disunion but actually favored a program of gradual emancipation."[14]

Of course "those who articulated their view publicly . . . assumed a quite different posture." And also of course, these great land and slave owners did little after the attempt of 1798–1802 to keep fresh male slaves out of Mississippi. But the question before us remains—what might have been done between 1784 and 1802 to prepare the way for the vast new opportunity presented by the Louisiana Purchase in 1803?[15]

The Third Opportunity—The Lower Mississippi Valley

The Louisiana Purchase opened a new arena where a yeoman republic might resume its struggle against the plantation system. The contest narrowly lost on the Southern seaboard, and lost a second time between the Appalachians and the Mississippi River, could be resumed in an arena where slavery was actually in decline. The President, at the time, was Thomas Jefferson, famous for his earlier antagonism to slavery. Yet after its purchase, the lower Mississippi Valley was organized under his magistracy to become more akin to the Old Order of the Chesapeake than to a New Order in the Universe. The planters were enabled to accelerate their preemption of the best agricultural land between the Atlantic and the Sabine. Eden had beckoned. An Empire of Freedom was possible. Yet, in the new empire of servitude, slaves plodded westward toward a frontier that was not a promise but a threat.

The most appalling prospect before a Virginia slave, aside from immediate physical abuse, was to be sent west and south into deeper enslavement. Between 1790 and 1810, Maryland and Virginia sent 56,000 people in servitude to Kentucky, 25,000 to Tennessee, and more than 5,000 to Mississippi and Louisiana. From 1810 to 1820, nearly 140,000 more were sent from the Chesapeake to the other side of the Appalachians.

As the slaves were driven westward during the presidencies of Jefferson and Madison, free farmers of the Mississippi Valley awaited them with legitimate apprehension—and at that juncture were assaulted from a most unexpected direction. The Virginian theorists in charge of national land policy had come to set a higher value on delaying industrialism than on sustaining free farming. The planters were the winners. North of the Ohio River, free farmers were thriving in interaction with the emerging small local industrial towns, expressing the benign and distinctively American result of diffusion of sources of water power and of habits of mechanical tinkering. But Jefferson and Madison were so prejudiced against an urban and industrial economy that they did what they could to discourage a similar evolution in the lower valley.

As the Purchase opened the Mississippi to commerce, subsistence farming in the southern reaches of the valley began to be replaced by staple production for international markets. Madison rejoiced—and the British textile manufacturers rejoiced with him. It was as if the acquisition of new opportunities to put slaves to work would avert the possibility that the Delta might become a sort of boggy Appalachia:

> By this expansion of our people, the establishment of internal manufactures will not only be for many years delayed, but the consumption of foreign manufactures will be continually increasing with the increase of our numbers: and at the same time all the productions of the American soil required by the nations of Europe in return for their manufactures will be proportionally augmented. . . . For 20 or 25 years we shall consequently have few internal manufactures in proportion to our numbers as at present, and at the end of that period our imported manufactures will be doubled. . . . Reverse the case and suppose the use of the Mississippi denied to us, and the consequence is that many of our supernumerary hands who in the former case would [be] husbandmen on the waters of the Mississippi will on this supposition be manufacturers on this [side] of the Atlantic . . . obliged by want of vent for the produce of the soil and of the means of purchasing foreign manufactures, to manufacture in a great measure for themselves.[16]

Madison and Jefferson were seeking a development plan midway between the urban and industrial society they feared, and that "semi-barbarous" condition of yeomen too far in "advance of civilization." They knew what the corrupt and plaguey cites were like. They had also seen enough of the hollows of Appalachia to entertain few illusions about the consequences of subsistence farming on small plots. They did not want their countrymen to live in isolation from a world economy, as hillbillies of the low country, and so prodded the people of the West to be up and out in the world, to do their economic calisthenics in service to an international market, as the tobacco and cotton farmers of Virginia had done. Otherwise subsistence farmers could be expected to sink into a "state of listless indolence and dissipation . . . that rude, uncultivated state, which has excited the derision and contempt of other communities."[17]

Allen Bowie Magruder of Kentucky agreed: it was, he said, "absolutely necessary" that the people of the Mississippi Valley have access through New Orleans to "an active commerce" with the world.[18]

> [If they did not,] the natural luxuriance of the soil would produce the worst impression upon the morals of the people. Without . . . a market to the products of agriculture, that agriculture would languish. . . . The immense fertility of the soil, where life is supported without that constant labor which requires an assiduous employment of time, would produce the same effect upon morals that acquired luxury does.[19]

Madison had told the Constitutional Convention that "the safest depository of republican liberty" was "a population of freeholders." Furthermore, he had been willing to accept the premise that *ultimately* "our country must be a manufacturing as well as an agricultural one." Yet he and Jefferson sought to sustain as long as they might a middling state of things in which the yeomen would give way and foreign influences would be welcome to keep things lively through exposure to an export market. Then, and only after a period deliberately extended by high-minded planters, a mixed economy might reluctantly be accepted, to absorb "a growing surplus of laborers beyond a profitable culture of it." (Some further thoughts about Madison's reasons for taking this position are offered in the Appendix; see "Jefferson, Madison, Adam Smith, and the Chesapeake Cities," p. 245.)[20]

As old age shriveled their aspirations, Jefferson and Madison accommodated themselves more and more to public and private lives disharmonious with their youthful professions of enthusiasm for yeoman culture. They were heard to utter derisive comments upon "agrarian laws and other leveling schemes," as if their own schemes had not been the noblest of these. Personally, Madison "eased comfortably enough into the life of a Virginia planter that the Revolutionary of the 1780s had resolved to avoid," in the words of a recent biographer, Drew McCoy.[21]

As Madison eased, the lower Mississippi Valley settled into a way of life dominated by the planter. The yeomen were crowded into the gullies and onto the hills. Two agrarianisms were developing, one grounded in Madisonian and Jeffersonian example and the other in their early rhetoric. "Each of these new agrarianisms found expression in imaginative and symbolic terms: that of the South in a pastoral literature of the plantation, and that of the Northwest in the myth of the garden of the world with the idealized Western yeoman as its focal point."[22]

Jefferson was the most potent political influence upon the several hundred thousand men, women, and children born in Virginia who took up homes in the West—four hundred thousand before 1850. Many had developed habits of deference to the opinions of the Sage of Monticello. Would these emigrants have continued to listen to Jefferson had he been more courageous in his opposition to slavery and in support for his Lost Cause? Some, certainly. Perhaps enough. Perhaps not. But, as the economic historian Robin Blackburn concluded, in Jefferson's silence "the Louisiana Purchase confirmed that . . . slaveholders would have their own reserved space" within the new American empire. "Because he was President, because of his reputation, because of his gift for compelling language, and because he was a Virginian, Jefferson was the only man who could have prevented that outcome."[23]

Though the population of the Old South declined relative to that of the Northern states refreshed by immigration, and though Virginia's seats in the House of Representatives, based upon its population, fell from twenty-three in 1810 to thirteen in 1860, and North Carolina's from thirteen to eight, those losses were balanced by seats gained in the new slave states of the West. Since all these might, with some effort, have been swung into the free-state column when first organized, the expansion of slavery might have been halted peaceably in 1792, 1796, 1798, 1802, or 1805–6. As it was, many "ayes" to slavery were cast for western constituencies in the accents of plantation Virginia by representatives elected by those new states.

As there had been two Virginias, one above and the other below the Thousand-Foot Line, there came to be two Souths, also divided topographically. The people of the highlands of northwestern Arkansas, southwestern Missouri, northern Alabama and Georgia, and Appalachian Kentucky and Tennessee drove cattle, raised most of their own food, planted no cotton, and held few slaves. By 1820, there were 1,528,000 people held in servitude in the United States, all but a handful of them south of the Mason-Dixon Line and below the Thousand-Foot Line. Four hundred thousand lived west of the Appalachians. By 1860, after the total number of slaves had doubled, two million lived in Western states admitted to the Union after 1789. Virginia still held 490,000 slaves after shipping to the West almost the same number.

Old Men's Dreams and the Memories of the Land

Writing as an old man to Edward Coles, Jefferson recalled his idealistic 1770s and early 1780s, acknowledging that the years of revolution and of possible reform had not radically disrupted "the quiet and monotonous course of colonial life." In his youth, he had disdained those who were unwilling to take large risks, whose balkiness cluttered the path of bold spirits like his, and from whom "nothing liberal could be expected." As to slavery, few "minds . . . yet doubted but that . . . [their slaves] were as legitimate subjects of property as their horses and cattle." When, wrote Jefferson, Colonel Bland, "one of the oldest, ablest, and most respected members" of the Assembly, "undertook to move for certain moderate extensions of the protection of the laws to those people[,] . . . I seconded his motion." Though "as a younger member," he was "spared in the debate," he learned a bitter lesson, for Bland "was denounced as an enemy of his country, and was treated with the grossest indecorum." That was the sort of thing that "irritated" Jefferson, and when irritated, he often withdrew from the field. In this case, he ceased seeking even "moderate extensions of the protection of the laws to those people." In 1779, as leader of a committee to revise Virginia's criminal code, he proposed stiffening the restrictions and penalties meted out to slaves, and he took no part in Virginia's easing of the rules governing manumission in 1782.[24]

The Lost Cause had languished by the time Jefferson recounted the events of the 1770s. Though independence was achieved, and a revolution of sorts did take place, by his account it did not alter the frame of things entire but left intact a way of life still disposed to "little reflection on the value of liberty." In 1815, responding to a plea from Coles that he emerge from his retirement to oppose the spread of slavery, Jefferson could only say that he had "outlived the generation with which mutual labors and perils begat mutual confidence and influence. The enterprise is for the young." The band of brothers had been disbanded. Though he himself was now a patriarch, he did not blaze with the fervor of Colonel Bland, and he complained to Coles that summoning him forth was "like bidding old Priam to buckle on the armor of Hector."[25]

The opportunity to be a Hector or even a Priam had passed. Revolutionary enthusiasm for manumission had lapsed. The laws of the Old Dominion had reimposed upon blacks a pre-Revolutionary harshness. As Jefferson noted, these restored strictures did "not permit us to turn them [the slaves] loose, [even] if that were for their good." Coles showed what he thought was for the good of his own slaves; he set them free. He was, however, too respectful of the old man either to remind him of that or to humiliate him by recalling Jefferson's cautionary words against doing so: "I hope then, my dear sir, you will reconcile yourself to your country and its unfortunate condition." Coles might "insinuate and inculcate" emancipation or manumission, but, anticipating little success, he should do so "softly but steadily, through the medium of writing and conversation. . . . It is an encouraging observation that no good measure was ever proposed, which, if duly pursued, failed to prevail in the end."[26]

During the years between Coles's manumitting his slaves and Jefferson's refusal to encourage others to do the same, the Sage of Monticello adopted the view that it was best "to do no more good than a country can bear." That was surely the way "to be loved by everybody," or at least by everybody who mattered. The opposite course had cost Colonel Bland dear. Though Jefferson had written that nothing was "more certainly written in the book of fate that these people are to be free," that book was not a bestseller in Virginia. "In the end," on the sidelines, he was lost in lamentation and rightly fearful of the future. His aspirations for an agrarian republic were now only "the dreams of an old man." His hopes for the elimination or containment of slavery had withered after "the occasions of realizing them . . . passed away without return."[27]

Writing in his late seventies, Jefferson reiterated his desire that emancipation might someday come—with deportation of any blacks who might be freed as a necessary and immediate consequence. Until then, it was always "not yet." He had learned in the 1770s, he asserted, that public opinion even then had not been willing to "bear the proposition, [and it would not] . . . bear it even at this day. Yet the day is not distant when it must bear and adopt it, or worse will follow. . . . Nor is it less certain that the two races, equally free, cannot live in the same government."[28]

A year earlier, Jefferson had written:

> There is no man on earth who would sacrifice more than I would to relieve us from this heavy reproach, in any practicable way . . . if . . . a general emancipation and expatriation could be effected; and gradually, and with due sacrifices, I think it might be. But as it is[,] . . . Justice is on one scale, and self-preservation in the other. . . . [I] regret that I am now to die in the belief, that the useless sacrifice of themselves by the generation of 1776, to acquire self-government and happiness to their country, is to be thrown away by the unwise and unworthy passions of their sons, and that my only consolation is to be, that I live not to weep over it.[29]

Whatever may have been said of Jefferson by writers to whom political history is a record of successes or failures measured by the achievement of power rather than its uses, he said of himself that he and the other members of "the generation of 1776" had failed in the full task of founding. His epitaph tells us that he chose to remember and to be remembered by only the events preceding, and those succeeding, his national public career.

The land itself remembered the Founders, for both their words and their deeds were recorded in it. Where the ideal of the family farm was pursued, the land prospered better than it did where that ideal was abandoned and the plantation system prevailed.

PART TWO
The Invisible Empire and the Land

Part Two is about economic dependence and independence among the citizens of the United States in the years between 1776 and 1826, and between those citizens as a whole and the international economic and political system. Domestically, dependence upon international markets for staple goods brought forth from the Southern planters a desire to sustain the subservience of their workforce. That had been true before 1776, when they had been largely dependent upon British markets and financing, and it became true again after 1783, and especially after the mechanization of cotton ginning in the 1790s. Their dependence and their demand for subservience had direct and terrible consequences for the land.

Following this story requires an expansion of view from domestic concerns to the larger international scene, following the widening of perspective on the part of the Founding Fathers as they met in Philadelphia in 1776. They were guided toward that breadth of vision by their most cosmopolitan members, especially Thomas Jefferson, whose final draft of the Declaration of Independence justified their revolution to an international audience on both political and economic grounds. Jefferson's language was of immediate interest to all colonial peoples, and he meant it to be so. The adversary against which he pitted his countrymen was not King George III taken alone but a colonial system which had become unbearable. That system had a history well known to Jefferson and his colleagues but, because of the rupture with Britain caused by them, not so intimately a part of the furniture of acquaintance with which we surround ourselves today.

The British had themselves been colonials, producers of crops to be manufactured by others, priced by others, and whose production was somewhat dependent upon being financed by others even in the Middle Ages. They had fought their way to a reversal of this demeaning status, and by the beginning of Jefferson's century they were able to impose it on others. Among the most important objectives of the American Revolution was to escape that British imposition.

That rebellion was not justified to humankind on that ground alone, however, for the Renaissance and Reformation had opened larger vistas to rebellious citizens—they might not only free themselves of political or economic shackles, but by doing so offer hope to others of a similar independence. When the American rebels proclaimed their New Order in the Universe, they asserted their reasons for cutting loose from the British colonial system in language offering humankind hope as well as explanation.

Others shared that hope of economic as well as political freedom, for persons as well as peoples. These others, therefore, felt themselves betrayed as the South reverted to the old plantation system, using slaves to do the work of planting, cultivating, and reaping. The South was recolonialized. Its agricultural products, of which cotton was the most important, were once again primarily devoted to the satisfaction of British demand. The process of producing them by slaves driven from new land to new land discouraged land-loyalty and did great damage to the earth.

7

Colonial-Imperialism

The Declaration of Independence conveys two kinds of information. Upon its surface, Thomas Jefferson and his colleagues stated their grievances and their aspirations—information by inclusion. Below the surface, as if in the "hidden text" in a computer memory, there lies information by omission: the passages Jefferson sought to include but failed, and further material that others on the committee of draftsmen, such as Benjamin Franklin, might have sought to have included but was left out. The legislative history of the Declaration is rich in discourse about why their suggestions were omitted, stimulating us to imagine what was left unrecorded, or even unspoken.

At the request of his colleagues, Jefferson drafted a committee report delivered on June 28, 1776, to the Continental Congress. The final document approved on July the Fourth was never called by that Congress "the Declaration of *Independence*," for independence had actually been declared two days earlier. The magnificent statement proposed by Jefferson was an explanation for that prior action, not the action itself. It is, therefore, especially important in seeking to understand how he and his colleagues wished to appeal to the "opinions of mankind" and whose opinions mattered to them.

The blacks, whites, and Indians inhabiting the "13 United States of America" at the time were separately mentioned in Jefferson's draft. The Native Americans appeared as "merciless Indian savages, whose known rule of warfare is an undistinguished destruction of all ages, sexes, and conditions." The blacks and whites fell within the general category of "all men," who were declared to be "created equal . . . endowed by their creator with inalienable rights . . . [including] life, liberty and the pursuit of happiness." The best evidence that Jefferson and the other members of the committee meant to include people of African ancestry within the ranks of "all men" lies within the "lost language" condemning the slave trade as "cruel war against human nature itself, violating its most sacred rights of life and liberty."[1]

Though this portion of the draft did not survive into the final version—for reasons to be discussed shortly—many people at the time took the Declaration to be asserting that blacks as well as whites had sacred rights of life and liberty. Many, as a consequence, believed that the new American Order in the Universe would no longer tolerate race-based, inherited human servitude. As if acting upon that understanding, more than half the states freed their slaves during the course of the Revolutionary struggle. Virginia, Maryland, Delaware, Kentucky, and North Carolina considered doing the same but failed in the task. Therefore slavery remained embedded in American life south of a line drawn roughly from Wilmington, Delaware, to Cairo, Illinois.

Three revolutions were being explained in Jefferson's draft of the Declaration. The North became successful in all three. The South achieved only the first, political independence of Great Britain. The second sought to strike off the shackles of the slaves. The third, freedom from British economic as well as political control, was also only successful in the North, though the South made a promising start during the war. Blockades, disruptions of commerce, and the self-abnegation of patriots weaned the Americans from the British imperial economy. The postwar policies of Alexander Hamilton were directed toward sustaining that independent growth. Jefferson's draft for the Declaration did not serve as the basis for support of a Hamiltonian program, for his complaints against British interference in American economic life were limited to those galling to the Southern planters, and, as it turned out, not to all of them.

Jefferson charged that the officers of the Crown had sought to batten the slave system upon the South; Royal Governors had been instructed to veto efforts by colonial legislatures to put a stop to the African slave trade, the "cruel war upon human nature . . . carrying them into slavery." Thus the Crown was guilty of seeking "to keep open a market where MEN should be bought and sold . . . [by] suppressing every legislative attempt to prohibit or to restrain this execrable commerce."[2]

Throughout the seventeenth and eighteenth centuries, British policy had encouraged slavery in all its colonies. The royal family itself had profited from the slave trade. The force of British arms had been deployed to drive off other European slave-selling competitors, and the British imperial wars of the eighteenth century had expanded the areas of North America and the Caribbean open to slavery. However, because Jefferson's fellow planters were accessories to the moral delinquencies he condemned, they struck these clauses from the Declaration before it reached its final form—hence the expression "lost language."

So much for what was cut out. It is equally interesting to note what Franklin and Hamilton had said in justification of rebellion that Jefferson did not choose to embody in the Declaration, for that omission offered a further presentiment of the future of the South. The industrial and commercial classes of the Northern states complained less against British attempts to *prohibit* colonial restraint upon commerce (the slave trade) than about restraints upon commerce itself. However, commerce was itself disagreeable to Jefferson. Inhibitions upon it did not arouse in him the passion evoked from such commercial persons as Franklin and Hamilton. While Pennsylvania's representative in London, Franklin had protested against the British for "restraining manufactures in the colonies," and Hamilton had been advocating economic as well as political independence lest "those things we manufacture among ourselves may be disallowed. We should then be compelled to take the manufactures of Great Britain upon her own conditions." The Americans learned that William Pitt had told the House of Commons that if they "should manufacture a lock of wool or a horse shoe," he would "fill their ports with ships and their towns with troops." But the final list of grievances prepared by Jefferson did not include repression of manufacturing.[3]

After political independence was achieved, the British role in the slave trade was resumed. A squadron of British slave ships hovered off Charleston in 1803, ready to land their cargoes as soon as the South Carolina legislature reopened the port to the traffic. A large share of Britain's offshore revenues were soon again derived from carrying staple crops produced by slave labor in the American South. Reciprocally, the South became again a major customer of British manufacturers. British ships unloaded in Southern ports thousands of cargoes of manufactured goods including millions of yards of cotton textiles. Another British squadron, composed of cotton freighters, awaited the American seizure of Mobile in 1813.

Colonies and Empires

By following those slave ships and cotton freighters back to their home ports, we may gain a sense of the people who sent them forth and of the reasons for their encouragement of the plantation system. The history of the British nation as a commercial people explains some peculiarities of the British ruling class, especially an affinity for commerce greater than that of similar classes on the continent of Europe except the Dutch. Britain emerged from colonial status in the early Middle Ages with such an affinity reinforced by success and set about evolving a set of managers for both empire and colonization—distinct undertakings, as we shall see.

The Dutch showed the British the way to "follow the fibers"—in much the same way that Deep Throat was reputed to have told Bernstein and Woodward to "follow the money" in sorting out the Watergate affair. The fibers we follow are those composing cloth, for the British Empire was as much a textile empire as the Mycenaean was one of bronze. After depicting the nature of British textile imperialism, we will continue to follow the fibers but confine our attention to cotton, as the British did in securing the resubmission of the American South. This was accomplished after 1783 with techniques so subtle

89

that they left behind not a thread of their operation—not even a word to denote the strategy. We must invent such a term by combining some common words we have been using all along: "colony" and "empire." Because the South was brought to heel by devices borrowed from both, the composite word used hereafter to denote this composite system will be "colonial-imperialism." That variety of it having the most indelible effects upon the southeastern quadrant of the American continent was textile colonial-imperialism.

Once we have defined our terms, we will turn to the roles of corporations and business partnerships as agents of colonial-imperialism. They were not new to the scene in 1783. They were among the "powers of the earth" determining the future of the upstart American Republic. No president, chief, general, or king could prudently commence a large action without taking into account corporate power of two main types, colonizing corporations and trading companies. In earlier centuries, in the infancy of modern capitalism, the two had been almost indistinguishable. The purpose of any European landing might be to open a trading post or to create a beachhead for true colonization. To put the matter in another way, it was seldom obvious whether an entrepôt such as Jamestown was there primarily to serve *imperial* purposes or *colonial* purposes.

The origins of these words are useful in directing us toward differences in the effects of each set of corporate intentions upon the land. The word "empire" has a downward valence, denoting *control* of a subject population, but it does not imply settlement. A colony is a placement of cultivators on the land; it remains a colony so long as it remains agricultural, whoever may control it politically. From the point of view of a lexicographer, therefore, the American South did not escape reintegration within an *empire* when it fell back under the economic control of the British, and it relapsed into *colonial* status when its leaders failed to diversify out of the condition of its founding.

Colonization had been learned by the English when they settled populations of strangers in Ireland. As Ireland was England's first colony, India was its first imperial possession. The English did not colonize the subcontinent. Very few of those who made their fortunes there had any desire to make their homes there as well. In the West Indies each island was its own case. Britain colonized some with white indentured servants, and some of those came to stay. Then, as black slaves replaced them, their owners behaved as if they were in the East Indies and came home to England as soon as they could repatriate their wealth. On other islands, the presence was imperial; the blacks were there before the British displaced the Spaniards or French who had brought them there. On these islands as on the subcontinent of India, there was very little British presence beyond the precincts of the governor's compound. Imperialism came to the greatest of Britain's acquisitions in 1615, when Sir Thomas Roe arrived at the Mughal court. Roe represented the East

India Company and began his discussion with "a salute of forty-eight guns" from the ships of the company's fleet lying just offshore. The force factors established, Sir Thomas assured his hosts that the company would be polite: it would eschew "the error of the Dutch, who seek plantation [or colonization] by the sword." The company did not have in mind using the sword or the plow, one the tool of empire and the other of colonization. It took it "as a rule," Roe asserted, "that if you will profit[,] seek it at sea and in quiet trade. . . . [I]t is an error to effect garrisons and land wars in India."[4]

Soon enough, however, India received corporate garrisons and suffered from corporate land wars. Lord Clive voided Roe's "rule" not because it had failed but because it had done its work of opening the way to empire, so India, never a British colony, became a triumph of imperialism. In North America, on the other hand, the trading companies evolved into colonizing companies with such success that the colonials became powerful enough to cut themselves loose. Though Canada remained within the empire, it was "a million acres of snow." When the thirteen plantable colonies to the south of it slipped away, William Pitt made principle from necessity, reasserting toward the North Americans Roe's formulation for India, declaring "schemes of conquest and extension of dominion" to be "measures repugnant to the wish, honor, and policy of this nation." The people of the subcontinent might be excused their bewilderment, while the people of North America were on notice that a new strategy was under development toward them, just in time to coincide with the need for great quantities of green-seed cotton.[5]

From Round Table to Board Table

After 1783, it became the "wish, honor, and policy" of the British to subjugate the American South by quiet trade. And who were "the British?" There are many ways to answer that question, but for working purposes we will restrict ourselves to the devices of old-fashioned history, describing the behavior of the small number of male persons who were generally in charge of things. They were a shrewd lot who managed the rise of a polyglot people inhabiting a little island of modest agricultural potential off the northern coast of Europe until it dominated the commerce of every ocean not under ice. By 1820, they were in the process of coloring much of three continents red.

And how did this elite learn commerce, colonization, imperialism, and colonial-imperialism? Their first instructors were the Baltic merchants of the Hanseatic League who placed on the London shore a fortified entrepôt that became known as the "steelyard." This occurred in the middle of the fourteenth century, the time of Chaucer and King Richard II. The King became the first of many British monarchs to charter commerce—not only to charter it, but also to take a piece of its action—as he entered arrangements with the

Merchant Adventurers of England and led his peerage toward becoming a mercantile aristocracy.

Thereafter, while the wars of Lancastrians and Yorkists provided Shakespeare with the gory stuff of drama, the merchants of London, Bristol, and Norwich were busy as well, supplementing the lessons of trade they had learned from the Baltic traders with financial techniques imported from Italy. The Florentines had quietly opened offices in London, instructing the provincials in the delights of limited liability. In scientific terms, limited liability provided sterile enclosures in which entrepreneurs could place their separate undertakings to grow or not grow without contaminating other holdings. Britain entered the commercial Renaissance in the fourteenth century. To this day the designation "limited" upon a brass plaque is taken in Britain to be a sign of honor as impressive, in its way, as a heraldic shield.

Florence prospered, and so, having learned Florentine lessons, did London. It too acquired domes, textile factories, painters, sculptors, and sweatshops. A half century after King Richard's first charter, London was no longer merely a squalid collation of docks where goods awaited other people's ships. It was becoming a city of dockyards, producing ships to ply the Baltic, the Caspian, the Arctic, and the North Atlantic. British traders first entered the larger world by driving eastward, repeating the Vikings' forays into central Russia and depriving the cities of the Hanseatic League of large parts of their trading territory. The great achievement of early British enterprise lay, however, in the opposite direction, westward across the Atlantic.[6]

By comparison to the undertakings of Spain, Portugal, and France, those of the English and Scots were remarkably private. British sovereigns *did* offer the protection of royal armies and navies to gentlemen in trade whom they legitimated by becoming their partners. The throne *did* become the fulcrum upon which Britain swung from the Middle Ages into the age of imperial capitalism. Yet royal sponsorship was not so important to the British as it was to continental sovereigns. When John Cabot and the people of the North American mainland discovered each other in 1497, only one of the five vessels under his command was provided by the King. The others were all corporate craft owned by syndicates of merchants. So, statistically, North America was discovered by a corporation.

This was not happenstance, for the old military elite of England was already differentiating itself from its Spanish or French counterparts. The warrior class took stakes in global trade and also in settlement devoted to the production of staple crops to supply that trade. By the close of the reign of Queen Elizabeth, the energies of their class that had previously gone into crusading and Wars of the Roses were channeled into colonization and empire. Ireland was already serving as the training ground for settlement. Swashbuckling colonizers such as Walter Raleigh, Humphrey Gilbert, and George Peckham made use of John Bull's Other Island as their neighborhood primary school in plantation. Leaving America for a time to the French and the Iberians, the English practiced colonization in Ireland. Then, hardened for the task, they set sail for the West Indies. Francis Drake and John Hawkins, knights of England, profitably soiled their hands with both blood and commerce. Gilbert became transmogrified into a joint-stock company, the London Virginia Company.

Reinvesting the Loot

John Maynard Keynes tells us that when Drake returned from the Spanish Main in 1580, the half of his loot that went to his Queen was more than the annual revenues of her Exchequer:

> The booty brought back by Drake in the *Golden Hind* may fairly be considered the fountain and origin of British foreign investments. Elizabeth paid off out of the proceeds the whole of her foreign debt and invested part of the balance . . . in the Levant Company; largely out of the profits of the Levant Company there was formed the East India Company, the profits of which during the seventeenth and eighteenth centuries were the main foundation of England's foreign connections.[7]

Generally, however, the British grew rich by subtler methods than piracy. As the eighteenth century opened, England was already a country of cities. The death rate was declining, the survival rate increasing, demand for food rising with it, and the wealth of territorial magnates rising as well as they sold foodstuffs to the townspeople.

The landed class in England, having learned to treat land as a commodity, skillfully transferred the rents and revenues derived from soil—and what had been found under the soil—into shares of stock in corporations, reinvesting food profits not only in textile plants but also in industry, transportation, and mineral extraction, providing Europe with the spectacle of canal-building dukes and coal-mining marquises. Though a small island, England is extended. It is more arms and legs than trunk, with more shoreline than many a larger land mass, so the owner of many a great house need not build a tower to catch a glimpse of the sea or at least of a stream that could bear a boat to the sea. He might look through his windows beyond his hedgerows to the ocean and be reminded of intercontinental trade.

The British were not alone in deploying the corporate form to capitalize international trade—and after trade, colonization and empire. East and West India Companies were also organized by the Dutch, French, Swedes, Danes, and Scots, and—laggardly and without much enthusiasm—by Spaniards, Austrians, and Burgundians as well. After the Muscovy Company, founded in 1555, became England's first use of the Florentine form of joint-stock company to outfit commerce abroad, it was followed by the Levant and Turkey Companies, in 1581, and by the East India Company, chartered in 1600. Operating as an agency of royal purpose, the English Muscovy Company explored Hudson's Bay, while the Dutch East India Company, founded in 1602, employed Henry Hudson to inquire into the coasts of what is now New England and New York, seeking apertures into the fur-producing interior of North America. Between these two hostile corporate salients lay the St. Lawrence Valley, controlled by the Company of New France, the consequence of observation by the ministers of kings of France of the successes of the Dutch. Making use of far greater resources than those of Holland, those ministers delegated to their chosen capitalists state-like functions, including the recruitment of armies and navies. The Company of New France employed Samuel de Champlain to found Quebec in 1608 as a trading post in the Dutch pattern. This French and Dutch emphasis upon trade rather than settlement explains some otherwise baffling chronologies: Albany (Fort Orange) was established far inland before the West India Company's New Amsterdam (New York). So, too, the French inland posts at Natchez (1715) and Natchitoches (1714) preceded the founding of New Orleans, in 1718, by Jean-Baptiste LeMoyne de Bienville for the Company of the West.[8]

The British founded "the Governor and Company of Adventurers of England Trading into Hudson's Bay" in 1670 to succeed the Northwest Passage Company of 1612. (The Hudson's Bay Company remained a quasi-sovereign until, exhausted by a ferocious war with the Northwest Fur Company, it handed those governmental functions back to the Crown in 1858.) We will review the British learning process, as they were instructed by the Dutch to produce textiles and to market them at gunpoint, until they were able to knock their instructors out of the international cloth trade and, in their boldest coup, they followed their defeat of Dutch commerce with the acquisition of a Dutch merchant prince to be their king. In 1688, James II went into exile. The British grandees rallied to Willem of Orange and made him their sovereign. Within a half century, he and his successors had created a "fiscal-military state" characterized by a large civil administration, a standing army and navy available when the subtler devices of economics were insufficient, a sustained tax burden, a system of debt to finance important territorial acquisitions, and "high finance" as exemplified by the Bank of England. In the process, they achieved a remarkable balance between tolerance for free expression at the center and a ferocious and oppressive imperialism at the fringes.[9]

Landed Gentry

The Dutch had shown how to get rich in trade and finance despite a poverty of arable land; one does not think of a Dutch "landed interest." After 1689,

Willem—now William—and his coterie quickly saw to it that the British tax base was changed to favor trade: burdens previously borne by trading companies and manufacturing monopolies were shifted to landed estates. The aristocracy went along, abstaining from revolts to avoid taxes and actively supporting great commercial wars fought at the nation's expense. Thus was created "a form of capitalism headed by improving landlords in association with improving financiers who served as their junior partners. This joint enterprise established a tradition of modernization and was itself the product of a modernization of tradition that both conserved gentlemanly values and carried them forward into a changing world."[10]

By 1721, King George I was able to set forth in his Speech from the Throne a crass and candidly commercial foreign policy. No other sovereign in Europe would have soiled his lips with it. Louis, the Sun King of France, would never have assembled the *noblesse* of France at Versailles to talk of trade. Neither would the Hapsburgs entertain their territorial magnates with schedules and tariffs, nor would the Hohenzollerns abandon the drill field for the countinghouse, nor the Romanovs cease from assembling armies to be sent into the Arctic mists merely for discourse upon customs and imposts. Yet the courtiers of King George were by 1721 as thoroughly commercialized as he. Hanoverian Britain was pledged to the glories of getting rich. Upon "our commerce," spake His Majesty, "the riches and grandeur of this nation chiefly depend." Henry St. John, First Viscount Bolingbroke, agreed: "Trade gave us wealth, wealth gave us power." Over the years, the straightforward brutality of Drake's brigandage had been refined into the dainty but deadly devices of mercantilism. The peerage had come to comprehend the differences among pillage (the way of their ancestors), colonization or occupancy (the method finally employed to control much of Ireland), and imperialism, or economic control. They were adepts. Trade occupied them all, from king and queen to baronet and squire.[11]

As suggested above, most of the new industrial undertakings of the seventeenth and eighteenth centuries were underwritten by peers. When the Stuart kings tripled the number of noblemen, they made room not only for their courtiers but also for landowners made newly rich by seams of iron or coal. When coalfields imperiled their ancient houses, these mineral magnates let them go, averting their eyes as sappers deposited villages and parish churches at the bottom of chasms. Those fortunate enough to own urban land drew more income from "housing estates" than from landed estates. The Earl of Durham grew so rich on coal that he was known as "His Carbonic Majesty" a century before that title passed to Henry Clay Frick. After the Duke of Sutherland added the revenues from his million acres of moor to his winnings from canals and railroads, he was said by Charles Greville to have become "the richest man who ever died."[12]

By the end of the seventeenth century, new people had entered the ruling class, many of them with no significant attachment to the land. The term "squire" was no longer limited to country gentlemen. It could now apply to "a mere urban office-holder like Samuel Pepys." Cousins of titled proprietors practiced finance, manufacturing, trade, and agriculture and enjoyed profitable captaincies at sea and on land. As the Industrial Revolution commenced adding to their wealth, Daniel Defoe wrote of them that "the declining gentry in the ebb of their fortunes frequently push their sons into trade and they . . . often restore the fortunes of their families. Thus tradesmen become gentlemen, by gentlemen becoming tradesmen." A decade earlier, Sir Richard Steele asserted that "the best of our peers have often joined themselves to the daughters of very ordinary tradesmen." In the seventeenth century, the social arbiter Edward Chamberlain had declared that no gentleman could go into trade, but after 1700 it was allowed that "to become a merchant of foreign commerce . . . hath been allowed as no disparagement for a gentleman born, especially to a younger brother." And, as Jane Austen reminds us—quietly, but often enough for the point to settle—if several of the country gentlemen in her pages had not owned a plantation on Antigua and battalion of slaves to work for them there, their fine old houses would have gone to the next risen tradesmen to come into the county aspiring to gentility.[13]

Here and there in eighteenth-century England, hidden away in the folds of its sheep-mowed hills, "backwoods" squires in cross-timbered halls redolent of the feasts of centuries may still have welcomed liegemen for wassail and electoral instruction, but the great houses of the neighborhood were likely to have fallen into the hands of stockbrokers, bankers, provisioners, admirals, and generals. After accounting methods learned elsewhere were applied to the land, "thrusting, calculating, profit-oriented, self-made men [who] turned their entrepreneurial skills into reorganizing agricultural practices" developed the most productive agricultural system in Europe, with the possible exception of the Dutch, while the cousins of "the leaders of the agricultural revolution" reorganized trade into a commercial revolution and manufacturing into the Industrial Revolution. Lawrence Stone tells us that "after 1650 the landed elite itself was willing to adopt economic and foreign policies designed to protect domestic industry and commerce and open up foreign markets by direct naval action around the globe."[14]

8

Textile Colonial-Imperialism

Swords might flash and spearheads clang upon breastplates, dirks and pisto-
lettoes might do their deadly work in alleyways, headsmen's axes might de-
capitate kings and poisons convulse dissident lords, but the weapon used by
the British nation to win world power was cloth. Cloth brought Britain out of
its own colonial status. Cloth brought India to heel. Cloth cargoes took British captains to Malabar and Cartagena, and the need for cotton fiber led Britain to use all its guile to induce the expansion of the plantation system across
the American South. From 1783 until 1861, colonial-imperialism, tested in
India and Ireland, was put fully to work to secure a steady supply of Southern
cotton for the British mills. There were a few misadventures along the way;
"perfidious Albion" was not always more clever than its competitors, even
when cloth was concerned. Sometimes it had to turn to brute force when
cleverness failed—as in an instance off Sumatra: the first of the East India
Company's vessels to attempt trade on that coast found that the natives had
little interest in heavy woolen vests and long-wearing work trousers from
Devon. Undeterred, the English hijacked a Portuguese ship lying nearby and
sold its trade goods to the Sumatrans.

   Competence in using textiles as weapons of empire emerged from a thousand years of experience. Scots and Englishmen learned about colonialism
from their own past. During the Middle Ages, the green meadows of Britain
supported a nation of shepherds, the Basques of the North Sea, providing
wool for manufacturers situated elsewhere. Others grew grain as the Poles of
the West. In the thirteenth century, the English landed gentry stood toward
Flanders as, in the nineteenth, the American planters stood toward the descendants of those gentry who had taken office as directors of banks and chartered mercantile companies. The great Flemish historian Henri Pirenne has
observed that in those days the medieval and colonial British "devoted themselves to producing more and more wool, for which there was always a sale"
in Ghent and Bruges, the medieval equivalents of Victorian Manchester and
Leeds.[1]

Bruges and Ghent were brought low by the French, English, and Spanish armies pillaging their way through endless dynastic wars. As these Flemish cities declined into picturesque desuetude, the British undertook what is now known as "vertical integration" of their economy—from lamb to loom. Having broken their dependency upon the Flemings, they established themselves as millers, selling their products in Flanders into the teeth of their former customers. Then they turned their basilisk gaze upon competitors in Holland, who were disadvantaged for having been too long in the modern world: their workers had become accustomed to wage capitalism and were free to negotiate. The British "enclosing landlords" had but lately turned their peasantry off the land and into the towns, where they became desperately available for wage-work. While the Dutch haggled, the British abandoned the production of "the undyed, unfinished, all-wool 'old draperies' they had produced up to then" and "took to the production of 'new draperies'—mixtures of wool with silk, linen, or cotton—as well as lighter worsteds. . . . They were able to produce these more cheaply than the Dutch, first by shifting production from the urban areas into the [impoverished] countryside, and later by the mechanization of the textile industry." Once assured of a compliant workforce, the English manufacturers kept their wool and flax at home. No longer would they provide to others the raw materials for manufacture. Now they manufactured for themselves and produced enough surplus to assault the Flemings and Dutch on their home grounds. This made Britain richer and ready for the Indian market—the real prize.[2]

India Is Conquered by the Mechanics

The Indians placed themselves squarely in the line of fire by sailing into the situation previously occupied by the Flemings and Dutch. The Indians had been growing cotton for thousands of years and had been a commercial people much longer than the British. In the seventeenth century they responded to the rising market for clothing in Europe by delivering thither immense amounts of cotton cloth. Their arrival was memorialized in many of the words used for items manufactured from cotton, such as the "bandannas" worn by herdsmen and the "calicoes" produced at Calicut, on the Malabar Coast. For a time, Indian industrialists were able to seize the opportunity presented by the presence of trading vessels of the East India Company to reach Europe. Shiploads of printed cottons from India sold more merrily in England than the woolens of the Midlands. To keep Indian goods out, Parliament passed a series of acts from 1700 to 1720 forbidding "absolutely the import of printed fabrics from India, Persia, and China."[3]

Behind the stiff arm so administered, the British set out to industrialize a response. Indian women weavers were able to survive on even lower pay than

English women, for though British textile *weaving* had been mechanized early, cotton *spinning* had not kept pace. So British ingenuity was summoned to industrialize spinning amid ecological requirements almost as rigorous as those of cotton planting. Britain enjoys a humid climate, but it was not at first easy to determine precisely where its fogs and damps would be most salubrious for cotton manufacturing. As a consequence, cotton was being manufactured only for candle wicks; the "cottons" of British manufacture in the Middle Ages were actually wool, imitating the fustians of the Low Countries and the Levant.[4]

Finally, however, during the reign of Elizabeth the First, John Billston produced a little cotton cloth in Chester. It turned out that Chester was not quite right, so by 1727 it was replaced by Manchester, the humidity of which was of a better sort. "Some dampness," we are told, "is essential to make the fibers cling," but not too much. What was good for fibers was also good for employers requiring cheap labor: "The unpleasantness of the weather renders an indoor occupation desirable, and the scanty sunshine, combined with the unfruitful soil, prevents the absorption of the population for agricultural pursuits." So limited, the workforce was disinclined to negotiate vigorously for higher wages. Even with these advantages, however, textile production did not increase much until the eighteenth century, when British spinning machines caught up with their weaving machines.

While the political submission of India was achieved by the arms of Lord Clive, its economic submission was achieved by the machines of Lewis Paul, John Wyatt, James Hargreaves, Samuel Compton, Thomas Highs, John Kay, and Richard Arkwright. Making use of the water power of the Midlands, the first weaving machines were water-driven, as were 143 cotton mills producing cheap yarn by the end of the 1780s. Then steam mills began to operate, for England was blessed with coal as well as with rivers, and these natural assets were placed at the disposal of a disciplined, skilled, and relatively healthy workforce. A full-scale industrial offensive was then launched against Indian textile manufacturers. Until the final third of the eighteenth century, they had no difficulty selling cotton products in England, but thereafter the massed machines of Lancashire were able to drive the Indians out of the British market. Next, Manchester delivered in India itself goods both better and cheaper than those produced by the hand looms of Indian cottage industry.[5]

In 1779, one machine, Crompton's "mule," could draw out fibers and spindle several at once. Unskilled women and children operating "mules" could produce in three hundred hours a volume of cotton thread requiring fifty thousand hours of handwork by Indian workers. Comparative wages ceased to be important. The difference between India and Britain now lay in productivity per worker. Manufacturers who had cried for protection now howled for free trade and got it. British capitalism had been protected in infancy by state sponsorship of the privileges of trading companies and the exclusion of competitive goods from abroad. At the end of the eighteenth century, it shed protection and burst forth onto the world market. As Adam Smith derided the tired notions of mercantilism, a bewildered public observed "the spectacle of capitalism, in its liberal age, attacking and destroying that which had given it birth."[6]

British production of printed cloth—once the Indians' specialty—grew from twenty million yards in 1796 to nearly three hundred fifty million in 1830; Clive and Hastings had extorted booty enough from India to finance the engines of its destruction as a textile-producing nation. British power looms and jennies reversed the flow of cotton fabric, and the Indian textile industry was suffocated under layer upon layer of British cloth. By 1840, the chief of a British firm trading in India chortled that bandannas were "the last of the expiring manufactures of India."[7]

Solving the Problem of Supply

Britain became the dominant textile power in the world by solving the mechanical problems of production and by eliminating competition. But it could not make cotton grow on its own ground. Sheep might safely graze its meadows, and flax might prosper in Ireland, but the mallows remained intractable. British mills could produce—and British merchants could sell—much larger quantities of cotton cloth than could be obtained from the long-staple cotton grown on the islands of the British West Indies, in the Bahamas, and along the Georgia shore. Only that variety could be economically released from bolls by the technology then available. Cotton was being separated from seed by a primitive comb (or "churka," as it was called in China and India until the World War of 1914–18). The rakes and combs of early eighteenth-century Virginia and those invented in the Bahamas did not improve much on the churka.

Then the famous gins developed in the 1790s effected a "technological fix." These new devices could strip out fiber by sending the cotton bolls down a tilted iron bed through whirling notched discs, producing fibers to be pulled away with revolving brushes. But this harsh system damaged the long, easily detached fibers of sea island cotton and was therefore uneconomic. It did not matter much that short-staple, green-seed cotton refused to grow much above the Thousand-Foot Line, until gins were devised to make it a commercial product. Gins were harsh and wasteful, but even after the waste they could deliver the volume of usable fibers demanded by the mills.

Having solved its technological challenge, Britain turned to a political dilemma of its own creation—its second major miscalculation of the utility of North America. In the 1490s, it had forfeited its opportunity to make use of the services of Christopher Columbus, and thus delayed its entry upon the world stage for more than a century. Recovering from their Columbian misstep in the seventeenth and eighteenth centuries, the British created a maritime empire of their own. Then, in the early 1770s, just as the age of industrialized cotton manufacturing was about to be coupled with the mechanized conversion of upland cotton bolls into fiber, they blundered into the loss of the world's best cotton land by exasperating their American colonists into rebellion. The cotton fields of the future fell behind enemy lines and remained there by the terms of the Treaty of Paris in 1783.

That might not have mattered much in 1750, but the Cotton Revolution had intervened, and those fields would be required to clothe the world. In the early eighteenth century, only the rich in temperate climates could enjoy the pleasures of fresh-laundered "linen," of cotton smallclothes and underwear, of sleek, long-lined dresses in the neoclassical style, of starched cravats, of cotton "bathing clothes" known later as "swim suits," of cotton overcoats that did not spot in the rain as silk does, of window curtains and chintzes. British exports of cotton yarn to continental Europe grew from a value of thirty-eight thousand pounds sterling in 1794 to more than a million pounds a decade later, as the millers of the Midlands learned how to make fashionable imitations of expensive Indian prints, just in time for neoclassical fashion to renew the upper end of the market.

American women read the same magazines as their English and Scottish counterparts, as we discern from the designs worn by George Washington's ladies sketched by Benjamin Henry Latrobe while standing on the verandah at Mt. Vernon. They wore neoclassical cotton frocks, scandalous from the point of view of Abigail Adams in their neoclassical susceptibility to the caress of every breeze and their Hellenistic revelations of the contours beneath and the withdrawal of their bodice-lines to the very frontier of decent coverage.

In 1789, the British consul in what was still called "the Quaker City" withdrew his gaze from the mincing ladies and gentlemen of Society Hill long enough to observe dangerous puffs of smoke from little manufactories along the Schuylkill. He was alarmed—it was all very well for the Americans to consume fine cottons, but quite another thing for them to produce them. The consul had been recommending for some time to his employers that they encourage the former and discourage the latter by dumping cotton goods at low prices. In 1789, he was able to report some success to the Duke of Leeds: the price war was going considerably better than had Lord North's military war six years earlier. Though the Americans were "under the necessity of purchasing and importing vast quantities of British and other European manufactures . . . Manchester cotton goods are sold for 25% less than the Philadelphia cotton goods. . . . [T]he cotton manufacturers in England have lately reduced their prices . . . and this has given a sensible check to the progress of the cotton manufactury in Philadelphia."[8]

A check, but not a permanent defeat. The contest was underway. And the question became: where would the planters take their stand? For they had Mr. Jefferson as their leader, and he was a host in himself.

The Americans Are Put on Notice

The American Revolution demonstrated that the clumsy clamps and containers of mercantilism could not constrain the energies of the Americans. After 1783, having learned that lesson, the British turned to other means, pressed toward the indirect and undiscernible by Lord Sheffield. Sheffield later gained immortality as the friend of Edward Gibbon, though he himself lacked Gibbon's gifts for epitomy or irony. His prolix and pedestrian arguments for mercantilism as the means to avoid the decline of British commerce required nearly as many words as Gibbon required for the *Decline and Fall of the Roman Empire*. Sheffield loathed free trade, perhaps because he had suffered from that branch of it being carried on by the young men of Sussex who preferred smuggling to net a guinea a week to working his estates for eight shillings. Like Jefferson, Sheffield expanded local experience into general theory, in his case warning his countrymen that without a reaffirmation of the financialmilitary state by other means, they might become "rich, perhaps, as individuals; but weak as a State."[9]

In 1783, Sheffield published his *Observations on the Commerce of the United States* urging Britain to return to the old religion of mercantilism and to reject the free-trade heresies of Adam Smith. The Navigation Acts, he asserted, had been "the basis of our great power at sea, [and] gave us the trade of the world." Though they had also driven the Americans to revolt, and from revolt to independence, Sheffield's response was that Britain should punish them by recolonializing them—subtly: "Great Britain will lose few of the advantages she possessed before these States became independent, and with prudent management she will have as much of their trade as it will be her interest to wish for, without any expense for civil establishment or protection."[10]

In Sheffield's account book, the scarlet panoply of empire became merely the expense of "civil establishment." Mace, scepter, ermine, emeralds, tall ships, and twenty-one-gun salutes should be brought into play only when they were cost-effective. A countinghouse imperialism could secure the protection of a cheap supply of cotton for the British textile industry by giving over to Southern planters the costs of expanding the cotton fields and the exertion of lashing the backs of slaves. Why lament the descent of a few flags from a few flagpoles, or the unemployment of a few former colonial governors? The American colonies had been "more loss than profit," taking account of the cost of governing and protecting them. Let those expenses be saved, and the money invested in manufacturing capacity. The Americans could be overwhelmed with cheaper consumer goods than they could make for themselves. The empire might be reestablished invisibly.

Some ingenuity was required, but the two crucial lessons had already been learned. The first of these was the failure of Lord North's imperialism, leading to the loss of the cotton fields to the rebels of 1776. The second was an unsuccessful effort to keep the entire development of cotton production within the British West Indian empire. The French on Haiti had been the largest source of cotton to the English millers until the French-American alliance of 1778 abruptly cut it off, instructing the British that essential raw materials ought not be left in the hands of foreigners. At the close of the Revolution, half the cotton imported into Britain still came from her own island possessions in the West Indies, and another quarter from Turkey and Smyrna. These sources were of limited potential, so immediately after the Treaty of Paris formalized American independence, the British attempted to see what might be done without North American cotton. The first effort was to obtain an adequate supply from the planters of Barbados and Jamaica, who were told to cut their plantings of sugar and to expand cotton production in their "own islands." In 1786, Lord Sydney, Secretary of State for the Colonies, directed each island governor to encourage those planters "as may be inclined to undertake the growth of cotton." The planters were made "aware of their needs and probably did much to popularize the adoption of more efficient cleaning and planting in the islands. . . . Between 1786 and 1790 the quantity of cotton imported from the British West Indies increased by almost fifty per cent," and those governors who had land left to grant, such as the governor of Dominica, made it available for that purpose. It was not enough. Those islands "were not capable of supplying the fast-growing needs of the industry." Much of their land had been sickened by tobacco and sugar and "would only yield small crops."[11]

Not long afterward, the Bahamas became suddenly important as potential cotton producers when Joseph Eve, the Bahamian Eli Whitney, unveiled his gin for cleaning long-staple West Indies cotton. Perhaps this new machine might justify a new crop. Agents of the Board of Trade and the Secretary of State for the Colonies gathered seeds from India, Africa, and Persia for experiment in the sandy soils of the Bahamas. Persian seeds cast aside in error on Barbados produced an efflorescence sent to be ginned by Eve's machine. Thereafter, bags of West Indian seeds were carried to South Carolina and Georgia by the Tory members of such bi-national families as the Moultries, McIntoshes, Livingstons, and Draytons, arousing a tumult of interest in the Bahamas, Florida, and the mainland states.

By 1800 or so, it was becoming manifest that there was not enough cotton-growing acreage on the islands under Britain's direct control to satisfy the immense demands of the textile manufacturers of the Midlands and of Scotland. Besides, the West Indian sugar planters were still powerful in Parliament, and they had no desire to serve the millers' interest rather than their own. Though the productivity of the West Indian plantations was declining with soil sickening—providing an unheeded lesson to the South—acre for acre, cotton growing remained a less lucrative use for poorer soil than sugar growing. Finally, the sugar plantations became so ravaged, and their workforces so excessive to the work to be done, that abolitionist virtue was able to triumph over the reduced influence of the sugar growers. Britain abolished slavery on the islands in 1833. The former slaves could then be left to fend for themselves on sick or exhausted soil.

Another thirty years passed, however, before the virtuous of Britain aggregated to a large enough body to diminish the appetite of the nation for goods produced by slaves driven by Americans. Meanwhile, to diminish the need for such a contaminated supply, Thomas Clarkson conceived the idea of serving the mills with African cotton grown on African soil. The Sierra Leone Company was established, and thousands of its acres were purchased directly by manufacturers. In the end, however, that sort of vertical integration failed. The millers went back to milling, having learned about insects, rot, piracy, and insurrection. Like "civil establishment" and "protection," those risks were to be passed to the American planters and to the American land.

Hamilton, Jefferson, and Tench Coxe Respond to William Pitt

The planters of the South were brought back into the imperial system by a wondrously complex marketing message. They could no longer be chivvied into doing so by Orders in Council or by peremptory instructions sent colonial governors. How might sensitive former rebels be beguiled?

They had revolted to achieve both economic and political independence. North and South, Jeffersonians and Hamiltonians agreed as to that. The successes of British economic mobilization under William the Dutch and the early Georges were instructive. As noted earlier, Hamilton was a student of those successes and sought to emulate them a half century later. His countrymen might make as good use as the British of "high taxes, a growing and well-organized civil administration, a standing army, and the determination to act as a major . . . power."[12]

Thomas Jefferson reached an opposite conclusion. He had no intention of seeing a fiscal-military state recapitulated in America. Such "changes in the nature of government and the character of wealth" were in his view pernicious, undermining those substantial landed proprietors who, by virtue of their extensive acres, were regarded as the 'natural' rulers of society," as contrasted to "a 'financial interest,' whose wealth was derived from dealings with government—as investors, contractors, and remitters—and held in the form of stocks and government securities." Regardless of who else thought them to be the "natural rulers of society," that was how they thought of themselves—and exactly how the British wished them to think of themselves.[13]

It would have been considerably more difficult to keep them in their place if they had thought of themselves as inheritors of the adaptations of the British upper class to trade and to industrial life. By ill luck, the personal prejudices of Thomas Jefferson reinforced those of his class, and the other American most competent to urge a more capacious sense of themselves upon the planters—and a more realistic appraisal of their antagonists—was Tench Coxe. Though exceedingly shrewd, Coxe was also exceedingly eager to please the planters.[14]

The appearance of textile milling in Philadelphia, so troublesome to the Duke of Leeds, was also being observed by Coxe, the leading economist of that city. Though he did what he could to encourage manufacturing at home, he was also assiduous in consoling the planters with assurances that "it is well known that the cotton manufactures in Great Britain will take any quantity." Demand for raw cotton had risen "to such a pitch . . . the price has risen by 50%. This article must be worth the attention of the Southern planters." Coxe himself certainly was worth their attention, and he made certain he received it, telling them what they wanted to hear.

Coxe had taken the Tory side in the Revolution, was captured, but after a brief incarceration made a switch in time. Having broken with the imperial political cause, he opposed its economic hegemony as well. A fierce Federalist until dismissed from his post in the Treasury in 1797, he executed another political pirouette just before Jefferson's election to the presidency in 1800, releasing private correspondence embarrassing to his former party colleagues. He was rewarded with the Purveyorship of Public Supplies. He held the post until it was abolished during the Madison administration, providing arguments for the expansion of the planters' realm and for the system of slave labor after his Hamiltonian phase ended, and ceased to urge with equal vigor the development of textile milling in competition with the British.

Though remarkably prescient both as to winning sides and economic trends, Coxe was neither an ecologist nor a humanitarian. He did not caution his Southern friends about the consequences for the land and labor force of intense, slave-based, staple-crop agriculture. After aiding the Virginians to defeat John Adams, he gave them satisfaction in the expansion of slavery by showing them how it would absorb their overstock of slaves as "the value of slaves would rise as more cotton was grown."[15]

Coxe apparently thought that Aaron Burr shared his views, for he wrote Burr in 1802 offering "the evils of Negro insurrection" as justification for encouraging a "liberal naturalization law" for "foreigners with property," especially white refugees from Haiti. Though the ferocity of these planters toward their slaves was notorious, Coxe wrote Burr that they should be welcomed as "a good counterbalance for the blacks." He was not aware, apparently, of the joint efforts of Burr, Hamilton, and John Jay through the New York Manumission Society to protect slaves who had escaped to New York from being reenslaved by "counterbalancing" squads of slave catchers prowling the streets of the city.[16]

Jefferson and the Cotton Business

Perhaps under the influence of Coxe, perhaps unconstrained by any foolish consistency between action and theory, Jefferson was willing to abandon his resistance to coupling cotton production to its manufacture when his—or Virginia's—peculiar interests were at stake. While Secretary of State in 1793, he received from Eli Whitney a drawing of his cotton gin. The two had not been introduced, for Whitney was a mere schoolmaster to planters' children. Jefferson was still protecting his reputation as an opponent of industrialism. His response was cautious. All he would say at first was that for a manufacturer of cloth "one of our great embarrassments is the clearing of the cotton of the seed." Yet, hedging, he expressed "interest in the success" of Whitney's invention "for family use" and later reopened the matter by asking that Whitney satisfy him as to the practicality of the gin. Was it, he asked, "yet but a machine of theory?" If not, he might be induced "to engage one of them." So introduced and so acquainted, Jefferson and Whitney became mutually convenient. As President, in 1801, Jefferson introduced Whitney to Governor James Monroe of Virginia as "a mechanic of the first order of ingenuity," urging Monroe not to content himself with household manufacture of cotton but to recruit Whitney for "our manufactory of Richmond" on the strength of his invention of "the cotton gin now so much used in the South."[17]

Having done what he could to assist the South with machinery for cotton, in 1808–9 President Jefferson suffered what he called "some noise . . . [for] a little transaction of mine," another service to the brotherhood of planters. His Embargo Act of December 1807 had forbidden any transaction with Britain or France, blighting American foreign commerce. Despite the anger of the merchants, the President did not cease to serve the planters' interests. The Agricultural Society of Paris had informed him that "they were cultivating the cotton of the Levant and other parts of the Mediterranean, and wished to try also that of our southern States. I immediately got a friend [John Milledge of Georgia] to have two tierces of seed forwarded to me." Milledge had also received some fine French rice seeds, which he distributed promptly to his fellow planters. Jefferson expedited the Georgia cotton seed on its way to Baltimore, where he knew the merchants were not squeamish about embargo-running. From there it was to be sent to New York and on to France. The merchants of Baltimore were, however, indisposed to accommodate a President who was bankrupting them. By his own account, Jefferson's cotton-seed order seemed to them "something very criminal, and . . . [they put it] into the newspapers." Ever resourceful, Jefferson turned to a friend, John Hollins, who saw to it that the seed got to Europe, "it being necessary I should not commit myself again to persons [of] whose honor, or want of it, I know nothing."[18]

As late as 1821, five years before Jefferson's death, Virginia was producing twelve million pounds of cotton, more than Louisiana, Mississippi, or

North Carolina. Its soil was sadly depleted, however, and its climate prob-
lematic. Though fading from that competition, it was doing so slowly and
obviously. Forewarned, the planters might have taken this to be an opportunity to reconsider diversification had the agrarian myth not already taken hold
in a peculiar Cavalier expression. Virginia's ample water power and its vast
supply of coal were left to be exploited by "new men." Few planters redi-
rected cotton profits toward manufacturing.

Who, then, would vie against Britain? In the North, despite the efforts of
that British consul in Philadelphia and his masters, textile independence was
following political independence. Models of Arkwright's loom had been
smuggled to the United States in 1786. The first American cotton mill had
been built in Massachusetts in 1788. Samuel Slater put a water-frame in motion in Rhode Island a decade later. By the 1830s, there were eight hundred
mills in the United States, nearly all in the North, using about a quarter of the
amount of cotton devoured by the mills of the British Midlands. Despite
Jefferson's effort to assist the manufactory at Richmond, there was no equivalent effort in the South. The possessors of Southern capital had become accustomed to easy fortunes derived from cheap land and slave labor, disdainful
of smoky towns and urban masses. They were also in the habit of thinking of
themselves as "natural leaders" elevated above "mechanics"—including Arkwright, Watt, or Eli Whitney.

The planters settled into a mood admixing pride to resentment. Increasingly they were patronized as well-mannered colonials by both the
British and the Yankees. "The South," wrote a correspondent to *DeBow's
Review* in 1847, "stands in the attitude of feeding from her own bosom a vast
population of merchants, shipowners, capitalists, and others." Sunk into
dependence upon debt-financed production, the planters became elegant
sharecroppers. They bought on credit and overpaid. Having failed to create
banks on a scale sufficient to compete with the Scots, the British, and the
rising "cotton Whigs" of the North, they were offered sympathetic snob-
bery and high-rate loans. As their land degenerated around them, many a
proud planter degenerated as well, falling among those who, according to
John Randolph of Roanoke, were raising slaves "for the market, like oxen
for the shambles."[19]

Slaves as Cash Crop

When Jefferson was writing Monroe about Whitney, Virginia was the most
populous of the states of the American Union. She remained nearly so even
after the shipment to the West of three hundred thousand slaves and more
than half her young white men. Without a substantial manufacturing economy,
Virginia's most important cash crop after tobacco, cotton, and wheat was slaves

bred for market. Few could be sold in the highlands immediately at hand, so a market had to be produced or found beyond the Appalachians.

The Cherokees, Choctaw, Chickasaws, and the tribes of the Creek Confederation had to be removed from the sales territory. Furthermore, the sellers of slaves had to solve a second problem: "seasoned" slaves, grown from childhood on eastern plantations, held their value in the West only if they could be kept uncontaminated by diseases introduced from Africa or the West Indies by new arrivals. The records of human death in the West Indies demonstrated that "fresh slaves" from Africa infected those already present with "fresh" African diseases. Since Virginia no longer imported many slaves and was not much contaminated by new arrivals, the death rate of its slaves was lower than that of the Lower South. (Conditions may also have been milder on some Virginia plantations than farther south; such matters lie beyond easy testing statistically.)

During the negotiations toward the United States Constitution, Virginia had purchased alliance with the Deep South by agreeing to constitutional protection for continued importation of slaves from Africa until 1808. This was not a popular concession around the Chesapeake, for those with slaves to sell did not welcome price competition from slaves brought in from abroad, nor did they wish to risk morbidity carried from abroad to their own stock. Thus the natural humanity among Virginians averse to a resumption of the international slave trade found reinforcement from others whose instincts were not in the least philanthropic. When 1808 approached and Congress took up legislation to bring to an end African competition and contamination, there was no important constituency in Virginia for keeping open the African trade.

However, Virginia was as committed to the interstate slave trade as South Carolina was to the international trade. Coffles of manacled people were driven westward from the 1780s onward, some of them sold by Jefferson himself. Eighty-five percent of the eight hundred fifty thousand slaves sent to the West between 1790 and 1860 came from Virginia, Maryland, and the Carolinas. Three times as many were sold in the last half of that period as during the first, for the demand for slaves continued to be subsidized by the taxpayers of the entire nation through an expansionist foreign policy bringing new cotton fields into the Union.[20]

At the end of his life, a "long succession of stunted crops" from gullied and eroded land reduced Jefferson to substituting the fecundity of his slave women for that of his fields. He wrote one of his overseers: "I consider a woman who brings a child every two years as more profitable than the best man of the farm, what she produces is an addition to capital, while his labors disappear in mere consumption." When the price of slaves fell during the cotton recession of 1819, Jefferson lamented that "beyond the mountains we have good slaves selling for one hundred dollars, good horses for five dollars, and the sheriffs [in bankruptcy sales] generally the purchaser."[21]

In 1790, the number of slaves in the Old Dominion had exceeded the entire population of the state of New York—white and black, slave and free. But since slave employment declined with the productivity of land, the abandonment of soils impoverished by the pernicious effects of growing tobacco and cotton could be measured by the rate of disposition of surplus slaves. By 1830, three hundred thousand blacks had been moved across the mountains. It is probable that more people were sold *from* the Old Dominion to work in the fields of the plantations in the West than were sold *to* Virginia during the entire history of the international slave trade. The price of Virginia's slaves was determined not so much by the amount of wheat, tobacco, or cotton they might draw forth from the depleted soils around the Chesapeake but by their predicted valuation by the planters of Tennessee, Kentucky, Mississippi, Alabama, or Missouri.

The Millers Send Out Their Salesmen

The British were meanwhile making their own calculations. They no longer had slaves to sell. Their product was cotton cloth. Its price was set by demand in the presence of competition, and its profitability depended upon the difference between that price and the cost of raw cotton produced for British mills by the planters, especially those of the American South. The Americans were, therefore, both on the demand side and the supply side of the British computations.

Flanders, Holland, and India were no longer serious competitors. Though the Yankees were making irritating efforts to mill a little cotton on their own, and though some small factories were under way along New England waterways, they were still, from the British point of view, a nation of customers. A consortium of Lancashire manufacturers pointed out to the House of Commons that "the annual value of British manufactures, exported to the United States[,] . . . exceeds ten millions sterling, and . . . our consumption of produce [largely cotton] from that country falls far short of that amount." Colonial-imperialism was working very well. The North was buying finished goods and the South selling raw cotton. At this juncture, "the success of the cotton manufacturers rested on the planters' ability to increase the quantity and quality of cotton from their plantations, and so keep the spinning machines working."[22]

To increase that "quantity and quality," salesmen were trained and sent out to visit planters and factors in Charleston, Philadelphia, and Savannah. Chief among them was the charming John Milne, of Stockport, a cotton manufacturing town six miles from Manchester. Milne rehearsed his arguments for two years in Georgia before making his crucial sales call at Mount Vernon, in February 1789. As it happened, the name bestowed upon the Washington estate by the President's elder brother Lawrence commemorated the family's association with another Stockport family, the Vernons. Lawrence Washington was introduced to military life in a Caribbean campaign forty years earlier under the command of Admiral Edward Vernon. Stockport had been built around the ancient seat of the Lords Vernon. Mount Vernon was the seat of the most influential man in the United States. Milne was not a man to let such a fortunate coincidence pass.

After the salesman from Stockport had fulfilled his task, his host reported to Thomas Jefferson on the success of Milne's mission of "stimulating and instructing the planters to the production of cotton. . . . [I]t is said that cotton may be made in such abundant quantities, as to prove a more profitable species of agriculture than any other crop." Washington went on to tell Jefferson that a pursuit of cotton agriculture could be "of almost infinite consequence to America."[23]

Washington was correct, though in ways he could not have anticipated. Those "consequences" were first felt in the reintegration of the economy of the South into the British imperial web. Though scattered units of independent yeomanry held out, the larger elements of Southern life were quietly but irresistibly brought within a skein of economic force commencing in "servers" in Manchester (to borrow some metaphors from the internet) and running through milling machines in the Midlands to bankers and factors in London, New York, Liverpool, Mobile, Galveston, and New Orleans and cotton gins operating from Southside Virginia to North Florida and westward into Texas.

The susceptible extremities of this system responded to signals from the servers with what one traveler in Georgia called "a kind of cotton insanity." John Davis observed its effects early, as a party of "cotton manufacturers from Manchester" were found one evening at Dillon's boardinghouse in Savannah: "Cotton! Cotton! Cotton! was their never-ceasing topic." Frederika Bremer, the Swedish novelist, passed the same spot on a steamer fifty years later, and the madness was still abroad in the land: "On deck, a few gentlemen, planters, who were polite and wished to talk, but talked only of cotton, cotton, cotton." Mesmerized and destabilized, the South became a vast flux. When prices were high, an endless flow of raw fluffy stuff was sucked away; the rivers were white with it; the Gulf of Mexico bore currents of it from Mobile and New Orleans eastward past the Keys and on across the Atlantic into the Irish Sea, to Liverpool and Manchester. William Cullen Bryant described "long trains of cars heaped with bales, steamer after steamer loaded high with bales coming down the rivers, acres of bales on the wharves, acres of bales at the railway stations."[24]

We may imagine that sometimes in the 1830s and 1840s, when there was no wind and the night was silent of all local noises, there came upon the South another sound—the rackety-clacketing of the looms, the insatiable looms, unrelenting, monotonous, and imperious. After Alabama had been in bed four hours, Manchester was already at work. Yoked to the looms insensibly and invisibly, the people of the South, rich and poor, black and white, inhabited the largest labor camp ever constructed, extending from the James to the Brazos and from the Gulf of Mexico to the Ohio.

Independence?

The central myth of antebellum Southern life was the independence of each plantation, a theme sounded time after time by John C. Calhoun. If there was independence, it was not to be felt in the plantations but, instead, among those "free and independent yeomen," white or Indian, remaining on the fringe of things. A planter might own hundreds or thousands of acres of cotton and preside over a columned citadel surrounded by the cabins of his workforce, but he and his peers were not independent. They relied upon borrowed money to raise their crops. When those crops were ready for market, they could be sold only in the quantities and at the prices acceptable to the very persons (or the cousins or partners of those persons) to whom the planters would have to return for more money, to grow more crops. Powerless against the vagaries of the international market, the planters nonetheless sought to persuade themselves that they were living in self-sufficient communities insulated from the world outside.

The architecture often chosen by the planter and his lady was a proclamation of such a delusion. It was rectilinear, blanched of the colors found in nature, and barricaded against it by an array of white columns. Though those columns implied stability, British demand oscillated wildly up and down, and by sympathetic motion each little community of the South oscillated too. Payments for luxury goods, mules, vacations, and interest on loans had to be made from very erratic revenues. The balanced blessings that come to better-diversified farmers were denied the Cotton South; it knew bonanza at best, bust at worst, and volatile prices all the while.

American cotton exports multiplied sixty times between 1790 and 1800 as the gin and the mule and the jenny got under steam. Though Jefferson's embargo cut those exports by three quarters in 1807 and 1808, a new boom set in as they expanded again by a multiple of six until the War of 1812 cut off the market and cotton became virtually valueless. The American planter was dragged in the dust as the chariot of cotton careened from price to price. From a price-relative of nearly 300 in 1816, cotton fell to 92 in 1831, rose to 170 in 1835, fell to 87 in 1840, rose to 103 in the next year and collapsed to 60. Five years later, the index was at 102 again, fell back to 66 in the next two, doubled in the next year, fell to 82 the next, but shot back to 100 the next.[25]

British buyers and bankers set both the price of money and the price of cotton—a price determining in turn the planters' capacity for repayment. During one fairly typical deflationary episode reported by the Mobile *Register*, "the British . . . demand payment in cotton at 7 to 12 cents a pound, for merchandise which was measured when sold by the same cotton from 14 to 19 cents. They have thus a right to require two bales of cotton where only one was originally contemplated." Was this independence?[26]

By the time the agrarianism of Jefferson and Madison struggled through the 1790s and into the nineteenth century, the freeing of slaves was no longer one of its tenets. Nor, in effect, was true freedom of action on the part of the planters themselves. The South became a harp for Manchester and Liverpool to play at their pleasure. When the British had all the cotton they needed, American wharfs and warehouses overflowed, planters defaulted, port cities were boarded up, and bankruptcy notices went up in the backwoods; the cotton panic of 1819 brought Savannah to its knees, and many merchant-factors in New Orleans packed up for Texas. Six years before, that schooner from Liverpool sighted earlier appeared in the port of Mobile on the day the city was brought within the territorial limits of the United States. A succession of subsequent visits made Mobile one of the thriving ports of the world, until in 1836 it learned Savannah's lesson. The British once again concluded that too much gold and silver was flowing toward the Americans selling cotton. Their discount rate was elevated, and they refused to accept American bills, including the obligations of such cotton states as Alabama. The Rothschilds called for payment of debts owed them by cotton banks, and the Barings soon did likewise, inducing a run on gold in Mobile. Cotton prices collapsed; seventeen-cent cotton became eight-cent cotton. All four banks in town closed their doors. Slave prices, always hitched to cotton prices, fell from $1,200 or $1,500 per slave to $250 or $300—depending upon condition, of course. As the British worked off their excess inventory, many of those planters who survived the initial impact of the crisis were brought to their knees. Those still left standing after a five-year depression returned to dependency upon British buyers, British credit, and British prices.

No one believes that Britain's prosperity, and its role as the world's dominant economic power, were redeemed for it solely by the author of the American Declaration of Independence. However, Jefferson was the most convincing advocate of Southern agrarianism, and an acquiescent South became the first province of the new invisible empire. The most eloquent ideologist of the winning side in the separation of the thirteen most valuable of Britain's North American colonies in 1776 happened to have a sentimental preference for an agrarian republic and also happened to lack the fortitude to insist that it be a republic without slavery. The poet of agrarianism came inadvertently to Britain's aid just when it required such a poet rather than an ideological or moral zealot with steel in his spine.

The British and the Plantocracy

While the cotton gin began its transformation of the Southern economy during the decades immediately after the Revolution, American politics were plastic and unpredictable. Aversion to slavery was still running strong. During those decades, Britain resumed its role as the dominant external force operating upon the American economy and got what it wanted: its imports from its former colonies nearly quadrupled. Half that volume was cotton. One British economist observed that the old colonial commerce had been a mere "peddling traffic compared to that vast [new] international intercourse, the greatest the world has ever known." Britain had suffered no injury from the "disseverence of the United States." At the start of George Washington's first term, American exports to Britain had been worth less than 180,000 pounds sterling. By the middle of Jefferson's, they were two hundred times greater—or, if one prefers to weigh *things* rather than to count money, in 1800, cotton shipments to Britain weighed nearly twenty million pounds, rising to ninety million pounds by 1810, *before* most of the South was brought into the Cotton Kingdom. Between 1815 and 1855, the value of cotton exports quintupled. As cotton still made up more than half the American produce sold to Britain, four fifths of British imports were in cotton.[27]

A horrid symbiosis bound the slave-system to the milling system, as the *London Times* acknowledged:

> We know that for all mercantile purposes England is one of the [slave] States, and that, in effect, we are partners with the southern planter; we hold a bill of sale over his goods and chattels, his live and dead stock, and take a lion's share in the profits of slavery. . . . [W]e are clothing not only ourselves, but all the world besides, with the very cotton picked and cleaned by "Uncle Tom" and his fellow-sufferers. It is our trade. It is the great staple of British industry.[28]

This was not a pretty picture. British manufacturers secured their supply of cotton and returned the American South to dependence upon a single crop sold into world markets. The British economic-military-political complex was able to guide the ascent of their empire from the humiliations of 1776–83 to the dominance of the commercial world. Though from time to time the millers and bankers lost perfect control of what accountants call their "sources and uses," and though they had to manage their way out of cotton depressions, generally speaking they were far more secure in their circumstances than were their primary suppliers, the uncoordinated and therefore individually vulnerable Southern planters.

Land to put under cotton was provided to the planters by the displacement or despatch of the Indians that had been occupying it, by its subsequent inclusion in the American public domain, and by its sale thereafter to individual growers of cotton. Slaves purchased in Africa and the West Indies were sold in Alabama, Mississippi, or Texas. Armies were mobilized, militias called to the colors, and gunboat boilers gotten under steam, as the boundaries of the Cotton Kingdom were expanded into Louisiana, Texas, and Spanish Florida. The rural South was drawn away from a continental economy within which its people might have enjoyed choices of occupation as diverse as those of Northerners and lapsed into dependence upon an invisible empire manipulated from London and the Midlands. The consequence was the withering unto death of future possibilities for the Southern land, reducing its long-term capacity to support a variegated economy and, in the short term, depriving even free white Southerners of the full range of choices accessible to their Northern cousins.

Let us recall that one of the justifications offered by Jefferson and Madison for a purchase of Louisiana was that it would permit the products of the upper Mississippi Valley to flow unvexed to the sea. A subtext to that argument, we recall, was that stimulating the production of those crops for world markets would keep the people producing them from turning instead to manufacturing. Madison had said that if relieved of perturbations at New Orleans, the upstream population would not be "obliged[,] by want of vent for the produce of the soil and of the means of purchasing foreign manufactures, to manufacture in a great measure for themselves."[29]

From the vantage point of those taking a therapeutic view of land, the farmers of the interior would be left in contact with the land's beneficent influence. Yet because they would be at work satisfying the world's requirements of them—such as growing cotton—they would not loll about in Arcadian squalor. From the British point of view, this meant that they would become extensions of the workforce of the mills. Madison further gave assurance that he and Jefferson would do all they could to discourage "manufacturers on this [side] of the Atlantic." What musical phrases! The British had developed a deep aversion to competition from others, having escaped at the cost of much blood and treasure the staple-producing status into which Madison and Jefferson now proposed to consign the Western population of their own country.[30]

In 1800, native peoples comprised the largest component of the population of the Mississippi Valley. They had their own views on the matters discussed in this chapter. So did the people brought from Africa to do the hard work of the plantation system. Part Three will offer some examples of how the displaced, the forcibly placed, and a group of dissident Europeans resisted the onrush of the plantation system.

PART THREE
Resistance to the Plantation System

By 1800, the Indians living in the American South had been resisting assaults by Europeans for three hundred years. Spain had made the deepest inroads into Indian territory. The armored cavalry commanded by de Soto had crossed the Appalachians and headed west by 1540, reconnoitering for successors who managed to situate forts in Tennessee, while the Jesuits placed missions as far north as Chesapeake Bay. But Indian resistance had beaten Spain back to a line of presidios and missions across Florida from St. Augustine to St. Mark on the Gulf Coast, where the British found them in 1702, burnt them out, and massacred their populations.

Spain retained the shell of Florida until 1763, when it went to the British, to be remanded in 1783. Meanwhile the French had withdrawn as well, abandoning the mainland of North America in 1763, to return to Louisiana for only a few months in 1803 for the astonishing transaction discussed in the final section of this book. From the Indians' point of view, the French came and went, the British came and went, the Spaniards clung to their entrepôts in Florida and along the Gulf of Mexico, and until 1790 the Americans, who succeeded in some mysterious way to the British, were still being held within a few miles of the Georgia coast.

Then things changed. The Americans seemed suddenly to be turbocharged, and so they were—by international textile colonial-imperialism. Opposing them were Indian nations weakened by disease and social dislocation only too late augmented by maroon reinforcements, and then in very small numbers. The maroons were people of African descent who had been enslaved but had managed to escape to form their own communities. (The formation of such colonies is called "maronage." For further etymology see "Creeks, Seminoles, and Numbers" in the Appendix, p. 255.) In combination, these Indians and blacks could still put more fighters into the field than the Americans could in regular armies until 1820 or so, so it became one of the chief tasks of American diplomacy in those years to keep the Indians from uniting with each other and with the maroons.

Ranged beside former slaves resisting reinslavement and Indians resisting conquest were former Tories resisting the further successes of the winning side in the Revolution; Irish émigrés, in the service of the Catholic Majesty of Spain, resisting the Protestant English and their Protestant American successors; people opposed to slavery on principle; people opposed to expropriation of Indians on principle; and pure adventurers. At the very end of this story, some yeomen joined the resistance out of a desire to prevent the expansion of a system from which they felt they had suffered as well.

These are the large themes of Part Three. It is organized somewhat more granularly than Parts One and Two have been, to permit more attention to individuals—unfashionable as such attention may be—both because their biographies are interesting and because they may help us show how great forces and individual lives interacted. Economic and demographic impulses endorsed the desires of some and warped and frustrated others less famous than Thomas Jefferson or George Washington. But they made history, too.

True—American ambition and British textile colonial-imperialism operated as invisibly as magnets under the table. True—multitudes of lives slipped into patterns on the glass surface. True, all true. But love, laziness, hate, habit, idealism, a desire to be companionable, and lust for power worked upon individuals separately and, in some cases, caused individual men and women to refuse to behave as iron filings. The great rips and scours of the Southern landscape were not caused by them. Yet their twists and turns left larger effects than mere scratches. As they offered ways of organizing life and using land as convincing as those of the planters, some of them succeeded just enough to permit the conclusion that the South would have been healthier had their proposals been heeded.

All those who resisted were not heroes. There were knaves among these losers, probably proportionately to the number among those who won. Yet knaves or not, their opposition in battle and in debate to the panoply of force assembled against them tested the true intentions of many more famous figures, including Jefferson himself. His ideal community did not include Indians, nor did he and his immediate circle qualify among its "chosen people" those blacks who had made themselves free. Jefferson's policy for both blacks and Indians was that they should be "removed." Blacks, if freed, should be shipped to Africa or to Haiti. There was no place for them in close proximity to whites: "Nothing," he wrote, "is more certainly written in the book of fate than that these people are to be free; nor is it less certain that the two races, equally free, cannot live in the same government." If set free and not removed, wrote Jefferson, the blacks would be so ferocious that "all the Whites south of the Potomac and Ohio must evacuate their States, and most fortunate those who can do it first."[1]

The term "evacuate" is not a happy one, but it does suggest voluntary movement, and for a time Jefferson seemed to offer that option to Southern Indians. Their refusal to accept his offer led him to abandon any conciliatory stance and to offer evacuation only at gunpoint. Yet the recalcitrance he faced was itself instructive in some subtle ways. It showed most obviously that the Indians were attached to land where they had been growing crops over several thousand years. It showed as well that they were not eager to rid themselves of it on prudential grounds—they had not ruined it. It had value. They had not sickened it as planters did.[2]

McGillivray

> He possesses an atticism of diction, aided by a liberal education, a great fund of wit and humor, meliorated by a perfect good nature and politeness.
>
> (John Pope, writing in 1791 of Alexander McGillivray)

On a summer evening in 1788, three magnificent characters gathered at "Tallassee," the home and place of business of a fourth, Alexander McGillivray. It was also McGillivray's capital city as Great Beloved Man—*isti atcagagi thlacco*—of the National Council of the Creek Confederacy. Waiting in attendance upon him were Philip Nolan, later cartographer of Texas, cowboy, scientific correspondent with Thomas Jefferson, and spy; William Augustus Bowles, actor, soldier, painter, merchant, later traveler of the world from Newfoundland to Manila, and still later self-elected Director-General of the Muskogean Republic; and Louis Milfort, traditional representative of the French to the Creeks and often their war leader against the British. Each of the four, in his own way, resisted the spread of the plantation system, though that resistance was more overt on the part of the two who became blood enemies—Bowles and McGillivray—than in the cases of Nolan and Milfort.[1]

The four were gathered at Tallassee to deal with the delayed consequences of the Treaty of Paris of 1783, concluding a world war of which the American Revolution was one theater of operations. Within that theater there had been two scenes of action: that along the Atlantic and Gulf coasts, where uniformed armies contended for cities and fought formal battles in the European fashion, and that of the interior. McGillivray had led a coalition of Southern Indian nations allied to the British against the United States. His later campaign against Bowles was the contest of one former Tory against another. The British betrayed these Indian allies when they became signatories in Paris to an agreement with France, Spain, and the United States deciding among themselves how the continent should be divided. In response, McGillivray organized a conference of the Southern nations in July 1785 to issue their own declaration of independence:

> We chiefs and warriors . . . do hereby in the most solemn manner protest against any title claim or demand the American Congress may set up for or against our lands, settlements, and hunting grounds in consequence of said treaty of peace between the king of Great Britain and the States of America.[2]

Despite the boundary-drawing in Paris, the chiefs solemnly informed the kings and prime ministers of Europe that the "lines of the lands in question" meant nothing to them, for they "were not parties" to these "divisions and assignments." With fervor equivalent to that of Thomas Jefferson listing the misdemeanors of King George III, in 1776, McGillivray remonstrated that "His Britannic Majesty was never possessed by cession or purchase or by right of conquest . . . [of the] territories . . . the said treaty gives away."[3]

Though the author of this modest assertion was half-Scottish by blood, and by culture a man of the Atlantic world, there was no doubt of his nationality: he was a Creek. That designation was not an Indian one, but he accepted it when corresponding with Europeans. He had much correspondence of that sort, for he was both the son of a woman holding a powerful position in a matrilineal society and a chief by his own prowess. When McGillivray told the world, "We are a free people and mean to continue so," he left no doubt that he expected the Americans, British, and Spaniards to accord to him and his people the rights of self-determination claimed by the white Americans in Jefferson's Declaration of Independence.[4]

McGillivray had defined his own nationality by affinity, not by color or by any bundle of genes. His Creek "people" were of many nations, and the Indian-ness he chose for himself extended beyond the Creeks to include the neighboring Cherokees, though perhaps he might have responded to their difficulties as he did purely out of motives of compassion. On one occasion, he reported: "A party of my warriors lately went into the Cherokees and collected some of them from their hiding places, and attacked a body of the . . . [American] troops that was laying all waste before them, and completely routed them. . . . It has revived the dejected spirits of the Cherokees."[5]

The Creeks had long had a tradition of bringing into their leadership powerful or wise men born of other lineages, through marriage with women of the Wind Clan. After the arrival of the Europeans, this tradition was first extended to the French, who from 1700 to 1760 were the most energetic European intruders upon the Muskogean Middle Ground until they were replaced by Scots. A Creek woman named Sehoy became the spouse of Captain Marchand de Courtel, who commanded at Fort Toulouse. They had a daughter, also named Sehoy, "cheerful in countenance, bewitching in looks and graceful in form," who married one of those Scots, Lachlan McGillivray. She bore him one daughter, Jeannet, who became the wife of Milfort, and, on December 15, 1750, she became the mother of a boy, Alexander McGillivray, the first of the sons of Scots traders to be accepted by the Muskogees as displaying the qualities of a chief. A third child, their daughter Sophia, was later married to a black man of whom we know all too little beyond his name: Durand.[6]

Around the time of Alexander McGillivray's birth, his uncle Archibald McGillivray, head of the family firm, explained to his clients that he was selling his interest. He, his brother, and the Creeks had built a company with a virtual monopoly of the trade in deerskins, carried by 183 horses and managed by twenty-eight packers. Archibald McGillivray's trans-Atlantic voyage was made in style, and, when he strode into the great hall at Moy, the ancestral castle of his clan, far from the stench of pelts and sweaty horses, he laid before Sir Aeneas McIntosh £10,181 in silver to purchase the estate at Straithnairn. Returned from the West, Old Lochinvar settled upon ancestral land and married—in the ancestral Scots way, this time—to Lucy McIntosh.

Mixed People and Mixed Motives

Meanwhile, back in Alabama, the question of what land was ancestral to whom was being asked by other McIntoshes, Weatherfords, McQueens, and McGillivrays. These were people bearing genes of the diverse peoples of Scotland—Picts, Celts of various sorts, Norse, Angles, Saxons, Norman-French—and also of the medley of nations who lived in Alabama in the eighteenth century. Many of these Indian leaders bearing Scottish patronymics had French antecedents as well, and thus were truly "mixed bloods" representing two mixing-pots, the northwestern corner of Europe and the southeastern corner of North America. The result of so much admixture appeared in the weapons used on the Southeastern battlefields: claymores (broadswords), blowguns, atlatls (a lever for increasing the velocity of a spear), simple bows, compound bows, muskets, rifles, rocks, planks, war clubs—and artillery. Until the eighteenth century was nearly gone, kilt-wearing, claymore-wielding Highlanders often went into battle beside cousins in blankets, breechclouts, and war-paint.[7]

Such complexities were—and are—irritating to people who wish to make taxonomies of persons on the basis of a quality they chose to call "race," rejecting the patent experience of humankind that the clusterings that matter are those of affinity. In the year 2002, on a pueblo feast day, ceremonial dancing is done by people of all sizes, shapes, and skin colors, belonging by declaration, by participation, by choice. Each pueblo has its own culture, and often a language different from that spoken in the next. So it was in central Alabama in 1790. Within an easy half day's walk of Tallassee one could be greeted at a village gate in any one of seven languages—two of which, Yuchi and

Muskogean, were as distinct from each other as Zuni is from the Tewa of some Rio Grande pueblos and the Keres of others. The Natchez had fled recently from European assault. The Yuchi had been resistant—how long? Does the question have an answer? They were as resistant to change in language or in custom as the Zuni—or the Basques. The Hitchiti and the Alabamas were "Creek," too—by choice.[8]

The political circumstances of these disparate groups had brought them—like the member tribes of the Iroquois Confederacy—to cleave to each other. They had been swept into the same riverine, forested, fertile landscape by epidemic, warfare, and the demoralizing effects of the fur trade. The life ways of them all had been traumatized by gunpowder, metal instruments, horses, draft animals, alcohol, and holocausts of the fur-bearing animals with whom they had interacted. The radical changes wrought since the advent of European diseases, tools, and armed forces were apparent each time a metal shovel was thrust into the earth in a field that not two centuries before had been the plaza of a city.

The intellectual trend of the times was hostile to understanding such polyglotery. In the 1790s, the Enlightenment was still delighting the European intellectual classes with filing systems. The world was being minced into "entries" in encyclopedias. A passion for order abhorred uncertain boundaries and shifting affinities. In this Age of Taxonomy, Thomas Jefferson was North America's taxonomist-in-chief—and also the only encyclopedist with the power to enforce a politics of tidiness and a land use of forced grids. The 200-by-235-foot "squares" (his term for them) of his grid-plan for the University of Virginia, and his five-mile-square school districts for Virginia itself, might, he wrote, be "enlarged to any extent." And so they were—into 640-acre townships marching across the Northwest, the Mississippi, and the West until finally supervened by the Rocky Mountains. As William Macdonald, the great scholar of the Pantheon, once wrote, "Jefferson was a Roman, and must try to conquer and order the unknown."[9]

Alexander McGillivray resisted such Romanizing as his Scots forefathers had resisted the Romans themselves. A "mixed blood" leader of a mixed people, he resisted either racial categories or geographic grids that took no account of homelands and common cultures. His nation was "orderly" neither in its anthropological composition nor in its geographic disposition. Wrong people. Wrong place. Jefferson's difficulty with them was not just that they were impediments to the economic objectives of his friends. They affronted an impulse in him even deeper than a desire to please those friends. Intransigents such as McGillivray were resisting both the anthropological and the territorial compartments into which philosopher-statesmen such as Jefferson wished to confine him. McGillivray represented a people whose very lives bespoke feelings—especially loyalties—rather than categories, cultures rather than colors. And they were in the way. The ambiguous boundaries of the Creek nation did not fit into Jefferson's plans for the rectilinear division of the land of the West. Nor did McGillivray's insistence upon traditional occupancy. Self-selection, as the basis of nationhood, did not accommodate the desires of the planters. McGillivray's proposal that his mixed-blood, polyglot Creek nation be left in possession of the richest farmland in the South was not acceptable to Jefferson. He could not tolerate the formation of such a nation into an independent political state, oddly bordered, inconveniently situated, and comprised of a collage of people.

Indian Statehood

The startling notion that the Creeks might even become a State within the United States brought Jefferson and McGillivray into full confrontation, intellectually, culturally, and politically. Their differences were never stated in opposing manifestos because they never negotiated across a table, and neither was fully aware of the preconceptions or the purposes of the other. We will have to piece them out. Several Indian leaders were proposing statehood at the time, and some of the Founding Fathers were encouraging them. At Fort Pitt, in 1778, the commissioners of the Continental Congress signed a treaty to keep the Delawares neutral in the Revolutionary War, pledging in its sixth article that the Congress would consider admitting such friendly nations into the Confederation as states. In 1785, at the Treaty of Hopewell, another set of Confederation negotiators assured the Cherokees that they could "send a deputy of their choice" to Congress. Two years later, McGillivray sent his own prospectus to John White, agent for the Congress to the southern tribes. The central government of the United States should, he urged, benefit from the energies of its "natural allies" the Creeks to combat both the "greedy encroachments of the Georgians" upon the Creek lands and their separatist intrigues against the United States.[10]

The Southern tribes represented by White were being assaulted by Georgian speculators and planters seeking their lands, sometimes by force and sometimes by "treaties" negotiated with rivals to McGillivray such as the Fat King, who accepted large bribes to arrange fraudulent sales of tribal lands. The same speculators bribed the Georgia legislature to transmit the land purchased to them in grants.

McGillivray fought on two fronts, against the Fat King in the Creek National Council and against the Georgians in the councils of the American government. Because he lacked the power to hold the intruders back on his own, he acknowledged that to bring his "natural allies" in the national capital to his side he would have to concede to the Georgians a strip of Creek land along the Oconee River. In return he promised to be "the first to take the oath of allegiance" to a state formed for his people to ensure continued possession of their homeland. All the Congress had to do was to "form [such] a body to the southward of the Altamaha." White appears to have been embarrassed at "something so singular" but sent a report along to the Secretary of War, Henry Knox. Knox was known to be in favor of setting aside large reservations in the West—but, so far as is known, had not suggested reservations-in-place, to say nothing of Indian states.[11]

(The idea of an Indian state did not languish completely. The Cherokees renewed it when they asserted their independence from Georgia in 1827, drew up their own constitution, and in 1837 in the Treaty of New Echota were promised the right to send their own delegate to Congress. In 1830, the Choctaws asked to send their own delegate as well and went further, proposing statehood in the lands in Oklahoma to which they were being removed, but by the 1830s Indians were being classed with blacks: "Some Southern men took issue on the color line, announced themselves as opposed on principle to a prospective Indian State, and declared a negro State would be just as proper and to them just as [un]acceptable.")[12]

Jefferson offered instead that famous plan for a tidy West contained within the same "Report on Government for Western Territory" that included Timothy Pickering's provision for the abolition of slavery in the region after 1800. Neither got very far. The reasons for the demise of Pickering's proposal were discussed in Chapter Six, but Jefferson's was more serious than an amusing example of his pleasure in putting names to things. He possessed the most vigorous intellect among the leaders of his country and had furnished it with encyclopedic knowledge of cultures as ancient as the Medes and Persians, and as exotic as the Incas and Chinese. Yet was he not looking out from his terrace at Monticello upon a Western terrain occupied by other people, having customs and preferences of their own, and recommending to the possessors of the most formidable military forces on the continent that they divide the Indian homelands into neat rectangles for which he felt free to suggest such names as Sylvania, Cherronesus, Metropotamia, Polypotamia— and Washington?[13]

He also suggested Michigania, Pelisipia, Saratoga, Assenesipia, and Michigania, which have an Indianish sound. That was not, however, because they were associated with people living there; they were instead selected from certain place names of the region whose sounds commended themselves to him. Jefferson knew that there were Indians living in the West and that they had their own ideas of which territories were theirs and which were not. But they were for all practical purposes nonpersons to him. A few years later, when he had purchased Louisiana, he wrote that "when we shall be full on this side" of the Mississippi, "we may lay off a range of States on the Western bank from the head to the mouth, and so, range after range, advancing compactly as we multiply." It did not happen that within the Louisiana Purchase rectangular states were formed called Sylvania or Cherronesus, but he did get his posthumous way with Wyoming and Colorado.[14]

We will come later to Jefferson's grid plan for the division of Indian territories west of the Mississippi. Jefferson would not tolerate proposals to incorporate Indians in their own chosen associations and in their traditional homelands within the United States. He was willing to consider them in planning for the West only to the degree that it might be necessary to offer them something to get them out of the way peaceably. The lands of the Delawares, Creeks, Choctaws, Chickasaws, and all the other current inhabitants of the region between the Mississippi and the Appalachians were to be "purchased of their Indian inhabitants and offered for sale by the United States. . . . [Only then would they be] formed into distinct States bounded . . . as nearly as such cessions will permit . . . northwardly and southwardly by parallels of latitude," and easterly and westerly from points along meridians at intervals producing ten boxes. The mind of Thomas Jefferson was remarkable for its bold simplicity and its rejoicing in radical innovation. By contrast, that of Alexander McGillivray produced only messy problems of cultural continuity.

McGillivray's Nationality

Alexander McGillivray was seven years younger than Jefferson, of the same height and ruddy Celtic coloring, and even "sparer made." He remained "remarkably erect in person and carriage" even when cancer was eating at his vitals. He was not a professional soldier and avoided war, though he fought well when he was forced to defend his people or to honor his word. The governor of West Florida described him to Lord George Germain as "a gentleman of fortune" as if he were laird of Straithnairn rather than his uncle, and he acted the laird as well.[15]

> His eyes were large, dark and piercing. His forehead was so peculiarly shaped, that the old Indian countrymen often spoke of it: it commenced expanding at his eyes, and widened considerably at the top of his head. It was a bold and lofty forehead. His fingers were long and tapering, and he wielded a pen with the greatest rapidity. . . . When a British colonel, he dressed in the British uniform, and when in the Spanish service, he wore the military dress of that country. When Washington appointed him as brigadier-general, he sometimes wore the uniform of the American army, but never when in the presence of the Spaniards.[16]

And how came he to possess all those uniforms? Let us commence that story with his own statement of his position among nations:

> Our Indian news is in the old strain. The [American] Congress on the one hand pretend to hold out the white wing to all the southern nations, on the

other the back settlers of North Carolina are overrunning the Cherokees, driving them into the woods, murdering women and children, as if they wished to extirpate those poor wretches.[17]

His addressee, William Panton, was another Tory. After the Revolution Panton become the greatest merchant of the southwestern quadrant of the North American continent from bases in Spanish Pensacola and St. Augustine. Panton's Spanish clients were at that moment seeking accommodation with the Americans. Therefore McGillivray was told that he "must treat of peace" both by Panton and by Governor Esteban Miró of Spanish Florida. He replied that he would make gestures in that direction only after he had won enough battles to have "power to offer and insist upon any stipulations." He would not accept "any conditions which they may chose to dictate to us. . . . [E]xperience has proved that such matters are only to be attained by the longest fire and at point of sword, particularly with the Americans." That being true, McGillivray proposed to throw "some obstacles in the way of the present treaty" and then, as the leader of "a free people . . . [meaning] to continue so," he would make what arrangements seemed to him wise, including accepting whatever blandishments the Americans might send his way.[18]

McGillivray had been disappointed by the Spaniards as he had been by the British. So in the summer of 1790 he tried the Americans, or, to be more precise, an American, traveling to New York at the head of a cavalcade of chiefs to meet with President George Washington. Secretary of State Jefferson was not disposed to take an Indian—even a half Indian—to be a peer, treating McGillivray as if he were an agent for the formerly Tory merchants whom, like all merchants, Jefferson despised. Such tradesmen, he wrote, were McGillivray's "principal sources of power." The Tammany "Sachems" showed little more respect, thronging about his hotel garbed as Indians, using lamp black on their faces as their version of war paint. Tammany's blackened faces led Abigail Adams to write that she expected McGillivray to be black, too, though she should have known better: Scots burn red in the sun, while Muskogees merely turn a deeper copper. She described the warriors standing about their ruddy chief as the "very first savages I ever saw." To her surprise, McGillivray was not only dressed "in our own fashion" but also spoke "English like a native." On inspection, she added, McGillivray was "not very dark . . . and . . . much of a gentleman." Fisher Ames, a "higher" Federalist and a lower order of being than Abigail Adams, could only bring himself to write that McGillivray was "decent and not very black." At an even less elevated station in the moral order were the journalists who complacently observed the bumpers of whiskey being dispensed. Yet even they conceded that the Scotsman in McGillivray stood the President's negotiators glass for glass and still retained his "recollection and reason."[19]

McGillivray and Washington

McGillivray required all his reason and his negotiating skill. He was confronting a confident American republic spoiling for an Indian war. Its regular army was lean and well exercised, and its militias numerous—though ill-disciplined by Creek standards. Great stores of unused munitions were left over from the Revolution, and American squadrons patrolled both the Atlantic and Gulf coasts. McGillivray had considered leading a "universal confederacy" of the Western tribes against this array, but after counting the odds he decided instead to seek peace with honor. Such a course led him into the shadow of assassination either by the hotheads among the Creeks or by the whites; many accommodating chiefs who survived execution by their own people were killed by those accommodated.

Washington was not in personal danger, but his presidency was at stake. An agreement with McGillivray would require him to repudiate the fraudulent treaties by which the state of Georgia purported to have purchased millions of acres of Indian lands. Jefferson was not yet President. Washington was still holding open the possibility that in the Southeast the government of the United States could include nonconforming, Indian, independent sovereignties. Washington and McGillivray were both nation builders. The chief of the Creeks was bent upon forming a nation out of an association of tribes—a nation that would have sufficient unity and power to permit them to continue to live in the lands in which they found themselves. Though Washington was a Virginian, a planter, and a surveyor before he was a planter, he showed no compulsive need for grids and was capable of tolerating complexity. Two masters of action, action in the face of the insufficiently known and the indistinct, were both at work assembling nations out of wartime alliances. They were opposed by the same people.

For six bloody years after the Revolution, until the formation of Washington's first administration in 1789, the State of Georgia functioned independently of any national government and used every means to extort or seize Indian lands. The speculators and planters who controlled that state made their arrangements with the Fat King and began discussions with Choctaws and Chickasaws who might cede territory ripe for planting along the Yazoo River of Mississippi. Slow, swampy, and bayou-like, the Yazoo lacks grandeur, but its name excited raptures from a multitude of speculators. The Georgia legislature, some of whose members had been purchased and some intimidated by thugs hired by the "Yazoomen," offered real estate on the cheap all the way to the Mississippi and the Tennessee; early buyers of shares stood to benefit from a sequence of subsequent transactions increasing values by fraud. People close to the national administration, including one member of the Supreme Court of the United States, were bribed with grants of entire counties. Citizens of many states rushed to buy and resell portions of this empire of potential cotton fields.[20]

If Washington were to repudiate the initial Yazoo sale, this vast and spreading system of corruption would be cut off at its roots. Such an agreement with McGillivray would also slow the sweep of the plantation system across the South. That point was not lost on the planter-President, but he went ahead anyway. Only Washington could carry off the task, for neither Hamilton nor Jefferson had the personal prestige to defeat the hosts of corruption. McGillivray informed Washington that he was ready to go to war if the Yazoo Frauds were not repudiated. Washington made his decision and was hung in effigy in Georgia by mobs mobilized by the speculators. The "people" spoke, rallying to the anti-Federalist—now increasingly Jeffersonian—cause, some out of conscience and some out of cupidity.[21]

The prospect of the Creek Nation and the United States tearing at each other has subsequently—and quite recently—delighted bloodthirsty historians, who decry Washington and McGillivray for depriving them of the spectacle. At the time, the peaceful settlement aroused no more enthusiasm among agents of the French, Spanish, and British. Money was made available from the coffers of these governments to the Yazooites, while their agents in New York commenced a campaign to try to buy off McGillivray. An auction of sorts was attempted one evening in the parlor of the Secretary of War, General Henry Knox, as the Yazoo press denounced Washington for placating McGillivray, calling him "a half-breed Spanish colonel." That term apparently suggested to the Spanish minister that he offer the colonel a promotion to general and a fat pension, conditioned only on McGillivray's refusing to agree to a treaty with Washington. The British emissary raised the bid and coupled it to the threat that if McGillivray reached agreement with the Americans, and war came, his government would cut off the trade goods of the Creeks. Trade was McGillivray's living. His Majesty's Navy could quickly sink any American gunboat sent to protect the traffic in goods promised by Washington. When told of the state of play, the President countered by assuring McGillivray that in that event the United States would send by land any trade goods denied by the British. There is no better exposition of the grave, Olympian tone of the relationship between Washington and McGillivray than the first exchange between them at 39 Broadway, on July 20, 1790, as their eyes met six inches above the others assembled to observe them:[22]

> —I am glad you have come, Colonel. I have long felt that we had much in common.
> —I cannot flatter myself that much, Mr. President, but it has long been my ambition to shake your hand in friendship.[23]

For a moment, we may hope, they stood there, in the light of the Manhattan summer, enjoying the occasion. The Washington-McGillivray Treaty, establishing clear lines separating the Creeks and the planters, to be enforced by the armed forces of the United States, stood as the law of the Southern land until the inauguration of Thomas Jefferson in 1801.

IO

Resisters, Assisters, and Lost Causes

William Augustus Bowles was born in 1764 in Maryland of a Tory family that enrolled him as an ensign in the British army at the age of fourteen. His first post was St. Augustine, where, after being childishly insubordinate, he was cashiered and provided the occasion for his first grand gesture—he flung his scarlet uniform into the river. After two years among the Indians, he returned to St. Augustine in 1781, bringing with him warriors in aid of the British against the Americans. He was commissioned a captain at the age of sixteen. He must have been gentle born; had that not been the case, he would not have been given officer's rank. He was serving as Captain Bowles in 1783, when Britain returned Florida to Spain.

The Loyalist troops who had retreated to Florida from the American Revolution were left stateless. Bowles, deprived of a profession as well, made his way to the West Indies, where he found employment as a musician, then as a portrait painter, and, finally, as an actor, his true calling. A painting of him in the National Portrait Gallery in London shows him as a matinee idol, dark-eyed, saturnine, Tyrone Powerish, as ready to seduce as to conquer. He was acknowledged to be attractive even by those who thought him deplorable.

> His elegant and commanding form, fine address, beautiful countenance of varied expressions, his exalted genius, daring and intrepidity, all connected to a mind wholly debased and unprincipled, eminently fitted him to sway the bad Indians and worse traders among whom he lived.[1]

Bowles could also sway royal governors. He was rescued from life upon a petty stage in 1788, by Lord Dunmore, the sixty-year-old Scot who had been demoted by the American Revolution from his previous assignment as the King's governor of Virginia to the lesser post of governor of the Bahamas. Dunmore was a descendant of the Stuart kings of Scotland in the female line; in 1745 his father had followed the Catholic Bonnie Prince Charlie against the Protestant Hanoverians who held the British crown, was pardoned, and swore to uphold King George II. His son pledged fealty to King George III, thus determining the course of his life and bringing him into opposition to the next great rebellion against the Crown, that of the American colonists. In 1775, as Royal Governor, Dunmore was commanding the Virginia militia invading the territories of the Shawnee in the Ohio Valley when the American Revolution was launched by the First Continental Congress.

Dunmore rushed back to Williamsburg to defend his capital against the rebels. Up to that point, he, his glamorous wife, and his daughter were the pride of the colony. The Dunmores had named the daughter Virginia, and the Virginians had named for him two of their fairest counties—Dunmore and Fincastle (he was Viscount Fincastle as well as Earl of Dunmore). In April 1775, Dunmore had the colony's supply of powder removed from the Williamsburg Arsenal, where the rebels might seize it, and put aboard a warship. Mr. Jefferson's friends cried that without adequate powder they could not resist a rising of their slaves. Dunmore responded that if their rebellion continued, "by the living God he would declare freedom to the slaves and reduce the city of Williamsburg to ashes." Many blacks rose to the implicit invitation, presenting themselves at the governor's palace to offer their aid to Dunmore as chief of that set of whites acting in their interest. Then Dunmore provided one of the grievances listed in Jefferson's draft of the Declaration of Independence by offering "liberty to all the slaves who would rise against, or escape from their Rebel masters."[2]

Scots, Blacks, and Seminoles

For this emancipation proclamation, Thomas Jefferson and his colleagues blamed not only Dunmore but also the Scots traders who rallied to his side. This set of Scots merchants had absorbed "the greater part of the increase in the British tobacco trade after 1745" and had much to lose from any revolutionary change. Along the Chesapeake as along the Gulf, it was a rare trading post whose proprietor spoke English without a burr, and when that sound was heard it might be assumed that the speaker shared the views of the laird of Dunmore. Accordingly, it became a Whig habit to lump all Loyalists into "the Scotch Party." Only a last-minute action by John Witherspoon persuaded the Continental Congress to remove from Jefferson's draft of the Declaration an attack upon the Tory merchants specifically as Scots.[3]

By the middle of June 1775, Dunmore was aboard a warship off Norfolk, rousing Tory, Scot, and Negro resistance. In July, he was joined by a mulatto pilot, Joseph Harris, who led the British in a series of raids resulting in their "harboring gentlemen's Negroes," as the *Virginia Gazette* reported. In October, guided by Harris, Dunmore's squadron attacked the seaport of Hampton in the first battle of the Revolution south of those at Lexington and Concord. Two weeks later, Dunmore declared martial law and became the first of a series of British commanders over the next forty years to offer freedom to any Negro who took up arms for the King. Black sashes bearing the words "Liberty to Negroes" were issued to those who answered the call. Dunmore's successful recruitment became the greatest challenge to the Southern plantation system before the American Civil War.[4]

In London, Edmund Burke noted a movement in Parliament to promulgate "a general enfranchisement of slaves," while the commanders of British forces in North America succeeded in rousing as many as a hundred thousand slaves against the rebellious colonists. Eight hundred former slaves served in Dunmore's British Ethiopian Regiment under the command of Thomas Taylor Byrd, son of William Byrd III. Cherokees and Shawnees also joined Dunmore's aggregate of Tories, Scots, and Negroes. They came to arms too slowly to tip the scales against the Revolution, but the memory of their doing so at all explains the consternation among the planters when Bowles roused a similar coalition in the later 1780s under Dunmore's sponsorship. The Virginians had observed how the Indians' "caressing the Negroes" in the time of Pontiac's coalition twenty years earlier had been "productive of an insurrection." Similar fears stirred the Carolinas when the Cherokees and Creeks welcomed black recruits to their contest against the Americans, and during the Revolution the Tory Colonel Thomas Brown incorporated Seminoles and Negroes into his King's Rangers.[5]

Though the Cherokees, Creeks, and Seminoles held black slaves, they did not divide people along color lines. Master and slave might be of any color; division was along status lines. We are told by Claudio Saunt that the Creek villages "on the lower Chatahoochee and in north central Florida . . . adopted Blacks into their clans and gave them all the rights and obligations of other kin." William Augustus Bowles drew support from the Indian groups especially friendly to blacks—the Chickamaugas, the Creeks along the Chatahoochee, and the Seminoles of north central Florida. He was undoubtedly encouraged in this behavior by his wife, Mary Perryman, who was said to have been a "mestizo Hitchiti." Her Hitchiti ancestors had more anciently settled the Southeast than those of the other people the English called "Creeks," whose language differed from that of the Hitchiti. In Mary Perryman's time they were as famous as the Chickamauga-Cherokees for integrating Africans into their culture.[6]

The Firm

The primary opponent to Bowles's mobilization of these peoples against the plantation system was William Panton, the onetime mentor of Alexander

McGillivray—though among the Creeks McGillivray opposed Bowles for other reasons. Not many pages will pass in this narrative hereafter without some mention of Panton or his partners. They were more effective agents of the plantation system than many generals and governors, acting as phago-cytes of the plantocracy (to anticipate a biological analogy to be employed in Part Four). Nearly eight million acres were transferred by Indian nations to the United States and the plantation system in transactions managed by Panton and his partners acting as Panton, Leslie, and Forbes, and later as John Forbes and Company.

They *were* "The Firm"—from St. Augustine to Baton Rouge, with off-shoots from time to time in Cuba, the Bahamas, and the Carolinas. Their influence reached to the Ohio, the Arkansas, and the Yucatán. Though it might seem tidier to avoid mentioning Panton at this juncture, saving him for treatment in Part Four, where we discuss *assisters* as a group, we cannot ap-preciate the accomplishments of McGillivray or the endeavors of William Augustus Bowles without pitting the two, each in his own way, against The Firm. McGillivray declared his personal independence by setting himself apart from The Firm, and its partners arranged for the death of Bowles.

In the eighteenth century, Scots traders had settled into every port on the Atlantic coastline of North America from Nova Scotia to Key West, effecting a transition out of animal husbandry into commerce, from herd to ledger, from rainswept moors to palm-shaded patios along the Gulf. It is a curiosity of history that Panton, his partners—Thomas Forbes, Charles McLatchy, and John Leslie—and the McGillivrays all came from the same tiny, rocky, foggy, lochpent corner of Inverness. So did the McIntoshes, who like McGillivray began as traders and ended as chiefs. (Indeed, they are not ended yet—there was at this writing a McIntosh chief of the Oklahoma Creeks.)

These men of Inverness came to live at another Celtic Fringe. In Georgia and Alabama, these Scots and Irish, thrust once again to the extremities, sus-tained another marginal and adaptive culture. Some became resisters. At Autosse and Cababee Creek, leaders bearing Celtic names and Celtic blood but now acting as Indians fought invaders hostile to their new nationhood, as their ancestors had battled at Kilkenny and Bonar Bridge. Others became masters of profitable accommodation. William Panton, John Leslie, three generations of Forbeses, and their cousins and colleagues in the Bahamas, in Georgia, the Carolinas, Florida, and along the Gulf Coast facilitated the tran-sition from the old world of barons and merchants to a new one of planters and factors.

We possess neither a portrait nor a description of Panton, though some of the next generations of partners were photographed—hard, cold, purpose-ful men, looking as John C. Calhoun would have looked had he gone into trade. All we know of Panton comes from his letters to his partners and to the statesmen with whom he dealt. Yet this drab agent of an invisible empire was in his way a prince of the borderland. His first American base was Charles Town. He and his partners expanded into Florida and Georgia, trading in deerskins and furs. When the Revolution came in 1775, they joined the Tory hegira to St. Augustine. The former capital of Spanish Florida had been held by the British since 1763. When Florida was retro-ceded from Britain to Spain in 1783, the partners of The Firm assumed Spanish nationality and arranged shadow partnerships with three successive Spanish governors as they expanded their operations to the Gulf Coast and the Mississippi.[7]

Leslie made terms with Governor Patrick Tonyn, the Hispano-Hibernian governor of East Florida, as a Scot with an Irishman, repeating his success after Tonyn's departure with his kinsman Governor Henry White, and then with Governor Vincente Manuel de Zespedes. Though Spain and Britain were soon again at war, Zespedes convinced his government to permit The Firm to trade directly with Bristol and Liverpool and to supply British weapons, guns, cooking pots, cloth, and nails to the Creeks on the backs of Spanish horses. Suspending the missionary zeal that had created the towns of *St.* Marks, *St.* Mary's, and *St.* Augustine, the governor insulated the partners and employees of The Firm, and by extension all Protestant Scots in their employ, from religious persuasion. Boys were recruited by The Firm for placement with Indian families, to learn their dialects and customs.

Scots boys who did so might remain Scots, but their progeny were something other. So strong were the prejudices of the day that even when writing to McGillivray's proud father, Panton could not eschew a patronizing tone toward that half of the son that was not European:

> I advised, I supported, I pushed him on, to be the great man. Spaniards and Americans felt his weight and thus enabled him to haul me after him, so as to establish this house [The Firm] with more solid privileges than, without him, I should have attained. This being the case, if he had lived, I meant, besides what he was owing me, to have added considerably to his stock of Negroes.[8]

It is unlikely that Panton meant to add to McGillivray's "stock" of black brothers-in-law. Nor did it appear that he had remembered how McGillivray had cut himself loose from his patronage. Panton had informed him that the Spanish "governor and intendant [fiscal agent or chief financial officer] of New Orleans . . . [had] relinquished their claim of one fourth of the profits of your trade." This slice of the action Panton offered McGillivray as inducement to give The Firm trading preference among the Creeks. The chief responded:

> Such a procedure is extremely generous, and as for my part I now repeat to you what I told you more than twelve months ago. . . . I then observed that my nation was much benefitted by the honorable and liberal manner in

which you supported them with goods; that as my attention being wholly engaged about the concerns of my people, it could not be in my power to be of any essential service to your business. Therefore I could not, nor ought to pretend to claim or hold a share of your industry and risks.[9]

After the Revolution, the partners of The Firm contemplated yet another transfer of their affections, this time away from Spain toward the American government the planters dominated, despite any lingering aversion toward a republic created by rebels against the Crown. The magnets under the table were changing position. Cotton was becoming easier to mill and to gin. Like Panton and Leslie, the millers of the Midlands and the bankers of London, Glasgow, and Aberdeen began to perceive a concert of interest with the planters dominating the affairs of that republic. The former slaves of those planters and the Indians whose lands those planters were bent upon acquiring could not as yet apprehend these shifts under the table. They had supported the Crown against the rebels and expected the Crown to continue to support them. Bowles went back to Florida with Dunmore's backing, confident in these old expectations, and encouraged by a group of commercial gentlemen in Nassau. Organized as the firm of Miller, Bonnamy, and Company, they had brought in Dunmore as silent partner and directed themselves to displacing The Firm in the Creek and Seminole trade.

The Creek and Seminole trade? What was that? Who was a Creek, who a Seminole? The words are of English and Spanish origin. "Creek" comes from the description of "people living along the creeks" of southern Alabama and Georgia crossed by English and Scots traders from Charles Town in the seventeenth century. It came to be used for any Indians, whatever might be their tribal background or the language they spoke, who lived north of the 31st Parallel, the northern limit of the lands claimed as Florida by Spain after 1783, and who were not Cherokees, Choctaws or Chickasaws. The same person—whatever his or her language or affiliation—would be a "Seminole" if found south of it. The word "Seminole" is no more Indian in origin than is "Creek." It came into use after many who were asked their tribal affiliations responded that they were refugees, or *cimarrones*. That is what one accustomed to speaking Muskogean might think he or she was saying. Their language has no *r* sound, so they would substitute an *l* instead, producing the word "Seminole" that began to crop up in British records. (A little more information about the origin of the words used to describe these native peoples is to be found in "Creeks, Seminoles, and Numbers" in the Appendix, p. 255.)

These "cimarrones" had been thoroughly mixed genetically between 1500 and 1800 as people flowed into the mixing bowl of North Florida, replacing an original Indian population well-nigh exterminated by disease and massacre. There is a tale, unconfirmable by documentary evidence—or so far by DNA—that in a South Carolina beachhead established by Lucas Vásquez de

Ayllon blacks rose in 1526 to drive off their masters with Indians with whom they thereafter formed families, thus becoming the original Seminoles. Their subsequent survival may be explained by the fact that Africans carried immunities against Old World diseases, and also by their staying out of the way as the British, French, Scots, and English fought wars of competitive imperialism. (The section "Creeks, Seminoles, and Numbers" in the Appendix contains somewhat more data about the reduction of native populations by disease.)

In 1693, the King of Spain formally freed all those slaves who had come into his Florida possessions seeking sanctuary, Indian and black, who would turn around and face their former masters in battle. At the siege of St. Augustine in 1702, the British were defeated by a mixed force of 174 Spanish regulars (who were largely white), 44 white militiamen, 123 Indians, and 57 blacks. These were roughly the proportions found in the "Spanish" force that assaulted the British during the "Yamassee War" of 1715 and nearly drove the British into the sea. Only a last-minute intervention by the Cherokees and the recruitment of four hundred blacks kept Britain in the Carolinas. The "Spanish" forces had been made especially formidable after their enlistment of slaves including Muslim Mandingoes, the famous cavalrymen of the upper Niger. Other skilled blacks constructed "Negro Forts" outside the Spanish fortified missions of St. Augustine and St. Marks.

Behind the lines, the Seminoles laid out their cornfields, their cabins, and corn cribs and fed their cattle. After 1790, however, this "free and independent" mixed-blood yeomanry ceased pressing into new territory in the hammocks and hills of the depopulated interior as their numbers stabilized. They were no longer augmented by a refreshing flow of blacks from the plantations because the Spanish authorities abrogated their policy of offering sanctuary to escaped slaves, bowing to the pressure of the American planters. Some blacks still sought places of safety, however, whether royally sanctioned or not. More maroon settlements appeared along the border between Georgia and Florida and in the interior of Alabama and Mississippi. On the McIntosh Bluffs of the Tombigbee, above Mobile, a community of similarly mixed peoples called themselves "the Cajuns of Alabama."[10]

This story has not yet ended. Travelers who search for the ruins of maroon settlements come to the end of the 31st Parallel where it strikes the Mississippi River. Turning a little south, they encounter the chain-link perimeter of the State of Louisiana's maximum security penitentiary. It is named "Angola" and is almost exclusively occupied by people of African descent. The name comes from the plantation it replaced, so designated by its owner, the slave seller Isaac Franklin, to celebrate his success in distributing fresh Angolans to the cotton and sugar plantations nearby. A little to the southward, in the underbrush, are some remnants of a maroon colony of a mixed people who called themselves "Freejacks" sequestered in the swamps of the Tchefuncte River.

The Valences Shift

William Augustus Bowles built the magnificent anomaly of his regime upon the fervor for freedom on the part of such black refugees from the plantation system, Indians determined not to be displaced by that system, and colleagues of his own Anglo-American lineage. As suggested earlier, some were out for adventure and for booty. Others, however, showed over decades their dedication to the concept of freedom for people of all races. Among these were several who paid on the scaffold and before the firing squads for their unorthodox views during Andrew Jackson's conquests in Florida.

Whatever may have been his own motives, Bowles was glorious to look upon, energetic, intelligent, multilingual, and linked to the Creeks through one wife and to the Cherokees through another. His first assignment from Dunmore was to undertake that mission to McGillivray in 1787–88 that brought him to Tallassee. Was there a possibility that the chief and the adventurer—Colonel and Captain—might strike up an alliance? No—Bowles was too flamboyant for the subtle McGillivray, too full of his own pride to gauge the grandeur of the statesman into whose shadow he had come. Besides, an alliance would have required McGillivray to find common ground with Dunmore against The Firm, and however beautiful and clever, Bowles was not the man to overcome the chief's justifiable distrust of the British in general and Dunmore in particular. The Shawnees against whom Dunmore had waged his war in 1774 were closely related to the Creeks; Dunmore killed the father of the Shawnee war chief Tecumseh at the Battle of Point Pleasant. The widow was a Creek; it is probable that Tecumseh himself fought beside the Chickamaugas and Creeks sent by McGillivray against the Americans in 1788, and when it came time for Tecumseh to seek a Southern alliance in 1811 he went first to the Creeks.

After the failure of his mission to Tallassee, Bowles decamped first to the Florida Keys, next to Nova Scotia, and then to Quebec, where he assembled an acting company of Indians—prototypes to the Lakota recruited by Buffalo Bill Cody for his Wild West show—and took them to London. While his troupe performed in the Vauxhall Gardens, Bowles sought to convince the government of William Pitt to support him in the recapture of Florida from Spain, the overthrow of McGillivray as chief of the Creeks, and a campaign against the Americans. Pitt declined. His government was already considering ways to be ingratiating to the planters.

In 1791, Bowles went ahead, making another landing in Florida, on the Gulf Coast. This was not the first time he disputed treaties made by others, nor was it the last; on this occasion he sought to stir up Creek and Seminole opposition to McGillivray's treaty with Washington. Its fixed boundary between the Creeks and Americans was as repugnant to the Red Sticks, those Creeks who believed they could defeat the Georgians in open warfare, as to the expansionary planters. Bearing gifts from Dunmore, Bowles was able to convince the Red Sticks to anoint him as "General and Director of the Affairs of the Nation." Signing himself by that title, he wrote Arturo O'Neill, governor at Pensacola (another Hispano-Hibernian servant of the Spanish crown), offering alliance with Spain in return for an assurance of free navigation along the Apalachicola and Chatahoochee rivers into the Gulf.

By October 1791, surveyors were beginning their slashing and flagging of McGillivray's boundary with Georgia. As they approached, Bowles despatched to them from a fortified position a letter stating a determination to scalp any who dared approach. The surveying ceased. McGillivray, urged along by The Firm, put a price on Bowles's head. Bowles struck first, seizing Panton and Leslie's store at St. Mark. He had defined the contest. He had also overreached. He might have survived the animosity of the Spanish colonial bureaucracy and of the distant American government. He might even have held out for a time when their coalition was augmented by the Creeks led by McGillivray. But The Firm was too much for him.

The names of its partners will not be found engraved in plaques of bronze, nor are their equestrian statues to be found in town squares. It cannot be said of them that they have faded from the popular imagination, for they were never in it. Yet in laying his gage of battle upon their doorstep, Bowles affronted people capable of altering the fate of millions of Americans. More to the point, Panton and Leslie were taken very seriously by the textile manufacturers, bankers, and civil servants of Great Britain. They and their colleagues of the fur and skin trade bestowed upon us some words still in common parlance. A buck still denotes a dollar—which bought a buckskin until the 1820s and even beyond. The dollar was pegged to the Spanish peso, which in turn was composed of eight reales. Two reales, "two bits" of a peso, were worth a quarter—a quarter of a buckskin. A buck and two bits. Many a merchant left a lesser legacy.

William Augustus Bowles—The Second Act

Until Bowles seized the fur warehouse belonging to The Firm, his dramatic gifts had served him well. At St. Mark, however, he began to act as if his role were his life, as if the title, costumes, and props he had created could furnish him power to withstand the Americans, the Spaniards, and The Firm. Presenting himself as a gentleman among gentlemen, Bowles accepted an invitation to visit the Spanish governor in New Orleans, abandoned his bodyguard, and took the governor's word of honor for safe passage. That assurance was betrayed. Bowles was clapped into irons. As soon as a ship could be found, he was sent to Havana, then to Cádiz, and on to Madrid, where he languished for a year in the city jail while the Council of the Indies deliberated his fate. To its credit, the council's members took seriously the possibility that he was, indeed, a gentleman, and thus an inconvenience: the breach of a pledged word to one of their kind still embarrassed the hidalgos of Spain, and dealing straightforwardly with the difficulty by executing him would be a violation of their code. Besides, he might be a useful instrument against the Americans, later. The dilemma was resolved by the King himself, who decided not to decide, ordering Bowles to exile in the Philippines.

At Tondo, on the island of Luzon, he was put on a leash; he might wander about to make some sort of living so long as he reported each day to the local *corregidor*. Though Bowles was not in peril of immediate execution, his chances would diminish with time, so he commenced harassing the authorities, stirring up the local soldiery and demanding a pension. One of his lieutenants from Florida was also in the region, under similar "protection"; when, in February 1797, he, too, adopted the style of a Napoleon in exile, the *corregidor* and the governor packed both agitators back toward Cádiz aboard the *Concepción*. By the time the *Concepción* rounded the Cape of Good Hope, Bowles had once again demonstrated his skills in community organization by convincing the crew to dispose of the captain and seize the ship. He was frustrated in that design only by the defection of the ship's chaplain. The captain was no doubt frustrated as well, for he might have dumped Bowles overboard had he not been under instruction to deliver him back to Spain alive. So he merely transferred Bowles, with twelve others, to another vessel in the convoy.

Off the coast of Sierra Leone, Bowles escaped; on his arrival at a British fort, we are told, "he was well received by Governor Zachary Macaulay," Tory and Highland Scot, father of the historian-laureate of Whiggery, and Evangelical Christian deeply engaged in reform of the slave trade. Lady Macaulay was the daughter of a Quaker bookseller. The two, earnest in a Clapham earnestness, practical, sober, and unblinking in the face of evil, were sweating for their convictions on the slave coast, amid the most vicious of miscreants, black and white. And now they had in their midst William Augustus Bowles.

Making use of foolscap, pen, and ink supplied him by the Macaulays, Bowles dispatched from the governor's palace a twenty-page letter to Lord Grenville, recounting his adventures and announcing his intention to sail at once for the Creek country. Once in his "home," he wrote, he could restore to himself a kingdom. All he required was transportation for that portion of his journey that would traverse the old slave-trade route from Sierra Leone to Trinidad. From there he could ad-lib his way northward to Florida.[11]

He did exactly that. Pausing in Jamaica, he displayed the *gravitas* rehearsed in his Philippine exile and introduced "himself into the best company on the island, where every mark of respect and attention was paid him by the Governor, Sir Hyde Parker, General Churchill and the other leading personages of the place." Bowles enjoyed "the reputation of a very learned man," which "added to the singularity of the Indian dress he wore, made him much re-spected by every class of people."[12] History was informed of what was meant by "the singularity of the Indian dress he wore" as the result of the capture of his kit by the Spaniards some months later, in Florida:

> A green jacket and a blue cloak, both ornamented with gold braid; a fur turban adorned with glass pearls. . . . [H]is library . . . containing . . . Abbe Reynal's *Indies* in seven volumes; Milton's *Paradise* [the Spanish inventory does not state whether it was *Lost* or *Found*]; the *Letters of Junius*, various works of Moliere and Boileau; some treatises on physics, algebra, and paint-ing; a classical mythology; some dictionaries (English, French and Spanish) and several English grammars. There were also some miscellaneous items—an octant, two saddles, some hydrographic plans, a pair of spurs, two frag-ments of a flute, a picture of Venus and Cupid, . . . a sheet . . . and a bar of soap.[13]

How could anyone lack sympathy for a man who considered these to be the essentials of life? So caparisoned and equipped, Bowles boarded HMS *Fox* for Nassau, in August 1799, accompanied by a new set of recruits. He was disap-pointed on his arrival to find that Dunmore had departed and that Miller and Bonnamy had become dispirited. So, abandoning whatever plans he may have had for a descent upon East Florida, Bowles convinced the captain of the *Fox* to bear him around the peninsula toward St. Mark. Navigation in those waters was chancy. The *Fox* overshot the outlet of the Ocklockonee River and ran aground on the eastern sand spit of Fort George Island, where Bowles was discovered by Andrew Ellicott.

Bowles and Ellicott

Ellicott was the Quaker surveyor celebrated for having laid out the Federal City of Washington with the assistance of the black mathematician Benjamin Banneker. He appears in this narrative, however, for his role in clarifying the lines determining a larger tract—the "Natchez District," including much of the best cotton land of the present states of Alabama and Mississippi, bounded on the west by the strategic bluffs along the Mississippi River, vaguely ex-tending into eastern Tennessee in the other direction and utterly without definition as it reached toward Bowles's ephemeral domain along the Gulf of Mexico on the south. The Treaty of Paris in 1783 had left the Natchez Dis-trict so vague, though British West Florida had included much of it between 1762 and 1783. Arduously, a series of American diplomats succeeded in reach-ing an agreement with Spain that the District would go to the Americans as far south as the 31st Parallel—the final statement of their understandings was Pinckney's Treaty of 1795.[14]

Even before the advent of Bowles, this succulent region was so strongly held by the Choctaws, Chickasaws, and Creeks that Spain twice suggested that the United States join in guaranteeing to those nations its occupancy as a neutral state. Bowles may well have had in mind an expansion of his Muskogean Republic to fill the District with a confederacy of Chickasaw and Choctaw states. Though the Spanish authorities gave him no encouragement, neither did they fulfill their treaty obligation to remove their strong points within the District. Ellicott's assignment in 1798 was to lay these problems to rest. Until he reached Natchez he was not much aware of the ambitions of the cotton planters, but he was assigned a large bodyguard of cavalry to overawe the Indians and urge the Spaniards toward the 1795 treaty line, which he was thereupon to survey. The Creeks, Seminoles, and Choctaws were not easily intimidated; acting in the spirit of Alexander McGillivray, urged along by friends of Bowles, and no doubt stimulated by Spanish reminders of the proposed neutral state, they declared that they had not been consulted in the foregoing transactions and whetted their knives in response to Bowles's warning that any surveyors would be scalped if they trespassed into the territory of his republic.

In 1799, Ellicott had rejoined his survey party encamped on the west bank of the Chatahoochee River to determine how healthy it might be to press the survey onward. Bowles was then thought to have been removed from the scene, and to be in the Philippines, but even in his absence, Ellicott concluded, the Creeks and Seminoles were sufficiently dangerous to deter going beyond the Chatahoochee. Having accepted the advice of friendly Indians that he come at the problem the other way round, he set about circumnavigating Florida to start at the other end of the line, through the valley of the St. Mary's. However, as he descended the Apalachicola toward the Gulf to commence his journey, he received a messenger from Bowles, sent from the grounded but comfortable *Fox*: "I wish much to see you. Although we may differ in politics, yet as gentlemen we may associate."[15]

A storm blew in from the Gulf. For eight days, Ellicott waited it out aboard Bowles's flagship. His host was beyond his sober Quaker ken, "certainly a man of enterprise, and address, added to considerable talents"—yet more than a little crazy. "He speaks in the style of a king; 'my nation' and 'my people' are his common expressions." Still, Bowles was sane enough to know that he needed a boat that would float, and that Ellicott needed the charts Bowles had brought with him from Nassau in order to find his way around Florida. Though Bowles supplied the charts, the exhausted Ellicott failed to rise to the occasion. With uncharacteristic deference to the niceties of diplomacy, he informed both the Spanish and American governments of Bowles's intentions.[16]

They began assembling forces against him, while he proclaimed an alliance with Britain and issued a declaration of war "by land and sea . . . [against]

the goods ships and subjects of His Catholic Majesty." By February 1800, however, Britain had made its choice of alliances; the planters were of more utility than Bowles, so his little force on Fort George Island was left to fend for itself. As the Spaniards approached, he retreated to a fort at Wekiwa, where the Flint and Chatahoochee join to form the Apalachicola.[17]

"Execute Him on the Spot"

The interests requiring the elimination of Bowles coalesced in March 1800. The planters of Georgia needed the land he controlled and were determined to terminate the hemorrhaging of their slaves toward the maroon settlements augmented by Bowles with recruits from the Bahamas. Urged forward by The Firm and by both the American planters and its own, the Spanish government instructed its armed forces "to make every effort to capture . . . and . . . execute him on the spot."[18]

In response, Bowles assembled another multiracial force of Indians, blacks, and miscellaneous Europeans, once more captured the Panton, Leslie store at St. Mark, and added the Spanish fort nearby. So formidable was his reputation that when Thomas Portell, the commander of the fort, learned that Bowles's little navy had captured two cannon and one of The Firm's ships, he surrendered his garrison of 106 men and a stout structure of hewn stone, set in a virtually impregnable position.

Bowles had reached the apogee of his career, but he had a fierce antagonist in Governor Vicente Folch of Spanish West Florida. Taking personal command, Folch came after him with a force of grenadiers and militia aboard four schooners escorted by three galleys and two gunboats. When the sails of this armada appeared offshore, Bowles's undisciplined recruits abandoned him. Once more he took to the shadows and Spanish moss of aboriginal Florida, where once more the fox became a lion. Benjamin Hawkins, the agent of the American government in the region, who was always ready to derogate whites who fought beside blacks, insisted *later* that Bowles had only sixty men and that they were "more attentive to frolicking than fighting." That was not, however, what Hawkins said at the time. On the scene and at the moment, he told his superiors that Bowles was so formidable that Spain alone could not handle him and that it "must give up the Floridas or fight for them"—adding that it was "showing little evidence of doing" so.[19]

Since President Jefferson had already decided that Spain must give up the Floridas, Bowles might have seemed a welcome pretext to get on with the job. That might have been the policy of an Adams administration, for before the planters' ascendancy in 1800, Adams "had manifested no interest" in acquiring Florida and no more enthusiasm for helping Spain squash Bowles than for helping France quash Toussaint Louverture on Haiti. Jefferson "was more obliging" in both cases. (For Jefferson, Napoleon, and Toussaint, see Chapter Thirteen.) Like Toussaint's multinational republic, Bowles's example might also be contagious. Besides, his regime of runaway blacks, Indians, and whites lay directly in the path of the planters. Bearing this in mind, we must be skeptical of accounts by Jeffersonian historians dismissing Bowles as only an "adventurer." An adventurer he was, but he was more, just as McGillivray was more than a mestizo chief and Toussaint considerably more than "a savage." In the minds of the planters, Bowles and Toussaint shared roles in 1800 as dangerous as that of Dunmore in 1776. All three could stir up trouble among those in servitude in the plantations.

The Fox Is Run to Earth

When he assumed the presidency, Jefferson agreed to coordinate campaigns against Bowles, with the Spanish authorities, and against Toussaint, with Napoleon. His Secretary of War, General Henry Dearborn, was directed to write Hawkins that "no exertion should be wanting on your part for securing him [Bowles] if he should venture within our limits." Spain had put a bounty of a thousand dollars on Bowles's head. Dearborn urged Hawkins to advertise the blood money "among the Creeks . . . [so that] some individuals of them . . . [might be induced] to make an exertion to apprehend him. . . . [E]very justifiable measure should be taken for placing him in such a situation as will prevent his being mischievous."[20]

In May 1803, Bowles was told that there would be a gathering of the Southern tribes at Hickory Ground, a few miles south of Little Tallassee. Hawkins, John Forbes, representing The Firm, and Esteban Folch, agent for his father, the governor, lay hidden nearby at Lachlan McGillivray's old trading post. Though Hickory Ground was over a hundred miles within American territory, the younger Folch brought with him a contingent of Spanish troops with Hawkins's agreement. Bowles knew a price was on his head but brazened it out. When he came upon Folch, he warned him that he and Hawkins might be "caught in their own trap." On May 27, however, Bowles walked too great a distance from his bodyguard of Seminoles and was captured by a detail of Creeks in the pay of Hawkins. They bound him and presented him to the Americans, the Spaniards, and The Firm.[21]

Here is Forbes's version of what happened next:

> I was eager to see the villain . . . Stephen [Folch] and I attended with three or four other white men rode down to where he was. . . . He was standing with his hands tied behind him, and Brian Molton with a Spanish flag some distance in front. At our approach he turned pale and said he supposed his last hour was come. Mr. Hill said no you have nothing to fear from us [washing his hands, one assumes]. He then ordered the handcuffs to be brought,

which he [Bowles] allowed to be put on him without a struggle, observing that he had once been a prisoner, but was never tied before. As soon as the irons were riveted he was put on board a canoe and the crowd of women and children immediately pushed it off.[22]

Though Forbes gloated that the Creeks "retired perfectly satisfied" except for "Bowles's friends . . . crying in the corner," those "women and children" included some who did not mock him and set about setting him free. Ultimately, however, Bowles was recaptured and sent under heavier guard to New Orleans and Havana. In early 1806, his death was reported from the Moro prison.

The traveler who comes to Little Tallassee and Hickory Ground today will find strip malls where Hernando de Soto found fields and Alexander McGillivray piled his pelts. Discarded hamburger wrappers swirl in wind curls across parking lots where William Bartram strode across graded ceremonial plazas. Wal-Marts loom where Bartram discerned "areopogi." Not far away is a respectable reproduction of the stockade of Fort Toulouse, reminding us of Louis Milfort and the French. The closest memorial of British tenure lies in Cherokee country—an admirable facsimile of Fort Loudoun, near Knoxville, on the northwest flanks of the Smoky Mountains. One day soon we may replicate as well one or more of Forts San Pedro, San Juan, and San Paulo built by the Spaniards under Juan de Pardo, nearby, in the 1560s and 1570s, forty years before the English arrived at Jamestown, and in the upland Carolinas archaeology may yet discover the footings of his Forts Santo Tomás and Santiago.

The scarred and wasted land itself is the most eloquent museum of the harried, hasty passage of King Cotton.

The Firm Steps Forward

After William Augustus Bowles had been despatched to the Moro prison, The Firm emerged as a full-fledged, multinational force, acting in concert with the masters of the plantation South. Jointly, they brought under the sway of King Cotton eight million acres of cotton land, including the area once called by Bowles his "Muskogean Republic."

The economy of the borderlands was in transition from a subsistence agriculture of white and Indian yeomen, growing their own crops and supplementing their diets with meat secured by hunting, to a plantation system, growing cotton and rice for sale to international markets. For more than a decade, hides provided by the Creeks and Seminoles had gone to the Bahamas on Panton and Leslie's schooners and brigantines, to be stored in Panton and Leslie's warehouses. The Firm controlled the trade of East Florida with a dozen stations, five of them along the St. Johns River. And they did a lot of business. The Pensacola station alone received 250,000 hides in a year. Panton's salt works cured fish and hides; Leslie's lumbermen along the St. Johns produced wood for the West Indies, and his drovers herded cattle to the shore to be slaughtered for salt beef. From a new headquarters at Pensacola, their trading empire spread to Natchez, Baton Rouge, New Orleans, and the port then called Nogales, where the Yazoo enters the Mississippi. As if to memorialize their victory over Bowles, they set about repairing and occupying the trading post at Hickory Ground.

Deerskins, Rum, and Land

So many deer were slaughtered in the American South to provide gloves, belts, and luggage for fashionable Europeans that the ancient interactions between humans and animals were forever disrupted. Between 1780 and 1830, the buckskin-doeskin trade induced Indian dependence upon firearms to defend themselves, as well as to hunt out that crop of deer required annually to pay debts incurred to purchase those very weapons. Early in this process, the traders discovered that for many Indians rum was not a recreational drug but an addiction. While disabled by it, they drunkenly ceded land to pay the debts of drunkenness. In this chapter we will follow the consequences to the land of the use of a rum-debt-land sequence demonstrated on a small scale by the traders of Charles Town, Augusta, Pensacola, and St. Augustine and enlarged into an instrument of national policy by the Virginians controlling the federal government.

Some changes in the leadership in Washington City and in the borderlands were required to prepare for the full use of that process. Alexander McGillivray, who was not susceptible to such means of persuasion, died in 1793. George Washington went out of office in 1796, and John Adams in 1800. William Augustus Bowles was put out of the way in 1803. Whatever else might be said of him, he was never one to sell out his friends, and he had no illusions about either the planters or The Firm.

Neither did George Washington. Though sharp in his own real estate practices and his negotiations with the Indians, he had conscientious objections to raw extortion. During his travels in the West, he had many opportunities to learn about the methods of the Indian traders, of whom the most notorious in the Southwest were the agents of The Firm. Upon ascending to the presidency in 1789, he resolved to reform those extortionate traders or to displace them. Washington proposed that his government socialize the Indian trade, setting up its own "clean" posts, keeping honest books, and abandoning the use of rum, intimidation, and fraud. In 1795, two such trading stations were put in place at Tellico and Colerain, within the choicest markets of The Firm.

William Panton was one of the first businessmen to understand how conscientious administrators may be outflanked by appealing to the appetites of venal members of Congress. In 1796, he dispatched John Forbes to Tennessee, to call on Senator William Blount and his junior partner John McKee, "in order to arrange the affairs of the Panton firm and prevent the ruin of its trade." Blount was known to be vulnerable because he was heavily in debt. He had been speculating in Western lands, some of them within the territories of tribes whose members owed large sums to The Firm. To prevent his own "ruin," Blount had proposed to the British that they send an expeditionary force from Canada across the territory of the United States to seize New Orleans. This might provide him a handsome capital gain, for Blount had a "call" upon lands that would thereupon rise in value. With the businesslike British in New Orleans rather than the erratic Spaniards, agricultural products produced upstream, including cotton, could be sent more confidently toward the markets of Europe. The Senate of the United States declined to accept the premise that another British occupation was acceptable to achieve that end and thrust Blount from its ranks.

McKee was singed by that encounter but not burnt. He was a Virginian charmer and—better than that, as we shall see—educated at Liberty Hall, now Washington and Lee University. He had learned the life of the borders and the importance of The Firm. He returned Forbes's visit and was sumptuously entertained in Mobile and Pensacola. Since he was at the time employed by the United States government, he could assure The Firm that the United States would "facilitate the effectual and prompt collection of their debts within our Indian nations."[1]

As agent to the Cherokees, McKee took his orders after the election of 1796 from Secretary of War James McHenry, who was privy to a scheme of Alexander Hamilton's for an assault upon Florida, as was the Secretary of State, Timothy Pickering. McHenry, Pickering, and McKee perceived the utility of The Firm to a venture offering an alternative to Blount's proposal that foreign troops cross American soil. All the British had to do was to hover encouragingly offshore while Hamilton assembled an overwhelming force of volunteers, a "land force . . . the command . . . [of which] would very naturally fall upon me . . . [in] the most grand and glorious project in all the world. . . . [W]e should certainly look to the possession of the Floridas and Louisiana, and we ought to squint at South America." Thus it was that when Andrew Ellicott, who was not privy to any of this, wrote Pickering that McKee seemed suspiciously friendly to the Blountians in Natchez, Pickering responded that "the government was informed of McKee's activities and fully satisfied of his loyalty."[2]

Ellicott was already unpopular with The Firm because his task was to see to it that the terms of Pinckney's Treaty of 1795 were enforced, including the requirement that the Spaniards withdraw The Firm's monopoly position in the Indian trade. From Panton's point of view, Spain's acquiescence in this provision meant that he and his partners had been "entirely abandoned to the mercy of the Americans . . . [and must] bow our knees to those whom we have much offended and endeavor to soften their resentment in the best manner we can." Panton needed Blount and McKee to bring the partners closer to what Panton called the swelling "purse of the United States." The old Tories were ready to "solicit being the agents of Congress."[3]

McKee might help with that, though both Ellicott and the Spanish bureaucracy identified him with Hamilton and the expansionists, so it was scarcely surprising that some overeager Spaniards arrested McKee as he passed through Mobile and took him under guard to New Orleans. The Firm secured his release, showing its power within the Spanish bureaucracy. Its ties to the militant tribes had been demonstrated in the Cherokee War in 1792. As it turned toward the Americans, it had been in a position to protect the rear and flanks of Hamilton's contemplated descent of the Mississippi in 1798. Then, in cooperation with a new administration in Washington, it got Bowles out of the way.[4]

On June 11, 1799, just after McKee became agent to the Choctaws, Panton made a proposal to Hawkins: The Firm would induce the Indians to sell cotton land to the Americans, understanding that a goodly share of each payment arising from such a sale would be endorsed back to it. At the same time, Panton threatened that if the Americans did not move, the British or Spaniards might, and he urged Hawkins to use his political influence to get things moving. Otherwise "some other means" would have to be tried. As we shall see, even after the American government acceded to their plan, the partners of The Firm did try other means.[5]

The balky Federalists were removed from office by the election of 1800. Two years later, McKee proudly recalled the "promise made by the government *through me* [his emphasis] . . . they [Panton etc.] might reasonably look forward to such indulgences as would greatly facilitate the effectual and prompt collection of their debts within our Indian Nations." In 1802, it was considerably safer than it had been in 1797 or 1799 to avow a role in achieving an alliance between the planters and The Firm. There was a new Secretary of War, Henry Dearborn, and a new President, Thomas Jefferson. McHenry had been willing to deal with the Tories to accommodate Hamilton's transitory purposes, but that aberrant in him now became general and sustained Jeffersonian policy. As Hawkins, once an ardent Federalist, set his barque upon the new Jeffersonian current, McKee did so as well.[6]

Indian Yeomen and Governor Sargent's Lost Cause

In 1799, as William Panton and Benjamin Hawkins were discussing Indian "removal" through debt-for-land exchanges arranged by Panton's firm, Timothy Pickering, still Secretary of State and still operating under George Washington's Indian policy, proposed that the Indians be helped to remain on their ancestral lands, in a modified version of a Spanish suggestion of a decade earlier. Pickering wrote Governor Sargent of Mississippi Territory that he should assist the Choctaws to adopt "the arts of husbandry and domestic manufactures." As yeomen, growing and ginning cotton, they might be integrated into Mississippi Territory, as if they qualified for inclusion among those Jefferson had called "God's chosen people." There were only twenty or thirty thousand of them left, so they were hardly much of a threat.[7]

When Dearborn took office in 1801 as Secretary of War in the Jefferson administration, he directed that the definition of Indian "arts of husbandry" emphasize "the growth of cotton as well as grain." Cotton was the crop of the future, everyone agreed on that. The question was: whose future? Jefferson's suggestion was that agricultural Indians needed less space than hunting and gathering Indians and that the space vacated could be put under non-Indian plows: "The time will come when a cession of land may be necessary to us and not injurious to them. . . . [The Indians would learn] to do better in less land, [while] our increasing numbers will be calling for more land." The indigenous peoples, wrote the President, had land "to spare," while the planters "want lands."[8]

Jeffersonian agrarian doctrine might be extended to Indian yeomen growing cotton on their ancestral land, in accordance with his recommendation that they "settle out separately or in small villages, farm their fields and turn their minds to agriculture and the raising of stock for the support of their families." John McKee had advanced such a policy, asking permission to provide the Choctaws with a cotton gin, and then-Secretary McHenry had approved: "The gin for cleaning cotton may [give?] encouragement to the Indians to exert thems[elves in] the growth of that article." McKee went to Natchez to purchase parts, and though the Choctaws refused to accept the gin, the Chickasaws took it and started ginning. Soon the Choctaws, repentantly or competitively, were asking for their own gin—after that given the Chickasaws mysteriously burned.[9]

In 1801, McKee, still operating under the old rules, filed a report from the Chickasaw Nation that cotton spinning went on "in both these nations with considerable spirit, and every kind of industry is progressing, particularly in this nation—the Indians here are settling out of their old towns, fencing their plantations, and . . . they have pretty generally good stocks of hogs and the owners of cattle are increasing fast." Indian women were learning to spin and weave, and the chiefs began to contemplate sending cotton to market on fleets of canoes.[10]

When Dr. Rush Nutt, philosopher, planter, and physician, traversed the Natchez Trace in 1805, he reported yeoman Choctaws hard at those "arts of husbandry . . . building log houses and cultivating the earth in corn, cotton, and other garden vegetables." The Creeks of Alabama were growing enough cotton by 1803 to induce Abram Mordecai and the brothers John and William Price to establish gins at their trading stations. The Creeks accelerated cotton production so much by 1806 that their chiefs requested that the Spanish authorities waive duties on cotton sent through West Florida to the Gulf; if so encouraged they would be able to make further progress from hunting to agriculture, "as killing of deer is partly at an end."[11]

Might these be "chosen people" in Jefferson's view? Did he mean what he said to the chiefs of the Cherokee Nation on January 10, 1806?

> I cannot take leave of you without expressing the satisfaction I have received from . . . [seeing] with my own eyes that the endeavors we have been making to encourage and lead you in the way of improving your situation have not been unsuccessful. . . . You are becoming farmers, learning the use of the plow and the hoe, enclosing your grounds and employing that labor in their cultivation which you formerly employed in hunting and in war; and I see handsome specimens of cotton cloth raised, spun and wove by yourselves. . . . Go on, my children, in the same way.[12]

Had Alexander McGillivray been present, he might have commented that Indians had grown and woven cotton cloth for a long time before the ancestors of Jefferson ceased to cover their nakedness with animal skins.

For a time there were four sets of Southern pioneers using similar agricultural technology—Indians, slaves, planters, and yeomen. Many Indians were managing agricultural technology and animal power with equal skill to that of their Euro-American neighbors and competitors.

Yankee Yeomen

"Handsome specimens of cotton cloth raised, spun and wove" by white yeomen and their wives might already be seen in the Delta, though neither as the artifacts of Indian cottage industry nor of plantation culture. Before battalions of slaves arrived to drain and ditch the marshes and to plant cotton under the lash, there were yeomen on the scene, growing and spinning. They were, however, Yankees, many of them Burrites, and Jefferson treated them as invisible while treating the Indians as moveable. These Yankee yeomen had come to the shores of the Mississippi a generation earlier, induced to settle in the Natchez District by British land grants. Their leaders were Aaron Burr's early sponsors, the Putnams, and his relatives, the Lymans and Ogdens. Their villages in what were called the "Jersey Settlements" appeared like those of backcountry Connecticut, Massachusetts, and New Jersey, though in the 1790s they had begun to grow and spin a little cotton for rough clothing. "The ladies would fill their aprons with cotton to amuse themselves on the road picking out the seed."[13]

> The cotton gin transformed all this. . . . The first Whitney gin appeared in the Natchez District in 1795. . . . As early as 1800, Narsworthy Hunter, a leading Natchez citizen, could write that "cotton is at present the staple of the Territory, and is cultivated with singular advantage to the planter . . . we have as many black as white inhabitants, we cannot make much less than three million pounds of merchantable cotton."[14]

A half dozen reasons were given in the opening pages of this work why white family farmers in the South were, on average, kinder to the land than white planters, without imputing to the yeomen any special benignity. They were poorer. However cheap land might have been, it was seldom cheap enough for them. The planters could not only buy but buy in quantity, and they could thereupon reserve the best for themselves. As a result, there was less incentive to a yeoman to move to fresh ground and more reason to tend what he had. Family farmers did their own work and cared for their own machinery. Planters' slaves had no cause for care of the land they worked or for the tools put into their hands. It was the presence of cheap land secured

from Indians that drew the planters onward and discouraged them from solicitude for any home place. We recall Jefferson's writing to Arthur Young
that it was cheaper to buy a new farm than manure an old one.

How are we now to distinguish the effects upon the land of Indian cotton
farmers from those of white yeoman cotton farmers, or of Indian planters
from white planters? What were the consequences to the land of the political
decisions driving off Indian yeomen, all full-blood Indian planters, and most
mixed-blood planters, and replacing them with whites? Let us stipulate that
class for class they all came to possess and use the same tools and that both
Indian and white planters made use of slave labor. Indian removal replaced
people who had nowhere else to go of equivalent fertility with those who
knew they could always get more good cheap land. It substituted people whose
ancestors had been in migrancy for centuries for others who had been living
in the same landscape for a millennium or so.

There is a large body of opinion, in which I share, that Indians as a group
treated blacks better than did whites. Certainly the Seminoles, Hichiti,
Chickamaugas, and Texas Cherokees did. No one seems to dispute the idea
that few Indians bore the kind of racial prejudices that encouraged whites to
treat blacks badly. Conversely, human psychology would suggest that blacks
who worked for Indians would treat the land they worked better than would
blacks working for whites. And finally, there is good evidence that Indian
agriculture made greater use than the agriculture practiced by whites of the
soil-sustaining concord of the Three Sisters—corn, beans, and squash. Since
planters and yeomen, white and Indian, grew corn, that part of an Indian
yeoman or Indian planter's property would be in better shape after a time
than the equivalent patch of the farm of a white yeoman or planter.

As for cotton cultivation, the few Indian or part-Indian planters who owned
large numbers of slaves lived amid other Indians who did not cease traditional
farming practices. Whites regularly derided Indians for permitting "weeds"
to grow up around their cotton and corn plants. Weeds are diversifiers. The
weedy landscape was healthier than the monocrop landscape, hoed more than
the traditional two times. White observers also noted the presence among
Indians of "old fields," recovering from staple cultivation and also producing
berries and wild onions and drawing in deer. Grassy expanses were, therefore,
both wild gardens and means of livestock management.[15]

The greater damage done the Southern land after transfer from Indians
to planters was not caused by a sheer increase in numbers. In many areas the
newcomers and their slaves were much more numerous, but by no means
everywhere. Though the Indians *were* fewer in 1800 than they had been in
1500 (the best evidence is that only between 10 and 25 percent of them survived the epidemics of the sixteenth, seventeenth, and eighteenth centuries),
before 1500 many of them had lived in the same places practicing their kind
of agriculture for hundreds of years. Between 1500 and 1800 there were still

large populations in what later became prime plantation land. Before the advent of the Europeans the Native American population of the Gulf Coast was probably over one million, and the Mississippi Valley probably supported four or five times that many people for three hundred years or longer. There were not more than a million Euro-Americans in the entire West in 1800, and no more than 1.8 million in the Gulf Coast states in 1850 after much of the damage had been done.[16]

After a lifetime studying the Southeastern Indians, Charles Hudson, no sentimentalist, contrasted the propensity for the people of industrialized nations to assume that "nature exists for man to use in any way he sees fit, and that nature is infinitely forgiving," to the opposing view of the Southern Indians: "Man had to exploit nature in order to live, but . . . man should do so carefully, and that nature was not infinitely forgiving. If mistreated, nature would strike back. . . . [M]an can become too populous, and . . . when he does nature suffers. . . . [Theirs was a] concept of natural balance." The Indians did not "live lightly on the land." They lived with it, using it, shaping it, participating in its ways, and saving themselves much inconvenience as a result, for they could farm the same tracts for twenty generations and more. The book of the land recorded therefore another set of reasons for regretting the forced removal of Indians to accommodate the policies of Thomas Jefferson and Andrew Jackson. It would have been better for the land if they had been left where they were—and where they had been for so long.[17]

Jeffersonian Strategy and Jeffersonian Agents

The workings of the mind of Thomas Jefferson during the summer of 1803, as he anticipated the formal acquisition of Louisiana, are among the wonders of the modern world. His continental strategic vision and his neatly calibrated tactical sense were in combination almost superhuman. Within a single plan he solved an interactive puzzle requiring the manipulation of the avarice of the Southern fur traders, such as the partners of The Firm, as he had in the previous year brought around the Eastern sea traders, such as the Livingston family (see Part Four). He made use of the land-hunger of the planters and the desperate necessities of the leaders of the Indian nations. He channeled to his own ends the personal ambitions of the "Bonaparte of the Backwoods," Andrew Jackson, as he had those of Bonaparte himself. At the same time, he provided satisfaction of the avarice and ambition of Jackson's arch foe, General James Wilkinson, whom Jefferson chose to be commander of the nation's armed forces in the West. The President drew upon the patriotic instincts of the Eastern Federalists who might oppose, for reasons of conscience, his expansion of the slave-and-plantation system, and assembled a de facto coalition in the West of planters, upriver farmers, slave sellers, slave buyers, and tens of thousands of anonymous frontiersmen. He even found a means to have the Indians pay for the Louisiana Purchase.

Jefferson's design was grounded in the cotton lands of the West still held by the Indians, though said by the Europeans to be governed by Spain. We will in subsequent pages observe the transaction between Jefferson and Napoleon by which title to these lands—as Europeans understood title—was conveyed first to France and then in a twinkling to the United States. The price was, in round numbers, eleven and a quarter million dollars plus interest. As we shall see, he and Napoleon agreed that a sufficient portion should go to the merchants of the eastern seaboard of the United States to assure their enthusiasm for a transaction otherwise of primary interest to patriots, planters, and the upstream farmers of the West.

Where would Jefferson find the rest of the money? He would "work the spread," as the current expression goes. He would buy Indian lands through extortionate purchases or obtain them by forcing the tribes to exchange them for temporary refuge in the wild lands of the West. With the Indians gone, the government of the United States would sell their homelands to the planters at prices perhaps five times "cost," though still much less than what would have been required if the buyers had not been preceded by an army and a subvention from the other taxpayers of the nation. As Jefferson explained to his old confidant John Dickinson, once "the lands held by the Indians on this side of the Mississippi" were obtained, "we may sell out our lands here and pay the whole debt contracted before it comes due." Obviously there had to be a "spread" for that to work.[1]

Jefferson's letter to Dickinson was sent in August 1803, two months after he told his primary civilian agent in the Lower Mississippi Valley, William C. C. Claiborne, that it was "all important to press the Indians, as steadily and strenuously as they can bear." They might sell or exchange, but they would always face the threat of forced removal. Jefferson himself advised the chiefs of the Chickasaws that as his "children" they should "dispose of some of" their lands "to pay your debts." "We are," he assured them, "willing to buy on reasonable terms."[2]

Reasonableness would be defined by Claiborne and the partners of The Firm. The Southern nations would be "offered" land on the western side of the Mississippi. Failing "purchase," exchange would do. Jefferson explained to Dickinson, who had a tender conscience, that some refuges could be found that were "unoccupied" by other Indians and implied that once removed to such serene settings the newcomers would be left in peace. He was more candid to others. He delegated the removal process to Wilkinson, who readily admitted that there was no "empty continent" offering "unoccupied" land: the Osages and the other Plains warriors were indisposed to step aside for "the transfer of the Southern nations, to the West of the Mississippi." Mass removal would not produce any "solid peace between these nations and the Osages particularly." The opposite of peace is war. That was what was likely. The smiling commanding general wrote the Secretary of War that the best "plan of settlement" would be one that ignored either debt consolidation or exchange but was straightforwardly "founded upon conquest, which I believe is most natural." He would, of course, need a bigger army "to meet the occasion."[3]

While Wilkinson was offering to conquer the plains, Jefferson was writing Governor William Henry Harrison that he would brook no opposition from the nations on the eastern side of the Mississippi River. If they were "foolhardy enough to take up the hatchet" to resist, they should be "driven across the Mississippi as the only condition of peace." Would they have been wise to accept instead Jefferson's offer of land on the western side? Not if they had read the balance of his letter to Harrison. The President left no doubt that any sanctuary offered them would only be temporary. To make his point clear, he set forth his celebrated vision that "when we shall be full on this side, we may lay off a range of States on the Western bank from the head to the mouth, and so, range after range, advancing compactly as we multiply." No sane Indian would farm in the path of that juggernaut.[4]

Andrew Jackson achieved Jefferson's removal plan in two stages. By 1815, his wars of conquest had dispossessed the Southern nations of much of the land they did not cede in payment of debts, becoming the hero of those lusting for "Conquest." As President in the 1830s, he carried forward the "removal" of most of the Indian people remaining, sending them off to "Indian Territory." It was not because it was "unoccupied"; the Southern Indians who survived Trails of Tears faced the armed resistance of the Plains tribes including the Osages.

Though Wilkinson was not granted the occasion for an Indian war in the West, Jefferson achieved all that he had sought, including the arrangements by which the government of the United States successfully "worked the spread." As we will observe in the following pages, it acquired millions of acres of Indian land at a cost averaging about twenty-five cents an acre and was able to sell at a dollar and a quarter an acre and better.

The Louisiana Purchase opened terrain across the Mississippi to which the Southern nations were removed, releasing cotton land to the planters on the eastern side. It also added to the Cotton Kingdom new provinces on the western side, in Louisiana and Arkansas. Since sales of public land in the South were directly correlated to cotton exports, "the spread" was kept broad by demand for cotton. Many millions of acres of public land were sold to the planters at rates subsidized in effect by the other taxpayers who bore part of the acquisition cost, but the postconquest price was still high enough to exceed that cost very comfortably. The amount due—fifteen millions in principal and interest—went to the bankers who advanced cash to Napoleon and the Eastern merchants. Few at the time attended much to the cost to the land, the slaves, the Indians, and the yeomen.

Jefferson and Wilkinson

The relationship between President Thomas Jefferson and James Wilkinson is one of the enigmas of Jefferson's public life. Wilkinson was the primary agent of the Spanish intelligence system in the Mississippi Valley. Jefferson was repeatedly warned of this association, yet he relied upon Wilkinson as his chief agent to secure the movement of the Indian nations from their ancestral homes east of the Mississippi River to some destination west of it. Wilkinson apparently enjoyed both the work and Jefferson's explanations for its necessity.

Reciting presidential writ, he ordered Silas Dinsmoor, agent to the Choctaws, to "cooperate with [William] Simpson [the representative of The Firm] in obtaining the Mississippi cession because the President wants land on the Mississippi to form a barrier of hardy yeomanry on that solitary frontier and to strengthen the ligaments of national union."[5]

This was no doubt one of the occasions in which Wilkinson permitted himself a little flirtation with irony. Perhaps he was only testing Dinsmoor, whom he knew to have conscientious objections to slavery, and who was well aware that he had no interest whatever in cluttering good plantation land with "hardy yeomen" and cared little for the "ligaments of national union." The general was a traitor, spy, perjurer, forger, and on several occasions the director of teams of murderers, as well as a planter of cotton both in the United States and later in Mexico. He supplemented his profits from tobacco and cotton with bribes from The Firm and added to his pay as an American general his stipend as a Spanish spy.[6]

Wilkinson's little joke to Dinsmoor was made as an observation upon the transparent sophistry of Jefferson's justification for Indian removal. Must the natives be relieved of their land? Were they not already raising cotton? Were they not the quintessential "hardy yeomen," only differing from the people of the Jersey Settlements by their color? Yet, as Jefferson had said, the planters "want lands." So the Indians must go. And why? The residual rhetoric of the Lost Cause was still there to provide a response. Indian removal would provide open space to "form a barrier of hardy yeomanry on that solitary frontier."[7]

What was the history of that idea? And how serious was Jefferson about it? Before the purchase of Louisiana, he had proposed to enlist yeoman volunteers to be settled on the east bank of the Mississippi, as the Putnams and Ogdens had already done and as James Oglethorpe had settled the border with Florida in the 1730s. In 1807, Jefferson renewed the idea, this time for a settlement on the west bank, each yeoman to be allocated 160 acres. The theoretical, younger Jefferson might have thought apportioning of public land in this way to be justifiable both on defensive grounds and to improve public mental health. The practical, middle-aged Jefferson recommended armed settlements of yeomen as an act of economy, for armed yeomen came cheaper than regular soldiers. Despite Wilkinson's irony, they were not there to form an ideal commonwealth but to push some "foreigners" (the Indians) out and to keep other "foreigners" (the French Creoles) down. The newcomers, "Americans by birth," were to see to it that the Creoles were instructed in the ways of an English-speaking yeomanry and put to work by it. Characteristically, however, Jefferson did not follow through on either of these proposals. And characteristically Wilkinson augmented his list of betrayals with another little gleeful jab against a sponsor.[8]

Wilkinson's Clients

Throughout the 1790s, while Wilkinson was currying favor with Jefferson by sending him archaeological reports and specimens of Indian arts, he was corresponding with Burr and directing the blaze of his charm upon Alexander Hamilton. To Hamilton he initially suggested a "grand and glorious" attack on the Spanish dominions—the scheme he later proposed to Burr—while simultaneously seeking a retainer from Spain to prevent Hamilton's success. (His capacity for triple dipping was demonstrated again in 1806, when he was paid by Jefferson and also by the Spaniards to apprehend Burr, who had included Wilkinson in his list of beneficiaries of land grants.)

A man of ordinary tolerance for complexity might have exhausted his options with these, but not Wilkinson. The Firm was by then another of his clients. Until 1798, he had treated it as a competitor against his own trading operations. During that phase, as The Firm and Alexander McGillivray were attempting to secure from the Americans a free port on the Atlantic where the Creeks could bring their goods, Wilkinson had warned his Spanish clients that neither McGillivray nor the Scottish partners of The Firm could be trusted: "Scotchmen throughout the world," he wrote, "are governed by the basest interests." Having so defined them, Wilkinson began grooming their favor, granting their agents—still Spanish citizens—a monopoly right to remain at Chickasaw Bluffs after the post was to have been closed down by Ellicott's implementation of Pinckney's Treaty of 1795.[9]

Having calculated Wilkinson's utility to their interests, the partners of The Firm brought him in as another of their associates. His special assignment was to facilitate their relationship to Jefferson. The new President's first international agreement was the Treaty of Chickasaw Bluffs, in October 1801, executed by Wilkinson, securing a portion of the route of the Natchez Trace through Chickasaw Territory. In return, the Chickasaws were assured that no further territorial concessions would be required of them. At Fort Adams, two months later, Wilkinson and two other commissioners acquired the rest of the right-of-way for the Trace by treaty with the Choctaws. They then moved to the stockade in Georgia the general had named Fort Wilkinson, where they acquired for the nation a tract of Creek land on the west bank of the Oconee River. This time they were directly coached by John Forbes and William Simpson. The consequences of that transaction were observed a generation later by Fanny Kemble Butler:

> On Monday evening I rowed over to Darien. . . . A sort of dreamy stillness seemed creeping over the world and into my spirit as the canoe just tilted against the steps to the wharf. . . . A melancholy, monotonous boat horn sounded from the distance up the stream, and presently, floating slowly down with the current, huge, shapeless, black . . . against the sky, came one of those rough barges piled with cotton, called hereabouts Oconee boxes. The

vessel is really nothing but a monstrous square box, made of rough planks
. . . to attain the necessary object of keeping the cotton dry. Upon this huge
tray are piled the swollen, apoplectic-looking cotton bags. . . . This huge
water wagon came lazily down the river, from the upper country to Darien
. . . where the cotton is shipped . . . for . . . Liverpool.[10]

When he had completed his transaction on the Oconee, Wilkinson met with
Simpson to bind up their understandings, but first issued one of his subtle
threats: "If they [The Firm] calculated on further indulgence it became absolutely necessary for their House to consult the interests and dispositions of
our government"—no doubt meaning his own interests. His alternative, smiling, style was displayed in a letter to Forbes, saying that he was "doing whatever may with consistency and propriety be done to reconcile your interests
to those of the United States." His cupped hand was already out.[11]

In September 1803, four months after William Augustus Bowles had been
taken into captivity, Wilkinson was despatched to New Orleans by Jefferson to
accept Louisiana from the French. En route, the general found time to pause at
Little River to meet with John Forbes, to celebrate their victory over Bowles
and to plan steps to make use of the removal of such a significant barrier to their
plans. No doubt Forbes told Wilkinson a story he had recounted to others—
that as the canoe bearing the handcuffed Bowles disappeared around the bend,
Forbes and Hawkins were already discussing the conversion of Indian debt into
plantation land. Forbes later asserted that he told Hawkins that The Firm would
take less than a hundred cents on the dollar if the debts owed it by individual
Creeks and Seminoles were converted into land in the areas currently within
either the United States or in Florida—and if the government for which Hawkins
was agent would guarantee to buy that land.[12]

Everyone assumed that Spanish Florida was ripe for plucking, and within
that province The Firm had already done its own cherry picking. It had bribed
some tribal leaders to concede to it a great swath of land between the
Apalachicola and Wakulla rivers in return for its generous cancellation of a
debt two thirds charged for damages done to its storehouses and forts by
those tribal members who had followed Bowles.

The Firm Adapts and Collects

No accounting firm operating by twenty-first-century standards would have
given the rest of the accounts receivable on the books of The Firm in 1800 a
very high rating for collectibility. They were individual debts. Among the
Southeastern tribes, an individual was dishonored who permitted his own
obligations to be visited upon the tribe. The partners of The Firm and their
allies among the agents of the Virginia Dynasty broke through the barrier,
weakening that code by splitting into factions the leaders of the Creeks. "A

new class of assimilated Creek citizens [was cultivated] who were themselves becoming cotton planters and slave owners" and were assisted to rise to dominate the tribal councils. In 1812, "packed" councils ordered the execution of young men who had resisted the Americans by force or who objected to the cession of tribal land to the United States in return for payment of *tribal* annuities. As these tribal annuity payments were assigned to The Firm to pay debts incurred by council members and other *individuals*, the disgusted and humiliated Red Sticks went to war.[13]

Forbes and Hawkins, acting as ambassadors of The Firm and of the government of the United States, had launched a process that brought about the Creek civil war. Jackson's victory in 1813–14 was made more difficult because The Firm, in its eagerness to effect its diversification into real estate, had joined the United States government in stimulating resistance among Creeks who might otherwise have remained neutral.

> Persistent demands by the Forbes company and the United States government that trade debts be paid through cessions of land severely tested the patience of Creek villagers. Indian leaders contested debts that were accounted to the nation but that actually had been incurred by individuals whose tribal status they did not recognize. When the company tried to add interest to their account, the Creeks grew angrier, insisting that "there is no word for it in their language," and accusing their old trade partner of wanting "to tear the very flesh off their backs."[14]

With those final phrases in mind, we return to economics—the great magnet under the table: The Firm had advanced cooking pots, axes, clothing, gunpowder, and guns to individual Indians to be repaid in skins, with those of bucks preferred. Doe and fawn skins were, so to speak, the copper coins of the frontier; beaver, martin, bear, and mink were already too scarce to merit trade. The "skins payable" account upon the books of The Firm grew with the years as interest was added. As animals were hunted out, the Indians were unable to pay in furs, which were the local currency. Though the debtors did not possess land or other collateral as individuals, they were members of nations that did. Land-as-land was, however, as valueless to The Firm as skins-as-skins. Both had to be monetized—converted into cash—to be bankable. The elimination of Bowles, a joint venture among the younger Forbes, the younger Folch, and Benjamin Hawkins, may have required bribery, travel, powder, and shot, but it could be entered in the books either as a cost of doing business or as a down payment on the collection of contingent assets.

The Firm could not monetize its skins payable account unless it completed three preliminary transformations. First, debts in skins had to be stated as paper contracts to pay sums of money. Second, those promises to pay had to be restated as commitments to deliver land. Third, the land claims had to be converted into cash by finding buyers.

None of this alchemy would be possible until Bowles, McGillivray, and two sets of scruples were out of the way, the first being loyalty between traders and Indians. The terrible phrase "to tear the flesh off the backs" imparts a sense of the brutality of the betrayal of its clients by The Firm. To many of the Indians, the trading relationship had been more than a series of transactions. Conveniences became affinities, and affinities, in Gary Anderson's term, "kinship of another sort." Yet even kinship could not withstand the combined pressures of the avarice of The Firm, the land-gluttony of the planters, the remorseless appetite for raw cotton of the textile millers, and the imperial ambitions of the Jefferson and Madison administrations.

The second barrier of scruple to the monetization of the claims of The Firm lay in the partners' nationality. Their fathers had been Scots. They had been British loyalists and then citizens of Spain. Now they would have to work things out with the government of the United States. The Americans came bringing cash for purchases, an army, and a set of militias eager for conquest.[15]

In February 1803, Dearborn had written Wilkinson that he should meet with Forbes to consolidate their forces for a campaign to deprive the Indians of their cotton land along the Mississippi. That is not how the matter was put, but that was what was meant. Wilkinson did as he was ordered, pressing Forbes to repeat the process of The Firm's Creek-Seminole transaction, this time in territory conceded by Spain to the Americans north of the 31st Parallel, where the Choctaws, Chickasaws, Cherokees, and Creeks could be thrust aside by more debt-for-land swaps. On October 1, 1803, Wilkinson affirmed to Dearborn that Forbes was disposed "to promote the views of Government in our Indian concerns, by every means in his power."[16]

Wilkinson urged Dearborn to accept the embrace of The Firm so that when Jefferson moved against Spanish Florida the partners could efficiently transfer to the American government the Indian land previously acquired by The Firm from the Indians in extortions approved by the well-lubricated Spanish authorities. Alexander Hamilton still had influence, so, on November 15, 1803, Wilkinson suggested to him that he meet with Forbes, splendid fellow that he was, "honorable, . . . amiable, and . . . erudite, . . . of sound intelligence and sterling worth, [and partner in an] opulent and respectable House." Forbes could add to Hamilton's knowledge of Florida, and if Jefferson hesitated, Forbes might smooth the way for Hamilton's expedition into Florida. "With military eyes," Wilkinson wrote, "I have explored every critical pass, every direct route, and every devious way between the Mexican Gulf and the Tennessee River." The "grand and glorious adventure" was still possible:[17]

> I have extended my capacities for utility but not my sphere of action, and in the present moment my destination is extremely precarious. To divorce my sword is to rend a strong ligament of my affections [to go over to

Spain, or become a freelancer?] and to wear it without active service is becoming disreputable.[18]

By "destination" Wilkinson might have meant ultimate citizenship or loyalty to one political figure or another. Perhaps he merely meant a geographic location such as Pensacola, "a good [military site] . . . and the harbor divine. . . . The geographical relation of this place, to the Indians and American estates of the European powers, renders it in my conception immeasurably valuable; and the acquisition of the Floridas, is rendered additionally important, by the luxuriant soil."[19]

Wilkinson, Forbes, and Dearborn

Jefferson trumped Hamilton with the Louisiana Purchase on December 20, 1803. In June 1804, Burr killed Hamilton. In 1807 Jefferson brought Burr to trial, and in 1808, Burr went into exile. Meanwhile, the edges of the Louisiana Purchase remained so untidy as to invite military resolution. It was not clear whether or not Louisiana extended into Texas or, in the opposite direction, subsumed Mobile. In the absence of clarity lay opportunity, military as well as commercial.

James Monroe had told John Forbes, in London, that the Jefferson administration would contend that Mobile was included in the Purchase. On September 21, 1803, Leslie responded to that bit of insiders' information by suggesting to Forbes that the partners of The Firm resident in that city should transfer their citizenship to the United States. Some time thereafter, but before 1813, the partners bestowed upon Wilkinson Dauphin Island, controlling the entrances to Mobile Bay. To everyone's surprise, apparently, Spain refused to give up Mobile, so the partners began urging Wilkinson to seize the place for the United States. He did not do so, however, until it could come to his American employer from his Spanish employer with a minimum of fuss. After the British appeared in the Gulf and threatened Mobile, Wilkinson scraped together a force of six hundred and a few gunboats and on April 15, 1813, made his triumphal entrance into the only city to rival New Orleans as a cotton port on the Gulf.[20]

Two weeks earlier, his son Captain James Wilkinson wrote James Innerarity, the representative of The Firm in Mobile, conveying his father's continuing "exalted esteem and friendship" and his regret that there had been abrasions upstream along the Tombigbee between The Firm and less sympathetic American officials. It seems that they had refused to put American soldiers to work recovering slaves liberated from the partners by the British. The younger Wilkinson could not help much with that but did see to it that Fort Bowyer was built with lumber, bricks, and tools provided by The Firm.

When office supplies and building materials were required, The Firm received one third of the business, and when the United States needed warehouse space or officers' housing, The Firm provided it. When Captain Wilkinson required fish sauce, mustard, and four dozen black silk handkerchiefs from Pensacola, Innerarity furnished those as well.[21]

Debt for Land

In 1804, as Wilkinson and The Firm were adjusting matters at both the national and personal levels, Secretary Dearborn instructed the general that "if no other consideration will induce the Choctaws to part with any of their lands but that of paying off the debt they owe Panton & Co," he should let no scruples delay such transactions. He was to instruct Silas Dinsmoor to use his influence to convince the tribe to settle those debts by relinquishing their lands east of the Yazoo. On April 20, Ephraim Kirby, a land commissioner, reported directly to Jefferson that "through the agency of the white traders settled among them, they [the Choctaws] may be persuaded to exchange their country for a portion of the wilderness of Louisiana."[22]

Forbes was in Washington, arranging the details. The prime Cotton Belt land then held by the Indians would be sold to American planters by the United States government, which would have obtained it by purchase from The Firm. The Firm would get the land from the Indian nations without cash, by convincing the chiefs that debts owed The Firm by tribal members should be treated as tribal obligations, though there was nothing in Indian tradition or in the laws of Spain or the United States to justify holding entire tribes liable for the personal debts or the transgressions of individual chiefs. Before the Choctaws could be induced to relinquish their ancient lands, the resourceful Simpson reported that "much time, labor, and money" had been required "with the chiefs." That expenditure of time, talent, and bribes was a pittance relative to the huge sums to be secured by The Firm by way of the government of the United States from the taxpayers of the United States.[23]

(In Ireland, the English conquerors had made use of such devices, rehearsing the policies advocated by The Firm and by Wilkinson and adopted by the Jefferson administration. The Irish precedents are the subject of the section "Tribes, Land, and Ireland" in the Appendix, p. 255.)

It is doubtful that the planters could have acquired equivalent land at twenty times the price paid the government for the Indian property extorted in this process. So, in addition to a transfer of ownership of land from Indians to planters, a transfer of funds was made to those same planters from taxpayers situated in the other parts of the nation. As Forbes and his partners were picking up their piece of the pelf, he graciously assured the Jefferson administration that they would now step aside from further Choctaw business. That lucrative commerce, and the opportunity to be compensated for further cessions, could now go to American traders licensed by the administration.

Forbes was not quite through. Perhaps Jefferson, and Madison after him, would continue to be diffident about attacking the Spaniards in Florida. So Forbes hedged his bets. He called on the Spanish ambassador, the Marques de Casa Irujo, to inform him that he would be willing to create a planter-merchant cartel in Florida to reanimate Spanish influence among the tribes. All that was required was that individual Indian debts be converted into tribal debts to a Firm augmented with some new Spanish partners. Then—no originality here—those tribal debts would be converted into land cessions from the tribes to a new class of international planters with an interest in continued Spanish presence. An interest-free loan of four hundred thousand pesos from the Crown would lubricate matters by getting cash quickly into the hands of the augmented Firm. The Marques declined.

In May 1804, while Forbes was dealing with Dearborn and seeking to deal with Casa Irujo and while his son was eliminating Bowles, other officers of The Firm managed to complete a transaction whereby some anti-Bowles chiefs of the Seminoles and Lower Creeks agreed to cede to The Firm a million acres of Florida between the Apalachicola and Wakulla rivers. Wilkinson's response was to urge that they ask for more in Florida, all the way to the Flint. A year later he pressed Forbes to extend the Okmulgee cession in Georgia farther into Creek property. True to form, he could not resist little tests of fate, for he put both letters into insecure passage through Indian territory, and both fell into the hands of the Red Sticks. Even more perilously, perhaps, he again mocked the pieties of his employer, President Jefferson, as he had with his parodistic version of Jefferson's armed occupation plan for Mississippi. This time he wrote that securing ancestral land to liquidate individual debts had become the "leading feature of our policy [to] . . . inculcate and . . . cherish a sense of moral obligations and distinctions among our Indians." Next, he said, the administration would "establish among them a factory or factories for furnishing them with all the necessaries and comforts they may wish (spiritous liquors excepted), encouraging these and especially their leading men, to run into debt for these beyond their individual means of paying; and whenever in that situation, they will always cede lands to rid themselves of debt. . . . [W]hen the debts get beyond what individuals can pay, they become willing to lop them off by a cession of lands."[24]

Having taught moral obligations by monetizing them, and having used the money to purchase tribal lands at much reduced rates, the government of the United States placed those lands upon the bargain counter for sale to cotton planters. First to rush thence were members of Jefferson's own administration, most notoriously Postmaster General Granger. Granger had often joined Wilkinson in inciting Jefferson's fears of Aaron Burr as an abolitionist loose in the Spanish borderlands and of maronage. Wilkinson and Granger found another common interest in encouraging the planters' President to treat the Choctaw and Creek lands as "of first importance to us." Among the means recommended by Granger and Wilkinson, and adopted by Jefferson, was persuading compliant tribal leaders "by every act of justice and favor which we can possibly render them"—it required little imagination to translate that bland formulation into bribery on the ground.[25]

Jefferson knew what his subordinates were doing. He minced no words in his instructions to those who failed to understand what he had in mind. He wrote Governor William Henry Harrison that "when the debts get beyond what individuals can pay, they become willing to lop them off by a cession of lands." And to the officers of the Indian bureaus under his direction he gave direct orders to ensnare Indians into excessive debt. In 1806, John Riley wrote Return J. Meigs, the Cherokee agent, that "in conversation with Mr. Jefferson he asked him [a third party, Mr. Hocker] if he could get the Cherokees to run in debt to the amount of ten or twelve thousand dollars in the public store. Mr. Hocker told him for answer fifty thousand. Well, says he, that is the way I intend to get their country . . . to get them to run in debt to the public store and they will have to give their land in payment."[26]

Corruption of the clean trading posts established by Washington and Adams would take some time. Meanwhile, The Firm could be given more commissions to expedite matters, making use of its existing stock of accounts receivable. As Wilkinson pointed out to Dearborn, the trade of the "clean" agencies was "but a drop in the bucket" compared to The Firm's annual sales of forty thousand dollars. Jefferson was not personally drawn to merchants—he referred to the partners of The Firm as "certain mercantile characters"—but they had their utility, as Jefferson made clear to Claiborne. As a result, the governor instructed his subagent, Samuel Mitchell, to insinuate among "some of the chiefs" of the Chickasaws the idea that they could escape their own individual indebtedness to The Firm by transferring their liability to the tribe as a whole. The chiefs could see to it that the tribal council would be "willing to assume and pay the debts of individuals." The next step would be to liquidate that debt "by a sale of some of their lands to the United States."[27]

The Accounts of Silas Dinsmoor

The Choctaw cession was achieved in 1805. After some shifting of positions among the three sides in the triangular transaction, all but $7,500 of the $50,500 paid ostensibly to the Choctaws by the United States went instead to The Firm. The Choctaws were unwilling to part with Yazoo cotton lands, offering instead only the pine plains of eastern Mississippi. This affront to the imperatives of the planters was embarrassing for Jefferson, who was unwilling to send the Senate the proposed treaty. (Only in 1808 was that body offered its occasion to "advise and consent" by being informed of what had been obtained, and what had not.) Soon after the Choctaw cession, Silas Dinsmoor had been instructed to "prepare the minds of the chiefs" of the Chickasaws for a similar transaction. He and his friend John McKee still drew their pay from Wilkinson, but both were leery of him, as they would soon demonstrate by throwing sand in the gears of his arrangements to apprehend Aaron Burr.[28]

Though they kept such sentiments to their private discourse with each other, they also developed loyalties to the people of the tribes among whom they served as agents. Dinsmoor, therefore, did, indeed, "prepare the minds of the chiefs"—but not in the way Wilkinson or Dearborn intended. He was an independent spirit from the New England hinterlands, with a puckish—and for a government agent perilous—sense of humor. So with ample portentousness he informed the Chickasaws that "the United States was buying the land so that the Chickasaws could pay their Panton, Leslie and Company debts." To underline that final point, he read to them in excruciating detail Simpson's itemized account and formal demand for payment.[29]

So cautioned, the Chickasaws became balky. As Dearborn was learning of their response and totting up the value of the cotton land along the Mississippi they were refusing to relinquish, his attention was drawn to the account rendered by Dinsmoor and the other commissioners for the Choctaw negotiations. It "occasioned . . . surprise," he wrote, for it included a "bill for articles furnished the commissioners . . . of highest luxury, such as could not have been intended for Indians . . . the most delicate spices, anchovies, raisins, almonds, hyson tea, coffee, mustard, preserves, English cheese, segars, brandy, wine, etc., etc., etc. . . . Such accounts of expense at an Indian treaty have, I presume, never before been exhibited to our government." Thus a covert act of resistance to the coercion of friends was elevated to comedy.[30]

Dinsmoor continued his quiet revolt by retaining $5,461.37 from the pelf sought by The Firm, "either because of a misunderstanding of his orders or because of other reasons," plus $4,304.25 assigned to pay a trader's bad debt—the debtor having absconded with his winnings to Virginia. Thereafter Dinsmoor and The Firm exchanged lawsuits for many years. As late as 1820, he was intrepid enough to remonstrate against Andrew Jackson's forced removal of the tribes—directly to Jackson.

The Firm Wraps Things Up

To summarize these transactions: after the deaths of Alexander McGillivray and William Augustus Bowles, nearly eight million acres were transferred by Indian nations to the United States and the plantation system in transactions managed by The Firm. In 1803–4, immediately after the removal of Bowles, the Lower Creeks and Seminoles ceded 1,427,289 acres from the Apalachicola

River to the Choctawhatchee in exchange for absolution from $66,533 in individual debts to this partnership of traders. Next, the "Forbes Purchase" in Florida was achieved at a price of a little less than "two bits an acre." In the Choctaw cession of 1805–8, 4,142,720 acres were "sold" by the Choctaws in a transaction managed by Forbes. The price was again about twenty-one cents an acre, totaling $108,000, of which The Firm got $41,787. Finally, in 1819, the partners resold most of the "Forbes Purchase" to two merchants of Savannah for the total original price, retaining as their profit the most desirable 16,680 acres of mainland, plus the 9,812 acres of Forbes Island in the Apalachicola.

By 1815, The Firm had completed its transition. It had been a trading company in the hide business. Now it was a real estate firm organizing the cession of Indian lands useful to the expansion of the cotton economy. The partners had long taken part in that economy as proprietors of plantations along the St. Johns and St. Mark's, but only as a sideline to their mercantile activity. The inflection point in their affairs occurred during Panton's discussions with Hawkins and Dearborn at the end of the 1790s. Their accommodations to the Americans accelerated after the Spaniards refused Forbes's proposal that Florida, once thought to be only a swampy afterthought, might preempt the New World cotton market. Any residual affinities for Britain on the part of these old Loyalists evaporated during the War of 1812, when they and their sons and nephews determined that their future lay with the Americans.

The Firm made its final choice in July 1813. A hundred Red Stick Creeks and Seminoles arrived in Pensacola, apparently expecting The Firm and the Spaniards to continue to provide them with the powder, guns, and swords they needed to contend against the Americans. The local Spanish magistrate was a close associate of John Innerarity, the local magnate of The Firm, and refused the Indians' request. They turned next to Innerarity, who was only a little more obliging, and, as soon as they were out the door, warned the Americans that their foes were on their way back toward the 31st Parallel. Though the Indians were dry-gulched at Burnt Corn Creek, they fought back fiercely and might have prevailed had they not run out of ammunition. The contest commenced at Burnt Corn Creek did not come to an end until March 1814, when Andrew Jackson wiped out the core of Creek resistance, the garrison of six hundred Red Sticks at Horseshoe Bend.

A British fleet arrived two months later. Though their allies came too late, the Creeks settled into a bridgehead a half mile below the Forbes and Company stockade on the Apalachicola, apparently in the mistaken belief that the partners, once Loyalists, were still Loyalists. That illusion dissipated when a letter signed by Forbes, intended for his representative at the Apalachicola post, was intercepted by the Red Sticks. Forbes's instructions were that his employees were to put every obstacle in the path of the British and Indians because the Americans would be the winning side.

Andrew Jackson Takes Charge, with Some Help from Benjamin Hawkins

And so they were, though only because the Virginia Dynasty was willing at the last minute to waive its aversion to Andrew Jackson. In 1814, finally, after being subordinated to James Wilkinson, the Bonaparte of the Backwoods was summoned from Tennessee to face the British fleet and army threatening New Orleans. At the Battle of New Orleans, behind his famous barricade of cotton bales, Jackson stood off a force of veterans of the Napoleonic wars with a coalition of Indians, free blacks, Kentucky riflemen, Louisiana militia, soldiers of the regular army, sailors of the regular navy, clerks, cotton factors, pirates, gamblers, French revolutionaries, Mexican revolutionaries, Texas revolutionaries, cowboys, and keelboatmen. It was a magnificent moment. (There was a shadow side to the magnificence. Within its penumbra Jackson humiliated Fulwar Skipwith in an incident described in the Appendix; see "Fulwar Skipwith and Andrew Jackson," p. 260.)

Jackson was never more splendid than when fighting the British. His animosity toward them began in 1781, when he was a fourteen-year-old militiaman on the Waxhaw frontier of South Carolina. He had been captured in battle and ordered by a British officer to black his boots. Jackson refused, and the officer slashed the boy across his face and arm with a saber. Every reader of American history has learned of Jackson's implacable hatred for all things British, but not of his services to the British economic interests. He served the planters. The planters served the British. So, in effect, there was an undeclared and in his case inadvertent alliance among the millers, the planters, and the border chieftain. Jackson was a great captain, an adept in commerce and domestic politics, and a competent planter. He was not, however, accomplished in the esoteric realm of economic policy, else he might have winced at being so useful to British interests. He was moved throughout his career as often by wrath as by deliberation, so it is fair to wonder how he might have adjusted his behavior had he understood what was happening.

Jackson did not understand, and he served Britain's invisible empire more effectively than any other American statesman except Thomas Jefferson. Together they saw to it that the textile millers received an ever-expanding supply of raw cotton from an ever-expanding supply of land. Thus, because the planters were so destructive of that land, these two great men not only gave aid to their professed enemies but also failed to serve the progeny of their friends.

Other matters deteriorated at the same pace, among them the potency of the ideals expressed by Jefferson in his Revolutionary years. Nonetheless, those ideals were still expressed by eloquent voices in the United States. Likewise, though the planters' counterparts and colleagues the textile manufacturers prevailed in setting an imperial economic policy indifferent to the moral problem of slave-produced goods until the 1860s, public aversion to plantation slavery increased in Britain, bursting ahead when economic interest was muted by wartime necessity during the American Revolution and the War of 1812. At the outset of the second American war, it became good manners for British statesmen to remember Lord Dunmore's proclamation of abolition in Virginia in 1776, to recall his deliberate disruptions of the plantation system in the 1790s, and even to credit him for his support of William Augustus Bowles— who was only seven years dead. Many who had no moral repugnance to slavery embraced Dunmore's strategy of discomfiting their American enemies by stirring up the slaves. The most hard-headed of Britons could see the value of weakening the Americans' economy and diminishing their military capacity by every soldier that had to be dispatched to put down rebellious slaves. Though stirring up slaves against the cotton suppliers did not become long-term British policy, there was plenty of stirring done between 1812 and 1815. Each time the British established beachheads along the Gulf Coast, they renewed their ties to the Creeks and Seminoles. Some warriors could still take the field despite Jackson's slashing campaigns against them, and slaves were always seeking ways to escape. Dunmore's program was revived. Slaves who joined the struggle against their former masters were offered land, guns, and freedom, and some actually received them.

In 1814, the British, finally free of Napoleon, could redirect their forces against the Americans and began to arrive along the coast in force. The officers in charge of their expeditionary forces were badly briefed, however. The Creeks and Seminoles were consistent, but the partners of The Firm were switching sides. James Innerarity was entrusted with weapons and supplies for the Indians and to keep up the good work of stirring up the blacks. Innerarity withheld those supplies put into his care, whereupon the Seminoles and Red Sticks showed their economic sophistication by annulling the cessions of land just made to The Firm and scalping those of its employees who strayed into the backcountry.

Still under misapprehensions about the loyalty of the former Tories, the British commander at Pensacola informed its Spanish governor of his plans to attack Fort Bowyer, Mobile, and then New Orleans. The governor confided in his confessor, Father James Coleman. Coleman promptly passed the word to another visitor to his confessional—Innerarity. Innerarity dispatched an agent named McVoy posthaste to Fort Bowyer, to acquaint the Americans with what the British had in mind. Forewarned, the garrison made a massacre of the British assault. Finally the British understood. After retreating to The Firm's plantation next to the fort, they freed nine hundred slaves and put to the torch all its buildings. Some of those slaves subsequently joined the coalition against the Americans, as did many released from The Firm's plantations in East Florida. An indignant Innerarity wrote John Forbes: "Time was when the name of Englishman was honorable, now it is synonymous with nay it is a term to designate a man capable of every thing that is low, vile, base, villainous, atrocious."[31]

Comfortably within the fortifications of Mobile, Jackson laughed at the British flotilla beyond the barrier islands and commenced moving at his own pace against Pensacola, the possession of Spain, a neutral state. Though agents of The Firm increased his knowledge of the British operations, Jackson did not trust turncoats. He was aware that the accommodations between The Firm and the Americans had been arranged by Wilkinson, and for that gentleman he had nothing but contempt. During the Burr trial in Richmond, in 1807, Jackson had challenged Wilkinson to a duel, and he had suffered retribution from Wilkinson early in the Creek and British War. He was not, therefore, disposed to be gentle with Wilkinson's partner Innerarity, whose horse and pirogue he seized and whose twenty-five slaves became his booty.

After the War of 1812, the energies of the surviving partners of The Firm were consumed in endless litigation, seeking to recover from the Crown compensation for their slaves who found sanctuary upon British warships or on islands held by British admirals.[32]

PART FOUR

Agents of the Master Organism:
Assistants to the Plantation System

A petri dish is a small, sterile container wherein a laboratory biologist can isolate a complex process. Without distractions or contaminants, unjostled and unconfused, the history of little organisms can unfold and be observed. As suggested at the outset of Part Three, the scene in which our story has been fulfilling its imperatives, ecological, economic, social, and psychological, is not a petri dish. It is considerably larger and, because the element of choice is so important, messier. History is not biology. Nonetheless, our understanding of complex historic sequences may be encouraged by biological analogies. Under our scrutiny have been two processes: the occupation of the most fertile portions of the South by the plantation system and the prevention, thereby, of the full development either of a continuing native culture or of a republic of free and independent yeomen—white, black, or Indian.

Engorgement by an overmastering organism is called in biology "phagocytosis." The operative portion of that word comes from the Greek for "eating," inviting us to imagine the plantocracy as a squid or octopus of continental size. Phagocytosis is not quite the same thing as biological "epiboly," or the hegemony of one species. Many such superventions over an insufficiently robust or resistant group of competitors by a more vigorous set can be observed in the fossil record. I am told by Douglass Erwin, a paleobotanist and hiking companion, that a fossilized epiboly extends across four hundred miles of what is now the state of New York, representing the dominance of a single species some millions of years ago. Certain social customs in areas of the United States where plantation slavery prevailed may be taken to be more recently fossilized social epiboly.

As early as 1784, political phagocytosis commenced in the American South by the deliberate extension of tendril-like extensions of the plantation system into Indian country and the Spanish borderlands; from this point forward in this narrative we will call this "amoebic imperialism." The traders, generals, admirals, and adventurers who were its phagocytic advance agents required no Greek words to describe what they were doing, nor until the mid-1790s did they have the fertilizing encouragement of British capital to advance their subcells and fibers. Before then, upland cotton had been merely another mallow. Then came the gin, altering the ecology of a third of a continent, and cotton became a geopolitical force.

We have spoken of master organisms, tendrils, subcells, and fibers. We will now speak of filibusters* and chiefs, of generals and admirals, operating in complex interactive systems with sponsoring planters and millers, bankers for millers and planters, speculators in land, and merchants converting accounts receivable into land, to be put under the planters' plows. Still, we must not let biological analogies to political outcomes import into such a discourse any tincture of determinism or hint of inevitability. Ideas and intentions do not, so far as we know, play roles in phagocytosis or epiboly on the microbiological scale, but they do in human affairs. Very little is inevitable in the experience of our species. That is why in Part Three we opened our narrative to other possibilities, other intentions, and other forces.

We do not know what amoebas are thinking when they send forth phagocytes to occupy space previously occupied by other organisms, overwhelm them, and consume them. We know more about what the planters' leaders were thinking when they sent forth filibusters to form ephemeral states—such as the Republic of Florida or the Republic of West Florida—which would seek incorporation of the acquired land into the planters' realm. Those political leaders told us what they were thinking.

---

*Historians have long made two uses of the word "filibuster." One denotes an extended speech in a legislature intended to tie up its processes. The other designates a private military adventure, though it may be extended to include state-sponsored adventures. It is odd that the term should evoke in the New World jingling spurs, pennants flying on the lances of dusty riders, rifle fire from adobe walls, hot nights and the shrieks of parrots, and shallow pools of alkaline water amid the cacti and sagebrush, for it originated amid the fogs, shoals, eddies, and quicksand of the estuary of the Rhine. It came into English usage from Dutch pirates' use of scampering light craft they called "fly boats" to emerge from the mists and pounce upon prizes becalmed by the baffling winds or beached by the errant currents of that perilous delta. The Dutch word *vrijbuiter* to denote a "flyboater" or petty pirate came into English usage as "freebooter" in the sixteenth century denoting a land pirate. Thereafter its usage was expanded to include any violent political freelance. The French then picked up either the Dutch or the English word and commenced to write of *filibustiers*. The French *filibustier* became the Spanish *filibustero*, and that in turn became the American "filibuster," used with American informality to cover seaborne invasions, overland piracy by private armies, and, finally, purloining other people's *time* in a legislature.

In Part Four, we continue to follow the lives of some of the commercial *assisters* and add to them these armed men. Both were required to expand the planters' domain, though the most effective agents of that phagocytosis were not soldiers nor statesmen but merchants. Many of the planters' conquests were achieved by contract rather than cannonade:

> The conjunction of slavery, colonialism, and maritime power permitted the more advanced European states to skew the world market to their own advantage . . . by transferring forced laborers to parts of the globe under European control, and favorably situated for supplying European markets with exotic products. But monopolies decreed from European capitals were of limited efficacy unless they were backed up by a host of independent merchants and planters, displaying entrepreneurial qualities.[1]

"Transferring forced laborers"—we hear the groans, and smell the sweat. "Supplying European markets with exotic products"—we picture flatboats loaded to the scuppers with towering stacks of cotton bales. And upstream—a ravaged land.

13

Fulwar Skipwith in Context

The partners of The Firm were crabbed little men, however shrewd they may have been and however efficacious as agents of the expansion of the plantation system. Fulwar Skipwith was also important to that movement in American history, but, great of heart and grandly proportioned in body, he served with a panache denied to Panton or Leslie or Forbes. Not a smiling sentence was left to us by any of the three, while Skipwith wrote of dances and songs and antic adventures before he settled down to the tobacco business, the diplomatic service, espionage, cotton planting, and a land office in West Florida.

Having observed the progress of the partners of The Firm from small-scale operations as fur merchants of Charleston to their roles as real estate agents on a continental scale, we will now follow Skipwith through the same time period and much the same terrain, but coming to them with an entirely different perspective. Skipwith took the Whig side of the American Revolution, survived the Quasi War, assisted the Louisiana Purchase, and became President of West Florida, aiding the government of the United States in acquiring that formerly Spanish province and then in bringing Louisiana fully into the slaveholders' territory. He was then asked to revive an American presence in Haiti, infuriated Andrew Jackson during the Battle of New Orleans, and found safe haven within the patronage system of his "particular friend" James Monroe.

Skipwith was not clever, nor did he cogitate policy. He was, so to speak, always an iron filing on the surface of the table and seldom conscious of the grand geopolitical and geoeconomic impulses playing upon his life and career. Though he was himself a merchant of tobacco and wine before becoming a diplomat and planter, he did not show much talent for commerce or comprehension of the immense power of the commercial magnets under the table. The partners of The Firm—called by his mentor Jefferson "certain mercantile characters"—were not his sort. He and they were, however, on the same side of things.

Skipwith was abroad—in the West Indies and in France—while The Firm was arranging the transfer of eight million acres of Indian lands into the hands of the planters. He was, however, an active participant in a second grand-scale transfer of land—the southern portion of the 828,000 square miles of the Louisiana Purchase—into the hands of those planters. All the citizens of the United States benefited from these vast additions to its territory, but the planters derived special blessings from both. So, too, did groups of merchants enjoying the favor of the planters' government. These men of trade and the planters they served twice enjoyed what was in effect a transfer of wealth to them from the other taxpayers of the country. In the case of the Indian cessions, those merchants were the partners of The Firm. The greatest private beneficiaries of the Louisiana Purchase were the Livingston family, enjoying another arrangement that was in effect a cash-for-debt-for-land exchange.

As observed in the preceding chapters, the Indian lands not taken by force in wars (fought at taxpayer expense) were purchased with tax dollars from The Firm—which might otherwise have languished forever without repayment of debts owed it by Indians—and resold to the planters at very cheap prices. A substantial part of the funds used for that purchase went to the Livingston clan to liquidate debts owed it by the French government. The Louisiana Purchase was largely negotiated by Chancellor Robert Livingston, with some assistance from Skipwith, who was charged with facilitating quietly a part of the process especially important to the Southerners he represented.

The Livingstons and the other merchants to whom Skipwith made awards had otherwise no better chance of getting Napoleon to pay them than the Firm had to collect from the Indians its claims upon deer skins. In the chapters to follow we will watch Skipwith working with the New Yorkers as these "mercantile characters" were well paid to support the addition to the planters' domain of the southern third or so of the Mississippi Valley.

Before ascending to the grand and global, however, we should once more ground ourselves in the specific, the physical, local, and personal, beginning by getting our pronunciations right. I am told by linguists that it is probable that at home either in Southside Virginia or among his peers in West Florida, Fulwar Skipwith was addressed as "fuller" and the family name spoken as "skip-ith." His family seat was at Prestwould—pronounced "pressed wood"— on the Roanoke River. He completed his career residing on a plantation called Monte Sano—"montay saw-no"—now within the city limits of Baton Rouge, Louisiana, where he died in 1839. It is a place where many of our themes converge: agriculture had been practiced along the banks of the Bayou Sano for thousands of years. Skipwith first cultivated cotton between earthworks built by people who had formed civil societies five thousand years before his arrival. He then made way for more cotton by training his slaves in the use of

Monticello, as sketched in 1802 by Anna Maria Thornton, showing the house and dependencies. Private Collection. Photograph courtesy of Museum of Early Southern Decorative Arts, Winston-Salem, North Carolina.

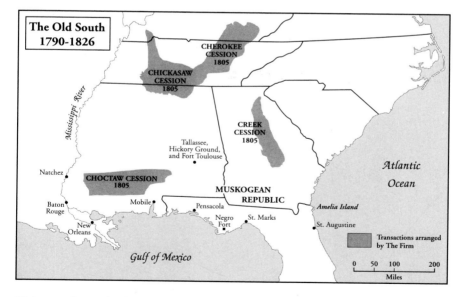

This map shows the first testing-ground of Mr. Jefferson's Lost Cause: The Old South, 1790–1826, showing cessions of land from Native Americans to the United States, transactions that were arranged by The Firm. This map and those following are based on data from *The Atlas of Antebellum Southern Agriculture* by Sam Bowers Hilliard (Baton Rouge: Louisiana State University Press, 1984).

Thomas Jefferson, the ambassador, at forty-four. Courtesy of the National Portrait Gallery, Smithsonian Institution. Bequest of Charles Francis Adams.

Cotton to the gunwales, sketched by Karl Bodmer in the 1830s, near the plantation of Fulwar Skipwith, near Baton Rouge, Louisiana. "Cotton Boat Near Baton Rouge: The Lioness" by Karl Bodmer (JAM.1986.49.109). Courtesy of the Joslyn Art Museum, Omaha, Nebraska. Gift of the Enron Art Collection.

George Washington, the soldier, at forty. "George Washington in the Uniform of a British Colonial Colonel," 1772, by Charles Willson Peale. Courtesy of the Washington/Custis/Lee Collection, Washington and Lee University, Lexington, Virginia.

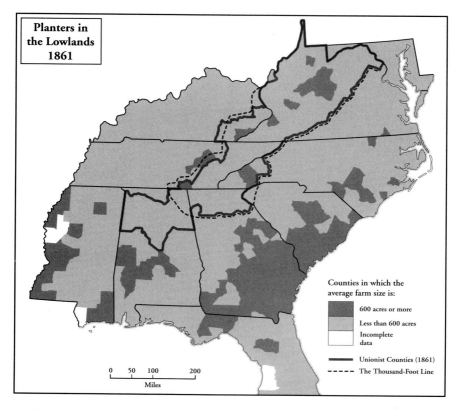

Planters in the Lowlands 1861

Counties in which the average farm size is:

- 600 acres or more
- Less than 600 acres
- Incomplete data

— Unionist Counties (1861)
- - - The Thousand-Foot Line

0   50   100   200
              Miles

In this map, the dark areas show where, east of the Mississippi, farms larger than 600 acres made up a majority of all landholdings. On these plantations were large concentrations of slaves.

William Augustus Bowles,
mezzotint by J. Grozer,
London, about 1791. Courtesy
of the National Portrait
Gallery, Smithsonian
Institution.

John Innerarity of "The
Firm." Courtesy of Special
Collections Department,
John C. Pace Library,
University of West Florida.

James Wilkinson. Courtesy of
the National Portrait Gallery,
Smithsonian Institution.

Andrew Jackson, the
Bonaparte of the Backwoods.
Engraving by Goupil.
Courtesy of the Historic New
Orleans Collection, Acct.
Number 1991.34.29.

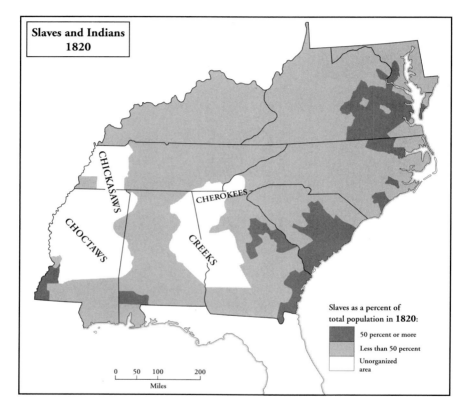

**Slaves and Indians
1820**

CHICKASAWS

CHEROKEES

CHOCTAWS

CREEKS

Slaves as a percent of
total population in **1820**:

50 percent or more

Less than 50 percent

Unorganized
area

0   50   100   200
Miles

As well as showing the percentage of slaves in the total population in the South of
1820, this map also shows the lands still belonging to various Indian tribes.

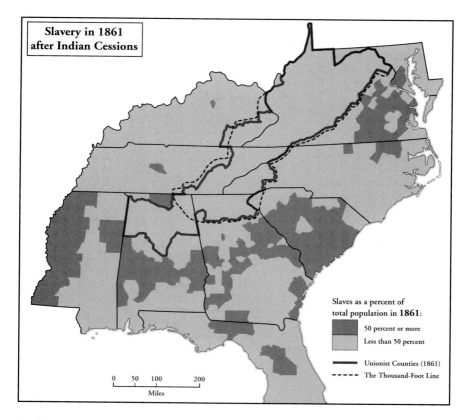

Slavery in 1861 after Indian Cessions

Slaves as a percent of total population in **1861**:

- 50 percent or more
- Less than 50 percent

—— Unionist Counties (1861)

- - - The Thousand-Foot Line

0 50 100   200
Miles

As this map shows, by 1861 the land that had been occupied by Indian tribes in 1820 had a large percentage of slaves.

Lelia Skipwith Robertson Skipwith,
daughter of Fulwar Skipwith.
Courtesy of the Prestwould
Foundation.

Fulwar Skipwith. Courtesy of
the Prestwould Foundation.

Prestwould. Photograph by Roger Kennedy.

drag-lines to plane down those earthworks, layer by layer. These newly scoured spaces showed an exotic tincture from clots of a strange reddish clay bearing ferrous oxide, for when the sod was torn from the surface of the mounds a layer of that clay was exposed. It had been more than two or three inches deep when laid down by Skipwith's predecessors five thousand years earlier. (Ferrous clay is not found near Baton Rouge; the name of the city is derived from red sticks marking the boundary between two tribes rendered extinct not long before Skipwith's arrival.)

Skipwith was not bent upon destruction or desecration but only upon raising cotton for the British market. He destroyed out of ignorance, and with even greater ignorance he exposed to the erosive deluges of Louisiana rain the friable earth that had lain beneath that poultice of sod that under his orders his slaves had ripped away. Most of the ferrous oxide went into the Gulf of Mexico with the topsoil. Finally, after a few more decades of cotton planting, the land became barren. After the 1940s, chemicals were restored to it, but not salutary chemicals: the corporation now possessing the land of Skipwith's plantation requires that female visitors certify that they are not pregnant before venturing upon the premises without anticontamination gear. All vestiges of ancient architecture, and of Skipwith's barns, sheep folds, and slave cabins, have been destroyed and replaced by a noisome cacophony of toxic wastes. Under a tank farm and waste ponds lie the splinters of Skipwith's cognac bottles and of the steatite bowls and trenchers used by his predecessors at a symmetrical remove in time from the birth of Christ. A bridge bearing Highway 180 bisects their ceremonial center and Skipwith's cotton lands.

Skipwith the Jeffersonian

Fulwar Skipwith, the proprietor of all this agricultural history, was doubly Thomas Jefferson's kinsman. Sir William Skipwith, cousin to Fulwar, had two sons, Robert and Henry, who married sisters—Anne and Tabitha Wayles—whose third sister, Martha, married Jefferson. Though of great political significance, the Jefferson connection was less fruitful fiscally to the Skipwiths than the alliances of the *elder* brother of Robert and Henry, Sir Peyton (7th Bart.), who married, in succession, two daughters of a Scottish merchant, Ann and Jean Miller. From resources so accumulated, Sir Peyton built the family seat, Prestwould, within ten thousand acres the 6th Bart. had won from the improvident William Byrd III at three-card draw.

Fulwar Skipwith represented the generation of Virginians who migrated to the Old Southwest after 1790, responding to the opportunity created by mechanized ginning and milling. Cotton was becoming the great staple of the region. Until then few planters had gone west. They speculated, but only small groups of yeoman farmers were willing to risk the perils of Indian Country. After the gins came into play, however, men such as Skipwith followed the expulsion of the Indian nations of the interior with the expansion of the planters' realm as far as Texas and the Everglades and forced Spain from Florida. "Millions upon millions" of taxes raised in both the North and South were "lavished in war and diplomacy to annex and spread slavery"—as Senator William Henry Seward later summarized the story.[1]

Though Seward was engaged in stoking Northern resentment of what he rightly called "the Slave Power," he did not exaggerate. His formulation did, however, impart the impression that all those millions had been spent with confidence, almost with bravado. That was not always the case, for many millions went to assuage fear. The purchases and conquests did provide fresh soil for cotton planters to exploit in Louisiana, in the Floridas, and in the provinces they wrested from the Indians. Yet these were apprehensive men. They feared that unless they obliterated the sanctuaries, "maroons" would form alliances with Indians, attack the plantations, and rescue the planters' workforces. Many of the "millions upon millions" that passed through the hands of Skipwith and others were spent to prevent maronage, sometimes tactically, Negro Fort by Negro Fort, and sometimes strategically, through a foreign policy grounded in the fear that Florida, Louisiana, and, later, Texas would become vast maroon colonies.[2]

These fears were not new. In the 1770s, while Jefferson was sending George Rogers Clark to keep the Pennsylvania abolitionists out of the Western territories desired by the planters, and to reassure the French slave owners of Illinois that they had nothing to fear from the Virginians (as noted earlier), maronage was already a problem in Kentucky. The "favorite slave" of John May was reported to have fallen in "with some worthless Negroes who persuaded him to run away and get with some Indians," and May told his fellow planters that the frontier was "a bad place to bring slaves to, being so near Indians that they will frequently find their way to them."[3]

Toussaint's Yeoman Republic

The most fearsome example of maronage lay offshore. A series of rebellions on Haiti from 1789 onward demonstrated the military effectiveness of slaves bent upon freedom. Then, once established, Toussaint Louverture's government encouraged a system of family farms in the first experiment in a yeoman society largely indifferent to international markets since that of Oglethorpe in Georgia a half century earlier. That example was as distasteful to the planters as Oglethorpe's had been, but more dangerous. Oglethorpe's was easily and peacefully overwhelmed by the Carolinians, but Toussaint's was fearsome to all the imperial powers, as well as to planters from Brazil to Maryland.

As things turned out, the economy of Haiti was destroyed by invasion, disease, and civil war. Alex Dupuy, writing in our own time, has told us of the circumstances of Haiti when Thomas Jefferson came to the presidency in 1801:

> Above all, the slaves aspired to become independent farmers. . . . Those with enough cash bought land for themselves; others with insufficient money pooled their resources and bought land collectively . . . [following] an alternative economic model . . . based on decentralized and small-scale farming, or the transformation of plantations into collective farms owned and run by the workers. The system of production they anticipated did not call for the export of raw materials and the importation of manufactured goods, or the need for foreign markets and foreign investments and technology.[4]

Another expert on the matter, Franklin Knight, tells us that this second independent republic to be established in the New World was the first to take seriously a preference for yeomen over planters:

> The Haitians dramatically transformed their conventional tropical plantation agriculture . . . from a structure dominated by large estates (*latifundia*) into a society of *minifundist*, or small-scale marginal self-sufficient producers, who reoriented away from export dependency toward an internal marketing system supplemented by a minor export sector.[5]

Jefferson commenced negotiations with the French toward the extermination of the "cannibal republic" in 1799, before either he or Napoleon had become a chief of state. Their discussions continued throughout 1800 and 1801, drawing in the Spaniards and the British to join in disastrous invasions of the island. After Napoleon lost more than thirty thousand troops, the British only a few fewer, and the Spaniards an unknown number, all these offshore powers determined to cut their losses. Without the sugar production of Haiti, Louisiana was of no value to Bonaparte, who had seen it only as a source of food, lumber, and draft animals to service the Caribbean plantations. So he sold it.

Alexander Hamilton observed that Louisiana came to the United States only because Napoleon had been driven to sell his claim to the property by "the unforseen course of events . . . [including the] courage and obstinate resistance . . . [of the] black inhabitants" of Haiti. Thus "by an accidental state of circumstances, and not to wise plans, . . . this cession" had redeemed what "the feebleness and pusillanimity of . . . [Jefferson's] miserable system of measures could never have acquired."[6]

The influence of the Haitian revolt was felt on the mainland in slave revolts and new maronage along the borders of the plantation system. The planters wanted the land beyond those borders, they wanted the runaway slaves, and they sought to eliminate the possibilities of further attrition of their labor force. Fulwar Skipwith was one of the agents of a Jeffersonian policy to acquire that land and reacquire those slaves.

The Career of Fulwar Skipwith

Skipwith was the scion of a great family of "Southside," the medieval quarter of Virginia, where one feels to this day a deeper antiquity than in the red-brick-and-white-trim of Williamsburg. Southside takes its tone from the Gothic: the traveler can still find at Smithfield the spiky Church of St. Luke, built between 1632 and 1638, and the Arthur Allen House ("Bacon's Castle") of 1665—one might think its construction date to be 1465 if it were upon the Isle of Wight rather than in Isle of Wight County. Here is the true "old Virginia," extending upward and westward into a strange, bare, and now impoverished countryside, where, on the eroded banks of the Roanoke and its tributaries, are to be found vestiges of the hegemony of three families, the Randolphs, Coles, and Skipwiths.[7]

What were they doing way out there? They were swept westward as the plantation system "passed like a devastating scourge over the upland soils of Virginia, [and] . . . the greater part of eastern Virginia . . . [was] reduced nearly to a barren waste." As we have seen, the Carters, Byrds, and Lees had been unable to sustain themselves for long even in "the rich valleys of the James and Rappahannock." Jefferson's branch of the Randolph kinship clung to their perch near Richmond, but others of the family emigrated to western Virginia. As the James and Rappahannock carried less and less tobacco into international commerce, the rivers of Mecklenburg and Halifax counties—the Dan, Roanoke, and Staunton—came into their own, bearing dugouts, canoes, bateaux, and barges laden with both cotton and tobacco.[8]

Upon a bluff above a now impounded Roanoke, amid ancient trees, lies Prestwould, magnificent in its isolated setting, providing a better sense of eighteenth-century Virginia than more closely crowded mansions along the James. Lady Jean Skipwith's great gardens are being restored. The interior of the seven-bay house of locally dressed sandstone needs little restoration, for it is virtually intact, retaining fine nineteenth-century French wallpapers.[9]

The Skipwith Cavalier associations came from Sir Gray Skipwith, the founding baronet, who is said to have been driven into exile by Oliver Cromwell. Sir Gray had, perhaps, anticipated such an event, for he had already invested in lands in Middlesex County, Virginia. The heir to Sir Gray, Sir William (5th Bart.), had four sons, including Sir William (6th Bart.) and Fulwar. That Fulwar in turn begat another—our Fulwar (1765–1839). Though cousin Thomas Jefferson's revolutionary reforms deprived the Skipwiths of primogeniture and entail, and though the baronetcy accompanied the 8th Bart. to England, the Virginian Skipwiths retained pride, land, slaves, portraits, silver, and houses. In the generation after Jefferson's—the generation of our Fulwar, who was only six years old when Jefferson was married—they acquired another remunerative mercantile connection through yet another double marriage. This time they took into their fold two Coleses, sons of a trading family recently from Richmond. Sir Peyton Skipwith's daughters, Selina and Helen, married John Coles III of Estouteville and his brother Tucker.

The American Revolution did little to alter the serenity of Prestwould, where the eighteenth century lasted until the Civil War. Skipwith matriarchs received gentlemen from Richmond aspiring to marry Skipwith heiresses as if Southside tobacco could fumigate the aromas of the countinghouse. When ladies came to call, they found that "such another family scarcely exists" living according to the old rules and the old routines. One of the Coles daughters reported as she was brought into the family with a wedding feast of a sort scarcely to be experienced anywhere else after the turn of the nineteenth century:[10]

> We all took our seats and found . . . a gold spoon and silver knife and fork. . . . Presently they brought from the next room soup in plates for everybody; then the plates were changed and we all had a piece of turkey and one vegetable and so continued until the plates were changed fifteen times for the meat course and twelve times for the desert.[11]

Fulwar Skipwith did not inherit much of that crockery and silver. He married a fortune, fortunately; he was no more adept in business than in the intricacies of espionage. He was not intellectual, whatever his kinsman the Sage of Monticello might have hoped for him when he took him and his cousin Robert under instruction. Robert Skipwith received from Jefferson in 1771 a famous manual in self-instruction, complete with booklist and annotations. In a broad sense, Fulwar, Robert, and James Monroe were all Jefferson's students, provided the same curriculum—and not only as to books.[12]

In 1781, at sixteen, Skipwith broke off his studies at William and Mary and served in the siege of Yorktown. He was in Richmond three years later, taking a flyer as a tobacco factor, though engaged, he admitted, primarily in "fiddling and dancing" while waiting for trade to pick up after the peace. In 1785, William Short, a cousin of Skipwith's and Jefferson's, wrote the latter from London that Skipwith was there. A year later he was there again, accompanying Jefferson in a shopping expedition for whale oil lamps and receiving instruction in the *Notes on Virginia*. The book became, he said, his "creed." He learned from the *Notes* of the possibilities of Virginia's trans-Appalachian provinces, where recompense might be found for the degenerated productivity of old lands. Skipwith wrote Short that their friend Fitzhugh had cleared two thousand pounds on a fast turnaround in Kentucky. Short took note—and died a very rich man thanks to Western transactions like those where Fitzhugh was operating, and thanks as well to the generosity of the Dutch bankers to whom he, Jefferson, and Skipwith all turned in adversity and opportunity.[13]

Skipwith had neither Short's shrewdness nor his luck. His Richmond warehouse, stock of goods, and a group of houses owned by his mercantile house, Skipwith and Eyre, were burnt in the Richmond fire of the winter of 1786–87. Later that year, Eyre went bankrupt in London. Skipwith returned to Europe in 1788, keeping ahead of his creditors as he looked about for markets for Virginia wine as well as tobacco. He was nearly caught after he sent a letter to a lady in Paris bearing his address in Dijon. It was intercepted, and with the terriers back on his trail, he was off again, having borrowed the transportation money from Short—whom he assured that, despite the haste "which from my cradle has haunted me," he had found time for "the language, vine, music, and dancing."[14]

The Quasi War and Spoliation

In the spring of 1789 Jefferson returned from his mission to France to take up a higher post, Secretary of State. Skipwith accompanied him, still dogged by debt, tugging at his sleeve seeking "favors . . . [he] had hoped to live without." However, with the directness of one gentleman to another, he asked Jefferson to assess his "morals . . . character . . . [and] slender talents" and to secure for him "one of the Consulships abroad . . . that of Lisbon, Bordeaux, Cádiz, or Marseilles." He settled for Martinique, in June 1790, but did not cease soliciting from Jefferson reassignment to a more pleasant place—such as Paris— accompanying his pleas with shipments of guava jelly from Guadeloupe, where he retreated from a slave uprising on Martinique. Finally, he seems to have given up on the prospect of help from Jefferson, for he was in Paris on his own in May 1793.[15]

Paris became his base for fifteen more years, most of that time as American consul, learning painfully the traps laid for blithe spirits by the peculiarities of the financial arrangements made by the new United States government for its consular service. Consuls and commercial agents were not salaried. They were expected to generate their own income from fees for doing favors for American merchants and captains. In the West Indies, Skipwith sometimes received funds for the relief of indigent Americans and for burial expenses to keep starving seamen or American corpses from becoming public embarrassments. Sometimes he and others were paid to commission American merchants to do chores for the government. There were many such merchants working in the sea lanes of the West Indies.

During the decade prior to Skipwith's arrival in Paris, the flags flying over the warehouses of the islands had not been important to the Americans. They had traded with the French islands when France was an enemy power until 1763, and traded with the British islands when Britain was the enemy from 1775 to 1783. Indifference to insignia became indifference to skin color after Toussaint's revolt in the early 1790s. Why should commerce be abandoned merely because the customers were black? The French, so recently allies, now became once again the enemy—but now enemy to trade as well. Skipwith the Francophile observed his countrymen with growing distaste as they put their old wartime privateering skills to work against the French blockade of Toussaint's Haiti. Harbors full of American armed merchantmen became harbors full of American privateers. Skipwith's counterpart on Haiti itself, Edward Stevens, boyhood friend (and possibly half-brother) of Alexander Hamilton, aided them with a will, for he and Hamilton were wholly dedicated to Toussaint's success. Skipwith did not share that enthusiasm, and the rest of his life was dogged with the financial consequences of the French response to American provocation.[16]

France armed its own privateers to capture American vessels, which were then sold in French and Spanish ports, depositing seamen ashore to be succored by Skipwith. As relations worsened, French privateers moved northward and ravaged the seas along the eastern coast of the United States. The losses of American merchantmen accumulated to a large sum—about $4 million in 1795 dollars, perhaps $170 million in 2002 dollars. These became the famous "spoliation claims" that occupied Skipwith for a decade and inflamed relations between France and the United States for a century. Though France and the United States remained formally at peace, the government Skipwith represented was after 1797 headed by President John Adams. Adams made available the Caribbean squadron of the United States Fleet to protect the armed merchantmen and privateers, and also the rebels on Haiti.*

Skipwith and Jefferson were dismayed as two of the three new republics of the age—France and the United States—fought "John Adams's Quasi War" over the persistence of the second in assisting the third, Toussaint's Haiti. American and French warships bloodied each other's decks. Adams proposed a sharp increase in naval spending—"millions for defense." The Jeffersonian opposition lapsed into cries for economy while Adams's new-built frigates sailed toward battle in the West Indies.[17]

James Monroe's First Mission to France

Three years before, George Washington had attempted to hold Jefferson and his friends in a coalition government with those of Hamilton. Though Jefferson departed his post as Secretary of State in 1794, to build what came to be

---

*These spoliation claims should not be confused with a second set, those which brought the United States and France to the brink of war in the 1820s and 1830s. These were not those arising in the 1790s but instead about $7 million in cargoes lost by American merchants captured or destroyed by Napoleon's vessels under the Milan, Berlin, and other decrees, after the Louisiana Purchase. Albert Gallatin had to find ways to finance the first set as Secretary of the Treasury and to avoid war over the second set as minister to France.

known as the "French party," Washington had already appointed James Monroe to be American representative in Paris. Monroe rescued Skipwith from his consulship by sweeping him into his entourage and taking him along to France.[18]

As soon as he stepped ashore, Monroe commenced making unauthorized and effusive speeches about an American alliance with Republican France, while, in London, John Jay was striving to convince the British that no such alliance was contemplated. Fulwar Skipwith left no doubt that he had chosen a side in this contretemps. Complaining of "the extreme jealousy of Mr. Jay's mission," he recalled that at Monroe's "first audience with the Committee of Public Safety at which I was your interpreter . . . their cold and severe deportment" betrayed their "rooted distrust of both yours and Jay's missions." Monroe and Skipwith warmed them up—but with the kind of flattery that transformed them into jurors of the bona fides of the policies of the government of the United States.[19]

It was the first week of August 1794. Only the most purblind enthusiasm could lead the Americans to defer to a body of bloodthirsty men who, free of any restraints of law, custom, or conscience, were continuing to make use of the guillotine to reduce the number of its members and to provide public recreation. The Committee of Public Safety was wallowing, one of them said, in a Red Sea of blood. On March 24, it had decapitated Hébert and his followers; on April 5, Desmoulins and Danton; on July 28, Couthon, St. Just, and Robespierre. Amid scenes like this, Monroe addressed the Committee and its parent body "the Convention itself . . . expressing the interest [of his government] in the French revolution" and declaring his admiration for "the fortitude, magnanimity, and heroic valor" of the French armies sweeping across the Low Countries "to the admiration and applause of the astonished world."[20]

Skipwith recalled some years later that as they left the Convention Hall, Monroe had remarked that "considering the state of parties at home, . . . [he] would not be surprised if the communication . . . should produce . . . [his] recall." It did, though not until Washington tired of attempting coalition government. He went out of office in 1796. Before the election of Adams in that year, however, Monroe made Skipwith consul-general in Paris in his final ministerial act. Skipwith remained for many years thereafter Monroe's mole in Paris—and Virginia's. From 1795 until 1808, he was the only continuing presence among the senior American officials in the capital of France. Though he made occasional voyages back to the United States for instruction and took one sabbatical, he was in effect chargé d'affaires until 1800 and official commercial agent until 1808, when he migrated to Louisiana to enjoy the fruits of his diplomatic labors.[21]

The great achievement of the Paris embassy was the Louisiana Purchase. It was not an easy transaction. Napoleon had extorted from Spain a right to acquire Louisiana, an asset he had no wish to hold but knew to be of great value to the Americans. Though the planters' government appeared willing to pay for it, the merchant classes of the eastern seaboard were making it known that they had no desire to pay taxes for the purchase of free navigation of the Mississippi or for remote plantation land. They could be brought around if Bonaparte would concede that the traders aggrieved by attacks on their trade in the Caribbean by the French fleet might have a right to compensation and that part of what he was paid for Louisiana could be siphoned off for their "spoliation claims."

Thus they could convert bad assets into good hard cash in the same way The Firm converted claims upon hides into land and then into cash. Honoring the merchants' claims would be giving them in effect a sort of commission for acquiescing in the planters' project. It worked out that they were paid about $3,750,000 in 1802 dollars—twenty million francs at 5.33 francs per dollar. The total paid for the land turned out to be 60 million francs, or $11.26 million. Though a variety of financing schemes and bankers' discounts adjusted these amounts somewhat, it is safe to multiply them by about forty to get valuations in 2002 dollars. The Livingstons and their immediate associates went home with at least $750,000 to $800,000 of the merchants' claims—a tidy sum when multiplied by forty.[22]

From Napoleon's point of view, such a settlement would divert some of the flow of funds, yet his righteous indignation was muted by the sound principle of finance that large commissions may be paid to get something you might not get otherwise. He was being paid for something he did not own. The treaty by which he had taken Louisiana from Spain was explicit that if he disposed of it Spain must have a right of first refusal. Then, too, the French constitution under which he held office was equally explicit that he could not dispose of such property without approval of its legislature. He made no tender offer, nor did he bother with the legislature. But neither did Jefferson have constitutional authority for the purchase. Recognizing that infirmity, he drafted a retrospective amendment, but then thought it best to do without it. Thus grandly was the Purchase achieved by a coalition of economic interests. An empire of land was secured by the South for plantation. Under the planters' regime, Louisiana's maroon colonies and Negro Forts could be obliterated. And a fortune in cash was transferred from the general treasury of the United States to a small group of Northern merchants.

Skipwith, the Livingstons, and Louisiana Cotton

The decisions made in Paris in 1802 and thereafter in the organizing of the territory won by the Purchase determined how the best cotton land in the western half of the Mississippi Valley would be allocated and used. Fulwar Skipwith was present at the making of many of these determinations, struggling to find an honorable course of action amid the rivalries between the Virginia and New York factions in Paris after Monroe's departure. Recalling his sentiments then, he wrote of his "devotion to the Republican Party of those days, in concert not only with the wishes of the French minister, Mr. Talleyrand, and some of the members of the French Directory, who never wished for war between the two nations, but, also, in accordance with the wishes of my personal and political friends at that critical period; Mssrs. Jefferson, Madison, Monroe and [Elbridge] Gerry." Those were not the wishes of Adams or of the American captains fighting the Quasi War, so Skipwith was brought home by Adams in the summer of 1799. After Jefferson won the election of 1800, Skipwith returned, bearing a commission as commercial agent and commencing work immediately as a confidential courier conveying messages from Jefferson and Secretary of State Madison directly to friends in France such as Lafayette and Dupont de Nemours. This back channel was not disclosed to his immediate superiors, the New Yorkers.[23]

The man in charge of the ministry was Chancellor Robert L. Livingston, patriarch of the faction that, together with the Clintons and Aaron Burr, had brought New York into the Republican column and Jefferson to the presidency. The Livingstons had plantations in Florida and on Jamaica and shared with the Virginians a grasp of the full potential of cotton growing on an imperial scale. Skipwith did not, apparently, think of them as fellow planters, for he failed to include Livingston among the recipients of a state paper coupling "the possession of Louisiana" with "the production of rice, cotton, and lumber." He did, however, accompany this prospectus with confirmation to Jefferson of rumors that Napoleon was laying in train a twofold policy for the Western Hemisphere. He would seek first to reinstate slavery on Haiti— Skipwith's glozing formulation was that the French wished "to qualify the principles of emancipation in its colonies, of its slaves, as to leave them but the name of being free"—and would then take over Louisiana from Spain.[24]

So much dust was thrown up by both sides in the Louisiana Purchase negotiations that it is easy to pass quickly by Skipwith's reference to cotton and to think that when Livingston sent his memorandum on the province to the French his own failure to mention cotton indicated that he did not know what Skipwith knew. But the Livingstons had been in the cotton business for a long time, possessed plantations of their own, and sought to acquire cotton property in West Florida in other transactions with Napoleon. Every important planter—including the President of the United States—knew that cotton was growing and was being ginned along the lower Mississippi. A Whitney-style gin was operating in Natchez as early as 1795, and Jefferson's correspondent there, William Dunbar, kept him fully informed of the "very great success" of his planting, reaping, and ginning.[25]

Dunbar was the leader of a sophisticated group of cosmopolitans who participated in the plantation-to-mill network, operating along the vectors of force proceeding from Louisiana and Natchez to the paneled offices behind the counting-rooms of the cotton brokers of Britain. Dunbar's chosen brokers were Green and Wainewright in Liverpool, who paid for his cotton with cash, Madeira wine, blankets, window curtain fabric, carpeting, scissors, handkerchiefs, lace, bonnets, necklaces, earrings, umbrellas, buttons, "striped blue ginghams . . . pink check . . . Russia sheeting . . . cotton holland . . . paints, brushes, pencils . . . Rochelle Salts . . . glauber salts," and black leather trunks "for putting behind a carriage."[26]

In 1806, despite the loss to fire of seventy thousand pounds of ginned cotton, Dunbar was able to promise delivery of a hundred thousand pounds "from the two plantations I occupy" and said that he would continue to improve its quality:

> I have made two small experiments of new cotton, one is the nankin, . . . the other is a species from Mexico, which I think excellent; it is of a fine rich color, very silky, fine and strong and rather a little longer . . . than our own staple; I send you a sample of each of those, requesting you to get it examined by your manufacturers and other good judges . . . so that I may judge whether . . . to extend plantations of either species for the ensuing year.[27]

Dunbar was always eager to extend plantations. One means of doing so after the Purchase was to agree with Jefferson to send Peter Custis up the Red River to follow up French and Spanish reports of its fitness for cotton. In May 1806, Custis reported directly to Jefferson:

> Most of the Red River lands are either of a clayey or marlaceous soil and appear to be not worth cultivating, but far from it they are found to be more productive than the best Mississippi lands and the cotton always commands a higher price than that of the Mississippi.[28]

Custis was confirming information already present in the American archives: in 1720, Jean-Baptiste Bénard de La Harpe had told his French employers that the shores of the Red—like those of the Ouachita—were well suited to cotton production. The founder of Louisiana, Pierre Le Moyne, Sieur d'Iberville, had anticipated such good news by importing exotic cotton seeds, for the Indians' indigenous variety was only good for making homespun. In 1733, a Father Beaubois had built a model of a gin but could not make it rake. In 1795, Daniel Clark's success in catching up with Eli Whitney's achievement was made possible by the young mechanic Clark put to work building a gin from a newspaper account. Piracy was a New Orleans tradition. By piracy of an industrial sort it made its own way into the Cotton Revolution. By 1800, cotton in commercial quantities was descending toward the Gulf from Natchez, and north along the Mississippi a series of slow-moving tributaries such as the Yazoo beckoned planter interest into the hinterland.

Dunbar's other service to Jefferson, as President, was to send other agents up the Ouachita River, where, as a grace note of history, they visited the Spanish Fort Miró. The grace was imparted a few years later when the fort was given its present name, "Monroe," to commemorate the arrival there of the international cotton market—even though the citizens arranging the matter were ignorant of James Monroe's role in presenting that corner of Louisiana to the planters in 1803. A steamboat named for him—he was then President James Monroe—had rammed and dodged its way through the snags and bars of the Ouachita River to arrive at the docks, eliciting paroxysms of joy from a welcoming committee of planters headed by the local judge, Henry Bry. The committee broke apart early so that its members might scramble for places for their crops aboard the *Monroe*'s voyage toward Liverpool.

The Chancellor, Indolent Maroons, and Thomas Sumter

The foregoing paragraph setting forth events more than a decade after the Louisiana Purchase has been inserted here to underline the point that the planters knew what they were getting. At the time of the Purchase, however, Livingston did what he could to dissemble and thus to diminish the opinion of Louisiana's plantation possibilities held by the French. In August 1802, he presented them with a compendium of disinformation, insisting that Louisiana was not an asset worth holding and omitting any mention of cotton. If organized into manors or seigneuries like his own on the Hudson, he wrote, its tenants could offer their lords no more than "twelve bushels of wheat per hundred acres," and though Louisiana's people might grow products "not produced in the West Indies . . . [such as] lumber and rice," even that was doubtful. "In the United States, lumber for the islands comes from the free north, not from the slave-laboring south." Furthermore, Livingston wrote, New Orleans was "a small town built of wood . . . [surrounded by] barren sands and sunken marshes . . . into which slaves could escape . . . to live a life of indolence with the natives."[29]

The planters of the upland Carolinas were painfully aware of such problems. Their slaves had been escaping to "barren sands and sunken marshes" for many decades. Yet they needed new lands to replace those they had themselves been rendering barren, and such risks must be taken. Besides, though they were attracted to the borderlands they knew that their slaves were attracted to them also. Therefore Florida and Louisiana must be taken—if not for the plantations they might become, then for the maroon colonies they must cease to be. These uplanders had, as their representative in Paris, Thomas Sumter, the son of a famous Revolutionary guerrilla captain who had set himself up as a planter with slaves taken as booty. Like his ally Skipwith, young Sumter reported directly to Jefferson and Madison, hiding outgoing despatches from Livingston and from Livingston's successor and brother-in-law, General John Armstrong. Sumter's excuse, like Skipwith's, was that Livingston was animated by "blind and insatiable vanity, if not corrupt and criminal motives," and that Armstrong was both corrupt and stupid. More precisely, they asserted that Livingston was using his office to preempt the best cotton land of Florida for himself. In proof of this, Sumter reported that one day he burst into a private room to find the minister in deep discussion over a map of Florida with Daniel Parker, an expatriate Bostonian, who was busy demonstrating to Livingston his inside knowledge of the Spanish lands. Though uninvited, Sumter shouldered his way into the discussion, informing Livingston and Parker that as a South Carolinian he knew Florida better than either of them. Having thus ingratiated himself, he went on to offer his judgment that little of value had been left over after the British and the Tories had locked up the best merchandise between 1763 and 1783.[30]

According to Sumter, Parker replied that he knew that Charles-Maurice de Talleyrand-Périgord, Prince of Benevento, foreign minister for Napoleon, had assessed the situation differently: there was plenty of value left unmined; fortunes might be made for the Livingstons and for Talleyrand as well; though the King of Spain might still be Florida's nominal sovereign, the luckless Carlos could be pressured into making grants the Americans would have to honor, when, as everyone anticipated, they took Florida. Skipwith and Sumter told their superiors in Washington that Livingston then made a personal deal with Talleyrand, through Parker. As if to confirm what they said, Livingston began urging his government to permit him to make a peculiar proposition: though West Florida and New Orleans would be purchased outright from Spain by the United States, East Florida would be left in French hands for a sufficient interval for such little transactions to be accomplished.[31]

(Though beyond the scope of our discussion, the speculations by the Livingstons in West Florida concurrently with their participation in both the Louisiana Purchase and the subsequent West Florida negotiations are so interesting that some further suggestions about them are made in "The Livingstons and West Florida" in the Appendix, p. 257.)

Mister Sumter Is Shocked

Discussion about slicing up Florida and Louisiana divided the factions within the American legation, opening rifts that became irreparable when they considered how to divide the portion of the purchase money that would go toward the spoliation claims. Sumter had declared his antipathy to the Livingston family interest, so the Chancellor-minister-claimant situated Major J.C. Mountflorence, his personal claims agent, in Sumter's office. Sumter withdrew to the sheltering arms of the American ministry to London, whereupon

Skipwith took over his role and entered into his own private discussions with the French. He was discovered by the Chancellor, who sequestered a thousand dollars of his salary and transferred it to his own agents. Skipwith protested to Madison, who protested to Jefferson. Both Skipwith and Sumter contended that Livingston could not be trusted, while Livingston told his friends that the "Virginia faction" was betraying his efforts to deal with Talleyrand in the national interest.[32]

The Virginians were no more sure of Livingston than Livingston was sure of Sumter. The planters wanted Louisiana and Florida on their own terms, and Livingston could not be relied upon to get those terms precisely right. Besides, the plantable provinces would be prizes, and, in politics, prizes are not to be squandered. Monroe was sent off to Paris by the fastest ship available. On April 12, 1803, while he still at sea, Skipwith dined with Livingston, who became either bibulously or imprudently candid, admitting that he resented being replaced after he had brought "everything to a proper conclusion," knocked off the ladder just as the apples were ripe. And that is what happened: Monroe arrived to take charge of—and credit for—the final stages of the negotiations, making certain that he and Jefferson got the credit for the Louisiana Purchase. And he gave a final tweak to the documents that had immense consequences for the future of slavery, agriculture, and the land in the territory purchased.[33]

The Third Article

Article Three of the Louisiana Purchase contract between France and the United States provided that the residents of the territory acquired would be protected in the "rights, advantages, and immunities" of citizens of the "acquiring power." It has frequently been said that the author of this clause was Napoleon. It is difficult, however, to believe that he harbored any solicitude for the "rights, advantages, and immunities" of the citizens of Louisiana, nor is there any evidence that this language was present in the draft handed by the French negotiators to the Americans. The far greater likelihood is that it was inserted as a "slight alteration" by Monroe.

Its effect was to assure Louisiana's slave owners and Virginia's slave sellers that those who possessed slaves in the region could retain them, and those who wished to market their human inventory there would not be impeded. In each contest in the Mississippi Valley from 1803 to 1860, the "rights" of Article Three were interpreted to include the rights to hold slaves and to buy more, and the term "advantages" was taken to mean the advantages of owner over slave.

Though the merchants' claims had been accommodated by Livingston's exertions, Article Three was not among the matters brought to "proper conclusion" by him. In the fog surrounding those final frantic days we can discern the figure of Skipwith—Monroe's man—shuttling between him and the French carrying drafts and revisions. On April 23, Napoleon drew up a "Projet of a Secret Convention'" that still did not include the crucial language about "rights" or "privileges." To the best of our knowledge, it said no more than that "in consequence of the said cession, Louisiana, its territory, and its proper dependencies shall become part of the American Union, and shall form successively one or more states on the terms of the Federal Constitution." [34]

Monroe later asserted that he showed these terms in draft to Livingston, who did not propose alterations. Monroe did not claim credit for inserting the poisonous language of Article Three on his own initiative, but nonetheless, by the terms of the contract as he then negotiated it—and as subsequently interpreted by him, by Jefferson, and by the Southern bloc in Congress—the United States agreed to protect slavery in Louisiana. [35]

So cherished, the malignancy throve, and the Southern land suffered irremediable havoc. Because the damage was neither immediate nor apparent, absentee landlords or absentee customers might prosper without any environmental qualms. Some were no doubt much attached to their own acres, but the eroding loess of the Delta and the vulnerable pinewoods of the upcountry were very far away. Did it matter to any of them that the opportunity to establish a yeoman republic eroded even more rapidly than the land itself?

The Louisiana Purchase brought great profits to the planters, and also to the gentlemen of England. Assured of a supply of cotton by the acquisition of a new empire by their old friends the American planters, the British could take special satisfaction in their having gotten it on the cheap from Napoleon, whose self-deception was so overwhelming that he was heard to congratulate himself that he had made the gift so as "to prevent the danger to which the colossal power of England exposes us." As Henry Adams reminded his readers:

> The colossal power of England depended on her navy, her colonies, and her manufactures. Bonaparte proposed to overthrow it by shattering beyond repair the colonial system of France and Spain; and even this step was reasonable compared to what followed. He expected to check the power of England by giving Louisiana to the United States—a measure which opened a new world to English commerce and manufactures, and riveted England's grasp upon the whole American continent.[36]

Skipwith and the Floridas

Fulwar Skipwith returned to the embassy in Paris in March 1806. Monroe had departed for London, with a side trip to Madrid. Chancellor Livingston had been succeeded by his brother-in-law General Armstrong. At this juncture,

American newspapers learned that there had been secret sessions of Congress to follow up the Louisiana Purchase with an appropriation of two million dollars "probably for the purchase of the Floridas," and the press correctly speculated that Skipwith was bearing the vouchers. He carried as well a note from Madison asking Lafayette's aid in putting the money where it would do the most good: "Mr. Skipwith has been a considerable time among us," wrote Madison, "and proceeds immediately from the focus of our political affairs. I refer you to him for everything."[37]

Florida was back in play, and Federalist scruples were no longer in vogue. During the XYZ Affair in 1797–98, an indignant John Adams had refused to pay bribes to Talleyrand and his friends, and the cry went up: "Millions for defense, but not one cent for tribute!" Now Skipwith was to bring two million dollars to France to bribe many of the same men, though the new moralists in charge of American diplomacy were willing to add three million for conventional, old-fashioned, purchase money. A nice ratio—two to three, bribe to purchase. A historian of this ugly period, Isaac Cox, observed that men such as "Talleyrand . . . received their training in an environment where intrigue, craftiness and mendacity were the accepted weapons[;] their American competitors claimed to be men of a different stripe . . . [but] when diplomacy descended to the plane of sordid bribery, the executive and his councilors were willing to profit by it. To such depths did his obsession for the Floridas entice Thomas Jefferson."[38]

The only flaws in this statement are the implications that a Florida "obsession" was peculiar to Jefferson and that—as an "obsession"—it arose from some darker and deeper region of his nature than his calculating intellect. In fact, no planter who had read William Bartram's eulogies to the possibilities of Florida as a cotton-growing region could fail to lust after it even before the Tory planters displaced to Florida, including the partners of The Firm, gleefully reported how nicely they were doing with cotton to their Whig cousins. By 1800, the Tory branches of the Moultrie, McIntosh, and Livingston clans were growing cotton there with immense success; it is likely that the Whig Virginians' aversion to William Augustus Bowles was inflamed by their disinclination to permit a cotton bonanza in Florida to be reaped by an old enemy, Bowles's sponsor, Lord Dunmore. How could any planter not be a little obsessed at the prospect of a place that Bartram described as growing either tobacco or cotton on easily plowed land requiring no replenishment, and that had a 280-day growing season extending into December—when in some places cotton continued to boll?[39]

Fulwar Skipwith was sent back to Paris to bring Florida within the planters' realm. His first act was to transmit to Armstrong instructions from Madison and Jefferson for the management of the bribe fund and the purchase money. His second was to establish a direct line to Madrid and Monroe. To make sure there were no slips, Monroe made it his practice to summon documents from Paris directly from Skipwith, urging him not to inform Armstrong that they were being sent. Skipwith had to walk a maze. He had helped Monroe tincture the Louisiana Purchase with the planters' interests; he had carried to Europe, from "the focus," bribe money toward the acquisition of the Floridas. He was doing what he could to improve his own financial condition by serving as agent for the Livingstons in their spoliation claims while they speculated in Florida real estate and, at the same time, serving Talleyrand's competitive speculations both in the real estate and the spoliation claims. There is some indication that Talleyrand may have financed the purchase by Skipwith of some of those claims and some of that real estate for his own account.[40]

Under the consular system, uncorrected from the days of his West Indian posting, Skipwith was still an independent contractor, not a government employee in the modern sense. He was still expected to earn his salary. Under the terms of the arrangements following the Louisiana Purchase Agreement, the consul was to recommend which American merchants were to receive payment of their claims from the Louisiana Purchase money. There was not enough to go around—perhaps not more than half the amount required. Skipwith was placed in a gatekeeper's role; his compensation was to be paid in commissions out of what he urged the French to pay the favored ones. He settled more than a hundred claims cases, splitting the commissions with another claims agent. He also purchased for his own account some of the claims he recommended for payment. Trouble was inevitable.

The Louisiana Purchase did not do quite everything it was intended to do. True enough, the planters got their cotton land, the New Orleans market was opened, the threat of a European power in the Mississippi Valley was removed, the nation got an unknown interior beyond the Mississippi, and the Livingstons got a large amount of money. Yet even they could not manage to secure all they wanted. They blamed Skipwith for what they failed to get, and they had allies. As a claimant himself, Skipwith was blocking satisfaction of the following formidable folk: Stephen Girard, the Philadelphia banker, who had the support of Secretary of State Madison; James Swan, a speculator under the patronage of Chancellor Livingston; Chancellor Robert himself; John Armstrong, the Chancellor's brother-in-law; John R. Livingston, who had for a time engaged Skipwith as claims agent and was also the Chancellor's brother-in-law; another Robert, the Chancellor's son-in-law and secretary, who was married to Margaret Maria Livingston, a cousin; and Peter Livingston, another cousin and the Chancellor's future brother-in-law.

At this juncture, it became widely known that Skipwith was being rewarded for his personal services to Talleyrand, who influenced the claims payments, while publicly advancing Talleyrand's proposal that *douceurs* be paid him and his noble brother in the form of grants of cotton land in Florida, to "smooth the way by reconciling public measures to the interest of influential individuals . . . to procure the salutary purposes intended."[41]

Conflicts of interest proliferated and intertwined. Nothing seemed out-rageous. Skipwith got lost in the jungle and put in writing to his employers in Washington a request that the bribing of Talleyrand be left to him. If Armstrong were kept out of it, he wrote, Talleyrand's land grants could be subtracted from the two million dollars, producing a considerable saving over an "all-cash deal." As it turned out, there was no purchase of Florida transac-tion at that stage, so the two million dollars were left unspent. Frustrated, Skipwith attributed the impasse to the legacy of Livingston, "that old villain from New York."[42]

Consul Skipwith Goes to Jail

The "old villain" and Armstrong had long arms and long memories. In 1808, finally, they had enough of Fulwar Skipwith. There is no proof—how could we expect they would leave any?—but it is surpassingly likely that they were the leaders of a cabal to get him out of the way in Paris and into a jail cell on the Isle of Wight. The evidence for this comes in part from the painter John Vanderlyn, who had been sponsored in his studies in Paris by Aaron Burr and who through Burr had many friends in the Republican party of New York. In March 1808, Skipwith complained to Jefferson that he was about to be "sent forthwith out of the Empire," citing Vanderlyn as his source. Vanderlyn was right: soon enough Skipwith was told to depart on board the *Hope*, Captain Haley, master. Apparently the French authorities, perhaps Talleyrand him-self, attempted to warn him not to trust Haley, for he was cautioned by his wife that "something has been brewing to vex you anew, in a place and cir-cumstances where you could not help yourself." He went aboard anyway. Haley made a stop at New Port on the Isle of Wight, behind the screen of the Brit-ish fleet, and thus beyond the reach of Jefferson's arm. The British authori-ties, having been informed of Skipwith's imminent arrival, made the news known to the English creditors of his Richmond factoring days. When the *Hope* docked at New Port a constable ran up the gangplank with a warrant for his arrest for debt. After some time in a cell, Skipwith found the necessary money and, vowing "to return no more among those transatlantic scoundrels," set out once more, arriving in the United States in the spring of 1809.[43]

Destiny by Intention

When Fulwar Skipwith arrived to take title to his plantation in what is now Louisiana, then within the Baton Rouge district of Spanish West Florida, the plantocracy in the United States and the textile colonial-imperialists of Great Britain were in one of their sympathetic phases. The American Revolution was over. The comb-like cotton gin was the technological wonder of the age. Steam-powered mills were sucking up every fluff of cotton plucked between Columbia, South Carolina, and the Mississippi River. Skipwith had become the willing instrument of those forces. His shift of venue permitted him to continue to be useful to them. A little time had passed since he came from the "focus"—but he could still serve the Virginia Dynasty.

By the time the phrase "Manifest Destiny" became common currency in the 1840s, the planters' government had frequently helped destiny along. Scarcely a year passed without some new "state," "republic," or changeling enterprise appearing upon the southern or western frontier of the United States. Repeatedly, agents of the federal government would suggest to a chosen set of citizens of Spanish Florida (or, later, Spanish Texas) that they pretend independence just long enough to provide to the American government what is known as a "call" in investment terminology. Control was imperfect, however, so some of them, including Skipwith, allowed their individual fantasies to expand enough to rupture their instructions. Then, in their presumption, they acted as though they had been provided, instead, a "put," as though they could require their "principal"—the United States government—to complete the transaction at their request, rather than the other way round.

While President, George Washington had set forth a policy against using private armies to assault the territory of nations with which the United States was at peace. His intention was to frustrate assaults upon neighboring Indians and against Spanish Florida. After his death his Indian policy and his Neutrality Act of 1794 still stood for a time against cotton wars fought by private and regular armies. Then those inhibitions were perforated by Jefferson and his successors, though the Neutrality Act remained on the books.

Presidents are sworn to uphold not only the Constitution but also the laws of the land. Aaron Burr was broken as a political figure because many people believed the charge made against him by Jefferson that he contemplated treason and had violated the Neutrality Act, though he was never convicted of either charge. None of the other major figures who actually did violate the act were punished; indeed, as we shall see, several, including Skipwith, were amply rewarded after a pause and a little painless knuckle-rapping. True, before the rewards were distributed there were moments when the violators were threatened with punishment: even agents of Manifest Destiny must acknowledge Presidents to be Presidents, retaining certain prerogatives, among them that "deniability" later made famous by Richard Nixon. Indeed, the first definition of "deniability" was provided by John Randolph of Roanoke, who, with a sort of admiring disgust, looked on as Jefferson and Madison "advocated . . . measures . . . until they were nearly ready for execution, when they hung back, condemned the step after it was taken, and on most occasions affected a most glorious neutrality."[1]

As early as 1790, Jefferson had reached the conclusion that Spanish Florida was ripe for the taking and was devising deniable means to take it. As Secretary of State in George Washington's administration, noting that the Spanish governor of Florida had been so imprudent as to invite "foreigners to go and settle in" his province, he offered a sly recommendation to the President:

> This is meant for our people. . . . It will be the means of delivering to us peaceably, what may otherwise cost us a war. In the meantime we may complain of this seduction of our inhabitants just enough to make [the Spaniards] believe we think it very wise policy for them, and confirm them in it. This is my idea of it.[2]

Washington did not endorse Jefferson's "idea," but after 1801 it became the charter of amoebic imperialism: the master organism, the United States, sent forth a nucleus of colonists to cross a border into somebody else's territory. Most frequently, the unwilling "host" was an Indian nation, though in the case at hand it was Spain. Once in place, the nucleus formed a cell that then declared itself independent. Then, to no one's surprise, the ostensibly independent organism demurely discovered dependence and, like a maiden of the time in the presence of her swain, shrank into the protection of the United States.

The swain, bearing arms, was always there awaiting the call—"hanging back," but only just enough. When Jefferson became President, it was not yet certain that Napoleon would resolve the "Mississippi Question" by robbing Louisiana from Spain and then selling it off to the United States. So Jefferson urged an Irish merchant, Daniel Clark, and Pierre Laussat, the French prefect in New Orleans, to raise "an insurrectionary force of the inhabitants to which ours might be only auxiliary. . . . [Thus] all this should be made as much as possible the act of France." Clark and Laussat distributed black cockades to their friends in New Orleans and set about raising "volunteers" in Kentucky, Ohio, and Tennessee, of whom the most famous was Reuben Kemper. Five hundred regulars and the Mississippi militia were to affect "a most glorious neutrality," in Randolph's words, and to come over the northern horizon only if all else failed.[3]

In 1794, four years after his Secretary of State had proposed his "idea" of imperialism by subterfuge, and while Jefferson was encouraging French agents to recruit in the United States for invasions of the Spanish and British dominions, President Washington issued the executive order anticipating the Neutrality Act.

The Adventures of George Mathews

After Napoleon, Monroe, Livingston, Marbois, and Skipwith arranged the Louisiana Purchase, Clark and Laussat could put down their insurrectionary plans and enjoy the new commerce flowing through New Orleans. Three years later, Burr looked beyond Louisiana toward Texas and took up the idea of raising troops in Kentucky and Tennessee. Despite efforts on his behalf by Jackson, Henry Clay, John McKee, and Silas Dinsmoor, however, he was betrayed by Wilkinson, who delivered him to Jefferson. While Burr was being tried in Richmond, Jefferson directed Governor Claiborne of Louisiana to out-Burr Burr. Claiborne—a territorial governor—was to press forward a plan approved in a secret session of Congress "to take possession and occupy all or any part of the [Spanish] territory . . . in case an arrangement has been or shall be made with the local authority of said territory for delivering up the possession of same, or any part thereof, to the United States or in the event of an attempt to occupy the said territory or any part thereof by any foreign government." A fund of a hundred thousand dollars was allocated—without repealing the Neutrality Act—to encourage some such "local authority" in Florida. The fund might have been as large as Skipwith's two million, but former Governor George Mathews of Georgia had reported that "the inhabitants of the province are ripe for revolt" and would act their amoebic roles cheaply. Though "incompetent to effect a thorough revolution without external aid . . . they would commence the business, and with a fair prospect of success . . . [if] two hundred stand of arms and fifty horseman's swords were in their possession." In July 1810, Mathews was given the opportunity to show he was right.[4]

Mathews was a Revolutionary War hero and a two-term governor of Georgia. He had made the error of becoming an accomplice of Blount and McKee at the end of the 1790s, and when nominated as governor of Mississippi Territory, he suffered the humiliation of having his name withdrawn because of that odiferous association. Besides, while governor he had signed the Yazoo Act and helped sell seventeen and a half million acres of land in three Georgia Counties that contained only one and a half million. Nonetheless, because the buyers were mostly from out of state, Mathews remained popular in Georgia.

Mathews's popular following was what counted to the none too scrupulous Robert Smith, Secretary of State in James Madison's administration; that, and Mathews's reputation for following orders, qualified him to use Georgia's soil to launch a filibuster against Spanish Florida. Smith offered him the job on June 20, 1810, through Senator William Harris Crawford of Georgia: he was to go "without delay into East Florida, and also into West Florida, as far as Pensacola" to reconnoiter how those territories might be brought within the planters' realm. Crawford and Smith informed Madison of their choice of Mathews; the President expressed himself as "perfectly satisfied" and invited Mathews to the White House.[5]

The Neutrality Act was still on the books.

The general appeared in full Revolutionary regalia, holding a three-cornered hat and wearing knee britches, high military boots, and his sword. Madison vouchsafed him private audience in a room where for nearly two hundred years privacy has often implied intimacy and deniability. The accounts left to posterity of their discussion by Madison and Mathews differ radically: Mathews told everyone who would listen that Madison urged him to set up an independent Florida republic and to transfer it thereafter to the United States. Madison later denied being so explicit but waited two years to disavow Mathews, and then with affirmations of presidential esteem.[6]

Only the Secretary of the Treasury, Albert Gallatin, seems to have expressed disaffection from this sequence of actions and events. His loyalty to Jefferson had kept him silent on racial matters. He had even been willing to offer a defense of the campaign against Toussaint. But now Gallatin was beginning slowly to emerge toward that passionate opposition to the plantocracy he expressed in the 1830s. In 1810 and 1811, he merely pointed out that Britain was at war with France and that Spanish Florida was in the hands of Spanish authorities favoring Britain. Provoking them would provoke the British as well, and what for? To secure plantation land? To recover slaves? To eradicate maroon colonies? Gallatin warned Madison and Monroe that public opinion would not support such a war and that it would be opposed by both Russia and Great Britain.[7]

"You know," wrote Gallatin, "that to take by force any place in the possession of another nation, whatever our claim to that place may be, is war." Monroe's response was a peremptory "question settled," with the implication that Gallatin should get back to his ledgers. But Gallatin was proven right as British warships appeared off Amelia Island, on the Georgia-Florida border, sending Mathews scurrying back to Georgia. The war with Britain was on.[8]

War, Commerce, and Race

From the British point of view, the Americans had been aiding France as the contest with Napoleon came into its deadly final stage. Thus for the second time those former colonists were making matters difficult: they had achieved their independence in 1783 in common cause with a royalist France previously treated as a blood enemy. The Quasi War between 1797 and 1799 had seemed to restore the Americans to the proper side of the immemorial struggle between Britain and France, yet in 1812 the Americans were once more betraying their ancestors and cousins.

Under such circumstances, the ripening commercial alliance between the British millers and the Southern planters was set aside. For the next three years, until Bonaparte was finally defeated at Waterloo, the Americans were no more to be treated as "family" than the Westphalians or any other allies of France. Besides, Britain could assume the moral high ground: their disreputable kinsmen were using their alliance with the tyrant Napoleon to put more land under slavery.

So, with virtue "riding shot-gun," short-term military policy could trump long-term commercial policy. Never mind the role of the British in conveying slaves to America. Never mind the profits enjoyed from the "low-wage suppliers" on the plantations—*non*-wage, indeed. Never mind that as far back as the Yamassee War of 1715, the British had themselves justified assaults on Florida with the cry that the Spaniards were "arming the barbaric Negro." Now, in the Florida borderlands, the race card could be laid face up on the table with full moral assurance. George Mathews played into the British hand by explaining that his invasion of Spanish Florida was required because Spain and Britain were threatening to land two regiments of Negro troops in Florida. According to Mathews's colleague John Houstoun McIntosh:[9]

> Our slaves are excited to rebel, and we have an army of Negroes raked up in this country, and brought from Cuba, to contend with. Let us ask, if we are abandoned, what will be the situation of the Southern States, with this body of black men in the neighborhood. St. Augustine . . . will be a refuge for fugitive slaves; and from thence emissaries can, and no doubt will be detached, to bring about a revolt of the black population of the United States.[10]

Georgia's Governor David Brydie Mitchell actually *encouraged* an uprising among the Creeks and Seminoles to "afford a desirable pretext for the Georgians to penetrate their country, and break up" the mixed-blood settlements. Maroons were "an important evil growing up under . . . [British and Spanish] patronage." Their being so supported was "so savage and barbarous that it is impossible for an American to hear it without feeling the utmost indignation." Mitchell was a mere amateur at waving the bloody shirt of racism and inciting fears of maronage; the specialist in separating poor Southern blacks from poor Southern whites was McIntosh. The first American McIntoshes had participated in James Oglethorpe's synthesis of Scottish philanthropy and Roman colonial policy, opposing slavery and deploying yeomen as legionaries to garrison the frontier against Spain. Nonetheless, by the time the second generation came to manhood, philanthropy had flickered out, and, under the leadership of the cotton planters, the garrisons had progressed from defense to offense. The paradigm for this generation of McIntoshes was no longer the abolitionist Oglethorpe but the imperial slave driver Wade Hampton.[11]

The plantation headquarters for McIntosh was Fort George Island, now part of a national park. It had been the scene of a Spanish mission town and of a British stockade—hence the name. McIntosh purchased it from Don Juan McQueen, a slave dealer and cotton planter, in whose hands it had provided instruction in racial politics and the social economics of cotton culture. One day in 1795, McQueen was visited by a Hitchiti shaman called Cohiti, accompanied by a black named Peter, who had been a slave of the grandfather of McIntosh and was now notorious in the neighborhood for "spreading the news of the 'good life'" to be enjoyed by joining the Seminole resistance. When McQueen ordered the two to cease operations, Peter laughed in his face and held him at bay at gunpoint while Cohiti recruited the field hands. McQueen had been a pirate-privateer and was no coward. He was reaching for a knife when the leader of those hands, whose name was Titus, "threatened to cut out McQueen's bowels" if he gave Cohiti any trouble. McQueen offered no further threats but remonstrated in a tone Peter found offensive, drawing forth from him the response "with much haughtiness" that "his master [Cohiti] and every other good Indian were as good as [McQueen]."[12]

One of the reasons for McIntosh to invade Florida was to demonstrate that Peter the Seminole was wrong, but after circling St. Augustine with many threats and posturings he and Mathews were driven out by a "Spanish" army including many blacks and Indians. McIntosh returned to a Georgia plantation called Refuge, complaining that the lawlessness that he and Mathews set loose in North Florida was everyone else's fault:

> Had the wishes of our old and worthy friend, George Mathews[,] been carried into effect . . . had [the] . . . advice . . . of the President been followed a few years ago . . . [Florida] would not have been a flourishing country under the government of the United States. . . . Could I live in St. Augustine under the government of the United States, I believe that many years would be added to my life. . . . And those years would be yet increased by that delightful and healthy climate.[13]

As Ponce de Leon discovered during his bloody search for Florida's fountain of youth, its climate might be delightful and healthy but only if one did not stray too far beyond the walls of a fortress or a well-garrisoned stockade—

unless, of course, one was a Seminole. It was far from delightful for George Mathews. In May, 1812, after sixteen years of chores for the Virginians, he got one of Monroe's disavowal letters. The administration had suddenly remembered Washington's Neutrality Act, which, wrote Monroe, "forbids such procedure under severe penalties." Though the law he had broken would not be enforced against him, Mathews was told to go home and nurse his wounded pride. Monroe was gentle: "I have thought it improper to mention this fact in an official letter to you, but it is one which had its weight in the part the government has taken."[14]

Assisters and Resisters

The agent selected by the Madison administration to clean up the mess left by Mathews and McIntosh and to minimize the Seminole-maroon menace was Thomas Adam Smith. This young Virginian had performed confidential services for Jefferson when his immediate superior was General Wilkinson. Smith had been told to carry despatches in the soles of his boots, directly to Jefferson in the White House, and to remove boots and despatches only in the privacy of the presidential chamber. Those boots had had hard wear amid the murk and mosquitoes of the swamps of the Delta, where Smith had been assigned by Wilkinson to try to kidnap Aaron Burr—Wilkinson's second attempt of that sort in advance of any judicial proceeding. Smith did his duty in Arkansas, Mississippi, and even the "damnable province" of Florida.[15]

By April 1812, Madison had disavowed Mathews and McIntosh. He had not, however, disavowed their conquests. Though the United States was not formally at war with Spain, Smith's regulars and Mitchell's Georgia militia were backed by American gunboats commanded by Commodore Hugh Campbell. Smith's instructions were to hold the position before St. Augustine and to confront the two companies of black Cubans that had recently augmented the Spanish and Negro troops holding the town. During the ensuing parlays, Mitchell reiterated McIntosh's emphasis upon a conflict of races, insisting that the United States would not tolerate armed blacks in the Spanish possessions. Monroe then confirmed the General Orders issued to the Tennessee volunteers under Smith's command that they should burn out the Indian villages and execute all Negroes found in arms.

As the War of 1812 got underway, senators who shared Secretary Gallatin's views reminded their colleagues that the nation's meager armed forces could better be deployed on the Canadian frontier or defending the nation's capital. The Senate went so far as to rebuke Madison's proposal that it endorse the seizure of the Floridas. Undeterred by constitutional problems of that sort, the President kept Smith, Campbell, and Mitchell on station while he and Monroe sought "a new cause" for their invasion of Florida. Jefferson, rallying to their side, declared that the Congress should cease its grumbling and let the administration persist in its campaign: "Their [the Floridas'] inhabitants universally wish it, and they are in truth the only legitimate proprietors of the soil and government."[16]

That "universal approbation" was not heard from those "proprietors of the soil" who were the British, Spanish, former Loyalists, Negroes, and Indians. *Their* wishes were being expressed, instead, in a series of nasty swamp fights against the invaders. A free black named Prince became a Seminole war chief, leading a force of seventy blacks and six Indians in forays close to the American camp. The Spanish regulars observing the smoke of these battles were joined by black militia, including former slaves from Georgia. As familiar faces peered down from the ramparts of St. Augustine upon the advance pickets of McIntosh's force, he exhorted his Georgians: "Will you in poverty become the sport of slaves and the abhorred army in St. Augustine[?]" After McIntosh retired from the scene, breathing outraged dignity and racial fear, some of the remaining "Patriots" set out for the interior of Seminole territory, where, in 1814, they honored Mitchell by naming their fort after him. Asserting that they were at war with "savages of all color," these representatives of "the District of Elotchaway of the Republic of Florida" sought admission to the United States. By then, however, the incompetence of the Madison administration's management of the war against Britain had so diminished its following that it was ready to disavow its Florida venture, Secretary Monroe declaring that "no countenance can be given by their government to the proceedings of the revolutionary party in East Florida, if it be composed of Spanish subjects—and still less can it be given to them if it consists of American citizens."[17]

Senator William Hunter of Rhode Island was not impressed with such post-hoc formalities. Though he had been warned not to add fuel to the "flame which had been raging in Congress and in the country," he forced the Senate to face the real objects of Madison's Florida operation: the seizure of more cotton land and the recovery or execution of slaves who had escaped. Hunter left no doubt that his sympathies lay with those in bondage—that "unhappy species of population which prevails in our Southern country." Driving his point farther, he extolled the successful runaways as "black soldiers and black officers dangerous well beyond the reach of their arms" because their example encouraged others to "likewise be soldiers and officers." On January 26, 1813, as the Senate debated Madison and Monroe's Florida War, Hunter mocked their avowal that the Mathews-McIntosh rebellion represented "a really deep, honest, spontaneous revolutionary movement." It was, he said, "on the contrary, an artificial, concerted, contrived, petty, patched-up, miserable treason, paid for by our money, fomented by our people," and intended to justify a "wicked . . . robbery of Florida."[18]

While Hunter was descanting to the Senate, a former slave named Tony, said to be the best interpreter of Indian languages in Florida, was serving the same educational purpose closer to the scene. He had been kidnaped by Mathews and given the task of cozening the Seminoles into giving up the blacks who had found sanctuary among them. Tony was no fool; knowing that Mathews could not be aware of what he was saying, he told his audience: "These fine talks are to amuse and deceive you. They are going to take your country. . . . The old people will be put to sweep the yards of the white people, the young men to work for them and the young females to spin and weave for them." The work "the young men" would do was in the cotton fields, supplying the fibers to be spun and woven.[19]

As Tony spoke for the indigenous resistance, Vice Admiral Sir Alexander Cochrane was riding the waves offshore in his battle fleet. Renewing Lord Dunmore's strategy of 1775 and 1794, Cochrane encouraged the Creeks and Seminoles once more to welcome escaping blacks to their ranks, offered to equip them from the sea, and issued a manifesto threatening that his mounted Negroes would sweep upon "Mr. Madison and his worthless associates . . . to give a complete drubbing before peace is made." The admiral had little time to assemble his black Cossacks, for the war sputtered on for only a few more months, but he was able to land fifteen hundred troops on Cumberland Island in December. While it was in British hands its slaves were free.[20]

The Green Flag of Florida

The "Patriots" of the "District of Elotchaway" were still waiting for amoebic imperialism to absorb them when three years later one of the corsairs of the Caribbean, Gregor MacGregor, hove into the port of Amelia in a fleet of five vessels. Like many buccaneers, MacGregor employed black crews but also traded in slaves. He was willing to share the latter activity with his neighbors in Georgia and let it be known that he would consider a proposal to include Amelia in the United States if first permitted to do a little state building. That, from a pirate, meant phagocytic state expansion, as MacGregor demonstrated by sending reconnaissance parties toward the outskirts of St. Augustine.[21]

MacGregor was a grandson of a laird of Inverardine known by the Gaelic name that translates as "Gregor the Beautiful" and famous for performing feats with the Lochaber axe and claymore. The piratic grandson of the laird was beautiful, too, when painted in his middle thirties, though a little pudgy and by no means as staggering in comeliness as William Augustus Bowles. Fame first came to him as a hero of Francisco de Miranda's second campaign for the independence of Venezuela. In 1812 he married a cousin of Simón Bolívar, whose army he joined next and who promoted him to become general of a division. After the failure of Bolívar's first campaign for Venezuelan independence, MacGregor persuaded the rebels of Mexico, Venezuela, New Grenada, and Argentina to commission him to do what he could to embarrass the Spaniards. A base for such operations was necessary; Amelia commended itself. On June 28, 1817, having gathered a fleet and army sufficient to over-awe the Spanish garrison, he raised over the island the "Green Cross of Florida"—a green St. George's cross on a field of piratic black.

Under that ensign MacGregor assembled a larger multiracial coalition including Jared Irwin, a former Pennsylvania congressman, and Ruggles Hubbard, formerly "high sheriff" of New York City. Next upon the scene, in September 1817, was George Woodbine, a British subject allied to Robert Christie Ambrister—later notoriously executed by Andrew Jackson. After conferences aboard Woodbine's flagship, the *Venus*, MacGregor sailed for London to recruit further aid. Ambrister returned to the Caribbean to launch a new venture. He was to recruit an army of fifteen hundred blacks, com-mencing with some who had fought for Britain in the War of 1812, and to establish a base at Tampa to assault St. Augustine from the south while the reequipped MacGregor was to renew his assault from the north.

This prospect was not pleasing to the American government. The gover-nor of Spanish Florida had already blown on the coals of fear aroused by McIntosh and Mathews, reinforcing his garrison at St. Augustine with several hundred free black soldiers from Cuba. When the United States Navy dis-patched the brig *Saranac* to the port of St. Mary's, just across a little bay from Amelia, to put a stop to such importations, it was attacked by the Spaniards and blacks on September 13, 1817. They were driven off, emboldening Irwin and Hubbard to defy both Spain and the United States. MacGregor's north-ward-inclining, independence-followed-by-acquisition policy was repudiated, and a southern orientation announced instead. MacGregor had once offered to be the advance guard of the planters. Irwin and Hubbard now became "the Northern Company for South American Emancipation." As if to confirm this 180-degree turn—and the fears of the planters—on September 17 a fleet of thirteen vessels came into the port of Fernandina commanded by Luis Aury and bearing an expeditionary force of black troops.

Aury was a contemporary of MacGregor, born in a suburb of Paris in 1786 or 1787. He joined the French navy, left it for piracy between 1803 and 1810, and set himself up in Galveston with the help of the New Orleans mer-chant Abner Duncan and Edward Livingston, a younger brother of the Chan-cellor. Both Duncan and Livingston no doubt took shares in Aury's operations and encouraged his providing a Galveston base for the operations of a succes-sion of Latin American revolutionary leaders, who, in return, commissioned Aury in their navies. Emboldened by these dignities, on September 21, 1817, Aury took down MacGregor's Green Flag and hoisted over Amelia Island the revolutionary flag of Mexico. (For more about Duncan, see "Fulwar Skipwith and Andrew Jackson" in the Appendix, p. 260.)

Things had been bad enough for the planters when Ambrister threatened to recruit an army of free blacks, and worse when the Spanish governor actually did so. Now a New Orleans reporter gave the full alarm: Aury's shock troops were "about one hundred and thirty brigand Negroes—a set of desperate and bloody dogs." Desperate they may well have become. They had been betrayed several times—though never by Aury. In 1814, under the command of a Haitian refugee, Major Joseph Savary, they had rallied to Andrew Jackson's army in New Orleans. Lest their prowess teach other blacks the lessons to which Hunter of Rhode Island referred—that they too might "likewise be soldiers and officers"—they were harried out of town by Governor Claiborne. They followed Savary and Aury to Galveston, saved Aury from a mutiny, and then went on to Amelia.[22]

Aury had issued a proclamation to "men of all nations[:] we are freemen; let us forever be united by the love of liberty and hatred to tyranny." This was not the sort of thing that could be left unanswered. On July 30, 1817, John Houstoun McIntosh wrote Crawford, his old sponsor of 1811, now Secretary of the Treasury:

> Aury's Blacks make their neighborhood extremely dangerous to a population like ours and I fear if they are not expelled from that place [Amelia] some unhappy consequence might fall on our country. It is said they have declared that if they are in danger of being overpowered they will call upon every Negro within reach. Indeed, I am told that the language of the slaves in Florida is already such as to be extremely alarming.[23]

George Graham, acting as Secretary of War for President Monroe, apparently agreed, for he dipped into the files of the department for a piece of secret legislation passed for the purpose of supporting McIntosh in January 1811. On the basis of its broad powers, Graham asserted that Aury and Savary had "taken possession of Amelia Island . . . without the sanction of any of the Spanish colonies, or of any organized government whatever, and for purposes unfriendly to and incompatible with the interests of the United States." The armed forces of the United States should, therefore, "break up that establishment."[24]

Though Aury was willing to improve his image in the neighborhood by selling slaves to the planters, he was unwilling to discharge the black core of his own force. This ambivalence was noted by Monroe, who explained to the Congress that Aury had "assumed a more marked character of unfriendliness to us; the island being made a channel for the illicit introduction of slaves from Africa into the United States, an asylum for fugitive slaves from the neighboring states, and a port for smuggling of every kind."[25]

In December 1817, an American fleet blockaded Amelia Island and its largely black garrison, while the planters' Secretary of War, John C. Calhoun, assembled an army. Early in 1818, Calhoun ordered General Edmund Pendleton Gaines to move his troops to St. Mary's, where he was to coordinate his land operations with a squadron of the navy. (Like Smith, Gaines had earned the confidence of the administration by service in Jefferson's campaign against Burr.) To the relief of McIntosh and the other planters looking on from the bluffs of the St. Mary's River, the Navy's gunboats were successful in nosing their way through the shallow estuaries that Captain Campbell had traversed in 1811, while Colonel James Bankhead assumed the role of Thomas Adam Smith. The garrison of Amelia Island went quietly.

Instead of returning the island to Spain, however, Gaines's orders were to hold it and to stay within range of the guns of one of Henry's corvettes, the *John Adams*. Soon thereafter, the claims of Spain to Florida were purchased away, while those of a substantial portion of the "legitimate proprietors of the soil" were left to be settled by another thirty years of Seminole Wars. Upon hearing of these achievements, John Quincy Adams, still dutiful to the Virginia Dynasty, offered public congratulations for a victory over "a motley tribe of black, white, and red combatants . . . parti-colored forces . . . [of] Negro-Indian banditti." Adams declared himself to be unmoved by pleas "in the name of . . . the rights of runaway slaves."[26]

15

Louisiana and Another Class of Virginians

We have been most cruelly disappointed. After all our expectations and hopes, after all the assurances we have received from General Mathews and Governor Mitchell and others, that we would never be abandoned by the U. States Government . . . we are surrendered . . . after we have attempted to throw off oppression.

(John Houstoun McIntosh to James Monroe, April 16, 1813)

[The messenger was] to mount his horse, if necessary, to travel among and stimulate the inhabitants of Florida to declare themselves independent and that he Governor C. or the government would defray the expenses. . . . I would conclude that both Gov. C. and the President both were highly delighted at seeing us led on and that the President . . . [was] determined to occupy this country, after we should subvert the Spanish[, . . .] yet felt some embarrassment in doing it.

(Fulwar Skipwith to John Graham, January 14, 1811)

We now return to Louisiana and West Florida, where the currents of economic force and imperial ambition observed in the previous chapter were also at work, and with similar effects upon the land.

The portion of the present state of Louisiana including its capital at Baton Rouge and extending nearly to Gulfport, Mississippi, remained part of West Florida for seven years after the rest of the state was purchased from Napoleon. These "Florida Parishes" were part of a sandy plain extending from Baton Rouge on the southwest and from Natchez on the northwest to Mobile on the east, looking southward upon a humid expanse seeming neither sea nor swamp nor shore but all confusedly at once. Even today, the Florida Parishes are remote from the picturesque plantations along the River Road to Baton Rouge, the roiling swell of the great river, the tourists, nostalgia, ghosts, and sugary recipes. The plains people are connected to the Mississippi along one of its old channels that left a west-to-east chain of shallow hazy marshy brackish lakes—Maurepas, Pontchartrain, and Borne—

oozing eastward through ever saltier marshlands gradually abandoning all surface greenery to become a long submerged shelf underlying the Gulf of Mexico.

The north bank of this old riverbed of the Mississippi rises two or three hundred feet through deeply eroded gullies to the plain extending to Natchez, but east of the loess hills along the Mississippi, unbroken by topographical excitement all the way to Tennessee. From the brink of this terrace, amid longleaf and loblolly pines, one can look southward upon the lowlands of cypresses and palmettos. Turning about to face northward, one progresses into a different country, populated by the people of the plain, not of the marshes. These pinelanders are Southern, not Creole. They have never been rich, nor have they made others rich, for the land itself was never rich and was impoverished early by failing endeavors to make it cotton country. It is unfitted for mallows; the prime plantation lands lie along the Yazoo and the Mississippi and the Black Prairie to the east.[1]

The most desirable cotton land of West Florida had been formed southwest of those sand plains by the outwashes and meanderings of the Mississippi and the blowing up upon its banks of more wind-driven particles of fine loess to form immense dune-like hills. Fulwar Skipwith's Monte Sano reposed on the lower fringes of those loess hills. Natchez lay at their center, its bluffs marvelously combining the virtues of splendid agricultural land and a military position commanding the river at a relatively constrained point. Ellicott's acquisition of Natchez was therefore as important to the planters for agriculture as to the free farmers of the upper valley for strategic purposes. Their products could most conveniently reach world markets by passing Natchez and Monte Sano and emerging at New Orleans.

After 1803 and the Louisiana Purchase, Orleans Territory was defined to include that city itself, the rest of the Louisiana boot, and claims toward the Rio Grande in one direction and the Florida Parishes in the other. Texas and the Floridas—East and West—remained under the nominal rule of Spain but were only spasmodically and patchily governed by anyone. The Spanish governors of Texas could assemble substantial military forces when they summoned their energies against an external threat, and did so to oppose Jefferson's expedition up the Red River in 1805 and Wilkinson's deployment of an army on the Sabine in 1806.

Florida, like Texas, and like Louisiana before 1803, was governed by officials drawn from many Catholic nations united only by loyalty to their Church and Crown. The affiliation to the Spanish Empire of the white population of Florida, already weakened when the Spanish authorities attempted to deny the planters replenishment with fresh slaves from Africa to make up for those who escaped to the Seminoles, snapped in 1808 when Napoleon substituted his brother Joseph for the legitimate Bourbon king in Madrid. The West Florida planters turned to the United States for "stability," defined by them as an ability to field a functioning army to keep down a servile workforce and to assist in recovering escaped slaves. Spain was no longer able to give them that assurance, so they were ready to listen to proposals from north of the border.

The messages brought them between 1798 and 1811 by agents such as John McKee, and thereafter by the partners of The Firm and General Wilkinson, were transmitted not only from the administrations of Jefferson and Madison but also from several sets of private interests. Jefferson, Madison, and James Monroe represented the slave sellers and the planters. Kentucky's John Breckenridge spoke for both these parties together with the upstream farmers. Vice President Aaron Burr and General John Adair represented the filibusters who discerned the silver mines of Mexico beyond Texas. As President, Jefferson achieved a concert of interest among planters, farmers, and slave sellers, dextrously shunting aside Burr and Adair while sending his own filibusters into territory disputed with Spain. Half the westward expeditions of his administration were directed in the guise of science toward the provinces at the portals of those mines. These provinces to be scientifically explored were also potential cotton lands.

Zebulon Pike was sent to test the defenses of New Mexico and Chihuahua, while Lewis and Clark probed along the Missouri, Custis the Red, and Dunbar the Ouachita. As noted earlier, whatever might be learned of use to science or toward the augmentation of the future American store of silver, these armed inquiries were of immediate use to the advance of slave-worked agriculture. That point was made by Jefferson's giving direction of the Ouachita and Red projects to William Dunbar and James Wilkinson.

Wilkinson could generally be counted upon to pause in what he was doing for Spain to serve Jefferson's provocations, whether against Mexico, Mobile, or West Florida, or driving Indians out of the plantation lands of Mississippi. In West Florida itself, the President's primary political agents were Virginians, of whom the best known were W.C.C. Claiborne and Fulwar Skipwith. Skipwith was the agent who had been said by Madison to have been "a considerable time among us," proceeding to his duties "immediately from the focus of our political affairs."[2]

Much the same might be said of Claiborne. During the impasse over the 1800 election, when Jefferson and Burr received an equal number of votes for the presidency, he was a very young congressman from Tennessee, staunchly supported the planters' cause, and was rewarded with the governorship of Mississippi Territory in 1801. Both he and Skipwith were gentlemen of modest wattage but impeccable lineage; both were thoroughly "broken in," as the expression goes in some intelligence circles. (Claiborne's loyalty to Jefferson nearly cost him his life in a duel with Daniel Clark in the aftermath of the Burr Trial in 1807, a story of implications too complicated to place either here or in an endnote. It is summarized in the Appendix in the section entitled "The Claiborne–Clark Duel," p. 258.)[3]

The Third Opportunity Reconsidered

Wilkinson, Claiborne, and Skipwith had their work cut out for them. While the Haitians were shriveling the plantation system on their island, a similar expansion of small farms was occurring in Spanish Louisiana. Had the great powers of the world not intervened when they did in Haiti and Louisiana, it is entirely possible that both places might have provided subtropical tests of Mr. Jefferson's ideal of a society of free and independent yeomen. Louisiana's French governors through 1762, and Spanish governors thereafter, had learned some sharp lessons about the perils of being white masters isolated amid a far more numerous population of people brought in chains from Africa. In 1729 the Natchez Indians and blacks led by Bambaras seized the French outpost at Natchez. Two years later the Bambaras launched their own rebellion, inducing the French crown to decree the first cessation of imports of slaves from Africa. As a result, only one slave ship brought a new "supply" during the forty years thereafter. Over the same period, world wars shattered the export trade of the Spanish and French colonies, depriving them of the labor force to refresh a plantation economy. Therefore, "rather than penetrating the backcountry . . . the population hovered around the port of New Orleans. . . . In the absence of a staple commodity of the kind that induced planters elsewhere in the Americas to drive slaves to the limit, the harsh regime of former years mellowed." The slave population of the Spanish possessions in the Mississippi Valley was confined within the immediate neighborhood of New Orleans and a few plantations along the Mississippi. There was very little agricultural servitude in the villages upriver. Had these enclaves been allowed to shrivel further, the valley might have been organized into free territories instead of slave territories.[4]

Louisiana backed up on Texas, and Texas had virtually no slaves, leaving its future course open. The 1792 census showed thirty-four blacks and 414 mulattoes in Texas, and as late as 1819 there were only seven black slaves in the largest town of Texas, San Antonio. There were three times as many Indians in the whole province of Texas as whites—perhaps 12,000 to 15,000 as against 4,100.[5]

In this still malleable setting, a model of society similar to that espoused by the young Jefferson had been advanced by two non-Spanish governors serving the Catholic Hapsburgs and Bourbons, one Irish and the other Flemish. Under the leadership of Alexander O'Reilly and the Baron de Carondelet, Louisiana had been evolving away from a plantation economy, and its land tenure system was being reordered in ways Jefferson might have undertaken had he still been serious about his Lost Cause. Germans, Canary Islanders, and after 1763 displaced Canadians—Acadians—were brought to Louisiana and given small allotments along the Great River and on the Gulf Coast. In 1769, O'Reilly, then governing Spanish Louisiana, promulgated a program for slaves to buy their freedom in installments (by *coartación*). Manumission was already common, especially among people of mixed parentage. Thus an increase in the proportion of free blacks in the society was planned, not accidental, as the result of policies directly opposite to those instituted after 1783 in Virginia. O'Reilly's program was producing a "self-purchase" per week until the Spaniards caved in to American pressure to stop it. The antimanumission reaction was thereby expanded from the Chesapeake to the Gulf.[6]

Like O'Reilly and Jefferson himself, Carondelet was a son of the Celtic Fringe. Though his father was a Burgundian nobleman, he was descended from the Irish Dunsanys on his mother's side. Like a good Celt, he resisted the English and the Anglo-Americans and seeded the countryside with yeoman communities better representing the Jeffersonian ideal than anything Jefferson himself achieved. In New Orleans he encouraged a multiracial culture including free blacks, and welcomed refugees from the successive revolutions in France, including several of Jefferson's old friends among the *Amis des Noirs*, still, after many buffetings, opposed to both the enslavement of Africans and the damage wrought upon the land by the plantation system.

In 1770, O'Reilly had supplemented his encouragement of a class of free blacks—and implicitly, mulattoes—with a veritable Homestead Act. Under its terms, farmers could gain title to land by clearing it and commencing its cultivation. Further, the Spanish government offered to build houses and supply breed stock, rations, and cash subsidies. The settlers were encouraged to put their cattle out into common feedlots, to refresh their fields, and to confine their habitations to villages.[7]

Hedgerows and tree lines marking long strips of land fronting narrowly on rivers are the footprints of French and Spanish land use. Rarer, but still observable to this day, are villages set amid strips of land greener than elsewhere, indicating places where people still go forth to farm as they did in the eighteenth century, returning to those villages rather than scattering out in ranchettes and rectangular farmsteads. Villages imply continuity, and continuity implies careful land use. These villages and strip-farms show that all the flat land was not "improved" into great plantations owned by absentees. Community life went on. The visits of magnates, such as the Hamptons and their kinfolk, were no doubt of great interest to the people of the "quarters," but not necessarily to the yeomen who managed to sustain the way of life the Baron de Carondelet had sought to install—before the Americans took over.

Village-centered, primarily subsistence economies were not peculiar to pre-Purchase Louisiana. They arose intentionally throughout Latin America as alternatives to proto-capitalist plantations yoked to world markets. The Jesuits, especially, advocated a well-diversified agriculture of villages. Where Jesuit doctrine worked its way into practice and was left undisturbed long enough to become tradition, there were often racially diversified populations as well. Lewis Cecil Gray, the magnifico of American agricultural history, wrote of the virtues of the pre-Purchase way of life, as compared to that engendered by the plantocracy: "French villagers and small farmers were characterized by industry, thrift, and stability, with a society patriarchal in organization and spirit." Such stability and thrift are generally associated with careful land use.[8]

This kind of society in Toussaint's Haiti had been destroyed by the invasions of the British, French, and Spaniards, with the encouragement of the Jefferson administration. In Louisiana, too, there was the beginning of a "society of . . . small-scale marginal self-sufficient producers." One could not expect Jefferson to embrace the example of a black yeomanry, in a "cannibal republic," but the O'Reilly-Carondelet system for Louisiana was largely manned by white yeomen. It was, therefore, an acceptable third opportunity after the first two discussed in our early chapters.[9]

Jefferson's first choice as governor of Louisiana—or so he said—had been Lafayette, one of the *Amis des Noirs*. In the 1770s and early 1780s, Jefferson attended to the views of such men and remained fond of Lafayette. After the fall of the Bastille, however, the decapitation of the Bourbon king and a large number of his friends of the old regime, and the accommodation of others to the series of tyrannical governments in their own country, the influence of these theoretically agrarian Frenchmen was no longer heavily felt. Lafayette survived unblemished, but only as a relic of former hopes. Indeed, Lafayette lived on so far into the nineteenth century that he was still expressing his old ideals in the year that Abraham Lincoln entered the Illinois legislature. Lafayette was not a theoretician; the poetry we associate with him is the poetry of action. Though they shared a revolutionary past and a classical tradition, Jefferson was another kind of being, a master of language, often an embarrassment in action. Or in inaction.[10]

The Hillhouse Debates

Lafayette did not go to Louisiana to join the *Amis des Noirs*. Jefferson did not use his powers as philosopher, rhetorician, or President to advance the cause of yeomanry. The sharpest test of his commitment to his Lost Cause came just after the Louisiana Purchase. As the Senate debated the organization of what was purchased, and specifically the implications of Article Three for the future of slavery, the President who received Louisiana failed to exert himself. Jefferson took advantage neither from the shriveling of the slave system in Louisiana nor from the efforts of Carondelet and O'Reilly toward a yeoman's republic. Nor did he assist the strong party in Congress that sought to prevent the further contamination of Louisiana by slavery. The most vocal members of that body who had resisted the organization of Mississippi as a slave territory in 1802 were still present. As the debate of 1805–6 began, they achieved a majority vote for keeping in place Carondelet's prohibition against further importation of slaves. Jefferson did nothing to help them, nor did he exert himself to assist the collateral endeavors of James Hillhouse of Connecticut, the leader of the antislavery cause.

Hillhouse had gained fame in 1779, at the side of Aaron Burr, leading the Yale students who fought off a British attack on New Haven. After the Revolution, he became a member of Congress, a senator, and president pro tempore of the Senate. In the debates of 1805 and 1806 that bear his name in a still almost evenly divided Congress, Hillhouse took up the cause George Thacher had urged in 1802, seeking to stop slavery where it was. He did not pretend that slavery was not already present in the area then being organized as "Orleans Territory," asking only that Congress prevent further importation of slaves from Africa or from the slave-selling states. When, at one stage in the debate, he took the conciliatory stance that though importation of slaves might be permitted if accompanying *bona fide* settlers—not slave dealers—he elicited from Jonathan Dayton, a proslavery senator from New Jersey, a comment embarrassing to the Virginians: "You are about to prohibit African slaves . . . and to admit the worst slaves—such as the southern planters wish to sell."[11]

Though slave-selling planters were almost as powerful in Delaware as they were in Virginia and Maryland, one of its senators, Samuel White, supported the proposal made by Hillhouse that Congress "prevent this horrid traffic in human flesh" and refused to be quieted by references to Article Three: "There is nothing in the treaty that guarantees to the people of that country the power, I will not say the right, of holding slaves." John Breckenridge of Kentucky at first agreed: "The treaty does not in the smallest degree authorize that people to hold slaves—much less does it pledge the faith of the union to this unjust, unnatural traffic. . . . I consider slavery as an evil—and am for confining it within as small a compass as possible." Later, however, Breckenridge changed his mind and commenced arguing that shipping slaves to the West would "disperse and weaken that race," an argument Jefferson had been making since 1787. Having averred that he thought slavery to be evil, Breckenridge seems to have checked with his party managers, for when he came back to the floor he proclaimed that "our Constitution recognizes slavery—it does more[,] it expressly protects it." And so did Article Three, as Jefferson's kinsman and business partner, Senator Wilson Cary Nicholas of Virginia, hastened to assure the Senate: the "rights" of Louisiana's planters included buying more slaves from his constituents, though Nicholas said he was "for prohibiting the people of that country from importing slaves from foreign countries."[12]

Cotton, slavery, and Article Three of the Louisiana Purchase Agreement were parts of the same package, so far as Georgia's Senator James Jackson was concerned. Though Jefferson and Napoleon had secured the western half of the Mississippi Valley, Jackson warned his colleagues that it would soon be lost again "without the aid of slaves. . . . Neither coffee nor cotton can be raised" without them. Louisiana was too hot for white men to farm, Jackson insisted. Without slavery, the whole territory would be so useless that "it must be abandoned."[13]

The upstream farmers had wanted the Mississippi opened to the seas, and the antislavery Senator McClay of North Carolina responded to Jackson that "that country was purchased to serve as an outlet for the U.S.[;] to admit slaves there will defeat that object." Jackson swept aside that geopolitical consideration along with another, the strategic argument that New Orleans must be denied to any hostile power. For him and the planters he represented, it came down to naked, sectional, economic interest; Louisiana was a new province for cotton growing, slave holding, and slave selling. Slave importers in South Carolina and Jackson's Georgia insisted through him that Article Three stipulated that "slavery must be admitted into that territory [Louisiana]" and drove the bumbling Senator Bradley of Vermont and John Smith of Ohio, an investor in West Florida, to acquiesce. Bradley conceded that "by the treaty we are bound to grant it [slavery] to the Louisiana planters," and Smith, though deploring slavery, took the view that Article Three seemed to ordain that "slaves may be admitted there [Louisiana] from the United States"—though not from Africa. Perhaps he simply did not care enough about the slavery question to disagree with another Senator Smith, Samuel, merchant of Maryland, who took the view that because "the people of that country wish for African slaves . . . we ought to let them have a supply."[14]

Those who had been observing the South as it divided along the Thousand-Foot Line already had heard from McClay of North Carolina the voice of the upcountry Southern yeomen who had no slaves and grew no cotton. His colleague, Jesse Franklin, remained silent through most of the debate. However, as the trimmers of the North found solace in Article Three, and the planters mobilized the votes of the new slave states of the West as well as the old ones of the seaboard, Franklin acknowledged that the antislavery forces could not win but insisted that the moment be marked in American history. When others contended that prohibiting direct importation to Louisiana would only encourage the slave markets of Charleston to provide them, Franklin rejoined: "I have no objection to sending a frigate to Charleston to prevent the landing of slaves from Africa imported by South Carolina—and frittering those nefarious traders to pieces."[15]

William Plumer of New Hampshire, who had kept the notes, summarized the outcome:

> It is obvious that the zeal displayed by the Senate from the slave states, to prohibit foreign importation of slaves into Louisiana, proceeds from the motive to raise the price of their own slaves in the market—and to increase the means of disposing of those who are the most turbulent and dangerous to them.[16]

The Lost Cause was truly lost when Wilson Cary Nicholas rose to declare obsolete Jefferson's aspirations of 1784. There should be no further talk of keeping slaves out of the West or freeing those already there, he cried. Only fools or Northerners—"strangers," Nicholas called them—could be so irresponsible. Louisiana already had too many free blacks, who, he said, "have a very ill effect upon slaves—they do more mischief than strangers conceive of." When the question arose as to whether or not free blacks had "privileges and immunities" they might carry over from Carondelet's regime in Louisiana—"privileges and immunities" in reverse, such as serving on juries—the Jeffersonians united in opposition to any such notion.[17]

It is noteworthy that during these debates of 1805–6 not a single Southern senator asserted the "positive good" theory of slavery later advocated by John C. Calhoun and others; none went beyond the dispersion theory of Breckenridge and the "new Jefferson"—the post-1784 Jefferson. Robert Wright of Delaware implored his colleagues to leave it to heaven:

> It is wrong to reproach us with the immorality of slavery—that is a crime we must answer at the bar of God—we ought not therefore to answer it here—for it would be unjust that we should be punished twice for the same offence.[18]

Though the forces behind the plantation juggernaut were very powerful, the Hillhouse Debates show how closely the nation was divided on the slavery question. Louisiana might have been made safe for individual husbandmen and for the Empire of Liberty. Settlement of the vast region had barely begun, and where there was settlement there was also the legacy of Carondelet—or, one might say, of George Washington's small-holder scheme for Mount Vernon—or of Oglethorpe's Georgia. Yet the President did nothing to advance the antislavery cause and without expressing a qualm, signed the law that made Louisiana a slaveholding territory.[19]

As the economic historian Robin Blackburn has commented:

> The Louisiana Purchase confirmed that the United States was an empire as well as a republic and it confirmed that slaveholders would have their own reserved space within that empire. Because he was President, because of his historic role and because he was a Virginian, Jefferson was the only man who could have prevented this development.[20]

Though the President withheld his hand and his voice, Hillhouse was able to secure "the strongest antislavery restriction imposed on any portion of the lower South between 1733 and 1865," an inhibition upon interstate commerce in slaves. Soon, however, his victory was obliterated when the Territory of Orleans was organized and the Chesapeake planters were permitted to ship their surplus stock to the cotton and cane fields. When the territory was converted into the state of Louisiana in 1812, and the rest of the Louisiana

Purchase reorganized as Missouri Territory, the planters were able to fight off yet another round of Hillhouse-type amendments, and the slave sales continued.

In 1818–20, three further battles were fought to arrest the onrush of plantation slavery. The first two would have stopped its advance northward along the western shore of the Mississippi River from Louisiana into Arkansas and then into Missouri. Jefferson, still very much a force in the nation, might have influenced these narrow outcomes but chose not to do so. In fact, he used his influence on the side of the plantation owners, giving as his reason an abhorrence of the prospect of Congress drawing boundaries for slavery. He communicated that severe view to President James Monroe, who may have been a little surprised; as noted earlier, Monroe had been beside Jefferson in the Congress during the debates over limiting slavery in 1784, when Jefferson had taken the opposite view. Then, Merrill Peterson assures us, "slavery had become in his [Jefferson's] mind a matter of fundamental national importance overriding questions of local autonomy." Then he had supported congressional action to decree "that after the year 1800 . . . there shall be neither slavery nor involuntary servitude in any of the said states, otherwise than in punishment for crimes, whereof the party shall have been convicted to have been personally guilty."[21]

In the debates of 1818 and 1819, the question of congressional line-drawing was raised by the Taylor Amendment freeing all black children born in Arkansas after 1819. That provision (so similar in intent to that Jefferson had supported in 1784 for the West except for Kentucky) was twice approved in the House of Representatives. It was defeated when Speaker Henry Clay broke an eighty-to-eighty tie, after Jefferson weighed in with the view that "spreading them [slaves] over a larger surface" would "dilute the evil everywhere." What was the evil he had in mind, we may ask? Was it slavery? If so, why had he done nothing to prevent its spread since 1784? Perhaps the evil he imagined was the presence of people of color, whether slave or free. As noted in earlier pages, Jefferson could not accept the concept of a multiracial society wherein free people of color would coexist with free people of his complexion; he did not share the high opinion of free blacks asserted by "noisy pretenders to exclusive humanity."[22]

There were two reinforcing ironies in this presence of the old Jefferson and the middle-aged Clay on the same side of the narrowly balanced scales. Both had been on the other side earlier. When Clay was young, in 1799, he had sounded like the young Jefferson, calling slavery an "enormous evil" and urging that slaves not only be freed but, once free, be given the "rights of citizens." An ambitious young politician could still say such things in Virginia in 1779 or in Kentucky in 1799. But by 1820 Clay had become the "Great Compromiser," always compromising between what the planters already had and the next thing they wanted. His next achievement was tipping the scales in Congress in favor of admitting Missouri as a slave state. That magnet under the table had grown in strength. And the Jefferson of 1784 had become the Jefferson of 1819. [23]

In 1822, the foes of slavery managed again to test the question of its expansion—for the last time during Jefferson's lifetime. They included language similar to that of the Hillhouse version of the Orleans Act in the draft of the plan of organization for Florida Territory. The planters were quick to discern the small print, however, and lest the benefits of Andrew Jackson's conquest of that new province be taken from them, they rallied and won— though only by a vote of twenty-three to twenty.[24]

The consequences appeared quickly. Within ten years "nearly all the desirable land in middle Florida had been purchased by speculators, much of it in large units which they held and then sold for ten dollars an acre." At the time, however, equivalent land in Alabama cost twenty-five dollars an acre. For comparison, we may note that the yeomen denied the best land could find in swampier places, or in areas more exposed to Seminole resistance, eighty-acre pieces at $1.25 per acre. The reason the land came so cheap, of course, was that the planters, speculators, and yeomen were subsidized by the rest of the nation's taxpayers. Not only did citizens of other states bear a large share of the cost of an almost continuous campaign against the Florida Indians. They also paid for the construction of the roads required to bring to market the cotton of inland planters: Florida's first highway was built for this purpose as a joint product of the army and a contractor driving slaves to do the work at public expense.[25]

Had the nation forbidden slavery in Florida, or west of some limit—perhaps that proposed by the New Englanders and supported by Jefferson in 1784, or perhaps that advocated by James Hillhouse in 1805–6, or those overcome by Clay's compromises—the system of raising staple crops with forced labor would have been compressed against that line. Amid the ensuing eddy, there would have been greater reason to heed the antislavery sentiment of the North and the Middle South. Without any such inhibition fixed upon human servitude, the frontier offered slavery a perverse version of Frederick Jackson Turner's famous "safety valve," a series, indeed, of valves. Having flowed through apertures opened before it in 1784, 1787, 1792, 1798, 1806, and 1820, slave-based agriculture spread its pernicious effects across the land. Sick and exhausted regions of the South became vast brownfields, acting, as brownfields do, to propel people to go elsewhere.

True, it was the loss of soil nutrients and the sickening of the land by favoring one set of microorganisms over another rather than the presence of chemical or dangerously radioactive contaminants that sent the planters and their coffles of enslaved workers westward. Nonetheless, the analogy helps us consider how pernicious land use accumulates negation, and how land adversely altered by human intervention retaliates by limiting thereafter what humans may do with it. Still, as noted in Chapter One, though choice may limit future choice, it may also force present choice. What if political choice had arrested the spread of slavery at a geographic line, and in the eddy so created the planters had been forced to decide what to do next?

Some of them anticipated some such event by taking steps to diversify their portfolios: one recalls Wade Hampton II at land auctions in Wisconsin and the investments of the Halifax Whigs of Virginia in Iowa farmland and in Northern industry, often in partnership with the Unionist nabobs of Natchez.[26]

Those who might have wished to remain on the land would have been forced to choose to replenish and renew what they already owned. In 1822, Elisha Mitchell of the University of North Carolina anticipated their need to do so before their dominance of the political process weakened, before they had to anticipate opposition to the use of the nation's armed forces and the public treasury to provide them with new lands through Indian removal, before the Arkansas and Missouri Compromises showed once more how difficult it was for the opponents of slavery to secure political limits to its expansion. Yet even in 1822, observing the degradation of the Southern landscape, Mitchell wrote: "As this system goes on, the planter will look down from the barren ridges he is tilling, upon the grounds from which his fathers reaped a rich harvest, but which are now desolate and abandoned, and enquire whether he cannot restore to them ancient fertility." How long must that system go on, we may ask, and how much land must be ruined? "Till he is driven by necessity to make this inquiry," Mitchell responded. Politics had not yet provided that necessity. The Ordinance of 1784 had failed. The Hillhouse Debates had had another outcome, and the occasion for benign necessity had been lost once again in the compromises just arranged in 1819–20. But it would come.[27]

16

The Virginians of Louisiana Decide
the Future of the Land

As soon as the Louisiana Purchase had been achieved, President Thomas Jefferson turned once more to its final negotiator, James Monroe. Having sent James Wilkinson to raise the Stars and Stripes over the parade ground of New Orleans at the end of 1803, Jefferson sought a more respectable yet equally manageable agent to conduct the civilian business of his new empire. Though his first choice may have been the Marquis de Lafayette, his more practical preference was for Monroe. It was traditional in colonial management that governors find personal profit in the territories put in their charge. Monroe had earned such a plum, indeed he had ripened it by arranging the acquisition of Louisiana on terms satisfactory to those with slaves to put to work and slaves to sell. Jefferson offered Monroe the opportunity twice.

He was refused twice, for Monroe interpreted the offers as manifesting Jefferson's desire to get him out of Madison's path to the presidency. Jefferson kept his temper and his settled plan, showing his irritation only when Monroe sought too often to secure for Fulwar Skipwith a profitable role in the affairs of Louisiana. On May 18, 1803, Monroe wrote Jefferson requesting that Skipwith be relieved of his guerrilla duties in Europe and granted retirement in a patronage post in the new province. Skipwith had admitted being "desirous of an appointment (Collector of the Port) at New Orleans," wrote Monroe, and "he has served long and faithfully here [Paris]. . . . Having known the direct and upright line of his conduct, through a period of great political embarrassment, I feel much interest in his future."[1]

Jefferson was unmoved and told Monroe that Skipwith must stay on station. He was, wrote the President, "much fitter for any matter of business (below that of diplomacy) which we may have to do in Europe." Below the level of diplomacy lay the tier of "scut work," in the language of intelligence. There would be no coming in from the cold. The Skipwiths at Prestwould were receding into Virginia's past and were of little use to the imperial Virginia of the nineteenth century.[2]

In the springtime of 1809, Skipwith appeared in Baton Rouge on his own—as he had appeared in Paris without Jefferson's sponsorship in 1793—to take charge of his lands along Bayou Sano. He had married a Flemish baroness in 1802. In 1805, his brother-in-law, an Anglo-Fleming variously spelling himself "Harris," "Herrisse," and "Harries," purchased for Skipwith the thirteen-hundred-acre property near Baton Rouge and a smaller spread next door for himself. Where did Harris get the money? Perhaps he and Skipwith were making use of the residue of the dowries brought them by their wives, daughters of a Flemish count. The sisters must have inherited considerable property, for the Skipwiths kept both a country house and a mansion in Paris. That was, however, before inflation swept Flanders in the wake of its conquest by the French, impoverishing many a landed family. It was also before Harris got his hands on what was left of the van den Clooster fortune. There is also the possibility that Skipwith was still in touch with Talleyrand, whose bankers were Flemings.[3]

When they first became established at Monte Sano, in 1809, the Skipwiths and the Harrises substantially elevated the social tone. It was not quite true to say—as it was said—that he was the *only* gentlemen, and she the *only* lady, present in the Florida Parishes; there was also the mysterious Edward or Edmund Randolph, a literary storekeeper of Pinckneyville. However, a Skipwith trumped a Randolph, and Fulwar Skipwith was remarkable even among Mr. Jefferson's students, "endowed," wrote an admiring nephew, "with more than average intelligence, well cultivated by a collegiate study, and by his cosmopolitan associations.... Of splendid physical development, he was more than six feet tall, straight as an arrow, with exactly enough flesh for his bone and muscle."[4]

Out of the Hills

In the Florida Parishes, awaiting this High Church scion of baronets, the Flemish countess he had married, and whatever carriages, portraits, slaves, silver, and retinue of servants they might muster, was a clan of Virginians of quite another class. The Kempers were sons of the hardscrabble, ridge, rock, and red-soil upland between the true Tidewater and the true Blue Ridge. Bitterly poor, they were hard men of a hard country who had learned to hate during revolutionary and civil bloodlettings, on a frontier where jayhawkers, bushwhackers, and Whig and Tory irregulars drygulched, ambushed, and burnt out each other. Worship on Sundays was in frame and log buildings not much larger than the slave cabins serving the estates of the Skipwiths. The Kempers' church was the one-room, one-story frame building with a stone chimney now known as the Bryan Baptist Meeting House. The hamlet of Sperryville, about a mile away from the Bryan church, was somewhat boutiquified in the 1990s,

but nothing can diminish the straightforward beauty of the scene it over-
looks, as the Thornton River comes tumbling out from hemlocks and granite
and begins to be domesticated into a brown, slow, and leisurely tidewater
stream.[5]

In another Piedmont church nearby preached the Reverend Craig, father-
in-law of Philemon Thomas, the man chosen in 1810 by the Kempers and
Skipwith to be commander of the armed forces of their West Florida Republic, when Thomas became known as the "Ajax of Revolution." There is a
splendid portrait of him by George Healy on display in the Pentagon Bar-
racks at Baton Rouge, looking every inch an Ajax, "tall and with a powerful
frame, with red hair, and clear blue eyes." (It might have gone easier for him
and his friends if they had had an Odysseus in Fulwar Skipwith. Skipwith
could spell—*that* he did better than Thomas. A local newspaper in St. Francisville, where Thomas maintained his "doggery" (grocery), reported in 1935
that he had displayed signs reading "Caughy for Sail" and "Akomidation fur
Man & Beest.")[6]

Thomas was as blunt an instrument as Ajax but without that ferocity the
Kempers showed when aggrieved. This is how they treated a man named
Kneeland:

> Reuben and Samuel . . . inflicted upon his naked back one hundred lashes,
> then one hundred more for their brother Nathan, who was absent. . . . [They]
> cut off his ears with a dull knife and permitted him to retire. These trophies
> of resentment were long preserved in spirits of wine, and hung up in one of
> the Kempers' parlor.[7]

Surely one would expect a different sort of bibelot in the drawing room at
Prestwould.

Around 1797, the patriarch of the Kempers, a Baptist preacher, and his
sons Reuben, Samuel, and Nathan, moved west, to Cincinnati, Ohio. They
were all over six feet in height and weighed over two hundred pounds. Reuben,
for example, was six-six, "as active as a cat, with a voice that rumbled like a
bass drum." In Cincinnati the father and all his sons found employment as
stevedores for Senator John Smith. Smith was also a Baptist preacher, but he
had turned storekeeper, provisioner to the armies sent by George Washington against the Indians, and land speculator in the Florida Parishes. His investments north of Baton Rouge and Monte Sano included 750 acres where
he announced plans to built a community called "New Valentia." He needed
a muscular garrison. The Kempers came to mind. Smith sent them forth to
New Valentia.[8]

The Kempers were of the right physique. But, Smith concluded—too
late—of the wrong temperament, for nature did not design them for subordination. Besides, there was that black cockade that Reuben Kemper had put on
his hat in 1803 in New Orleans. He and his brothers were Virginians, and

patriots, and averse to Spanish rule, while Smith's opportunity for a fortune in real estate—like Talleyrand's—depended upon making arrangements with the Spanish authorities that would remain good after American occupation. Reuben Kemper was just as much a rebel after Wilkinson's ceremony in the Place d'Armes as before; all he had done was to remove his incendiary intentions from the city to Smith's countryside, but still within the authority of Spain.[9]

Reuben and his brothers liked what they found in Smith's stockade and determined to stay. Smith sought a removal order from his friend the Spanish commandant, Don Carlos de Grand Pré. Don Carlos temporized, and by the time he summoned a posse against the Kempers they had made a fortress of their cabin. Grand Pré was forced to call out the militia; the Kempers fired some shots; Grand Pré called for cavalry and four gunboats from New Orleans.

As it turned out, neither the gunboats nor the reinforcements were required. Though the local militia was almost entirely American in origin, its members had acquired their land from Spain under the same procedures that had provided for Smith. No more enthusiastic about squatters than he, they drove the Kempers across the border into Mississippi Territory. The three brothers nursed their wrath in the village of Pinckneyville, finding common cause with Edward Randolph. Randolph may or may not have been among Jefferson's kinfolk descended from Sir John of Turkey Island (c. 1693–1736); he was certainly, however, a business partner of Clark's, and of Clark's partner, Don Juan Ventura Morales. That was pedigree enough in West Florida in 1804. Morales was feuding with Grand Pré and used Randolph to inflame the Kempers' resentment against his rival. Factionalism was as important as nationalism in Spanish West Florida.[10]

On August 7, 1804, the Kempers stormed back across the border at the head of a hundred men bearing a Declaration of Independence composed by Randolph for a Republic of West Florida. Anyone who doubts the value to revolution of literary skill at the Jeffersonian level should read the hash made on two great occasions in Florida. The first was composed by Randolph of Pinckneyville:

> When the sovereignty and independence of a nation have been destroyed by treachery or violence, the political ties which unite its different members are dissolved. Distant provinces no longer cherished or protected by the mother country, have the right to institute for themselves such forms of government as they may think conducive to their safety and happiness.[11]

The second was intended to give dignity to the Republic of East Florida but managed to leave out all invocations of grand assertions of principle derived from human nature, reducing them, as if embarrassed, to "interesting considerations":

> Whereas the inhabitants of East Florida, being called upon by a variety of the most interesting considerations to themselves and their posterity to emancipate themselves from the Spanish yoke and its galling effects and to take the management of their own affairs, into their own hand, and wishing to participate in the advantages of a government founded upon the principals [*sic*] of rational liberty [etc.].[12]

What was meant by "the sovereignty and independence of a nation"? Which nation? John Houstoun McIntosh and George Mathews were clear enough about that. They were leading a phagocytic filibuster to extend the American plantation system into East Florida, despite their self-description as "Patriots" and the formation by their followers of a "District of Elotchaway" of an ephemeral "Republic of Florida." On the other hand, Kemper and Randolph were almost certainly on their own. Though both the East Florida "Patriots" and West Florida Republicans were heading toward outcomes satisfactory to the Jefferson and Madison administrations, the West Floridians had failed to synchronize their watches with those being set in the City of Washington. President Jefferson was not disposed to permit his geopolitics to be conducted on a schedule set by eager volunteers. Thus the West Florida filibusters heard the whistle of an "offsides" penalty during the summer of 1804.

The Kemper Outrage

The Kempers withdrew again to Pinckneyville, and in the following fall the "Spanish" militia came after them into the territory of the United States. This new posse, sent by Grand Pré, was doubly provocative: it was led by Anglo-Americans calling themselves Spaniards, and it was supported by seven Negroes.

> The party were armed with armed with guns and clubs and provided with ropes. They forced the door, entered the room where Reuben Kemper was sleeping, dragged him from his bed, beat him with clubs, and then tied him. . . . Nathan was also severely beaten. . . . The party then gagged them by placing large sassafras roots in their mouths. Then tying a line around their necks they were made to run before the horses of the kidnappers, and were conducted to the Spanish line. At the same time a branch of this party had entered the tavern of Samuel Kemper at Pinckneyville, the proprietor of which they seized, beat with clubs, gagged and pinioned. . . . He, too, was conducted to the Spanish line, where all three of the unhappy brothers were delivered to Captain Solomon Alston.[13]

Though Alston, one of the area's medical doctors, was aligned with Grand Pré, another, Dr. Towles, had contrary political sentiments. Towles happened to be making a house call in the neighborhood and, as soon as he learned of the midnight events, he galloped to summon a detachment of American troops encamped across the Mississippi. When Dr. Towles arrived with them, they liberated the Kempers, captured the captors, and brought them all back across the 31st Parallel to appear before Judge Thomas Rodney, in Washington, Mississippi Territory.

The newspapers in the United States rose in righteous wrath about what they called "the Kemper Outrage," meaning what was done to the Kempers rather than what they had done. John Smith had set his match to tinder, though Governor Williams of Mississippi blamed Grand Pré. When John Randolph of Roanoke heard of the Kemper-Williams-Randolph version of events, he proposed to the House of Representatives that the army of the United States be sent forthwith into West Florida to set things right (perhaps the merchant of Pinckneyville *was* a Virginia Randolph).[14]

Armed intervention was not quite timely; it became so five years later, after the administration had time to digest the intelligence provided by Senator Smith. Smith was a Burrite and opposed to slavery, but he was also eager to get rich in Louisiana. Accordingly, he assiduously sustained his links to Burr, to Jefferson, and to the Spanish authorities. His networking was useful to the President, who sent the senator on an assignment to West Florida to sound out the sentiments of its Spanish officials in the event of a war with the United States. It was, said Jefferson, "inevitable." Smith had heard the same opinion from Burr and cheerfully agreed to make the reconnaissance. When he returned, he assured Jefferson that "the governor, the inferior officers, and the inhabitants generally, were not only friendly to the United States but were desirous of attaching themselves to it."[15]

1809–1810

James Madison became President in 1809, after Burr had been tried and exiled. Though Burr's experience as a warrior and statesman was no longer available for campaigns against the Spanish Empire, and though Madison was not of an imperial disposition, any disruption of the Spanish hold upon its colonies was an invitation to American adventure. The Spanish Bourbons had been deposed by Napoleon. Having defeated the French in Portugal, the Duke of Wellington was grinding his way northward toward Madrid to reinstall them, but so slowly that he took two years to reach the capital. In the meantime, the Creole elites of Spanish America were increasingly disaffected.[16]

On September 16, 1810, Padre Miguel Hidalgo y Costilla issued a Mexican declaration of independence, the *Grito de Dolores*. His revolution was at first successful: his armies seized the silver mines of the north, captured San Antonio, and appeared on the southern edge of that no-man's-land of brigands, escaped slaves, and refugees from political oppression some called "the

Free State of the Sabine." Hidalgo went no further, for the inhabitants of the Free State would acknowledge no sovereign.

James Madison was in a dilemma. Beset by a public eager for conquest, he had not the means to defend his own shores, much less the capacity to answer the testosteronic ambitions of an adolescent republic. With the tools at hand, the United States could not have stood off attack from any European power of the first class. The American "fleet" was so reduced in size that it would scarcely have composed a squadron for the British. Albion ruled the waves as Napoleon ruled the European earth. Mr. Madison's army was disgracefully led, penuriously provisioned, and undermanned. France might make a triumphal return to the Americas if Napoleon were to win in Europe. If things went otherwise, and the British managed to defeat him, Madison's puny armed forces could offer no effectual obstruction to the British should they desire to scoop up the remnants of the fiefs of Spain in the Americas. The immediate, irremediable fact was that without provoking the British he could not provide any measure of stability to those Spanish provinces bordering the United States.[17]

The Jeffersonian legacy of little government reduced the Administration in Washington to reliance upon sponsored filibusters to achieve its foreign policies. So weak was "the center" that sometimes those policies could be forced upon it by any large number of armed citizens willing to go to war on their own. George Washington had convinced Congress to pass the Neutrality Act of 1794 because he feared such a situation. Forgetting the stern standards of Washington's statesmanship, however, the feeble governments of Jefferson and Madison acquiesced in the territorial ambitions of the planters and inflamed the ardor of filibusters for glory and pillage. While George Mathews and John Houstoun McIntosh were launching their assault upon St. Augustine in 1810, Madison's governor of Mississippi Territory, David Holmes, wrote Secretary Smith to reiterate Senator Smith's opinion that the people of that Spanish province were—like the "local authorities" of East Florida—longing for liberation from Spain. Once again, a governor and the Secretary agreed upon a strategy of manufactured destiny, offering assurance of American support for an operation in the customary stages: a revolution, then day-lily independence, then merger into the United States.[18]

As usual, "local authority" would be required to provide the revolutionary nucleus, but Holmes wished to assure the "Patriots" that the distant authority would back them up. Naturally enough, they "feared to make known such a desire or to take the necessary step until they knew the attitude of [the] President." Smith drafted a response offering only measured encouragement and sent it for review to the President. Madison raised the ante, ordering Holmes to use "every means within the limits of executive authority" to take advantage of any "internal convulsions" that might be ignited. Was this too subtle? Madison inquired of Smith whether or not the administration's policy should be made more explicit: "Would it not be advisable to apprize Governor H[olmes] confidentially of the course adopted as to W[est] F[lorida] and to have his cooperation?" Holmes needed no coaching. He assured Smith that West Florida could be gained without bloodshed. On July 17, 1810, Madison instructed Secretary Smith to tell Holmes to keep the militia of Mississippi Territory mobilized "to take care of the rights and interests of the U. S."[19]

On June 14, 1810, Governor Claiborne, after his own conference with Madison, had written "under the sanction of the President" to William Wykoff in Mississippi, a territorial judge, militia colonel, member of the legislature of West Florida, and cotton planter. According to Fulwar Skipwith, reporting what Wykoff imparted to him, Claiborne's letter was written "urging him to mount his horse, if necessary, to travel among and stimulate the inhabitants of [Spanish] Florida to declare themselves independent and that he—Governor C.—or the government would defray the expenses." That is not exactly what the letter said, but it was reasonable to believe it to be what it was meant to be thought to have said. The Madison administration still had to consider the Neutrality Act of 1794. Madison ordered copies of his letter sent out to people who might be expected to make yet more copies, including Holmes and Mathews, both of whom were notoriously chatty. By using Claiborne as his intermediary to Wykoff, Madison was preserving deniability. As Skipwith soon demonstrated, misunderstanding was easy. Perhaps from Madison's point of view, it was desirable.[20]

Skipwith and Randolph

Skipwith later wrote that the claim of the United States to West Florida from the Mississippi to the Perdido had been discussed with "the European Powers . . . whilst I was at Paris" and that a candid assertion that that territory was included in the Louisiana Purchase would be "contrary to their policy and doctrine." It would be "more satisfactory" for a convention of "honest cultivators of the soil" to provide a "request" to be absorbed into the United States than for the American army simply to march in and take it. A year later, Skipwith, to whose doorstep rode Wykoff on his rounds, concluded "that Gov. C. and the President both were highly delighted at seeing us led on and that the President . . . [was] determined to occupy this country, after we should subvert the Spanish . . . [quite willing that] a Floridian [should] beat him [the Spanish governor] in battle, and conquer the country, and get possession of the public stores, and [then] . . . all [would be] washed, except the poor Floridian, in holy water . . . and . . . sweet to the palate of the . . . Administration."[21]

The rhetoric of the second West Florida Republic was improving. Skipwith had replaced Randolph as draftsman for declarations of independence, and he had been schooled in Paris to blend references to the Rights of Man into an appeal to law and order:

> Betrayed by a magistrate [the King of Spain] whose duty was to have provided for the safety and tranquility of the people . . . and exposed to all the evils of a state of anarchy . . . , it becomes our duty to provide for our own security, as a free and independent State . . . calling upon all foreign nations to respect this our declaration, acknowledging our independence, and giving us such aid as may be consistent with the laws and usages of nations.[22]

A little before dawn on September 23, 1810, eighty armed men, having so declared their political principles, appeared before a decayed Spanish fort at Baton Rouge defended only by a handful of sick, elderly, and untrained Spanish soldiers, commanded by a brave young lieutenant, Louis de Grand Pré, son of Smith's friend Don Carlos. The little garrison was apparently unaware of a tunnel into the stockade from the riverbank. A picked squad of assailants was led through it by a defector. Emerging from the tunnel, their leader brayed to young Grand Pré and his handful: "Ground your arms and you shall not be hurt!"[23]

> The young man thought himself bound in honor to maintain a trust committed to him; he rejected the summons to surrender, and when . . . [more] Americans swarmed over the ruinous bastions they found Louis Grand Pré almost alone defending his flag. He was killed.[24]

The attackers shouted, "Hurrah Washington!" One of them applied a rifle butt to the skull of the Spanish governor of West Florida, Charles de Hault de Lassus de Luzière, who was barely rescued by General Thomas from being bayoneted. The enthusiasm of the troops rose further when the strongbox of de Lassus was discovered, containing six thousand dollars. Three days later, the victors declared West Florida to be independent and made Skipwith chief of state. In his inaugural address he progressed rapidly from independence to dependence:

> The blood that flows in our veins like the tributary streams which form and sustain the Father of Rivers encircling our delightful country will return, if not impeded, to the heart of our parent country. The genius of Washington . . . stimulates that return, and would frown upon our cause should we attempt to change its course.[25]

Skipwith and his junta quickly communicated with Holmes, assuring him that their "unqualified declaration of independence" was a cardboard firewall. They professed to have no desire to stand between the United States government and the acquisition of West Florida. Instead, they claimed an "unalterable determination to assert rights as an integral part of the United States" and solicited a "body of militia"—and perhaps some gunboats—to paralyze further Spanish resistance. Holmes was asked to inform Madison of their desire to be taken "under immediate and special protection, as an integral and unalienable portion of the United States."[26]

Skipwith—and Washington—had set the tone. The Kempers went on a mini-filibustering expedition against Mobile to join forces at McIntosh Bluffs with the regional gentry led by John and James Caller, both militia colonels eager for action. Kemper reported that the local judge, and the commander of the regular army garrison at Fort Stoddert, Captain Edmund Gaines, were "definitely friendly," as was Joseph P. (in this instance, for Pulaski) Kennedy, once an ornament to Washington society and now chief of the Mobile Society, whose charter was the acquisition of West Florida.[27]

With a multitude of motivations and a few score insurrectionists, Kemper and Kennedy marched on the Tombigbee. They were, they said, the advance guard of the advance guard. Civilization—slaves, staple crops, and planter-investors on a grand scale—was on its way. Kemper, Kennedy, and Caller provided flatboats and roused the neighborhood. We are told by a local chronicler that there were plenty of "ardent spirits" along the Tombigbee—literally. As a result, Kemper and Kennedy sallied forth befuddled to Mobile to stand below its battlements and demand its surrender from Governor Folch. Folch assessed their befuddlement, sent a few volleys of grapeshot over their heads, and sent them packing to the old Indian fields along Minette Bay. They awaited tents and reinforcements, but instead of tents they got a "keelboat laden with [more] whiskey, corn, flour and bacon. . . . The whiskey put the whole expedition into good spirits. Glowing speeches were made by Kennedy, who pointed them to ancient Mobile, which, he said, they would shortly capture." It began to rain. There was some shelter upstream, so the liberation army retreated another twelve miles to a grove where, "with an abundance of whiskey and several fiddlers," another celebration ensued.[28]

Folch, informed of their "frolic" by "an evil old man in the neighborhood, who often drank with them," unchivalrously sent two hundred soldiers and militiamen to accost them "while the poor fellows were singing and dancing. . . . At 11 o'clock at night, [the force from Mobile] fired upon them" as no gentleman would. After just this much gunfire, this "Kemper Expedition" collapsed.[29]

Complexities in Baton Rouge

Things went better for a time at Baton Rouge. Holmes reported that "the views of our government have been in a great measure realized," while Skipwith celebrated victory in messages to his friends in the Virginia network—his son-in-law Bolling Robertson, General John Mason, and John Graham of the State Department. But he overreached as he had in Paris, forgetting that he was in West Florida to serve Virginia, not to restore his fortunes. Apparently recalling Talleyrand's lesson about the importance of timing in West Florida land transactions, he sent to his betters in Washington a message to which he should have given deeper thought. Writing for himself and the other rebel leaders, he asked compensation for himself and his colleagues in land grants as well as reimbursement by the federal government for indebtedness incurred in the course of their performing what they clearly perceived as an assigned task.[30]

Despite all his years of training, Skipwith was naive. Madison was not a popular President and was not disposed to court impeachment by admitting that he had sponsored violation of laws he was sworn to uphold. Still—the Neutrality Act was on the books. Skipwith might expect some solicitude from Monroe, his sponsor all these years, but Madison no longer had use for him—in West Florida at least. With the Baton Rouge district already in hand, with its "local authority" on record as desiring it to be included in the United States, and with Napoleon once more occupying the full attention of the British, the time had come to assert that the area had always been included in the Louisiana Purchase. On October 27, 1810, the President so asserted: the United States, he told his Cabinet, had jurisdiction over the entire Gulf Coast between the Mississippi and the Perdido River. Madison did not say so very loudly, though, for he refrained from informing Congress of his claim until his annual message on December 5.

By then, Claiborne had hastened to Washington, Mississippi, from Washington, D.C. He arrived on December 1, bearing Madison's instructions to Holmes that the Mississippi militia should suppress any local advocacy of independence. Once in position, Claiborne wrote Secretary Smith that he was prepared to do his part "to guard against the intrigues of certain individuals . . . and a few adventurers . . . of desperate character and fortunes, who have lately joined the convention army." A detachment of troops from Wilkinson's command took their stations nearby while agents went forth to "ascertain the general sentiments of the people, and particularly the leaders."[31]

There was reason for urgency. The British were not quite absorbed by their contests with Napoleon, it appeared, and might, after all, weigh in to support their Spanish allies. The slave populations of Florida and Mexico and the Indians were unpredictable. When masters fell out, slaves and aggrieved neighbors might discern opportunity. There were the usual rumors of British or Spanish agents stirring up slave and Indian unrest, giving Holmes cause to write Secretary Smith that things could get out of hand quickly if steps were not taken to bring the West Florida republicans to heel.[32]

Skipwith at Bay

Skipwith was apparently bewildered by the approach of Wilkinson's troops. Amazed, he said, that there was such "an armed force in the neighborhood," he assured the Assembly of West Florida that they had a "right of self-government despite the imperative tone in which the President summoned them to submit." The assemblymen responded that they were willing "to unite with him in proper resistance." An assister had suddenly become a resister. Why? Did Skipwith feel betrayed, or did he still hope to add to his holdings of cotton land, or both?[33]

Whatever his motivation—my own guess is that his indignation genuinely expressed a sense of betrayal—Skipwith produced a succession of manifestos proclaiming that he had "retired to the fort of Baton Rouge . . . [where rather] than surrender the country unconditionally and without terms . . . [he would] with twenty men only, if a greater force could not be procured, surround the flag staff and die in defense of the Lone Star flag!" Melodrama is sometimes amusing, but Skipwith's was not in good taste. At the foot of that flag staff, ground into the dust and gravel, there were already bloodstains—those of Louis de Grand Pré.[34]

Claiborne had no desire to humiliate Skipwith, so he sought out Holmes as an intermediary—another Virginian of the same class. Holmes was to go to Baton Rouge escorted only by "a few gentlemen of respectability"—but not too far in advance of gunboats, a troop of Isaac Johnson's dragoons, and Colonel Covington's infantry. A day or two passed after Holmes's arrival, providing Skipwith with time for contemplation. Then, abandoning his flag staff, he wrote Madison that he would welcome instructions from the mother country—perhaps one should say "father country" in the light of his oratorical references to George Washington—insisting only that he wished to "resist dishonor [and] repel any wanton outrage to . . . [the] feelings" of his followers.[35]

Just before the gunboats appeared and Covington's regulars began landing, a series of dignified conversations with Holmes avoided any further fuss. Claiborne assured his superiors that his fellow Virginian had been moved to "imprudence of expression" because "his feelings were I suppose wounded." Skipwith made a concession speech in which he may well have been speaking the literal truth, declaring that he never thought of giving "an order that would lead to the shedding of a single drop of American blood." Claiborne congratulated him on his "correct" conduct, reporting to Madison and Smith that "we are on good terms, and I believe he is sincerely disposed to promote the interests of the United States. The sudden fall of the State of Florida evidently affected him, and I suspect he still thinks that the local authorities as established here by the people ought to have been consulted, and perhaps treated with previously to the taking possession of the country by the United States."[36]

Claiborne reported that others had informed him that Skipwith wished a formal recognition of sales of land under the Spanish authorities but that "it is very certain that few of the citizens hold lands under what are called Morali's [Morales] titles. I had suspected that Mr. Skipwith was concerned in that speculation, but I learn to the contrary, nor does he seem in his conversation with me to take any interest in the matter." Perhaps that is how it seemed to Claiborne, but Skipwith—like Senator Smith—did not disguise to others his interest in seeing Spanish land grants engraved in American title books. The land records at St. Helena, Louisiana, show that both he and his wife possessed not only their plantation land on the Bayou Sano but also other holdings in West Florida, some in the area disputed between the United States and Spain. Furthermore, he had written John Graham on June 20, 1808, saying that he was not only interested in West Florida but also in "a claim to an undivided part of a tract of land on the Ouachita, to which I must look for an asylum, or at least for the means of providing for a family." This was the Maison Rouge Tract he acquired through Daniel Clark.[37]

The Convention had instructed Skipwith as its President to seek statehood or territorial status for West Florida with a provision "that it should be recognized as having full title to its public lands" and that its proprietors receive a cash grant from the United States of one hundred thousand dollars. Other states and territories came into the Union without acquiring all public lands; in those cases those lands went to the United States itself, except for those granted back to them by the Congress. If Skipwith was treated a little brusquely, it was because those in charge of matters in Washington were making it clear to him that he was asking too much. He might serve the interest of the expansion of the United States and the Cotton Kingdom, but his masters would decide who would receive what benison in public land. Having administered a gentle rap across Skipwith's knuckles, Claiborne congratulated him on his new correctness and provided General Thomas with his sobriquet "Ajax of the late Revolution."[38]

Haiti Again

It has often been written that the leaders of the West Florida uprising were humiliated and forever disavowed by Madison and Monroe. It was in fact not so, as the State Department historian of the matter, Augustus Ingram, discovered: Skipwith "did not suffer in the estimation of the administration, for lengthy correspondence on file . . . indicates that in 1813 he was entrusted by Monroe . . . with a confidential mission to Santo Domingo or Haiti. A certain James Gillespie was also connected with this mission. It is believed that the object of his mission was to obtain permission from General Pétion to establish a base on the island for American vessels during the war with England."

One circle was now complete: Louisiana had come into the Cotton King-dom in 1803 because Napoleon and Thomas Jefferson had failed to starve out General Pétion's predecessor, Toussaint Louverture. In the process, however, the American government had forfeited the base provided it by Toussaint on the island. Ten years later, Mr. Madison, now President rather than Secretary of State, sought to strengthen the defense of Louisiana by reestablishing that base so that American vessels might harass the British from the rear.[39]

Skipwith was unable to find a captain who would convey him past the British navy to Haiti, but a subagent, a "Mr. Taylor," made it through and established himself at Port au Prince. Taylor was still under Skipwith's direc-tion on March 23, 1815, when they were informed that the peace treaty with the British signed at Ghent had made it no longer necessary to deal with the black regime of Pétion. The services of Mr. Taylor would no longer be needed. And Skipwith was sent a commission to go back to Paris, where the old re-gime had been restored by the allies victorious over Napoleon.[40]

It might have been like old times. Skipwith, the sender of guava jellies, had merely to return to the service of his kinsman Mr. Jefferson's protégé Mr. Monroe, who was still professing to regard Skipwith almost as if they were still the "particular friends" of 1794. Thomas Sumter wrote from Rio de Janeiro that, good fellow that he was, Skipwith had fallen into bad company who were responsible for the mess in West Florida. He had not, however, fallen out with Monroe. He did not undertake his third assignment to Paris, and as soon as Monroe became President he sent Skipwith another commission, now for the convenient, comfortable, and lucrative post of Receiver of Public Moneys for Lands at St. Helena, in the Florida Parishes. Though he failed in a run at the United States Senate, he remained a power in Louisiana politics; he was not only elected to the Senate of Louisiana but was elevated to be its presid-ing officer. (He occupied that role during Andrew Jackson's military occupa-tion of New Orleans in 1814–15, and the two had a bizarre altercation. Skipwith sought to preserve the prerogatives of the legislature and Jackson took him to be lukewarm in his patriotism. This tale had no conceivable relationship to land policy and no consequence except to deny to Skipwith a more lucrative patronage post. It is therefore relegated to the section "Fulwar Skipwith and Andrew Jackson" in the Appendix, p. 260.)

Other circles of history were closing as the Florida Parishes settled within Louisiana. Skipwith's office in St. Helena lay in the midst of his own cotton lands and contained title deeds for estates in the same parish that had been the subjects of the Livingston "cherry-picking" session in Paris interrupted by Thomas Sumter. Though the records of that epoch are not too easy to find in that land office, it is entirely possible that among them are other titles to other cotton fields bearing witness to Skipwith's discussions with Talleyrand about West Florida plantation land. And among Skipwith's files and ledgers resting within the library building at Louisiana State University in Baton Rouge there is a letter of recommendation for him from Talleyrand. No doubt it recognized Skipwith's role in the arrangements between Talleyrand's master and Thomas Jefferson for the sale and purchase of Louisiana and was also intended to take some of the sting out of Skipwith's humiliating exit from France after he had been so useful to Talleyrand privately.[41]

As the years passed, Skipwith's insistence that as President of West Florida he had acted as agent of the Madison administration became less of an embarrassment. The land claims he had sought in 1811 had been confirmed. He had been placed in charge of the land office where their continuity could be assured. In comfort of spirit and pocketbook, he could return to the leisurely life of his Virginian forbears.

> At candle-light he and his young associate would meet by the parlor fireside, on each side of which was a chair, some fancy model for his nephew, and on the opposite side was a cushioned big-armed, high-backed veritable chair of state, and when the governor reclined himself cozily in his familiar seat, memories of Marly, Versailles, Paris, Bonaparte, Barras, Sieyes, and Talleyrand flowed from his mouth in polished phrases as smoothly as water from a gurgling fountain.
>
> On one side of the chair of state was placed a small round table on which his servants had placed a long candle in a high candlestick, a large decanter of water, a sugar dish and tongs, a decanter holding a quart of whiskey, and a large meerschaum, by the side of which reposed a tiny tobacco pouch. On the other side of the chair of state was placed a basket full of seed-cotton and an empty basket to hold the cotton seed when picked. To pick that basket of cotton was the task of the evening. He might engage in animated narratives of interviews with the First Consul or the Emperor, or with some other great man of those days of great deeds, but the cotton picking went on mechanically and monotonously all the same. He never paused in his task while drawing the most fascinating pictures selected from the wildest panorama. . . . He did not even pause . . . to mix himself a drink. That indispensable part of the drama devolved upon his young relative who had become familiar with the properties of whiskey, sugar and water by nightly practice in mixing for the old gentleman.
>
> As the night wore on the results began to be more clearly developed. The candle was flickering in its socket. The water decanter was empty, the tobacco pouch was empty, and the basket of cotton-seed was empty. But the basket of picked cotton was nearly full, and the Governor was quite full!
>
> Nevertheless, after bidding his nephew a ceremonious good night, he would back himself out of the room with all the grace of a courtier of the ancien régime. When the curtain dropped on the last act . . . he was as majestic, dignified, and graceful in his carriage . . . as he was at the start; neither time, talk, or whiskey had the power to unsteady the legs of the late Governor of West Florida![42]

Fulwar Skipwith was finally home, the hurly-burly over, free to sit in the parlor of a Creole plantation house amusing himself by separating cotton seeds from cotton fibers in the old way, as it was done by slaves, Indian women, and the yeomen's wives of the Jersey Settlements, before Eli Whitney, Thomas Jefferson, and Andrew Jackson changed the world.

The great event of his life and Jefferson's was the Louisiana Purchase. Doubling the extent of the American imperial republic, it multiplied many more times than that its power and influence. Whatever crops might be grown along the Great River, control of that artery meant control of the body of the continent. The Mississippi had not been permitted to fall into the hands of a strong European power such as France or Britain.

And there were the Florida Parishes on the northern coast of the Gulf; no merchant could have wished to abandon to others a coast indented with such splendid harbors. It was essential that after the Purchase in 1803 the Virginia Dynasty should arrange to acquire that shoreline as well, in increments ending with the exhausted withdrawal of Spain from Florida in 1819. By then, that ancient empire had been chivvied out of its last holdings in North America by nips and bites, by filibustering, and staged insurrections producing brief independence, by coercive purchases and official American invasions.

Over the course of Skipwith's life and Jefferson's, and within the southern portion of the acquisitions bounded by the Gulf, the Atlantic, and the Spanish possessions lying beyond the Purchase, a sequence of decisions had been made consigning province after province of agricultural land to the plantation system. Hard fought on the land itself and justified each time by bare majorities in the Congress of the United States, these successive triumphs of the Slave Power might have been prevented. Had more energy been applied to achieve Mr. Jefferson's Lost Cause, the land might have been devoted instead to a culture of free and independent yeomen. In the absence of that commitment, the planters' lust for land was slaked, and those among them who had worn out the productivity of their soil for their chosen staple crops were provided new land to wear out and new markets for the sale of their surplus slaves.

Skipwith's Florida

We began our discussion of Fulwar Skipwith's service in Paris by recording his statement of "devotion to . . . the wishes of the French minister, Mr. Talleyrand, and . . . [to] the wishes of my personal and political friends at that critical period," especially "Mssrs. Jefferson, Madison, [and] Monroe." Thereafter, we observed how these great men showed their own devotion to expanding the plantation system into the rich lands of north central Florida, Talleyrand as a private speculator, and Jefferson, Madison, and Monroe as planters serving other planters. Once more, now, we return to the land, to follow the consequences of their success in bringing Florida into the realm of King Cotton.

Skipwith's properties were in West Florida, but the core of the Florida cotton belt lay around Tallahassee, in the region known to the Indians as

Apalachee. It had been farmed for centuries. Its open fields had been so densely populated by Indians that even after de Soto and a succession of epidemics swept through it, thousands of Apalachee could assemble in a single gathering to discuss a peace treaty with the Spaniards and a nearby nation (one friar reported thirty thousand, but let us assume half that number). Though numerous, they could organize themselves quickly for war, or for hunting, or for planting because they practiced a diversified agriculture. According to de Soto's chroniclers their fields of corn, beans, and squash stretched for miles. Though they kept the brush down, and drove herds of deer, with annual winter fires, they did not move from one swiddened forest to another. They stayed in place—until the diseases and the Spanish and the British arrived. After the Great Dying of the sixteenth and seventeenth centuries, and the holocaust of 1702–4, their now fallow fields filled with brush until they were reoccupied by Creeks and Seminoles. Both Alexander McGillivray and William Augustus Bowles influenced the lives of the new occupants: McGillivrary's Creek state might have included them, and Bowles's Muskogean Republic asserted dominion over them.[43]

When McGillivray and Bowles were gone, Talleyrand, Jefferson, Madison, and Monroe arranged for these native farmers to be replaced by cotton planters. Thereafter, according to Charles Hudson, "the impact of the Apalachees on the forest cover was as nothing compared with the impact of . . . cotton plantations. . . . Erosion and gullying were so great on the cotton plantations in the Tallahassee hills that the land lost as much as three-quarters of its topsoil by 1860." Twentieth-century maps showing the Florida counties requiring the most intense rehabilitation if there were to be any hope of restoring them to productive uses can be overlaid without much adjustment upon earlier maps of the concentration of slaves and the highest percentage of large plantations in 1850. These can in turn be readily superimposed on maps showing the densest locations of Spanish missions between 1575 and 1704. Those missions were placed in the midst of the largest numbers of sedentary Indians—Indians practicing sustainable agriculture. Overgrazing by cattle and sheep has destroyed much of the evidence of native agriculture farther south in central Florida, but though the friars set loose huge herds upon the Tallahassee hills they did not fundamentally alter their very topography, as well as their health, as did cotton culture.

The story of Euro-American use of the land of Florida has begun with family farming and has ended with plantations—with a great deal of statesmanship in between. A multitude of choices were made during the course of this long transition, and are still being made, changing at each point of decision the circumstances limiting what new choices are thereafter possible.[44]

Epilogue

The Jeffersonian Legacy:
The Civil War and the Homestead Act

As Thomas Jefferson predicted it must sooner or later, in 1861 the American nation came to a resolution of great questions long delayed:

Would limits be set to the expansion of slavery into the territories of the West?

Would the leaders of the United States advance the ideal of a republic of free and independent yeomen by giving them preference in the allocation of the public domain, or would they receive only what was left after its most desirable portions were wholesaled in aggregates to speculators and to plantation owners?

Would the South shake itself free of British colonial-imperialism by diversifying its agriculture and then enlarging the worldview of its planter elite?

Would the requirements of the land itself be heeded—would *its* voice be heard—before it was so weakened as to be incapable of supporting a diverse and independent economy?

The North had become able to manufacture nearly all its own needs and also to produce surplus food and fiber for both foreign and domestic markets. The South, by contrast, was still importing most of its tools, clothing, and luxury goods. Its obsession with cotton, produced in haste and by slave labor, depreciated its land, and thus reduced its ultimate power base. The reliance of its production system upon slaves was becoming disagreeable to a growing element of British aristocratic opinion. Quite aside from what they were doing to their slaves, the planters were alienating many enlightened middle-class people by their increasingly repressive treatment of other whites. It seemed to many that the South was turning the benign face of Jefferson's agrarian legacy to the wall and giving honored space instead to portraits of filibusters and backwoods caudillos.

Andrew Jackson was considerably more than a caudillo, a man of such complexity moved by such contradictory impulses and external pressures that we might have presented the final chapters of our story, as the South committed itself to the way of life that finally imploded in 1861, through his career. But Jackson came into his full powers after the course of Southern history had already been set; his famous Indian removal policy was Jefferson's, as was his disinclination to accept the diversification of the Southern economy. It seemed best instead, therefore, to follow Fulwar Skipwith through the earlier, formative phases of the tale, as he traversed mud-spattered the alleyways and forest paths while the carriages of the great ones and the bright uniforms of the cavalry—and the coffles of slaves—jostled him into the underbrush. Both Skipwith and Jackson fought in the Revolution and lived into the youth of Abraham Lincoln. While Jackson was building his political and military base, erasing the effects of multiracial resistance on the part of men such as William Augustus Bowles, and undoing by force of arms the achievements of the statesmanship of Alexander McGillivray, Skipwith was forfeiting his base in Virginia to serve the interests of the Jeffersonians in the West Indies, in Paris throughout the Louisiana Purchase negotiations, and in Baton Rouge.

When Skipwith and Jackson came to their confrontation in New Orleans in 1814, Old Hickory had managed to batter his way through the system of Virginian alliances that had used Skipwith to achieve indirectly what it could not do by Jacksonian methods. The central sections of this book set forth those intertwined stories in the context of economic forces, chiefly those of international textile colonial-imperialism. And we have tried to look outside, from time to time, through the windows of plantations, counting-houses, palaces, stockades, and factories, to observe what was happening to the land.

Statesmanship and Self-Deception

We have sought to attend as well to what could be seen only in its effects, as the wind must be seen, the swirl of invisible forces emerging from the magnets under the table. The most powerful of these were economic and environmental, though outcomes were altered time after time by human choice. The most important choices made by any single statesman for the future of the South arose from the preferences, prejudices, and policies of Thomas Jefferson. We have striven to present his choices within the range of possible outcomes provided him, and the South, by its own soil, climate, and topography, and also by the enormous suction exerted upon him and the planter class by demand for cotton from manufacturers in Britain.

Yet all the while Jefferson's character made some choices more likely than others, contributing two elements to the planters' self-deceptions. Though they did not mix their own labor with the soil, he provided his Proximity Principle, offering them derivative status within the chosen people of God. Those who were convinced of that gospel could therefore persuade themselves that they occupied a higher order of being from that of townsmen, merchants, or manufacturers. Secondly, there was Jefferson's beggar-thy-buyer policy, the contra-mercantilism with which, in the 1780s, Jefferson and Madison had responded to British inhibitions on American trade by seeking to change British behavior by inhibitions upon British trade. This policy reached its ultimate expression in Jefferson's Embargo of 1807, when, in retaliation against the British Orders in Council, he attempted to cut off international trade. It was successful neither in its processes nor in its objects. It was pounding a child's fist against a steel gorget. Yet Jefferson's example encouraged the South to think that sellers could control the behavior of buyers, even when those buyers had other sources of supply. Southern statecraft absorbed Jefferson's contra-mercantilist rhetoric along with a perverse version of his agrarianism. By the 1850s, the planters of South Carolina, led by James Henry Hammond, came to believe that by withholding their cotton they could force British intervention in American politics on Southern terms. In his "King Cotton" speech in 1858, Hammond posed his famous rhetorical question: "What would happen if no cotton was furnished for three years?" and offered his famously foolish answer: "Britain would topple headlong."[1]

Thus was Jefferson and Madison's policy of the 1780s revived and Jefferson's Embargo of 1807 reborn: Jefferson had written Charles Pinckney of South Carolina that the "manufacturing and navigating states" could be forced to abandon their resistance to the planters' pressing slavery into Missouri if Southern cotton were withheld from them. "After a little trial," he assured Pinckney, they would "think better, and return to the embraces of their natural and best friends."[2]

In 1861, the South tested that proposition by withholding its cotton in a neo-Embargo that merely completed the effects of a Northern blockade. The Confederate Vice President, Alexander Stephens, watched cotton pile up on the wharves and assured his compatriots that "our cotton is . . . the tremendous lever by which we will work our destiny." The *Memphis Argus* urged its readers to back up the process all the way, to "keep every bale of cotton on the plantation. Don't send a thread to New Orleans or Memphis till England and France have recognized the Confederacy—not a thread." This was simply a re-application of the delusion expressed by Jefferson in 1797: "Nature has given us . . . in our commerce . . . if properly managed . . . a better instrument [than war] for obliging the interested nations of Europe to treat us with justice."[3]

Stephens had insufficiently assessed the relationship between supply and demand. The Southern states had shipped so much cotton between 1858 and

1861 that the British millers had a huge backlog of finished cloth on hand. Nor had he realized how well the British had absorbed their own lessons of the years from 1775 through1795, when they had attempted without success to diversify their sources of cotton away from the American mainland toward new plantations in the West Indies. As noted in Chapter Eight, the owners of private land on those islands were doing so well with sugar that they had little incentive to accommodate geopolitics in which they had no stake. In the 1840s and 1850s, that experience instructed Britain how to provide incentives to landowners in Asia and North Africa to undertake conversion to cotton. In 1861, these default producers were able to meet those requirements left unsatisfied by the inventories of cotton goods the British had built in anticipation of Southern foolishness.

By that time, there was little danger that such a strategy would affront the American North. It was going its own diversified way. As a result of the success of family farming in the North, its profitable interaction with Northern industry, and the arrival of large numbers of immigrants becoming prosperous with astonishing rapidity, the North had become a better market for British manufactures than the South. Besides, Britain was a steady customer for its grain. Accordingly, King Corn replaced King Cotton. This new North Atlantic symbiosis throve; the South was left in a commercial eddy. When there were crop failures in Europe, the North was ready to supply food to the mills and the millers.[4]

Once upon a time, the Governor's Council of Virginia had assured the British manufacturers that if the planter aristocracy were assured a good market for the staples of its agriculture it would abandon any "new fangled" notions of manufacturing for their own needs. Amid the American Civil War, the Crown's Solicitor General was asked to consider the South's request that the Royal Navy break the Northern blockade of Southern ports and used the same phrase—"new fangled"—to dismiss such nonsense. Why should a nation that had made blockading a prime instrument of policy renounce it just to serve the needs of a distressed and fading trading partner? The Solicitor General concluded:

[There should be no] new fangled notions and interpretations of international law which might make it impossible for us effectively at some future day to institute any blockade, and destroy our naval authority.[5]

Mr. Gladstone, Britain's Prime Minister, had granted to Jefferson Davis that the South had formed an army and a navy and also seemed to be forming a new "power of the earth." In this rare instance, however, Gladstone failed to heed the sentiment of his own nation. Its moral precepts were finally coming into coincidence with its free trade principles, obviating any lingering nostalgia for the old planter-mercantilist alliance. Britain's abstention from support to the Confederacy and its refusal to break the Northern blockade were statements of a preference for customers—and for untrammeled commerce—over any single set of suppliers, however well-mannered and familiar.

The planters revolted from the United States in 1861 in the belief that fear of the loss of a cotton supply would also discourage the North from any action to arrest their departure from the Union. Davis's application of the beggar-thy-buyer doctrine, failing to take account of the moral force of abolitionism or the importance of Northern grain to European consumers, also discounted the value of Northern consumers to the British manufacturers. At precisely the right moment after the Battle of Antietam was fought at the end of 1862, Abraham Lincoln issued his Emancipation Proclamation, and British opinion swung decisively toward support of the North.

During the course of the War for the Union, the South was itself divided. The Thousand-Foot line reasserted its importance all the way from the ridge where Thomas Jefferson stood at Harpers Ferry, observing the confluence of the Shenandoah and Potomac rivers, to Lumpkin County, Georgia, and around the bend of the southern Appalachians to enfold the mountaineers who wished to remain with the Union. Though the countryside varies considerably, the highland sociology does not, and it was even more intact in 1862. West Virginia seceded from the Confederacy—or, perhaps, it would be better to say that it refused to secede with it. East Tennessee and eastern Kentucky stayed with the Union as well, as did a half dozen counties in North Georgia and several in Appalachian Alabama. From these Southern highlands rode the First Alabama Cavalry that escorted William Tecumseh Sherman to the sea.

Final Thoughts

Thomas Jefferson is Hamlet to our play. Virginia—his Elsinore—has been more important to this account than any stage set, for it was, in its silent way, another character. It was affected, as a set may be, by what the human characters did within and upon it, but it also did its own affecting. All along it refused to do certain things above the Thousand-Foot Line, such as growing cotton, and after being abused below that line, it refused to continue to support many kinds of agriculture. Sets are built to endorse, amplify, and symbolize human action. The soil of Virginia not only set limits to action but, after being acted upon, responded by becoming less accommodating. Nature itself ran out of patience. The land would no longer accept humans as its masters.

In the early chapters of this book, this story was observed repeating itself throughout Jefferson's theater of action. In the final pages it was seen again enacted upon the contaminations at Monte Sano and the eroded banks of the Sabine and Red. The land does not remain passive for very long. It is not inanimate.

We have brought forward characters recognized even by their families as being of secondary importance, and only a few whom their most admiring friends would describe as heroic. This supporting cast has been as necessary to our tale as the watchmen Bernardo and Francisco were to Hamlet's, for they have given bodily form to forces that would otherwise remain abstract. Without observing such leaves as these we cannot see the way the wind is blowing—though, of course, to those who loved them, each was the entire forest.

Like Rosencrantz and Guildenstern, the courtiers of our tale—the Fulwar Skipwiths—have been sent to undertake missions at great risk, and ofttimes beyond their understanding.

And at the end, Andrew Jackson, prince of Middle Tennessee, has entered with trumpets, playing Fortinbras.

Jefferson has been with us since his draft of the Declaration of Independence asserted that statesmen should improve the circumstances in which citizens seek happiness. Thereafter, he has spoken to us many times, offering his own version of events as his cause was lost and his own statesmanship contributed to outcomes he deplored. In the 1820s, he declared himself affronted by the condition to which his country had come, especially in the South, where his influence had been most potent. Let us take him at his word—his many, eloquent words. The triumph of the plantation system, grounded in slavery and thus in violence, was not what the young Jefferson intended. Nor could the elderly statesman take satisfaction in the condition of the Southern land in the 1820s, after that system had wrought upon it waste and desolation.

In the 1770s, he had contended that the earth should be regarded as a trust, passed either intact or improved by each generation to another—a usufruct only. Yet, close at hand, in Albemarle and Bedford counties, Jefferson witnessed the failure of his aspirations for land as well as for its people. From the porticos of each of his plantations he could see the dispiriting lessons of a plantation system putting excessive stress upon the land and upon a labor force of slaves. During the three decades in which Jefferson was the South's dominant political figure, it resumed its reliance upon slavery and that dependence upon foreign markets that consigned it to the production of a few staple crops. As they were then produced, these were not benign crops for the land, nor was the slave system benign for either master or slave.

Though Jefferson did not often display in public his religious convictions, he struggled from his youth to his last days with the moral dilemmas arising from the difficulties of living a life in accordance with his view of man's place upon the earth, in the sight of God. Therefore we must listen carefully to his confession of a dread of divine retribution for the failures of his class and his generation as he approached death and admonished his peers. The planters' triumph would not last and would bring a host of horrors in its wake. So he had warned a half century earlier in the *Notes on Virginia*:

I tremble for my country when I reflect that God is just: that his justice cannot sleep for ever: that considering numbers, nature and natural means only a revolution of the wheel of fortune, an exchange of fortune is among possible events: that it may become probable by supernatural interference! The Almighty has no attribute that can take side with us in such a contest.[6]

That contest was fought between 1861 and 1865. Many times before that, Mr. Jefferson had asserted his principles, yet never had he done so with sufficient vigor to arrest the descent of his nation into the valley of the shadow. The failure of the cause he proclaimed between 1776 and 1784 was a tragedy for him, for the slaves and for their owners, for the Indians who were thrust aside to make way for plantations, and for the Southern land. The tragic flaw central to this drama was Jefferson's timidity in risking affront to those whose approval he craved. The tragedy for them was that they had insufficient interest in the long-term health either of society or of the land to accommodate the inconveniences he espoused in his young manhood. When he approached the end of his life, he offered the two alternative verdicts upon his career set forth at the outset of this account, one carved into his epitaph at Monticello, omitting his national public career and designating him an author and educator, and the other in a letter in effect summarizing the public life of his country while he was its foremost statesman and concluding with the terrible words:

[I] regret that I am now to die in the belief, that the useless sacrifice of themselves by the generation of 1776, to acquire self-government and happiness to their country, is to be thrown away by the unwise and unworthy passions of their sons, and that my only consolation is to be, that I live not to weep over it.[7]

After Jefferson's death in 1826, there were many more occasions for weeping.

Then, commencing in 1861, Abraham Lincoln redeemed his country and Jefferson's Lost Cause. His first task was to reanimate Jefferson's language of the Declaration celebrating the New Order in the Universe. Slavery and wars fought to extend its sway had made mock of that glorious prospect. The South had settled back into an ancient and squalid order. But Lincoln restored to the concept of Union that moral content initially provided to it by Jefferson and largely lost in the intervening confusions, integrating the Preamble to the Constitution and Jefferson's Declaration of Independence into a single charter of freedom.

Lincoln's father had chosen to cross the Ohio onto free soil from a Kentucky still dominated by slave owners. Lincoln was himself a risen yeoman. As such he saw to it that practical use was made in 1861 of the opportunity for radical reform provided by the secession from the councils of the nation of the representatives of the planters. Two great pieces of land-use legislation were rescued from the legislative imprisonment in which the planters had kept them. The first was the Homestead Act and the second the Morrill Land Grant Act. Both were Jeffersonian in concept, and both were enacted as soon as the Congress could free them.

Homestead acts had been proposed for more than a decade: the House passed one in 1858, but it was turned back by a phalanx of Southern votes; in 1859 the planters' proxy President, James Buchanan, vetoed another passed by both houses. The Homestead Act of April 1862 provided that any head of household could work his (or her) way to owning 160 acres of previously public land by residing upon—and improving—it for five years. The period could be shortened to six months upon payment of $1.25 per acre. In the same year, two other Jeffersonian concepts for the use of public land were revived after a series of defeats by Southern senators. The Morrill Act limited its effects to the Northern states but provided seventeen million acres of federal public lands to endow colleges and universities; it also established a system of military training in these institutions harkening back to an idea of Jefferson's presaging the Reserve Officers Training Corps. After Reconstruction, the sixteen Southern states got their portions of the public domain.

Thus Jefferson was vindicated in the two aspects of his public career for which he wished to be remembered, his formulation of a moral basis for the American Union and his labors on behalf of education. The failures of his political leadership were washed away, though a just appraisal of that leadership required the men of the 1860s to take due heed of his responsibility for the high price they were paying for his mistakes.

The Economics of Land Use

In the end, they honored Jefferson for his eloquence, as we do. He found winged words for conceptions otherwise creeping about in the treatises of his less gifted contemporaries. He could thus affect profoundly and for the better the uses of land in the United States after the nation began ridding itself of the plantation system. His ideal of a truly independent yeomanry and his therapeutic conception of land use have become imbedded in the American mythos, moving legislatures to allocate vast sums to farmers and, by extension, moving private owners toward careful use of the land. It is only incidental to this achievement that we cannot any longer accept wholly the Jeffersonian hypothesis as reiterated by George W. Julian in 1851 and in countless orations since, that "the life of the farmer is peculiarly favorable to virtue. . . . The farmer lives in rustic plenty, remote from the contagion of popular vices." The public had an interest in the yeoman's presence on the land because it was good for him and would, as a consequence, be good for the nation.

Jefferson's therapeutic view of land won its proudest victory over a purely commodity theory of land in the Homestead Act.[8]

We should not leave this subject without noting that the act, though long delayed by the planters' opposition, was the final action of a remarkable series owing much to Jeffersonian theory, remarkable because the population had been rapidly growing, and ordinarily an increase of demand brings an increase in prices. Yet the warmth of Jefferson's language wilted all demand curves, and American democracy empowered the landless.[9]

From 1790 through 1862, largely as the result of the increasing power of small farmers in the North, more and more of the public domain of the West was broken into small units. The size of these units was important because the cost of buying them was on a per-acre basis. Most farmers could become their own landlords after working on someone else's farm long enough to be able to buy a small property. That meant that there had to be small properties available for sums a person might earn while hearty enough to want to keep on working afterward. In the first decades of the nineteenth century, large speculative buyers aggrandized themselves at the expense of individual farmers, but thereafter more of the public domain became available to nourish a yeoman republic—in the North and West.

Looking backward, some elderly gentlemen among those who secured passage of the Homestead Act in 1862 might recall that when Jefferson provided their ideology 90 percent or more of Americans "labored in the earth." Those draftsmen of the act who lived another thirty years could hear Jefferson's phrases still ringing in the rhetoric of William Jennings Bryan in the 1890s, when 30 percent still farmed. When the same phrases were uttered by Robert Lafollette in the 1920s, 17 percent of Americans gave their profession as "farmer." Only 5 percent were full-time farmers when Hubert Humphrey brought the litany forth again in his 1968 campaign. Along the way, Franklin Roosevelt provided his own version of the doctrine in his Farm Speech of 1937:

> Sturdy rural institutions beget self-reliance and independence of judgment. Sickly rural institutions beget dependency and incapacity to bear the responsibilities of citizenship. . . . [On the family farmer] continuance of the democratic process in this country to no small extent depends.[10]

Roosevelt's Secretary of Agriculture, Claude Wickard, brought home to Monticello the Ark of the Arcadian Covenant in 1944, leaving no doubt that he and his President endorsed Jefferson's precept that the "peculiar deposit . . . of the Almighty's virtue" had been placed with "those who labored in the earth . . . on their own soil . . . [with] their own industry." To the applause of a large audience, Wickard proclaimed the Sage of Monticello to be "the father of the idea . . . [that] the family-sized farm" was "the seat of liberty."[11]

Jefferson was certainly the first major American statesman eloquently to espouse that idea. He was, truly, a founder.

Despite all the failures, imperfections, and unfinished business over which the Stars and Stripes had flown, those who looked up to see it still flying over the dome of the Capitol in 1865 and in 2002 could see it take the breeze once again as the symbol of a Union dedicated to the proposition that all are created equal. In Lincoln's words, all "should have an equal chance." That was why the Union had to be preserved—why it was, and still may be, "the last best hope of earth."[12]

Appendix

Another Stream

At one stage in its development this was a much bigger book, attempting to tell the story along two parallel lines, one proceeding southwestward from Virginia and the other emanating from Wade Hampton's South Carolina. At a second stage, recognizing that everything cannot be done in a book of moderate length, the Carolina stream was reduced to an appendix. Even then, as I endeavored to suggest the differences between the origin, nature, and effects of the tobacco and cotton culture of the Chesapeake and those springing from the Low Country cultivation of rice, indigo, and sugar, and the equivalent differences between the intellectual elite of Virginia and that of the Carolinas, the appendix grew to book length. The men of the Chesapeake and those of the Low Country talked, wrote, and lived differently from each other; their architecture and their way of arranging their buildings on the land differed; their effects upon the land differed, as well. So trusting the reader to be willing to leave all that aside, here are the other subjects I think essential to rounding out discussions initiated in the text but which if pursued in place would impede the course of the narrative or analysis.

Jefferson, Madison, Adam Smith, and the Chesapeake Cities

Thomas Jefferson's encomium to the little seaport towns of the Chesapeake calls to mind John Adams's famous comment that his friend Jefferson was never happier than in the Paris of the *ancien régime*. The chasm between Port Tobacco or Norfolk and Paris is wide enough to include most of the cities of humankind, and all those having smokestacks. Yet the Chesapeake cities were handsome enough in a red-brick-with-white trim sort of way to induce many civilized planters—though not Jefferson or Madison—to take up residence in them from time to time. Henry Adams, measuring them by the standard of Boston, did not find them to his taste, and in his disdain went so far as to mislead his readers by omitting Chesapeake urbanism from his celebrated survey of the nation in that year. "The absence of city life was," wrote Adams, "the sharpest characteristic of Virginia, even compared with South Carolina." Actually, the *presence* of city life was so significant to Chesapeake culture that Jefferson was entirely justified in situating Virginia's "most improved state" in its seaport towns.[1]

Richmond, which Monroe and Jefferson proposed to develop as a cotton-manufacturing city, had been established by the Byrds at the fall line of the James and the Appomattox. Its water power was turning mill wheels before it became a seat of government; around the fur warehouses of William Byrd I soon appeared speculative buildings constructed by his son, and his son's son established a dream-city named "Manchester" at Rocky Ridge, on the south bank of the James. This second Manchester was extinguished by the competitive ferocity of the British and Scottish traders who undercut in price whatever its little factories might make, and there were only 684 inhabitants of Richmond when it became the capital city of Virginia in 1779. Thereafter, things grew apace; Jefferson's Capitol Building of 1792 dignified an industrial village of about thirty-six hundred. At the end of the decade, Richmond had become a little city of nearly six thousand, some of them working for the "manufactory of Richmond" toward which Jefferson sought to draw Eli Whitney. A town of 6,000 people may seem to us a mere village, but Richmond in 1800 was larger than Philadelphia and New York had been in 1700. Richmond throve upon politics, foundries, manufactories, slave-worked iron works, and munitions factories.

Norfolk, on the other hand, was repeatedly smitten by plague, fire, and ill luck. It might have risen to the magnitude and vigor of Baltimore had Pennsylvania been its hinterland rather than the Great Dismal Swamp, or had it been luckier in war. Much of the city was burnt out on New Year's Day 1776. Most of what remained was put to the torch thereafter by Whigs extirpating Tories. The merchants rebuilt their city, and Norfolk grew to house three thousand people by March 1796. After burning again in 1799, it rose once more from the ashes, but the swamp was still there, breeding mosquitoes and yellow fever. Nonetheless, Norfolk and Richmond had by 1805 demonstrated that Robert Beverley had been wrong in pronouncing that "neither the interest nor inclinations of the Virginians induce them to cohabit in towns." Actually, their interests and inclinations drew them into an intercontinental skein of economic interest that "stimulated and sustained the clearing of fields for cultivation of the staple [tobacco] and the construction of networks of roads, bridges, and ferries for the tobacco to be hauled to the warehouses and stores near the rivers, where it could be exchanged for English goods."[2]

Though not within the political boundaries of Virginia, by 1800 Baltimore was on its way to becoming the nation's second largest city, well within the horizon of Virginia's planter class, bursting with vitality, attracting to its markets many Virginians, black and white. It grew to become larger than John Quincy Adams's Boston and nearly half again larger than Philadelphia. Before the line between Virginia and Maryland was drawn in blood in 1861, Baltimore was the pride of both. It had commenced as a junior rival to tobacco-shipping ports such as Annapolis but took a more active role in the Revolution, putting to sea 248 privateers between 1777 and 1783, prospering mightily, and doubling in size. It became "conceited . . . and debonaire, growing up like a saucy, chubby boy, with his dumpling cheeks . . . fat and mischievous, and bursting incontinently out of his clothes." Norfolk and Georgetown did nearly as well and in the 1790s traded with both the French and British. During the first years of Jefferson's presidency, the Chesapeake ports throve, as undeclared wars against France in the West Indies and the Barbary States in the Mediterranean required ships, supplies, and men. Privateering sustained them through embargoes and nonintervention until the War of 1812, when Baltimore put three thousand men aboard its war fleet.[3]

Its backcountry, the wheat lands of northern Maryland and Delaware, was becoming a rural equivalent to the urban mixture of Baltimore—showing a similar interchange of city and country to that composing a culture of family farms in the Midwest, but with a difference: there were black yeomen in Delaware and a few in Maryland. Pennsylvania had been without slavery for decades; Delaware, though a slave state, was demonstrating the fallacy of the Virginian argument that free blacks and whites could not coexist. By 1820, three quarters of the black population of Delaware was free, a reversal of the proportions of 1790. That recalls to us that letter of 1785 from Madison to Monroe urging that he stimulate the planters "to reacquaint themselves with the science of commerce . . . and . . . [become] sensible of the utility of establishing a Philadelphia or a Baltimore among ourselves." The Baltimore model was beckoning to Madison so early as that. But the other planters did not follow through.[4]

There is an aspect of Jefferson's view of cities that seems to be in conflict with his enthusiasm for a society of free and independent yeomen. He and Madison shared with Adam Smith a dour Scottish model of culture and of "progress": virtue would decline as industrialism and urbanization increased—indeed, as refinement increased. Yet Jefferson seemed also to say that civilization *gained* in North America as altitude declined, until the best society was found, naturally enough, in the Piedmont, where his humbler neighbors were not so refined as the denizens of the seaport cities nor so raw as the men and women of the mountains.

Distinguishing refinement from morality, Jefferson appeared to agree with Smith, who wrote of the yeoman farmer with admiration equal to his own.

Smith's ideal citizen was also a farmer doing "little foreign commerce, and no manufactures but those coarse and household ones which almost every private family prepares for its own use." As their contemporaries placed such yeomen in the American landscape, they appeared as citizens of the Bacon South, or, later, of the Midwest. In the Far West—at a farther and farther remove over time—one would find the "lowest and rudest state of society," in which aborigines, and people desiring to live like aborigines, hunted, fished, found nuts and berries. At the other extreme of the continent, on its easternmost fringe, lay cities such as Charleston and Philadelphia, where commerce throve as it did in London or Edinburgh. In between, reported the *London Chronicle*, lived "the greatest part" of the citizens of America, "as yeoman farmers removed from the aborigines by a pastoral zone" and removed, on the other side, from the cities' trade and commerce. Those who think Smith prescribed laissez-faire, a market economy, industrialization, division of labor, and urbanization without calculating their costs may be startled to find how Jeffersonian he was. It was Smith, not Jefferson, who wrote: "How much the lower ranks of people in the country are really superior to those of the town, is well known to every man who either business or curiosity has led to converse much with both."[5]

The Romans, Armed Occupation, and the Homestead Act

As the Romans knew, the first necessity of land policy on a frontier is to garrison it. Otherwise it would lie open to reacquisition by those from whom it has been taken. The Romans had been quite clear about that, as we discern from this paragraph from an essay on the subject by Abel Hendy Jones Greenidge and Agnes Muriel Clay:

> The existence of public land, first in Italy, and then in the Mediterranean world, was the outcome of two ideas which are very familiar to students of antiquity. This land was the prize of conquest and was one of the means of defraying the current costs of state-administration. . . . But . . . the state is not wholly disinterested in undertaking such acts of assignment. It gains security and territorial control by planting garrisons in conquered territory, and it relieves itself of the necessity of providing for its poorer classes.[6]

For a time, during the tribunates of Licinius and Sextius, about 376 B.C., the Romans also allotted public land (*ager publicus*) for small holders: no more than 500 *jugera* (about 333 acres) was allocated to the homestead of any single cultivator. It is possible that Licinius and Sextius were proto-Jeffersonians and had ideological reasons for their allocations, though cynics (they are still with us) might say that they, like the Founding Fathers, responded to the armed demands of the yeomen for whom they were to act as representatives.

Rome needed future soldiers and did not need revolts from landless and proficient military athletes. Thus "the satisfaction of the individual needs of poorer citizens."

Conquered land, be it on the Tiber, the Suwanee, or the Platte, may be seen as endowment. It may be sold in blocks, or leased "to be occupied on the condition of payment of dues," in other words, to generate recurring income. Fee-paying occupants, or *possessores*, could pass their allotments to their heirs and defend them against others, much as ranchers may in American practice. Rome, like Virginia and Ohio, found that it could not limit to their first recipients those frontier holdings intended to sustain militias, nor could only its poorer citizens be satisfied. The Romans transferred entire provinces to generals and statesmen whose loyalty had either been proved or was doubtful. During and just after their revolution, the Americans did likewise, though shabbily. They did not mean to insult. Neither did they mean to be as munificent as the British had been to Marlborough and would be to Wellington. The states thought of themselves as nearly bankrupted by paying their war debts, and, more important, they did not fear *caudillos*. Though disaffected officers such as James Wilkinson, George Morgan, William Blount, George Rogers Clark, and the Baron von Steuben became disgusted by what they took to be the ingratitude of these states, and offered their services to foreign powers, none of them considered marching upon the national capital in the Caesarean fashion. George Washington was there. The Roman origins of the Armed Occupation Principle were well known to the officers of the Revolution who established themselves at Marietta, as they demonstrated in the names they chose for their landmarks. Their "Campus Martius" was approached from the banks of the Muskingum River along the Sacra Via (still so designated by a street sign), and they gave other Roman names to each of the Indian earthworks within which they built their village. After enactment of the Homestead Act, veterans, like other citizens, could easily and cheaply obtain less exposed federal land.

Jefferson and the Ordinances of 1784 and 1787–89

It is easy to become confused about Jefferson's role in the Ordinances of 1784 and 1787 (the Northwest Ordinance). I have myself erred in attributing to him a primary role in the Northwest Ordinance, having read it repeatedly said by his biographers that the essentials of proposals made by him in 1784 were carried over into it. In my misconception, I had given insufficient heed to Merrill Peterson's disposition of the matter. Peterson pointed out that much of the substance of the Northwest Ordinance was, instead, "a reaction" to Jefferson's plan of government, by which, in his absence in Paris, his opponents "tore from his plan the provisions for democratic government."[7]

Peterson did, however, leave to his readers the impression that Jefferson "proposed" the antislavery provision of the draft in his handwriting of the Ordinance of 1784. Jefferson accepted Pickering's suggestion and did place it within the draft, though Pickering is nowhere mentioned in Peterson's account. Peterson received mild remonstrance from Robert F. Berkhofer in what must surely be the definitive account of "Jefferson, the Ordinance of 1784, and the Origins of the American Territorial System," which identifies Pickering at page 248 as the person who set in motion "the subject of prohibiting slavery . . . outside Congress" and concludes that "Jefferson's contribution to the report appears to be less than scholars have assumed."[8]

Jefferson wrote Madison on April 25, 1784, that the Ordinance of 1784 had passed without the failing provision he and Pickering had suggested and extending "not only to the territory ceded, but *to be ceded*," underlining for emphasis the last three words. Only to this extent was Claude Bowers correct in saying that the antislavery provision of the Ordinance of 1784 (which he attributes entirely to Jefferson) "set a precedent for the anti-slavery clause included in the Northwest Ordinance of 1797." Bowers was clearly too enthusiastic in giving Jefferson credit for having "left a permanent imprint on the governments of Indiana, Ohio, Illinois, Michigan, and Wisconsin, and in none of them was slavery permitted long." The fight for admission of those states free of slavery was fought well after he had ceased the struggle. The Northwest Ordinance was not his work. The 1784 antislavery provision was not his proposal but Pickering's, though Jefferson did accept it for inclusion in his draft.[9]

The odd aspect of Jefferson's widely cited letter of chagrin to Madison is that he knew the recipient's mind as well as anyone, and Madison never showed any sympathy for the fixing of geographic limits upon slavery. The final draft of the Northwest Ordinance, as adopted by the new Congress, had drawn a line at the Ohio River against the spread of slavery into the territories organized north of it. Madison saw in this a bad precedent. If Congress could legislate where slavery could not go, could it not legislate where it might, or might not, remain? In *Federalist 38*, therefore, Madison asserted that the drawing of lines beyond which slavery might go in the Western territories had been done "without the least color of constitutional authority," leaving the clear implication that he remained rueful that "no alarm has been sounded." He went further, proposing a committee report in 1789 clarifying the point that the Northwest Ordinance should be construed "to mean that slaves living in the territory were not in fact emancipated." They could only be freed by action of *state* constitutions. Though Indiana finally abolished slavery in its one such constitution, as affirmed by its Supreme Court in 1820, slavery continued to exist there until 1830. In Illinois it was not finally extinguished until 1848.[10]

Madison got his alarm in 1819—Mr. Jefferson's famous "firebell in the night." Tugging the bell rope was "the new Jefferson," proclaiming to the world that the Missouri Compromise was unconstitutional because it drew a line against slavery. This "new Jefferson" thereby repudiated the line-drawing Jefferson of 1784.[11]

Debt and Land

Alexander Hamilton's funding scheme managed to restore the moral and financial credit of the United States. When he came upon the scene as the new nation's financial genius, the debt incurred by the American Revolutionary governments had been reduced only by inflating it away at the expense of the nation's moral credit. Many patriots had provided food, uniforms, transportation, powder, and guns to the Revolutionary forces, accepting in return promises to pay in paper money before prices stated in that kind of money ascended until promises to pay nearly $400 million in paper declined in purchasing power until they were not "worth a Continental."

The Constitutional Convention faced twelve million dollars in debts owed foreigners, forty million owed domestic creditors by the United States, and twenty-five million in obligations of the states. These in turn broke into two categories, domestic debts run up by the states to their own people in financing the war and debts to foreign bankers and governments. With such a burden upon them, the Founders found themselves writing a constitution not upon some Lockean blank page but upon pages bearing the word "debt" followed by large numbers. Even if the domestic debt were repaid gradually at 4 percent interest, its carriage and reduction would consume three fourths of the contemplated federal budget. Worse, during the shilly-shallying years of the Confederation, the most patriotic of citizens had lost faith that those debts would ever be paid. Many who had been willing to forget wartime inflation and to invest in government obligations had next to withstand a postwar depression by selling whatever assets they held, including their tattered, shredded, spindled, and torn notes from their government. By 1790, only about 20 percent of these government obligations were held by original lenders, and those held were heading downward in the direction traversed already by the Continentals.

In the peaceful revolution of 1787, Hamilton and Madison supported the new Constitution on the ground that the United States would assume the debt of the states. Though agreeing as to that, they differed as to the price to be paid for the outstanding paper: should it be valued at face value or at current market value, whatever that might be in the absence of any central market? Madison (and Jefferson's great modern biographer Merrill Peterson) argued for market price: "justice was revolted," wrote Peterson, by paying face amount, for it provided a bonanza for speculators. How one defines a speculator and how a patriot under these circumstances remains unclear, but

Jefferson was not, it seems, revolted, though he later insisted that he had been "duped" by Hamilton. As they discussed swapping the principle of face value for the location of the national capital on the Potomac, he was, he insisted, "ignorantly and innocently made to hold the candle" for what Peterson called Hamilton's "fraudulent scheme."[12]

The charge of fraud seems a little severe. There was no disguise in the transaction. Greater profits were made by speculators without incurring such a charge in the Chrysler and Savings-and-loan "bailouts" of recent memory. No one of Jefferson's intelligence and sophistication would have been "duped." There were no secrets hidden from him. He and Hamilton were both "realists." Each got what he wanted, and of the two, Jefferson had the greater economic interest in the agreement they reached. Hamilton got the difference between "face" and "market"—a matter of interest largely to the North, where most of the holders of the debt resided. Jefferson got the location of the national capital on the riverbank where his friends lived and speculated. Madison shrugged—and went along.

The next set of arguments erupted about which products should bear the excise taxes required to pay Mr. Hamilton's interest rate of 4 percent. Unrestrained by the Jeffersonians, the frontiersmen of western Pennsylvania and Kentucky rose against his whiskey tax. Finally, however, though tax collection was difficult, Washington and Hamilton found the money even in the depression years of the 1790s to honor the nation's debts both to foreigners and to its domestic creditors.

Jefferson's Doctrine of Usufruct

Joseph Ellis has this to say of Jefferson's doctrine of the usufruct: "There is no single statement in the vast literature by and about Jefferson that provides as clear and deep a look into his thinking about how the world ought to work. The notion that 'this earth belongs to the living' is in fact a multi-faceted product of his political imagination that brings together in one place his essential obsessions and core convictions."[13]

Perhaps. But let us see how Jefferson came to say that "this earth belongs to the living." In England, or in England's American colonies, those who inherited land bearing a mortgage had an obligation to make payments to the creditors so secured, lest the land itself be forfeited. In Jefferson's formulation, they had a further obligation to the next set of owners not to run up the size of the mortgage beyond the capacity of the land to generate sufficient income to pay the mortgage off. As a mortgage-burdened debtor, Jefferson made no secret of his resentment of the mortgage obligations running with the lands descending to him from his father, father-in-law, and mother.

Some writers—though not, as I understand him, Mr. Ellis—have attributed to Jefferson a view he never, in fact, set forth: that the concept of honorable life tenancy was an obligation to the land itself. The closest he came to such a statement was a phrase in a letter to a similarly obligated James Madison in 1789. It was, he wrote, "self-evident" that "the earth belongs in usufruct to the living." "Usufruct" is a concept of the English common law, grounded in Roman land law, holding tenants of estates to a standard of care that would leave those properties, after their use and enjoyment, in no worse condition than that prevailing when the tenant first took possession. The concept of usufruct was a weapon in the hands of residuary legatees to use against life tenants. In most cases, those having usufruct were parents, and those getting what was left afterward were children.

In the English experience, as well as in Jefferson's own, those who inherited land had a legitimate desire to receive it in good condition and unencumbered by liens. Their enjoyment to come might, therefore, be diminished by any excessive joys purchased by their parents with money secured by mortgage. In this construct, nobody spoke for the land. The living, represented by Jefferson, resented having to pay off debts incurred by the dead, though they did not object to receiving assets from their predecessors. And, of course, they were free to leave those debts unpaid if the net value of a piece of inherited land did not comfortably exceed the obligations burdening it. They could always walk away. Though Jefferson and Madison both complained about abuse of usufruct, neither did walk away.[14]

There was nothing very high-minded in this. Jefferson's principle was not a declaration of personal independence of all inheritance. It was instead a declaration that he would rather not make mortgage payments. Characteristically, however, he did not content himself with complaining but formed a theory out of his resentments: all who held land were, in effect, life tenants. (And characteristically as well, he did not let himself be inhibited by principle but in his own affairs added to the debt burden upon the lands he inherited and left them so encumbered that his heirs let them go.)

Private intergenerational bickering is not very interesting, but Jefferson's concepts of appropriate behavior toward land did leave implications making for excellent conservation doctrine. Here is the seed-pod of those implications:

> The portion [of land] occupied by an individual ceases to be his when [he] ceases to be, and reverts to the society. If the society has formed no rules for the appropriation of its lands in severalty, it will be taken by the first occupants. These will generally be the wife and children of the decedent. . . . [who] may give it to his *creditor* [my emphasis]. But the child, the legatee or *creditor* [my emphasis] takes it, not by any natural right, but by a law of the society of which they are members. . . . Then no man can by *natural right* [his emphasis] oblige the lands he occupied, or the persons who succeed him in that occupation, *to the payment of debts contracted by him* [my emphasis].

For if he could, he might during his own life, eat up the usufruct of the lands for several generations to come, and then the lands would belong to the dead, and not to the living. . . . What is true of every member of the society individually, is true of them all collectively. Since the rights of the whole can be no more than the sum of the rights of individuals. . . . The present generation . . . have the same rights over the soil . . . as the preceding generations had. They derive those rights not from their predecessors, but from nature. They then and their soil are by nature *clear of the debts* [my emphasis] of their predecessors. . . . [T]here is no umpire but the law of nature. . . . [O]ne generation is to another as one independent nation to another. . . . The earth belongs always to the living generation.[15]

As usual, Jefferson stated a principle, not a program. As Dr. Ellis puts it, he failed to "put forward his generational argument as a serious legislative proposal . . . but . . . clung to it tenaciously, introducing it in conversations and letters for the rest of his life." It is by no means clear what it was that he was holding so tenaciously, but it was not a conservation doctrine. It was instead a sense that as among several sets of men no one group had exclusive claim upon land. A good society was that in which "as few as possible shall be without a little portion of land. The small landholders are the most precious part of a state." That is a distributive theory, not one of care.[16]

There was an oddity in this akin to Jefferson's selection of a yeoman's cabin for his first home. It appears that he imaginatively linked his own indebtedness to the squalid condition of the peasantry of Europe. Because they, like his own slaves, worked to produce money for their owners, they in effect made the mortgage payments due creditors from their landlords. Thus they bore the burdens, but enjoyed none of the benefits, of the debt system. Peasants were rack-rented, and slaves worked to exhaustion, to pay off obligations undertaken to make luxurious lives more luxurious. Furthermore, "improving" landlords in Britain, France, and Virginia were notorious for increasing their rent-roll by throwing the peasants—some called them yeomen—off the land and replacing them with sheep. Sweating slaves and starving peasants composed a picture offensive to many good people, including Jefferson, who wrote in 1785:

The earth is given as a common stock for man to labor and live on. If, for the encouragement of industry [or the "improvement" of a landlord's property], we allow it to be appropriated, we must take care that other employment be furnished to those excluded from the appropriation. If we do not, the fundamental right to labor the earth returns to the unemployed. It is too soon yet in our country to say that every man who cannot find employment, but who can find uncultivated land, shall be at liberty to cultivate it, paying a moderate rent. But it is not too soon to provide by every possible means that as few as possible shall be without a little portion of land. The small landholders are the most precious part of a state.[17]

Tribes, Land, and Ireland

After the final rising of the tribal chiefs in 1603, the holocaust at Kinsale, and the "Flight of the Earls," tribal Ireland was done for—as tribal Mississippi was done for by 1830. In the decade after 1603, as Jamestown was being "planted" in Virginia, Articles of Plantation put five hundred thousand acres in Ireland in the hands of planters. A new population, largely Scots Protestants, was brought to the scene to supplement the native labor force. Though this was a greater exchange of populations and acreage than that brought about in the Chickasaw settlement of 1805, the methodologies of 1603 and 1805 were similar. The Irish tribal chiefs—the Earls of Tyrconnel and Tyrone— had risen against Queen Elizabeth I and had been defeated. The lawyers of the Queen and her Scottish successor, James Stuart, relieved the disgraced earls of their individual holdings, drove their farmers off, and aggregated them as Crown lands with tribal holdings beyond the earls' properties, to be distributed into the "plantations" of Protestant Scots.

Early in this narrative we noted that an acute observer of this process was Francis Bacon, one of Jefferson's "worthies" whose sculptured bust ornamented the anteroom at Monticello, and that Bacon had said of it that "the bane of a plantation is when the undertakers or planters make such haste to a little presentable present profit as disturbeth the whole frame and nobleness of the work for times to come." His disapprobation of this abuse of the earth did not, however, diminish Jefferson's willingness to make use of Britain's Irish devices in dealing with the tribal societies obstructing the expansion of the American plantation system.[18]

Under Jefferson's direct instruction, legal devices tested in Ireland were employed in dealing with the Chickasaws, Choctaws, and Creeks, with similar consequences for the land. Tribal land was confiscated and distributed in recompense for the debts or sins of some, but not all, tribal chieftains. The lawyers for the British kings had asserted that there was sanction "in Irish custom and the law of England" for this methodology. Jefferson was similarly assured with regard to American law. Yet, as Edmund Curtis tells us in his history of Ireland,

> whatever the power of the chiefs was, they certainly did not under the accepted principles of Brehon law actually *own* the whole land of their "country", nor can we imagine that in England [or Virginia] the rebellion of a few great men would have led to the dispossession of the whole body of their tenants in several counties.[19]

Creeks, Seminoles, and Numbers

Those Indians whose trade normally moved down the rivers of Georgia and Alabama on their way to Mobile, Pensacola, and St. Mark had no obstacles to cross—the wholly arbitrary 31st Parallel being invisible to them. Sometimes, however, they grew impatient with the prices paid by the firms chartered in those ports by the French and Spaniards, and after Charles Town was established in 1680 they often sought a British option. To get there, they had to cross great rivers and expanses of territory; in the conventions of English parlance, a distance is "up," so these distant people became "Upper" Creeks, while those closer in to Charles Town became "Lower" Creeks. Upper or Lower, the "Creeks" were so designated by the British by location, whatever might be their culture or race. No one is quite sure whether they were the people *of* the rivers and creeks or the people British traders could only reach *by crossing* creeks. (For similar reasons, the British placed Upper Choctaws to the west of Lower Choctaws.)

The word "Seminole" derives ultimately from the Latin *cyma*, drawn from the Greek term for a mountain fastness. Slaves who could escape their masters in the Aegean basin escaped to such places, so a cyma came to be a sanctuary for escaped slaves. Because the slaves of the Greeks were often procured from the Black Sea region, and were of a skin color ruddier than that of their sallow Greek and Roman masters, a person of the cyma was not thought of as necessarily "dark" until the fugitives from slavery included some from the other end of the Mediterranean, where slaves tended to be darker than their masters, having been obtained in Africa.

The word lost its topographical significance about the time it gained a racial implication, as sanctuary became found as often in marshes and swamps as among the mountaintops. So, by the time it worked its way into modern languages, the word for people of the cyma, *cymarrons*, meant anyone who escaped; only by extension did it mean an animal that would not be easily corralled. The Spanish word for escaped slaves became *cimarron*, the French, *marron*. As early as 1606, the word "symerron" entered English parlance, though replaced by "maroon" by the end of the eighteenth century. Characteristically, Thomas Babington Macaulay used the word pejoratively, to mean someone who fires from ambush; the master stylist among Victorian historians disdained slaves, especially those of a darker color than the English.

By 1503, the Spaniards on the island of Hispaniola had taken to calling any slave a *cimarron* who escaped—whatever might be his or her race. By the end of the seventeenth century, the Spaniards' need to recruit a workforce to create fortifications against the British led them to send expeditions to seize Indians to be put beside the gangs of Africans they deployed to do their hot work. Thus Africans were brought to America to replace Indians, anticipating the filling of the mainland South with black slaves to replace Indians who had been forcibly "removed."

The "removal" of most of the Indians of the West Indies and Florida had not been the consequence of policy, however, but of contagion. The best scholarly estimates seem to be that when Columbus landed on Hispaniola in

1493 with his disease-ridden crew and his influenza-bearing animals, 3,770,000 people were living on the island. Their number had been reduced to 92,300 in 1508 and to 15,000 in 1518. Then smallpox arrived, and a culture that had nourished nearly four million persons ceased to exist. There is a fierce scholarly battle about the population estimates of all these scholars, but none with regard to the general truth that a very large population of Indians was wiped out on Hispaniola first, and later in Florida.[20]

Florida's Indians suffered next. For millennia, double-hulled canoes had carried West Indian natives from Hispaniola along the coasts of Cuba to Florida, and in the other direction to Venezuela, with sufficient frequency to produce similarities in language between the Timucuans of Florida and the Warao of the Orinoco delta. After 1493, these seagoing craft also carried sick people from Hispaniola to Cuba, and from Cuba to Florida, where the precontamination population was probably about 350,000. Some were already dead of disease by 1539: malaria arrived in 1513–14, smallpox in 1519–24, (eliminating between half and three quarters of the people), measles or typhoid fever in 1528 (taking half the remainder), and an unidentified epidemic in 1535–39. Then Hernando de Soto appeared with hogs and horses, all bearing contagion. After de Soto came bubonic plague in the 1540s, typhus in 1549, mumps in 1550, and influenza again in 1559. In 1759, just twelve Timucuan speakers were still living in Spanish missions; 180 descendants of the people of southern Florida, including a few Calusas, lived within the present city limits of Miami. Forty-five Appalachee could be found living along the Red River of Louisiana in 1825.[21]

The Livingstons and West Florida

No doubt inflamed by Fulwar Skipwith and possibly by James Monroe as well, James Bowdoin, the American minister to Spain, asserted that his efforts to achieve a peaceable acquisition of West Florida were being complicated by John Armstrong's revival of Chancellor Livingston's speculations in Florida plantation land. According to Bowdoin, Armstrong was attempting to purchase three million acres for himself, making use once more of Daniel Parker. As Armstrong later wrote Madison:

> M. Bowdoin . . . in conjunction with M. Skipwith and by means which I shall take care to investigate, did obtain from an Irish ex-priest of the name of Somers a deposition, in which an attempt is made to implicate me in a land speculation, connected with the then intended purchase of the Floridas. . . . [T]his deposition was multiplied by several copies, one of which was inserted on the consular Register of this place—which . . . forms the true reason why that register has been so unwarrantably withheld by Skipwith and [Isaac Cox] Barnet [who was assisting Skipwith at the time]."[22]

Armstrong also brought into the discussion the name of James LeRay de Chaumont, a Parisian speculator who had already purchased vast tracts of Pennsylvania and northern New York and who was sponsoring the importation of Spanish merino sheep in partnership with Chancellor Livingston. (There is a chapter in my *Orders from France* about the architectural consequences of these relationships among the Livingstons and LeRay de Chaumont.)[23]

Armstrong had written Madison on October 10, 1806, that a "Mr. Chew of New Orleans" had told him that Chew, Daniel Clark, Skipwith, and Barnet "had in company, purchased from Morales, all the country in West Florida, worth having, between the Mississippi and the Pearl River." Clark and Don Juan Ventura Morales were partners in a number of ventures, some of them of intense political interest. Though Morales was charged with governing Mobile and Pensacola, he resided in New Orleans, where he made no secret of his views:

> [He] preferred to sell the province [Florida] to the Americans . . . [having assessed the] expense of maintaining a hopeless front against these restless neighbors, with no local revenues, and uncertain subsidies from Mexico, with fortifications in ruins and no possibility of increasing their defenders. . . . Pensacola and Mobile could not support their combined population of about fifteen hundred, including soldiery. . . . Baton Rouge . . . was so enclosed by neighboring American territory to be defenseless.[24]

Let us assume that Morales and Clark talked real estate as they talked trade and politics. Jefferson and Madison ignored Armstrong's charge against Skipwith and Bowdoin's against Armstrong. As Jefferson had said earlier of the Livingston-Skipwith fracas, it was "disgusting"—there were larger matters at hand.[25]

That was apparently still his view in 1810 when Armstrong brought the matter up again, and Jefferson and Madison again finessed without taking sides. Armstrong sought a comment from the two because, as a potential Cabinet member, his honor was at stake, and they had been sent copies of the deposition against him from Skipwith in 1806. Madison responded by assuring Armstrong that he had found no evidence of any involvement by him "in any land speculation whatever" and providing an enthusiastic character reference. Armstrong was a powerful figure; he had been senator from New York, and might be again—or, if not he, then another of the Livingston clan. There was no need to worry about Bowdoin's response: if he learned of their assurances to Armstrong, he swung no political weight; Bowdoin was a frail intellectual and philanthropist, from a Federalist state.[26]

The Claiborne-Clark Duel

When Claiborne arrived to take up his post in Mississippi Territory, the Louisiana Purchase had not yet been transacted. Napoleon was threatening to replace the erratic but feeble Spanish regime at New Orleans with something much more dangerous. Claiborne had ample cause to believe Wilkinson to be in the pay of Spain, but he was not known to have sold himself to France as well, so the two agreed to prepare a force to seize New Orleans. After couriers arrived from Paris reporting that the Louisiana Sale and Purchase had settled the question peaceably, Wilkinson and Claiborne rushed four hundred militiamen downriver to make certain there were no second thoughts on the part of the French or Spanish officials in the city.[27]

Claiborne was required by Jefferson to work for many years in a distasteful partnership with Wilkinson, though their methods were not the same. Claiborne was under instruction to avoid any open break. Though evidence of the general's treason had been repeatedly brought to his attention, he had followed Jefferson so deeply into complicity with Wilkinson that he barely escaped death in a duel with Daniel Clark.

Clark was one of those who insisted upon telling both Claiborne and the President of Wilkinson's treason. As a Burrite, Clark was ignored, but he took his evidence to the House of Representatives, charging in addition that Claiborne had refused to do his duty. Claiborne challenged. Though both survived, both shot to kill; Claiborne suffered a grievous wound in his thigh. However unpleasant their altercation was for Clark and Claiborne, we might put it down as merely another ritual bloodletting in a dueling age had it not given rise to "a rare view of Jefferson, as it were in undress, one that never appears in his own writing." That view has come to us from Isaac Coles, who was at the time Jefferson's secretary, writing to his friend Joseph Cabell, another Jefferson protégé.

> "I wish," said he, "that your friend [Cabell] would consent to go to Orleans. . . . There is the deuce to pay there. . . . Claiborne has left Orleans and gone, God knows where, to fight a duel with Clark, and if he falls there will be no one to represent the government. I wish Monroe was here, I think I could prevail on him to accept the office, though he has hitherto refused it—he would now be of infinite value to us there." After a pause of some moments he continued—"If Cabell would go, and Monroe should still refuse, I will make him governor."[28]

Monroe did refuse, as noted elsewhere, and in October 1803 Claiborne was elevated from governor of Mississippi Territory to become governor of Orleans Territory, with a clear opportunity to become governor of Louisiana when it became a state. As Jefferson dispatched him to Louisiana, he was reminded by Secretary of War Dearborn that he remained a "secondary character." The precise phrasing was that "no secondary character would have a better right" to the job. Monroe was apparently a "primary character." And, in "a frank private explanation," Jefferson "let him consider his appointment perhaps as ad interim only." One can commiserate with a person put onto the field by that kind of coach.[29]

Fulwar Skipwith and Andrew Jackson

In 1824, as the party caucuses were proceeding toward the next presidential election, it became manifest that the Chief Magistracy would pass from the Virginians to John Quincy Adams, their earnest and conscientious agent over twenty years, rather than to Andrew Jackson. Jackson was famously irritable even when things were going his way, and during the course of the campaign he heard that Fulwar Skipwith, Virginian in accent and demeanor, was contending against George Croghan for the postmastership of New Orleans. Croghan was a nephew of George Rogers Clark and was himself Jackson's friend.

Skipwith! That Jeffersonian troublemaker! Postmaster, indeed! Shades of Gideon Granger, ally of James Wilkinson and provoker of Jefferson against Jackson's friend Aaron Burr! Jackson set pen to paper to denounce Skipwith as a traitor to his country, recalling—or persuading himself that he recalled—that during the Battle for New Orleans he had told his troops that if Skipwith and his friends in the Louisiana legislature were doing what the gossips said they were doing, and if "I were so unfortunate as to be driven from the lines I then occupied and compelled to retreat through New Orleans, they would have a warm session."[30]

Abner Duncan, the New Orleans merchant, had been on the scene in 1815, and as the 1824 campaign heated up, he asserted that what Jackson had *really* done, on hearing the report of the legislature's willingness to treat with the enemy, was to order his men to find out if the report was accurate "and if true, to blow them up." Duncan was probably remembering what he wished Jackson had said. It made better copy for the newspapers. They tore into Skipwith, denying him his postmastership. He faded from sight, no longer useful to the expansion of the plantation system on any grander scale than growing a little cotton at Monte Sano.[31]

Whatever he may have said, it is undeniable that after the battle against the British Jackson was in no haste to lift martial law. He did not yet know that the Treaty of Ghent had been signed and that the British threat was over, and he fell into some of the practices that had brought odium to Wilkinson eight years earlier during the Burr Affair. It was the same city. Many of the same people were involved, though with roles reversed; Edward Livingston now had General Jackson at his side, rather than being hunted down by General Wilkinson. Jackson imprisoned the judge of the United States District Court, Dominick Augustin Hall; Wilkinson had threatened imprisonment of two judges, John B. Prevost (Burr's stepson) and Superior Court Judge James Workman.

Edmund Gaines, never a coward, was willing to head a military court and substituted for Hall; when Gaines found not guilty some of those Jackson disliked, Jackson kept them in jail anyway.

At length, things simmered down. Judge Hall was released and fined Jackson a thousand dollars. Jackson paid it with an admission that his treatment of Hall had been somewhat peremptory, and in 1844 Congress voted Jackson $2,732 to repay his fine.

Notes

Chapter 1

1. The two ladies had come into Jefferson's dutiful life after their own unsteadier comings of age, though they had passed through the sobering stage of being Quaker matrons of Philadelphia on their way to becoming charter members of the new establishment of Washington City. The mother of Dolley Payne Todd Madison had kept a genteel boardinghouse after Mr. Payne's bankruptcy and death. He was a person of principle who had been shunned in Virginia for manumitting his slaves and fell into bankruptcy after failing to find ways to earn a city living. His daughter Dolley had herself been widowed before she married James Madison. She was a small, smiling, buxom, courageous woman.

The mother of Anna Maria Brodeau Thornton had also been widowed early. She kept barely above poverty by becoming a schoolmistress. She accompanied the two lively younger women to Monticello, and beside them was Anna Maria's husband, Dr. William Thornton. Thornton was an active opponent of slavery, though the luxuries of his life had come not from medical practice but from his plantations on Tortola, in the British West Indies. He later enjoyed governmental sinecures provided by the Virginians, as well as commissions from them to design city mansions. He had earned his medical degree at Edinburgh and traveled widely in Europe, with many adventures. Indeed, thunder at Monticello and Thornton's role in the Washington City establishment bring to mind the story of this future Commissioner of the United States Patent Office and architect of the Capitol huddling under a skin tent, as a rainstorm swept the Isle of Staffa in the Hebrides, with the young man who a half century later, as James Smithson, established the Smithsonian Institution.

Thornton was one of the first investor-inventors in steamships, won the competition for the design of the Capitol (though President George Washington understood that he was too inexperienced to be entrusted with building it), and took an administrative role in the Capitol construction process, while serving as Patent Office commissioner. Much later, he assisted Jefferson with the designs for the University of Virginia. Thornton was probably—there are no drawings—the author of the design of the finest Palladian villa in the West Indies, a house on the island of St. Croix which anticipated Jefferson's rotunda house for his friend Governor Barbour of Virginia.

2. Since the first Monticello, a Palladian house, has disappeared, those who wish to see how it might have looked must travel to West Andover, Ohio, to see a somewhat smaller near likeness: the Edmiston House, designed by Leverett Osborn and built in 1845. I have told the story of the first and second Palladian Monticellos in *Orders from France* and *Greek Revival America*.

3. The visit of the Thorntons and Mrs. Madison in 1802 has been recounted in several biographies of Jefferson; indeed, one of the pleasures of reading them is to see how each writer makes use of this event. My favorite version—except my own, of course—is that of Jack McLaughlin, in his admirable *Jefferson and Monticello*. He starts as I do but goes in quite another direction.

4. My quotations come from ibid., pp. 3 ff.

5. Ibid., p. 32.

6. Quotation from Gray's treatment of this subject in his *Agriculture*, Vol. 1, pp. 166–67. Ox hide, Bonner, *Georgia*, p. 104. See also p. 98.

7. Piedmont described by Craven in *Soil Exhaustion*, p. 26. Description of Virginia country, to Jean Baptiste Say, March 2, 1815, *Writings*, Memorial Ed., Vol. 14, pp. 260–62.

8. My statistics and quotations are from Craven, *Soil Exhaustion*, pp. 27–28.

9. TJ on Noah's flood, quoted ibid., p. 28; the report on Albemarle County in 1790, in Peterson, *Jefferson*, p. 525.

10. Meinig, *Shaping of America*, Vol. 2, p. 289. We may all be grateful to Meinig for this splendid, capacious work, and for his determination over many decades to integrate history, economics, and geography, and to do so in plain English.

11. Incendiary agriculture has been used on all continents except Antarctica; in northern Europe it has been called "swidden farming," since the Norse used the word *swidden* to designate burnt ground. Replenishing may occur by crop rotation, by waiting for nature, or by bringing fertilizers. How long would a planter or yeoman have to wait? The nutrients removed in a single hundred-day season would, we are told, ultimately return "from rainfall and free bacteria in the soil." But few have the capital or the patience to await the ultimate, though it could be drawn closer if the bacteriological balance were restored by putting into the soil other plants upon which other microorganisms might feed and prosper. Some restoration would recur if the living matter in the soil were fed upon whatever portion of the crop was left to decompose in place after the tobacco leaves and cotton bolls had gone to market. The fastest replenishment would occur if all nutrients were plowed back. But why would the farmer do that? The purpose of growing cotton or tobacco, or grain, is to be able to sell the crop, containing much of the nutrients—pumped out of the soil and deposited by burning on the surface—to someone somewhere else. That is the message of the familiar pictures of huge spouts spewing grain into the holds of ships on the Chicago lakefront, and of bales of cotton piled high upon the wharves of Charleston harbor. The choice remained: replenish the land or reposition the farmer.

12. TJ, *Notes*, in *Writings*, Lib. of Am. Ed., p. 289 ff.

13. When a yeoman could stake a claim, by purchase, by veteran's grant, or by seizure, he partook in the benefits of the conquests by the regular army and the militias and was subsidized by the taxpayers of the nation as a whole, who bore the military as well as the purchase costs of expansion.

14. My quotation about the small farmer's priorities comes from Helms, "Soil," at p. 733. Manure from a milk cow or from a draft animal will do the work of many imported fertilizers, yet it is arresting to find in Helms's work the statement that the use of commercial fertilizers later in the nineteenth century "made possible a southern landscape [still] dominated by cotton" but made up of "smaller farms and a denser rural population." The reverse of that observation may be instructive in thinking about what happened earlier, when "smaller farms" returned to the Southern land more fertilizer per acre than plantations more devoted to nutrient-mining and exporting staples. His view is to be found on his p. 753.

15. TJ quoted in Craven, *Soil Exhaustion*, p. 34.

16. John Hebron Moore, *Agriculture in Ante-bellum Mississippi*, pp. 37–42. I thank Jack Elliott for leading me to Moore.

17. Ibid.

18. Taylor quoted in Craven, *Soil Exhaustion*, p. 38.

19. *Notes*, in *Writings*, Lib. of Am. Ed., p. 33.

20. I am quoting from Lynch, "Westward Flow," pp. 310–11. This process recapitulated that already seen in the West Indies, where "buying up and extending plantations" also "made smallholdings scarcer and hard to obtain," a century earlier. (The quotation and the numbers presented in this and the ensuing paragraph are to be found in Ralph Davis, *Atlantic Economies*, pp. 132–33.) On Barbados, for example, sugar had become a plantation crop in the 1640s, grown on large fields by slave labor and replacing small plots of cotton cultivated by yeoman farmers and their indentured servants. As the great planters engrossed the island, thirty thousand white yeomen and servants were driven elsewhere. This process was repeated on the mainland with cotton replacing sugar as the planters' crop inimical to a yeoman culture after the cotton gin. On Jamaica, a white population of fifty thousand in the 1650s, many growing cotton, was reduced in the next half century to no more than eight thousand, some still growing that crop, amid forty-five thousand sugar-producing blacks. A similar transition occurred in the elbow of the Tennessee River a century later, though the original population of independent farmers was in that case composed of Indian yeomen. See also Gray, *Agriculture*, Vol. 1, p. 184.

Chapter 2

1. TJ quoted in Craven, *Soil Exhaustion*, p. 34; Washington quoted in R. Smith, *Patriarch*, p. 138.

2. Washington quoted in Hirschfeld, *Washington*, p. 76.

3. My description of Washington is largely drawn from that of George Mercer in 1758, quoted in Flexner, *Forge of Experience*, pp. 191–92, and from descriptions of him on his deathbed. Jefferson was limned by the descendants interviewed by Henry

Randall and quoted in Fawn Brodie, *Thomas Jefferson: An Intimate History*, p. 20, and his skin was reported by his overseer Edmund Bacon, as quoted by Ellis, *Sphinx*, p. 29.

4. TJ to Dr. Walter Jones, Jan. 2, 1814, quoted in Kenin and Wintle, *Dictionary*, p. 768; and also those passages quoted in B. Mayo, *Jefferson Himself*, pp. 161–62.

5. John Quincy Adams, diary, Jan. 27, 1831, quoted in Kenin and Wintle, *Dictionary*, p. 419.

6. Washington's uniforms, now in the Smithsonian Institution's National Museum of American History, show his coats to be as large as a contemporary 41 Long.

7. Locke did not, however, give honored status to family farmers. He wrote to exalt the status of the British "country party" of large landowners over the "city" or "Court" party.

8. Locke, the Psalmist, and TJ quoted in Griswold, *Farming*, p. 36 ff.

9. Bacon quoted in *Encyclopaedia Britannica*, 11th ed., s.v. "plantation."

10. In scattered pages of the *Notes* and in some of his letters, Jefferson left some implications from which later conservationists have constructed an ideology of what the good yeoman should do with and for the land—the famous "theory of usufruct." Though under close scrutiny the result of their labors turns out to be nearly all commentators' glue and very little Jeffersonian shard, without the shards and the authority of the potter there would have been no glueing. When Jefferson wrote that "this earth belongs to the living" he was making a statement about each generation's obligation of care for the earth to protect the succeeding generation, not the earth itself. The shards and glue are deconstructed in the Appendix; see "Jefferson's Doctrine of Usufruct."

11. My statistics as to the importance of tobacco and cotton in the economy are drawn from North, *Economic Growth*, pp. 40, 75, 88, 102, 135, 169, 178–80, and 211.

12. What was essentially an epidemic disease of the earth was thought in the nineteenth century to have been purely a matter of chemical imbalance. It was said that things got too acid, or that the soil grew insufficiently "base" after cotton (or tobacco) consumed the limited supply of base nutrients naturally found in such clayey or sandy acid soils. I am drawing heavily upon the description of this process in Helms, "Soil," as adjusted somewhat in a conversation with Terry Sharrar. Helms's analysis of the importance of soil types to cropping methods and the location of roads and settlements seems to me to be very useful. It is arresting and, after a contemplative pause, stimulating to find a writer published in 2000 who eschews the word "slaves" when writing about the antebellum period, preferring the word "hands," and who attributes exclusively to "the disparity between the potentials of the southern soils and midwestern soils" the difference between "the numbers of rural youth available to fight the Civil War . . . [in] Alabama, Georgia and Mississippi . . . [and] Ohio, Indiana, and Illinois" (p. 726).

One hundred days vs. twenty years is also from Helms (ibid., p. 729), just before a derisive reference to the use of terms implying "a higher level of natural chemical fertility than actually existed." This is an important point, and surely Helms is correct in urging attention to the limited range of options available to many Southern farmers. My use of such terms is intended to draw attention to the difference between "before" and "after," not to imply the level of what "before" might be. And Sharrar has assisted me to see that the terms "soil exhaustion" and "soil depletion" may have an even more pernicious consequence: they may ignore the biology of the soil itself.

13. These statistics and much of the matter of the text are drawn from my longer accounts in *Greek Revival America* and *Architecture, Men, Women, and Money*.

14. "Cotton . . . uses, for example, less phosphorous and potassium than alfalfa . . . [but] corn takes thirteen nutrient elements from the soil and is a particularly heavy user of nitrogen and phosphorous. . . . [B]oth as a row crop and as a direct destroyer of fertility, the South's basic food, more than its commercial staple, injured the soil." Cowdrey, *This Land*, p. 77. William E. Doolittle has contributed mightily to our understanding of the relationship of corn to cotton, and of both to slavery and the land, in his monumental encyclopedia of native American land use. My quotations from individuals and much of the matter of the text are drawn from longer accounts in *Greek Revival America* and *Architecture, Men, Women, and Money*.

15. Ibid.

16. Where the cities of Selma and Birmingham now thrive, some millions of years ago there was a sandy shoreline upon which lapped the waters of tranquil shallow seas, leaving deposits high in calcium carbonates. The sediment-laying shallows left behind in central Alabama and Mississippi contained only a small percentage of large particles such as rocks or gravel and were thus much harder and more fertile.

Over time, these carbonate sands solidified into Selma chalk, hundreds of feet deep in places. This sterile, soft, white material is more easily eroded than nearby, harder limestones. Upon its "rotten" upper surface, loose sand crystals became mixed with loam, darkening to a toffee brown and increasing in fertility. The grasses brought forth wilt annually, decompose, and grow once again, depositing a compost of nutritious, deep, black loam.

Jack Elliott corrected my impression that the soil on top of the chalk washed down from the mountains. Instead, he tells us, it was produced by the weathering of the chalk itself. "In other words, all of the chalk has a certain percentage of the smaller clastics, usually clay, silt and smaller sands. As a result of chemical weathering the calcium carbonate in the chalk gradually dissolved at the top and was carried away by rain water, leaving as residual material the clastics which then formed the basis of the soil which accumulates at the top." Elliott in private communication, April 2000.

17. Quotation taken from Gray, *Agriculture*, Vol. 1, p. 446. See also Thomas Nairne, *Nairne's Muskhogean Journals: The 1708 Expedition to the Mississippi River*, ed. Alexander Moore (Jackson: University Press of Mississippi, 1988). In Madison County and elsewhere, the plantation system was succeeded by sharecropping, and sharecropping by agribusiness. Some of the Black Prairie is still under cultivation, though little of it is still very black.

18. John Hebron Moore, *Agriculture in Ante-bellum Mississippi*, pp. 37–42.

19. Ibid.

20. Bonner, *Georgia*, pp. 59–60, 64, 68.

21. Ibid.

22. Ibid. The Georgia Cotton Planters Convention then took its constituents in the opposite direction, encouraging more cotton cultivation and soliciting further credit and orders from the British. With British encouragement, the planters turned again to the South and West, reverting to an expansionist foreign policy dedicated to extensive, rather than intensive, agriculture—"extensive" in the geographical sense,

turning their energies outward, toward lands held by others, rather than inward, toward their own. "Nativity, friendship, kindred, comfort," fertilizing, contour plowing, crop rotation, and domestic industry could wait.

23. Ibid., pp. 100–110 and 125. On the Black Prairie, many slave-owning families remained in place, some out of a sort of affection, some out of necessity when they lacked sufficient capital to invest in a sequence of new plantations. Family names do recur generation after generation in some Mississippi counties. As Jack Elliott of Mississippi's Department of Archives and History wrote in June 2001 (private communication), his family "on both sides arrived in the 1830s and 1840s with the advancing cotton culture, and there they remained, as did many other families, whose descendants I grew up with. All of this illustrates that many, many of these planters did dig in and establish roots, while others continued hop-scotching westward."

24. Bonner, *Georgia*, p. 100 ff.

25. J. H. Moore, *Agriculture in Ante-bellum Mississippi*, pp. 37–42.

26. Eudora Welty, in her "Place in Fiction" (in *Essays*, p. 781 ff.), gives special attention to Faulkner's way of anticipating what might have happened in any of the Southern places—with the place so fully real for us that his anticipations seem inevitable. Cowdrey, *This Land*, pp. 6, 7. Northern writers had to await the Great Blizzard of 1888, the retreat from the Plains of the 1890s, and the coming of the Dust Bowl in the 1920s to reach an equivalently tragic sense of place. Southern land-loyalty was so intense that Welty's and Faulkner's evocations of Southern specialness almost permitted their readers to forget that Sarah Orne Jewett's Maine and Willa Cather's Nebraska were special, too.

Chapter 3

1. This is a good time to study Jefferson, because the fundamentals of his character, career, and ideology have been well stated for us in recent work of first-rate scholars. In 1997, Joseph Ellis produced his biography of Jefferson, *American Sphinx*. In 2000, Peter Onuf published his *Jefferson's Empire*, an intellectual history treating Jefferson's ideology. The book in your hands does not seek to do again what Ellis and Onuf have done so well. It is limited to one aspect of the man and of his career: Jefferson as a revolutionary planter-politician who had arresting things to say—and who did even more interesting things—about the proper uses of public land.

2. TJ in *Notes*, in *Writings*, Lib. of Am. Ed., pp. 289, 290–91.

3. Churchill, *Age of Revolution*, p. 182.

4. TJ to Priestley, March 21, 1801, quoted in Boorstin, *Lost World*, p. 228.; TJ on album, to John Cartwright, June 5, 1824, in *Writings*, Memorial Ed., Vol. 16, pp. 44–45.

5. Cutler quoted in Andrew R. L. Cayton, "The Conquest of Trans-Appalachia," in Ben-Atar and Oberg, *Federalists*, p. 85.

6. Jefferson's instructions are printed in *Writings*, Memorial Ed., Vol. 1, p. 262.

7. TJ to John Holmes, April 22, 1820, *Writings*, Lib. of Am. Ed., p. 1432.

8. TJ quoted in Fay, *Revolutionary Spirit*, p. 242.

9. For the accumulation of great estates, see Gray, *Agriculture*, Vol. 1, p. 399 ff.

10. Hamilton on primogeniture, *Report to the Society of the Cincinnati*, July 6, 1786, *Hamilton Papers*, Vol. 2, pp. 335-36.

Merrill Peterson has provided his assessment of this phase of Jefferson's career as revolutionary, though none could have expected that it would lead to the eradication of "every fiber . . . of ancient or future aristocracy and a foundation laid for a government truly republican," and it did not. Peterson tells us that "Jefferson never made . . . [the] mistake . . . [of imagining] that the overthrow of primogeniture and entail accomplished at one stroke a virtual democratic revolution in Virginia society. . . . The institution of fee simple tenure in the law of the commonwealth, while a radical act, was not socially revolutionary. . . . The eradication of [these] hopeless vestiges of feudalism . . . was only the first measure of his system." Peterson, *Jefferson*, p. 116. See also Stuart Bruchey in his article "Social and Economic Developments After the Revolution," in *The Blackwell Encyclopedia of the American Revolution*, p. 556.

11. Claude Bowers, in his *Young Jefferson*, p. 171, incorrectly assured his readers that "the Virginians prohibited it [the docking of entails by legislated termination] by law." Dumas Malone quietly pointed out in his *Jefferson the Virginian*, p. 253, that many entails were docked before 1775, including several at Jefferson's behest. TJ on emigrants and carapaces, *Autobiography*, in *Writings*, Memorial Ed., Vol. 1, pp. 6-12.

12. *Soils and Men*, p. 117. See also Edmund Ruffin, in Gray, *Agriculture*, Vol. 2, p. 647. Primogeniture and entail, which seemed to Jefferson's generation of Virginians to be retrograde feudal remnants to be swept aside to permit Virginia to get on with modernizing, actually helped to destroy feudalism in Britain. They drove able, healthy, well-fed, well-educated younger sons off the land and into trade. After the middle of the eighteenth century, such lively folk sought careers in the highly profitable army and navy, which by then had become implements of trade. Thus the custom of confining titles, and passing the bulk of estates, to elder sons fertilized British commercial life. Because they had no other way of sustaining themselves, the children of fighting families, deprived of estates and the retainers who came with estates, percolated into finance and commerce, as well as into the traditional professions of the church, army, navy, and diplomatic service. The British aristocracy may not have been readily entered at the top, but it was wide open at the bottom: "There was little to prevent most of the male children sliding out of it." On the continent, the landed gentry (especially the Poles and Hungarians) sliced and resliced landed estates among innumerable titled sons and forbade those sons by law to go into commerce. (The "sliding out" line is Lawrence Stone's, *Open Elite*, pp. 4-5 and 19-23.

13. TJ to Madison, Feb. 20 and Dec. 8, 1784, *Writings*, Ford, Vol. 3, p. 406, and Vol. 4, pp. 17, 18.

14. These could not be brothers of the sword like Hamilton's or Aaron Burr's, for Jefferson had not chosen to serve in the Revolutionary army. Indeed, after he ascended to the presidency a decade later, he pitted himself against their opposing brotherhood after it organized itself as the Order of the Cincinnati. The officers of the Continental Army had won supremacy for the new nation over a third of a continent, and many of them were already seeking to establish themselves upon vast tracts in the Ohio Valley, where they became his steadfast antagonists. Of the officer class, only Monroe became part of Jefferson's circle.

15. TJ to Jean Baptiste Say, March 2, 1815, *Writings*, Memorial Ed., Vol. 14, pp. 260–62.

16. TJ to Madison, June 9, 1793, *Writings*, Ford, Vol. 6, pp. 291–92.

17. Two years later, he wrote of his reelection as a personal vindication against the "unbounded calumnies of the Federal Party . . . [that] force my continuance . . . [despite] great desire . . . to retire at the end of the present term to a life of tranquility." Those "calumnies" had, it seems, contaminated his relationships not only to his domestic political constituency but also to his emotional constituency, the French. The Federalists, he complained, had "filled the European market" and thus obliged him "to appeal once more to my country for justification." A man who is driven by what he himself states to be such feelings is no invulnerable, impenetrable, calculating, porcelain figure, unmoved by the emotional climate about him. By his own account, confirmed by what men like Madison said of him, Jefferson was, like all good politicians, acutely conscious of what was said and thought of him, and implied about him. TJ in 1807–8, to Comte Diodati, March 29, 1807, *Writings*, Memorial Ed., Vol. 11, p. 182; to Dupont de Nemours, March 2, 1809, ibid., Vol. 12, pp. 259–60.

Henry Adams only rarely permitted himself to assert what Jefferson, or anyone else, longed for. John Randolph quoted, in Adams, *Jefferson Administrations*, Ch. 20, Lib. of Am. Ed., p. 1239 ff. Adams speaks for himself, ibid. p. 1058.

18. This subject has drawn some magnificent scholarship, from that of Fawn Brodie to that of Douglas Wilson and Kenneth Lockridge, but it does not bear upon land use directly enough for us to give it the space it deserves.

19. See Lockridge, *Patriarchal Rage*, and TJ quoted in Peterson, *Jefferson*, p. 242.

20. TJ to Monroe, May 20, 1782, quoted in Malone, *Virginian*, p. 395.

21. Madison, quoted in Marie Kimball, *War and Peace*, p. 161.

22. TJ as war hawk against Spain, see Stuart, *Half-way Pacifist*, quotations on p. 41.

23. TJ in *Notes*, in *Writings*, Memorial Ed., Vol. 2, pp. 225–28.

24. French theoretical writers of Jefferson's time referred to that kind of structural rhetoric as "speaking architecture." Association is important in architectural style. The designer-occupant says more than "This is me!" He or she also proclaims to the world that he or she is a member of an admirably cultivated subculture. In the theater or along a residential street, masks are larger than faces. Their features may be static, but they are also clear and may thus by symbolic expression become representative, rather than idiosyncratic, as human features are. The potency of symbols depends upon their having general meanings, not merely individual ones.

It is not easy for people of our symbolically impoverished period in the world's history to read the symbols offered by architecture or drama; the "close-up" in motion pictures has reduced our symbolic sensitivity, while audio enhancement has made it unnecessary for actors to talk above a whine or whisper. Sheer volume does not impart urgency, for it tells us nothing more than that the mechanical amplification has been turned up. We do not think a loud voice necessarily says anything more important than a soft one. There are many good books telling us how to read a suburb, how to read the distance between curb and facade or between rear wall and lot line. Placement matters, and so do shape and color, in imparting to our neighbors what our group is or what group we wish to be taken to represent.

25. My discussion of Jefferson's cabin is grounded in the work of Buford Pickens. It is a joy to be able finally to develop an idea Pickens urged upon me thirty years ago. He is not responsible for my conclusion that a yeoman's republic was a Lost Cause.

26. TJ to Madison, Feb. 17, 1826, *Writings*, Ford, Vol. 10, pp. 376–78. For quotations from him as to the fecundity of slaves, see J. C. Miller, *Wolf by the Ears*, pp. 240–41 and 251.

27. Durand quoted amidst Joseph Rykwert's exposition of these themes in his *On Adam's House in Paradise*, pp. 40 and 41.

28. The useful expression "Empire of System" is Andrew Cayton's; I quote his *Frontier Republic*, p. 21. He quotes Jefferson on p. 23. As public land policy evolved in the United States, an additional consequence emerged from Jefferson's advocacy of the use of the public domain to improve citizenship, and not merely as an asset to be pieced out to reduce taxes. That consequence took time to ripen, but it was fully manifested in the transfer of portions of the national endowment to endow the land-grant colleges, during the decade of the enactment of the Homestead Act.

29. TJ to Pendleton, Aug. 26, 1776, in *Writings*, Lib. of Am. Ed., p. 755. A fundamental reason for Jefferson's unwillingness to risk much democracy was, I believe, his limited faith in the *demos*, despite Woodrow Wilson's announcement that "the immortality of Jefferson does not lie in any one of his accomplishments but in his attitude toward mankind." Wilson did not deign to inform us exactly what that "attitude" was, though the British historian John Ashworth defined it as "mild condescension" (*"Agrarians" and "Aristocrats,"* p. 22).

Daniel Boorstin provided the Wilson quotation in the preface to the 1993 edition of his *Lost World of Thomas Jefferson*, p. vii. See also Charles Beard, in *Economic Origins*, p. 465.

Though one can hear it said, and even see it written, that Jefferson wrote the phrase "We the People," which opens the Constitution, he was not there to write it, being fully engaged at the time in Paris. Such language did not come naturally to him.

30. Ibid. As Daniel Boorstin concluded, Jefferson took the view that only "the corruptibility, the fickleness, the ignorance, and the crudity of the popular mass would surely prevent their conceiving or carrying through any grand design." Boorstin, *Lost World*, pp. 190–91.

31. *Notes*, in *Writings*, Memorial Ed., p. 215 ff.

32. Another elder statesman among historians, Edmund Morgan, provides us with the bone-chilling statement that what excited Jefferson "was the cutting edge of independence, the further emancipation of the already free, the progress in individual independence of that majority of Americans who were already ahead of the rest of the world." The people of Europe could wait for redemption from "ignorance, superstition, poverty, and oppression of body and mind." The masses of Latin America might forever remain incapable of "securing freedom and happiness . . . [or] of taking care of themselves." The theorists of seventeenth-century British Republicanism, whose accents can be readily discerned in familiar phrases of Jefferson and Taylor, had looked out their windows to the platoons of Nonconformist yeomanry moving to join Cromwell and Hampton and had made heroes of them. Their contribution to the Jeffersonian civic ideal was permitting him to treat Albemarle County in the eighteenth century as if it were Shropshire in the seventeenth, presenting "the yeoman

farmer," in Edmund Morgan's picture, to be seen "standing foursquare on his own plot of land, gun in hand and virtue in his heart . . . the ideal citizen of a republic." In Virginia, so long as this sort of farmer had a slave or two, he could be counted upon to see things as his greater neighbor did and to vote as he was told. Morgan, *American Slavery*, p. 377, and *Meaning of Independence*, p. 71.

By 1776, Americans had grown accustomed to the notion that governments were deliberate constructs to be held to stated *moral* objectives. The ideas of the *Mayflower*'s Elder Brewster and William Penn broke the path for Jefferson's. Penn had said that "government seems to me . . . a thing sacred in its institutions and end. For if it does not directly remove the cause, it crushes the effects of evil." Jefferson went on to associate both government *and the government's land* with the crushing of evil. Penn quoted, ibid.

33. Madison quoted in McCoy, *Last of the Fathers*, p. 245. TJ to Edward Coles, Aug. 25, 1814, quoted in Paul Finkelman, "Jefferson and Slavery," in Onuf, *Jeffersonian Legacies*, p. 209. Jefferson always proposed that slaves should be shipped out as soon as they were freed, unlike freed white indentured servants.

34. *Notes*, in *Writings*, Lib. of Am. Ed., p. 289 ff.

35. Jefferson is often said to have been a deist. I do not think this does justice to him; he was more and better than that and was, in fact, an animist. Deism was a creed based entirely upon reason rather than revelation, holding that though a supernatural agent may have formed creation, that agent no longer intruded upon it. The clockwork universe would tick along on its own, presumably until it needed new batteries. Jefferson sometimes wrote as if he were a deist, though he invoked God's blessings as if he believed they were there to be invoked and alluded on other occasions to "supernatural interference." The general tone of his writing was by no means indifferent to that possibility. My use of the term "animist" in this context is intended not to imply that we know Jefferson's mind about such matters but only to suggest that he gave indications of going beyond an observational and scientific stance toward nature in the direction of the greater reverence implied in the term: the Latin word *anima* is often translated as "soul." The distinction intended lies between observation of nature from outside it, by a detached scientist, and from within it, by an observer acknowledging participation in it. Those who wish to pursue the matter may find some interest in the "Animist Manifesto" to be found in my *Hidden Cities*.

36. Fitzhugh in *Debows Review*, January 1861.

37. Ibid., pp. 168 and 170. TJ in *Notes*, in *Writings*, Lib. of Am. Ed., p. 289. Though great landowners did not labor in the earth, the great John Locke had numbered them among the elect by virtue of their propinquity to those who did. Through their library windows, the English squires whose way of life Locke celebrated became virtuous by observation: out there between the hedgerows their tenants were farming. That was enough; gentlemen were landed, not dirty. Similarly, in Virginia, planters sitting on their piazzas might look across broad fields worked by slaves to descry, at the farthermost fringes, the cabins of yeomen, "chosen people" but not for the best real estate. Since slaves were disqualified from the ranks of the chosen people, it must have been the Proximity Principle that stamped the planters' passes: they owned the land; some of its "ennobling influence" would rub off on them. The Proximity

Principle was useful in adjusting a theory celebrating participation in the work of the land to justify a way of life in which some people owned other people who worked the land. It did not, however, beguile those who kept in mind Jefferson's precise language about how agrarian virtue arose from farming.

Chapter 4

1. The description quoted comes from Jefferson's answer to Query IV in the *Notes*, in *Writings*, Lib. of Am. Ed., p. 142 ff.

2. Ibid.

3. Description of Virginia country, to Jean Baptiste Say, March 2, 1815, *Writings*, Memorial Ed., Vol. 14, pp. 260–62.

4. Kulikoff, "Yeoman Classes," p. 105. Kulikoff's treatment is not only essential reading in itself but offers a bibliography which leads into the very rich literature which has been developed on this subject in recent decades. I have rearranged his categories a little and do not suggest that we see all in the same way.

5. Naturally enough, there is great scholarly dispute as to the degree to which the Virginia farmers were subservient to the planters. Opinion on the question shifted back and forth throughout the twentieth century and still does. I have offered my own conclusion, recognizing that others differ. My quotations come from Kulikoff, "Yeoman Classes," pp. 81 and 89. The full sentence which I have excerpted reads as follows: "Unlike yeomen, agrarian realists were committed to the search for foreign markets and rapid economic development." This might be read to suggest "economic development" in twentieth-century terms, meaning industrialization, but that was not, I am sure, Kulikoff's meaning.

Jefferson's lifelong affinity to things French may well have gained strength from his knowledge that the pre-Revolutionary French tax system in effect subsidized Virginian tobacco planters. It thus provided some stability to their prices. A percentage of price was taken, so it was in the Crown's interest to keep the prices of those goods high in order to sustain "tax-take." This quixotic French tax system was one of the casualties of the French Revolution, producing, as it happens, a sharp decline in the profitability of Virginia tobacco and the value of Virginia plantations.

6. Smith, quoted in the *WPA Guide to Virginia*, 1941 ed., p. 106.

7. I am following the account of Middleton, in *Tobacco Coast*, p. 282 ff.

8. Byrd quoted in Marambaud, *Byrd*, pp. 146–47, and in Thomas Jefferson Wertenbaker's essay on Byrd in Vol. 3 of the 1946 edition of the *Dictionary of American Biography*. It may be useful to extend the range of vision to point out that the wharves of the Virginian planters were so like those to be seen on the Vistula or the Pregel that it became a commonplace of nineteenth-century travel reports to liken the treatment of Negroes by the planters of Alabama and Mississippi to that accorded the Slav peasantry by the Prussian Junkers. The Virginians did not, however, have the stability of Junkers. Instead, the closest counterpart to a Virginia plantation was a Mexican hacienda of the nineteenth century, though the Virginia skyline of the eighteenth had not yet enjoyed the advances in technology providing industrial chimneys to the haciendas of Mérida and Yucatán, with their sugar mills, rope works, and pulque manufactures.

9. TJ to Angelica Church, Nov. 27, 1793, *Writings*, Ford, Vol. 6, pp. 455–56.

10. Boorstin, *Americans*, pp. 105–9. I have reversed the first and second portions of this quotation for purposes of clarity.

The maritime historian Samuel Eliot Morison has suggested that the virtually continuous military careers of the Lees, like that of George Washington, were merely the landward expression of the privateering bellicosity of their class.

11. TJ to John Jay, Aug. 23, 1785, *Letters*, in *Writings*, Lib. of Am. Ed., p. 818.

12. Ibid. In the 1920s, Norman S. Buck explored the progress of cotton production in Virginia during the colonial period and concluded that after the planters committed themselves to tobacco, raw cotton became as scarce as raw silk, though considerably less appreciated. Liverpool imported three bales of cotton from New York in 1770—obviously transshipped from somewhere, together with four from Virginia and Maryland and three from Georgia. Since Georgia was producing considerably more than three bags of sea island cotton, this tells us that the Georgians must have been doing a good deal of hand-looming of their own cotton fibers. (Buck, *Development*, p. 33.) In that year, the British West Indies sent six thousand bags.

In 1784, at the close of hostilities, when eight bags of cotton arrived in Liverpool on an American ship, they were seized by the authorities, who believed that their contents could not have been produced in the United States and must have been illegally transshipped. By 1810, 240,000 bales were arriving in Liverpool from American ports; yet it is worth noting that in that year Brazil sent nearly 142,000—though Portugese bales were only a third as large as American. (Ibid., footnotes on pp. 34 and 35.) The description of Berkeley outdoing the Yankees comes from Edmund Morgan in his *American Slavery*, p. 187; Beverley is quoted in Machor, *Pastoral Cities*, p. 76.

13. Newton had been directed to the study of probability theory by the work of the Dutch mathematician Christiaan Huygens and expressed his warm admiration for it. Soon thereafter, British insurers were making that theory the basis for business judgments. Merchants had all along dispensed with theory while directing their affairs.

The verse and the references to Newton's reading come from one of the works of my friend and sometimes partner Peter Bernstein, in his *Against the Gods*, at p. 93.

14. Commissioners, ibid.; and "tobacco swallowing all others," quoted in Gray, *Agriculture*, Vol. 1, p. 232.

15. Middleton, *Tobacco Coast*, pp. 176–77.

16. Commissioners, etc., quoted in Gray, *Agriculture*, p. 232 ff.; Pitt quoted in Friedenberg, *Life, Liberty*, p. 120.

17. Jefferson's theoretical—or, more rightly, his emotional—aversion to Scots and British merchants was shared by Madison, but only some of his antiurban bias. In 1785, while Jefferson was in Paris, Madison wrote Monroe to urge that he stir the planters from their torpor "to reacquaint themselves with the science of commerce and . . . combine in defense of their interests." They must be made "sensible of the utility of establishing a Philadelphia [Madison's own annotation at this point added: "by concentrating on commerce at Alexandria and Norfolk"] or a Baltimore among ourselves." Madison to Monroe, June 21, 1785, *Madison Papers*, Vol. 8, pp. 306–8.

The relationship of Jefferson and Madison to Virginia's own cities, and to the difference in their evaluation of pavement and cultivated fields, is a subject worthy of more extended treatment than the scope of an endnote, so I have put some further reflections and data in the Appendix; see "Jefferson, Madison, Adam Smith, and the Chesapeake Cities," p. 245.

18. Dunn, "Black Society," p. 75. In 1820, despite American discouragement of manumission, the percentage of free blacks in New Orleans had crept up to 18 percent, against 34 percent comprised of slaves, and 48 percent of whites, in a city that had grown from 17,000 inhabitants to 84,000.

19. Jefferson's attitude toward free blacks is discussed in Part Four. It is no wonder that in the year 2002 Cincinnati is building the nation's Underground Railroad Museum.

20. TJ quoted in Onuf, *Jefferson's Empire*, p. 20.

21. Price, "American Port Towns," p. 164.

22. I am grateful to the staff at Monticello for these measurements.

23. The twisting is important: without it cotton cannot be spun; for that reason, the peculiar, untwisted, wild species of the Hawaiian Islands may be handsome botanically but is commercially a bust. In India and Africa, cotton grows into a small tree, bearing orange or red blossoms, producing fibers intermediate in length between the long-fibered, black-seeded "sea island cotton" of the American coast and the short-fibered, green-seeded upland species of the Cotton Belt.

Cotton cloth was scarcely known among Europeans until the Christian era. Herodotus wrote of it as one of the wonders of India; the word itself is of Arabic origin—*qutun*—though the oldest cultivated plants so far discovered are not from the Old World. They come instead from Mexico and were cultivated so deep in antiquity as to astonish modern archaeology. In the 1960s and 1970s, archaeologists sweating it out in the bone-dry heat of southeastern Puebla Province determined that the cotton they found had been deliberately grown seven thousand years ago—before maize (corn) was put under cultivation, before beans, gourds, or squash. Writing in the *Athena Review* in 1999, Virginia Betz located "a fully domesticated form" in the Tehuacán Valley "dated 3500–2300 B.C." (p. 26), and Emily McClung de Tapia offers a table in her "Origins of Agriculture" showing a species of *Gosypidium* in the El Riego portion of that valley between 7000 and 5000 B.C. (p. 151). (I am grateful to Daniel Gelo for sending along the Betz article.)

How cotton came to Puebla is a difficult question. The "A genome" contributor for cotton is not found in the New World, but is in the Old; various suppositions have been offered, including exceedingly early human transportation of seeds or "oceanic drift of an A genome propagule." Cottons grow wild on the Galápagos Islands and in coastal Ecuador and Peru, and Betz says that "cotton may possibly have been introduced to Mesoamerica as an already domesticated form from the southern hemisphere where, in coastal Ecuador and Peru, cultivation of another species (*G. barbadense*) had been documented for much earlier periods. Yet most views favor the independent domestication of *G. hirsutum* in Mesoamerica" (p. 26). As I understand it, these sites in Ecuador and Peru have yielded evidence of domestic cotton as old as the oldest finds of cotton in Europe or Asia. (See Phillips, "Cotton." Thanks to my former colleague at the National Museum of American History, G. Terry Sharrer, I am able to rely upon this summary article.)

During what Europeans call "Roman times," a cotton belt developed in southern Arizona. Seven centuries later, while the Europeans were enjoying their High

Middle Ages, elite families of the Tucson and Phoenix basins were bound in alliance by filaments of cotton. Cloth produced along the Salt and Gila rivers was used to dower women marrying upstream—or so archaeologists suppose—and Arizona cotton even made its way into Chaco Canyon.

By the time Europeans appeared on the scene, cotton agriculture and the making of cotton cloth were so widespread in the valley of Mexico that the Aztecs taxed each commoner to deliver to the authorities one cotton cloak per year, producing a hoard from which distributions were made by traders for exchange as far away as New Mexico.

24. Webb informs us that annually, on average, during the brief tenure of the Cattle Kingdom—the *ensuing* fifteen years—280,000 cattle were driven to market. Forrest McDonald and Grady McWhiney have computed that the comparable number of hogs driven annually from the Southern hills in antebellum drives was 4,468,400. Webb's total for his fifteen-year Cattle Kingdom is 4,223,497 cattle. McDonald and McWhiney give us 67,026,000 hogs. ("The South," p. 1107.)

25. Kulikoff in his *British Peasants*.

26. The yeoman is quoted in McDonald and McWhiney, "The South," p. 1106.

27. Wilson, "American Agricola," p. 354.

28. Faulkner, quoted in McDonald and McWhitney, "The South," p. 1106, ibid. What had been true in the Appalachians was true as well in the Ozarks. Ecology ordained culture even in Arkansas, where, in 1836, the *Little Rock Times* wrote of the lowland delta lands of its southeastern counties as being "considered the great cotton region," and the northwestern counties as being "somewhat broken, but interspersed with innumerable valleys and small water courses" where all that might be grown were "corn, vegetables, and fruits," but providing "the cottages of the poor" with "substantial comforts." (Arkansas wonders quoted by Rohrbough, *Frontier*, p. 286.)

The *Times* was making a point of immense political significance. In Arkansas and Missouri, as in Georgia, South Carolina, North Carolina, Virginia, Kentucky, and Tennessee, non-cotton-producing upland counties were disposed to secede from any regime acting largely in the planters' interest—as they did secede, in some cases, formally, from the Confederacy.

The Appalachian highlanders have left us not only that legacy of erosion that comes to us in the photographs of the New Deal period and is recalled to us by any walk above the headwaters of the Rappahannock or Potomac or James. They have left us the blossoming of Appalachia in the spring and its reminder of the great achievement of the 1820s—its demonstration that a nation can break a collective addiction. Alcohol consumption was reduced in a decade to less than half its former quantity, and after that it declined further. The consequences to the land were delightful. The yeomanry of the mountains returned to subsistence farming, and the nation acquired an unofficial national arboretum—some of it planted later, when peach brandy and applejack enjoyed a resurgence, but much of it a tribute to early nineteenth-century abstinence. (See Rorabaugh, *Alcoholic Republic*.)

Though its origins were commercial rather than scientific or aesthetic, in the spring of a good year travelers on airplane flights from Dulles Airport to Atlanta's Hartsfield may divert themselves from their computers and romance fiction to observe below them, for two or three weeks, the entire eastern slope of the Appalachians flowering white and pink with peach and apple blossoms. This exquisite testimony to a generation of hardy arborists and distillers is slowly going wild; the apple trees are reverting to the forms and habits of their central Asian ancestors, growing gnarly and unkempt, while, deep in the chromosomes of the peach trees, North Africa stirs again. The native wild plums and redbuds stand amazed while, amid the exotic fruits, dogwoods, azaleas, and mountain laurels bloom white and pink, elegant enough for Laura Ashley.

Some highlanders have discovered the apple market, with its waxing, boxing up, conveyor belts, and refrigerator cars, but many others still peer downward upon the plains, remaining as little moved by what they see there as their forefathers were in Jefferson's youth.

29. Bonner, *History of Georgia Agriculture*, pp. 108, 110.

Chapter 5

1. TJ, *Autobiography*, in *Writings*, Memorial Ed., Vol. 1, pp. 53–59. Remonstrance to his majesty, Friedenberg, *Life, Liberty*, p. 150.

2. First paragraph of the Declaration of Independence, *Writings*, Lib. of Am. Ed., p. 19.

3. John Stilgoe's wonderful *Common Landscape* presents in a short essay a compelling picture of Spanish settlement and intention, p. 34 ff. My quotation from Bradford comes from Ahlstrom, *A Religious History*, p. 136.

4. The Russians' presence on Hawaii was discovered with delight by President James Madison during the War of 1812; Madison's agents were able to arrange a bailment of American ships with the Russian American Company to keep them out of the hands of the British.

5. Gray, *Agriculture*, Vol. 1, pp. 312, 333. Jamestown and Plymouth were both founded by an enterprise which we call "the Virginia Company" as shorthand for a complex synthesis of earlier ventures originating in Bristol and the West Country. The Massachusetts Bay Company followed with an entrepôt at Boston in 1629. In the light of this corporate history, Plymouth Rock might do as well as a corporate logo as the Rock of Gibraltar.

The earlier company had failed in its effort to place a settlement in Maine in 1606, but the Virginia Company succeeded at Jamestown and then issued a patent of settlement in 1620 to the Pilgrim Fathers of Massachusetts. The Mayflower Compact, like the Declaration of Independence, was a *statement of purpose* issued by a *company* of people. A "company" is an assemblage of persons breaking bread together—*com-panis*. As we commence our inquiry into what the founders of the American Republic had in mind in 1776, and specifically what Thomas Jefferson *said* he had in mind, then and thereafter, we must be clear about the tradition in which they stood. It was one of expository companying and ceremonial incorporating. It is too easy for us, in the age in which corporations vie with governments for power, to use words that leave the inference that *governments* may be "instituted among men" and women, through imposition, while economic organisms such as *corporations* are somehow more consensual and by implication less predatory. That was not Mr. Jefferson's view of the matter. When some of his civic purposes were subverted or frustrated by companies and by governments sponsoring and deploying them, foreign and domestic, Jefferson did not like it at all.

As we survey the powers of the earth among which the Founding Fathers situated their experiment, we must give a little more attention to the words they used in explaining why they did so. Unlike the Pilgrims, they did not often refer to themselves as forming a "company." They might readily have done so, for they knew Latin better than we and used words of Latin origin very precisely. We use "company" promiscuously, to denote large corporations, whose shareholders never broke bread together even metaphorically, for companies of players, companies of soldiers of less than regimental strength, good company, bad company, people we entertain, and for any individual who keeps us from being alone. Yet in common usage in the United States, a "company" is now generally distinguished from a partnership by its possession of a charter, which means that it does have a statement of purpose.

Let us note that the Pilgrims came very close to designating their compact as a corporation, when they said it was "a civil *body* politic." Though current use makes us expect the term "corporation" to designate a business firm, we also use it when we write of municipalities, churches, and, as Daniel Webster once instructed us, of much-loved small colleges such as Dartmouth. The word still denotes an artificial person— a *body* politic. Governments are by that definition corporations, though some were compacted as a snowball is compacted, and some, like that announced on July 4, 1776, grew together like a snow crystal.

6. R. Blackburn, *Making of New World Slavery*, pp. 6 and 11. Before the trading company's discovery of the profits to be enjoyed at "the conjunction of slavery, colonialism, and maritime power," slavery had been "marginal or non-existent in Western Europe," Blackburn writes. Only after the Age of Discoveries was "the slave plantation system itself . . . perfected as a productive enterprise," leading to the "prodigious growth of the various slave systems, set in the context of the eighteenth-century commercial boom and the onset of the Industrial Revolution" (ibid., p. 25).

7. Until Marshall and his concurring justices had their say in the matter, it had not been clear that a corporation had the rights of an individual under the Constitution. Scholars differ on the exact number of corporations organized to produce goods in the colonial period, but the best count seems to be that only six were formally chartered as such—two in the seventeenth century and four in the eighteenth. Three hundred and ten corporations were chartered by state legislatures between 1775 and 1800, of which only eight produced goods. The rest were issued for the formation of public utilities, colleges, municipalities, and the like. After the Supreme Court of the United States declared itself determined to see to it that corporate charters would be inviolate from state legislative tinkering, the great animals of the Jurassic age proliferated. New England alone gave birth to nearly two thousand corporations by 1830, half of which were for commercial or industrial purposes, and emphatically private in their benefits. My numbers of corporate charterings in the colonial period, and those of the post-Constitutional period, are taken from Stuart Bruchey's essay "Social and Economic Developments After the Revolution," in *Blackwell's Encyclopedia of the Revolution*, at p. 563, and from a footnote on p. 438 in J. E. Smith, *Marshall*. As Smith notes, the classic text on this subject is E. Merrill Dodd, *American Business Corporations Until 1860* (Cambridge: Harvard University Press, 1954).

8. My quotations come from Bailey, *Ohio Company*, pp. 203–5 and 208, and my treatment owes much to Friedenberg, *Life, Liberty*, p. 103.

9. Inhibition against settling Indian lands, Friedenberg, *Life, Liberty*, p. 214.

10. Turner, "State-Making," quoted in ibid., pp. 220–21.

11. Wallace, *Jefferson and the Indians*, p. 21.

12. TJ to Madison, Nov. 11, 1783, *Papers*, Boyd, Vol. 7, pp. 503–4, quoted in Wallace, *Jefferson and the Indians*, p. 48. Wallace on Cherokee land, ibid., p. 38. On pp. 46–47 Wallace concludes that there is no evidence in the Jefferson papers to confirm the assertion of a participant in the Henderson-Blount speculation that Jefferson was involved in it. If he was, however, this would provide another Claiborne association, for William C. C. Claiborne certainly was.

13. TJ to Madison, Jan. 30, 1787, *Writings*, Lib. of Am. Ed., p. 882. United in these undertakings were the Meriwethers, Lewises, Claibornes, and Jefferson. Having examined the record, Dr. Wallace was moved to assert that Jefferson's letter to Madison of November 11, 1783, "was a flat-out lie . . . probably intended to facilitate the conduct of his mission to France, unencumbered by suspicions that he had used or was using public office to promote his own private financial schemes." The verdict is just, though it does not mean that he intended to lie. He was a man of phenomenal compartmentalizing skills, able to remember just what he wished to remember, and no more, and also given to strict construction of unpleasant facts. Wallace gives a meticulously annotated account of these events, and their context, in Chapter One of his *Jefferson and the Indians*.

14. Boorstin, *Americans*, pp. 105–6. The juxtaposition of the term "laborlord" to "landlord" was suggested by Gavin Wright, in *Old South*, as part of a powerful exegesis of this matter, pp. 17–31. Randolph, *Domestic Life*, p. 408. The Nicholases, like the Walkers, Meriwethers, Clarks, and Claibornes, were plungers into real estate on a grand scale. The brother of Wilson Cary Nicholas, George Nicholas of Kentucky, was for many years a resident of that western extension of Virginia, watching over claims that eventually accumulated to more than a million acres. His associates there were James Wilkinson and Harry Innes, brother of the attorney general of Virginia (and Jefferson's source for the ancient Indian sculpture presented in the foyer of Monticello). The endorsement of a note, which Wilson Cary Nicholas asked of Jefferson in his old age, was the latest of a series of interchanged endorsements and guarantees arising from Nicholas's speculations. Nicholas defaulted. Jefferson was forced to find the money.

15. My quotations and part of this analysis are drawn from Cayton, *Frontier Republic*, p. 14 ff.

16. Ibid.

17. Cavalier glamour still shimmers from Carolina rivers such as the Ashley and the Cooper, named for courtiers who were called "landed proprietors." They did not go to live beside their rivers, nor did they inspect much of their proprietorships. And, so far as I can find out, none of the purchasers of Canadian baronies from the Stuart kings ever saw Canada—not even the Viscount Canada himself. These gentlemen of England and Scotland may have been enfiefed, but they quickly substituted real estate promotion for any anachronistic notions of collecting tribute from Eskimos or Yamassees. The Penns, Fairfaxes, Culpepers, and Calverts raised no levies and led no armies.

18. Jefferson and Locke quoted in Griswold, *Farming*, pp. 38-40. In two famous passages known by heart to many of the Founders, Locke had written a century earlier that America remained virtually in a state of nature, wherein "whatsoever . . . [a man] removes out of that state that Nature hath provided and left it in, he hath mixed his labor with it, and joined to it something that is his own . . . thereby making it his property." And again: "As much as any one can make use of to any advantage of life . . . so much he may by his labor fix a property in."

19. Fort Stanwix Treaty language quoted in Onuf, *Jefferson's Empire*, p. 40.

20. Roosevelt quoted in Friedenberg, *Life, Liberty*, p. 298.

21. Lee quoted in Finkelman, "Slavery and the Northwest Ordinance," in *New Perspectives*, p. 83, with extensive further bibliography on the point. The views of Cutler and the Mariettans are quoted from Cayton, *Frontier Republic*, pp. 37-39. I have dealt at length with one aspect of the Mariettan similarities to Jefferson—their respect for American antiquity—in *Hidden Cities*.

22. Ibid.

23. Oglethorpe quoted in Spalding, *Oglethorpe*, p. 50.

24. Washington to Arthur Young, quoted in Smith, *Patriarch*, p. 138. Washington on yeomen and small lots, quoted in Hirschfeld, *Washington*, p. 76.

Chapter 6

1. Michael Kammen entitled one of his best books *A Season of Youth*. Washington did not manumit all his family slaves until after the death of his wife. It is probable that Madison intended to free his, as well, but that his will was altered.

2. TJ in *Autobiography*, in *Writings*, Lib. of Am. Ed., p. 5. Paul Finkelman, a student of these intricacies, concluded that "Jefferson persisted in telling his European readers" something that was not true. Finkelman in "Jefferson and Slavery," pp. 196-99.

3. TJ to Madison, quoted in ibid., pp. 198-99; to Jean Nicolas Démeunier, June 26, 1786, *Writings*, Lib. of Am. Ed., p. 591.

4. TJ to Chastellux, June 7, 1785, ibid., p. 799.

5. Ibid.

6. TJ to Monroe, June 17, 1785, ibid., p. 805.

7. Peterson, *Jefferson*, p. 283.

8. Ibid.

9. I do not know how Monroe voted. So far as I have been able to learn, no record was kept of individual votes. I may be in error about this, but the account given in the text is the best I can provide.

10. Ammon, *Monroe*, pp. 53-54.

11. A fresh and detailed treatment of this matter is to be found in Stephen Aron, *How the West Was Lost*, p. 89 ff.

12. The Kentucky Abolition Society proposal appears in an excellent discussion of this subject in Meinig, *Continental*, p. 301. On Kentucky constitutions, see Ireland, *Kentucky*, pp. 2-3, and Abernethy, *South*, pp. 70-71.

13. Cotton and male slaves, Gray, *Agriculture*, Vol. 2, p. 688.

14. J.F.H. Claiborne, *Mississippi*, p. 467. Scarborough, "Heartland of the Cotton Kingdom," pp. 331–32.

15. Ibid.

16. Ibid.

17. My quotations are taken from a wonderfully lucid exposition of the progression of Madison's views by McCoy in his *Last of the Fathers*, on pp. 175, 193, and 233–36.

19. Ibid. I have also shadowed Leo Marx's view of the search for a middling state in politics as well as in ideal poetry. See his *Machine in the Garden*, p. 100 ff. TJ on seaport towns, quoted in Onuf, *Jefferson's Empire*, p. 20; Onuf himself, p. 69. In these pages I do not seek to present a complete picture of the evolution of Madison's political thought. He was, of course, not of the same mind on all subjects at all times. The sequence of his changes has been set forth by Drew McCoy in his *Last of the Fathers* (1989) and *Elusive Republic* (1980), by Jack Rakove in his *James Madison and the Creation of the American Republic* (1990), by Richard Matthews in his *If Men Were Angels: James Madison and the Heartless Empire of Reason* (1995), by Lance Banning in his *Sacred Fire of Liberty* (1995), and by Garrett Ward Sheldon more recently in his *Political Philosophy of James Madison* (2000).

19. Magruder quoted in McCoy, *Elusive Republic*, pp. 198–99.

20. Ibid.

21. Ibid.

22. I am quoting from Henry Nash Smith's treatment of the evolution of the two agrarianisms in his *Virgin Land*, p. 152 ff. Smith does not appear to be any more currently fashionable than Leo Marx, but they will be again.

23. R. Blackburn, *Overthrow*, p. 285.

24. TJ to Coles, Aug. 25, 1814, *Writings*, Lib. of Am. Ed., p. 1344 ff. Finkelman, "Jefferson and Slavery," pp. 198–99; Appendix to *Notes*, in *Writings*, Lib. of Am. Ed., p. 344.

25. Ibid.

26. Ibid.

27. Ellis, *Sphinx*, p. 173, and quoting TJ to Crawford, in 1816, on old men's dreams at p. 309. The abolition of the slave trade was an entirely different matter from the abolition of slavery itself. The productivity of Virginia's enslaved workforce was coming to exceed the productivity of its arable land, so the importation of more slaves was not in the interest of those who already had a surplus to sell. However, Jefferson elided manumission and the end of the international slave trade when recalling that "[in] the year '78" he had "brought in a bill to prevent their further importation . . . [that] passed without opposition . . . leaving to future efforts its [slavery's] final eradication." In 1780, when he began work on the *Notes*, the horizon of that "future" was already beginning to recede: "We must be contented to hope they [antislavery principles] will force their way into everyone's mind." The force was greater in the opposite direction, however, and the "future" had receded toward invisibility by 1821, when Jefferson wrote that "the process of emancipation and deportation . . . [must be carried forth] peaceably and in such slow degree as that evil will wear off insensibly, and their place be . . . filled up by free white laborers." "No more good," TJ to Dr. Walter Jones, March 31, 1801, *Writings*, Memorial Ed., Vol. 10, pp.

255–56; wearing off insensibly, *Autobiography*, ibid., Vol. 2, pp. 71–73; content to hope, *Notes*, ibid., Vol. 2, pp. 225–28; final eradication, *Autobiography*, ibid., Vol. 2, pp. 73–74.

28. Ibid.

29. TJ to John Holmes, April 22, 1820, *Writings*, Lib. of Am. Ed., p. 1432.

Chapter 7

1. Jefferson's draft, in the Declaration, *Writings*, Lib. of Am. Ed., p. 22.

2. Ibid.

3. Hamilton and Franklin quoted by Stuart Bruchey, in his article "Social and Economic Developments After the Revolution," in *The Blackwell Encyclopedia of the Revolution*, p. 564. Pitt quoted in Friedenberg, *Life, Liberty*, p. 120.

4. Forty-eight guns and Roe quoted in Buck, *Development*, pp. 77–78.

5. Ibid., p. 102.

6. The Baltic is the northern equivalent to the Mediterranean, but it endures a crueler climate and had no Middle East at hand to civilize it. After one try—"Varus, where are my legions?"—the Romans left it alone. Then the Muslims created commercial opportunity for the Baltic peoples, and ultimately for the English, by sweeping across the eastern provinces of the old Roman Empire, eliminating Mediterranean competitors, and inviting the blond, hairy northern tribes to establish trading connections between Denmark and Baghdad. Soon after the year 1000, the first organized crusading of Europeans against Muslims brought Germans descending those routes to join the fray, led by the Teutonic Knights. Trade and religious zeal were always admixed, as we learn from the tale that the first headquarters of the Teutonic Knights was a grounded trading ship salvaged during the winter of 1190–91 by merchants from Bremen and Lubeck to make of it a hospital where both armed men and physicians were trained for service either in the Holy Land or along the trade routes of the Baltic.

7. Keynes quoted from De Schweinitz, *Rise and Fall*, p. 43, from whom I have also derived the details of this transaction.

8. Had Hapsburg monarchs had the wit to resuscitate the medieval Flemish, South German, Austrian, and Italian financial and trading companies they had taken down in their bankruptcies of the seventeenth century as prototypes for Catholic corporate imperialism, the history of North America would have been otherwise, and Latin America would have entered the twentieth century with quite another set of elites.

9. The term, and concept, of the "fiscal-military state" was seen by its author, John Brewer, as "the most important transformation in English government between the domestic reforms of the Tudors and the major administrative changes in the first half of the nineteenth century" (*Sinews*, p. xvii).

10. Improving landlords and financiers, from Cain and Hopkins, *British Imperialism*, p. 101.

11. King George and Bolingbroke, ibid., p. 420. One did not acquire status in feudal times from acreage but from tenantry. And in later times a duke whose income came from land-leases in London might own a million acres of gorse, but if all he owned was the gorse no one would doff a hat as he passed. In America, it is not so.

Though no large fortune was ever made in this country on rural property without what Texans call "minerals," we retain an archaic regard for mere acreage, whether occupied or not. It is difficult to recall any American landlord since 1783 who actually led his tenantry into battle, though British gentry did so as late as the Second World War.

12. As to the Elizabethans, I am following J. V. Beckett, in his *Aristocracy*, p. 208. As to Durham and Sutherland, my quotations come from Cannadine, *Aristocracy*, p. 18.

13. "Mere urban office-holder" is a line of Lawrence Stone's, from his *Open Elite*, p. 7, from which I have taken my quotations from Steele and Chamberlain.

14. Ibid.

Chapter 8

1. Pirenne quoted in Wolf, *People Without History*, p. 121.

2. Ibid., p. 270.

3. Acts of 1700 and 1720, De Schweinitz, *Rise and Fall*, p. 121.

4. Weavers and spinners, ibid., p 120.

5. My account of the advantages of Lancashire in cotton manufacture comes from the stately eleventh edition of the *Encyclopedia Britannica*, Vol. 7, p. 283. See also De Schweinitz, *Rise and Fall*, pp. 121–22.

6. Spectacle, in Roll, *History*, p. 51. My numbers come from Wolf, *People Without History*, pp. 272–73.

7. Briton in India on bandannas, quoted ibid., p. 286. Production figures from Buck, *Development*, p. 166.

8. My account, and this quotation, come from Edwards, *Growth*, p. 65.

9. Sheffield quoted in Brewer, *Sinews*, p. 64.

10. Ibid.

11. Edwards, *Growth*, p. 65 ff., esp. 76 and 79.

12. I am quoting from John Brewer's admirable treatment of this matter in *Sinews*, pp. 137 and 199.

13. I am not quoting Jefferson but Brewer, ibid.

14. The title "father of the American cotton industry" comes from the biographical essay on Coxe in the *Dictionary of American Biography*, 1946 ed., Vol. 3, pp. 488–89.

15. Coxe quoted in Edwards, *Growth*, pp. 86–87. The line about the value of slaves is Edwards's summary, not Coxe's language.

16. *Burr Papers*, p. 658. There are earlier examples of correspondence between Coxe and Burr in the *Papers*, I have sought to provide an account of the alliance of Burr, Hamilton, and John Jay against the émigré planters in my *Burr, Hamilton, and Jefferson*.

17. TJ to Whitney, Nov. 16, 1793, in *Writings*, Ford, Vol. 6, p. 448; to Monroe, Nov. 14, 1801, in *Writings*, Lib. of Am. Ed., pp. 1095–96.

18. TJ to Monroe, Nov. 14, 1801, ibid., pp. 1095–96; to Hollins, Feb. 19, 1809, ibid., pp. 1200 ff. The references to TJ and Milledge are to be found in the Milledge Papers, in the Georgia Historical Society. See also Joyce Chaplin, in her *Anxious Pursuit*, p. 136 ff. with an extensive bibliography, and, as to Whitney's faking his demonstration of "interchangeable parts" for President John Adams and President-

elect Jefferson, see Robert Woodbury, in *Technology and Culture*, a magazine I am proud to have had a role in sustaining at the Smithsonian, Vol. I (1960), pp. 235–53. See also TJ on interchangeable parts in Paris, quoted in Peterson, *Jefferson*, p. 336.

19. Randolph quoted in Fogel, *Without Consent*, p. 65.

20. I am using the aggregate numbers provided by Fogel, ibid.

21. TJ to Randolph, ibid.; TJ to Madison, Feb. 17, 1826, *Writings*, Ford, Vol. 10, pp. 376–78. Quotations from him as to the fecundity of women are from Miller, *Wolf*, pp. 240–41 and 251.

22. Edwards, *Growth*, pp. 69 and 75.

23. Milne's visit and Washington's response, ibid., p. 87, and Flexner, *New Nation*, p. 166.

24. I have quoted Davis's, Bryant's, and Bremer's words from Mills Lane, *People of Georgia*, p. 154 ff. I confess to quoting a phrase or two from myself in these two paragraphs, for *Architecture, Men, Women, and Money*, in which I discussed this matter at greater length, is out of print. Besides, some terms are more appropriate here than they were there, and what was good enough for Rossini is good enough for me.

25. My statistics are taken from North's classic study *The Economic Growth of the United States, 1790–1860*, with its schedules after p. 280, and from Edwards, *Growth*, p. 75 ff.

26. Mobile *Register* quoted in Brantley, *Banking in Alabama, 1816–1860*, Vol. 1, p. 346.

27. "Peddling traffic," Eric Williams, *Capitalism and Slavery*, p. 128. For statistics, see North, *Economic Growth*, schedules p. 280 ff., and Edwards, *Growth*, pp. 75 ff.

28. Editorial in the *London Times*, 1857, quoted ibid., p. 176.

29. Quotations from McCoy, *Last of the Fathers*, pp. 175, 193, 233–36.

30. Ibid.

Part Three Introduction

1. Jefferson on free blacks, quoted in J.C. Miller, *Wolf by the Ears*, p. 218, in the midst of a brilliant discussion of Jefferson's differences with John Marshall; the book of fate is opened in a passage from *The Writings of Thomas Jefferson*, Memorial Ed., Vol. 1, pp. 72–73.

2. C. Hudson, *Southeastern Indians*, p. 159.

Chapter 9

1. For McGillivray's title, see Michael Green, *Politics*, p. 32 ff. McGillivray had a complex of plantations at Tallassee, upper, lower, and little. I have clumped them as a group after attempting with the aid of experts in their history to locate who was at which when.

This is not the book to offer biographies of Milfort or Nolan, for Milfort was gone from Alabama before the planters' assault upon that interior region was fully in train, and most of Nolan's celebrity arises from his exploits in Texas, beyond the boundaries we have set for ourselves. He does deserve a salute as he goes, however, for had he not turned back from a rendezvous at Monticello with Jefferson, some parts of this story might have come out differently. Nolan shared a death sentence with Bowles, which was executed upon each at an eight-hundred-mile distance.

2. McGillivray to Panton, Sept. 20, 1788, included in record of the case of *Johnson* vs. *Innerarity*, Docket #1156, Series New Orleans 1813–1846, Supreme Court of Louisiana Collection, Louisiana and Special Collections, Earl K. Long Library, University of New Orleans. I am indebted to John C. Kelly of those Special Collections for this letter. Statement of chiefs quoted in Caughey, *McGillivray*, pp. 90–93.

3. Ibid.

4. Ibid., p. 93. Claudio Saunt, in his enterprising *A New Order of Things*, sets himself against those of us who have found Alexander McGillivray "to be an appealing subject because of his status as an educated mestizo Indian who shared many of the values of his white antagonists and because of the abundance of letters he left behind" (p. 68). The term "mestizo" may explain some of Saunt's animus, I fear. Who since Adam has not been a mestizo? Saunt does good work in demonstrating how McGillivray as a slaveholder had much in common with the planters against whom, Saunt acknowledges, he contended for dominance. He also produces several instances, of what he says are many, of McGillivray's assisting American planters to recover lost slaves. He was a man caught between cultures, that is undeniable.

5. McGillivray to Panton, Sept. 20, 1788.

6. Sehoy described in Cashin, *McGillivray*, p. 72; the date of McGillivray's birth has been much debated but has been settled by Cashin. See his p. 73 and notes thereto. J. Leitch Wright, in his *Creeks and Seminoles*, cites Benjamin Hawkins as his source with regard to Durand's being a Negro. See Wright's p. 20 and his note 34 on p. 326.

7. I am grateful to Daniel Gelo for this definition of an atlatl and to Denis LaBat of the staff of Louisiana's Poverty Point State Historic Site for showing me how to use one. I was shown the killing power of a blowgun by an Alabama chief— for squirrels and birds. With just a little poison on the tip it could do for a human enemy.

George Milner does *not* place atlatls in the hands of Indians facing de Soto, but some laggards may well still have preferred them to the recurved bows that were replacing atlatls as weapons by the advent of Europeans in the New World. See Milner, "Warfare in Prehistoric and Early Historic Eastern North America," *Journal of Archaeological Research* 7, no. 2, 1999. Simple bows had been used in the Mississippi Valley since the seventh century, or even earlier, but they did not have the stunning power of either an atlatl-driven spear or an arrow discharged from a recurved bow. I am told that there is evidence that the Aztecs were still using atlatls against the Spaniards and were still employing simple bows, without recurving, against vulnerable animals. See also Steven A. LeBlanc, *Prehistoric Warfare in the American Southwest* (Salt Lake City: University of Utah Press, 1999) especially Chapter Three. I am indebted to Steven Lekson for these references. Claymores, muskets, leather leggings and kilts were conspicuous at Moore's Creek in 1775, among many other places.

8. Seven languages and the non-Creek chief, Wright, *Creeks and Seminoles*, pp. 11 and 17.

9. My quotations come from an extended essay upon this subject in my *Rediscovering America* entitled "How the University of Virginia Became Ohio, and Other Thoughts About Original Sin."

10. For what little is known about the proposals at Fort Pitt and Hopewell, and McGillivray's letter to White, see Abel, "Proposals," pp. 89–90.

11. Ibid.

12. Ibid., p. 97.

13. Jefferson's proposal, *Writings*, Lib. of Am. Ed., pp. 376–78.

14. TJ to Harrison, Aug. 9, 1803, quoted in C. Keller, *Philanthropy*, p. 60.

15. Quoted in Cashin, *McGillivray*, p. 296.

16. McGillivray described by a source quoted by Pickett, *Alabama*, pp. 431–32.

17. Ibid.

18. McGillivray to Panton, Sept. 20, 1788, included in record of the case of *Johnson vs. Innerarity*, Docket #1156, Series New Orleans 1813–1846, Supreme Court of Louisiana Collection, Louisiana and Special Collections, Earl K. Long Library, University of New Orleans.

19. My quotation of Jefferson comes from Saunt, *New Order*, and the sources he cites on p. 76. Abigail Adams is to be found in Cashin, *McGillivray*, p. 304. Fisher Ames quoted in R. N. Smith, *Patriarch*, p. 55. Smith effectively uses material from Arthur Orrmont's *Diplomat in Warpaint* and John Caughey's *McGillivray of the Creeks*, both admiring accounts, but appears determined to diminish the Chief's eminence by asserting that he suffered from syphilis (p. 55), took bribes, and "died a dissolute death" (p. 167). It is more likely that the cause of death was pneumonia and what those about him knew as "gout of the stomach." This sounds more like cancer than syphilis. See Cashin p. 307. McGillivray and drink, Flexner, *New Nation*, p. 264.

20. There are many rollicking accounts of the Yazoo Frauds, of which Friedenberg's (*Life*, *Liberty*) is a good example. My favorite remains, however, Abernethy's, for his cold contempt of the pious frauds. See his *South*, pp. 76 ff. and 136 ff.

21. The party of Jefferson has come to include many historians who have found both Washington and McGillivray distasteful because they were distasteful to their hero. The same affinities explain their washing the Yazooite speculators in the blood of the historiographic lamb—many of the speculators were associated with Jefferson. McGillivray has been subjected to the most rigorous of derogation. Among the charges made against him are complaints that instead of agreement with Washington he should have treated historians to a good rollicking war. Perhaps the Creeks would have been better off had they fought then; McGillivray had six thousand warriors to set against a considerably smaller American army, and his influence was great as well among thousands of Cherokees and Choctaws. Perhaps, in hindsight, we can rightly comment that they were weaker later, when Andrew Jackson went after them. But it is always easier to calculate than to do the fighting.

22. "Half-breed" in R. N. Smith, *Patriarch*, p. 56.

23. Ibid.

Chapter 10

1. Pickett, *Alabama*, p. 411.

2. My quotation comes from Douglas Egerton's *Gabriel's Rebellion*, p. 5. There is an excellent account of Dunmore's relationship to the blacks of Virginia in Woody Holton's "Rebel Against Rebel."

3. Scots and tobacco, in Gray, *Agriculture*, Vol. 1, p. 215. The large number of Southern Scots who followed Aaron Burr rather than Jefferson may be explained by either the experience of wartime Virginia or their shared Presbyterianism—or both. It may be recalled that Burr studied theology as a Presbyterian.

4. The recognition of the first battle south of Massachusetts, and my account of Harris and Dunmore, are drawn from Holton, "Rebel Against Rebel," p. 160.

5. Burke quoted ibid., p. 163; "caressing" at p. 162.

6. Saunt in his *New Order*, p. 111. Because Mr. Saunt and I differ so much on other matters, it is no doubt best that I add that, for clarity in context, I have reversed the order of the two clauses quoted, though, I believe, without changing their meaning. Saunt's footnotes provide an excellent bibliography for this point. For Mary's lineage see J. L. Wright, *Bowles*.

7. I am following William Coker's admirable account in the *Colonial Latin American Historical Review* of 1994, summarizing his book with Thomas D. Watson, *Indian Traders*, published six years earlier.

8. Panton to the senior McGillivray, April 10, 1794, ibid., pp. 430–31.

9. McGillivray to Panton, Sept. 20, 1788, included in record of the case of *Johnson vs. Innerarity*, Docket #1156, Series New Orleans 1813–1846, Supreme Court of Louisiana Collection, Louisiana and Special Collections, Earl K. Long Library, University of New Orleans.

10. Claudio Saunt is surely correct in his suggestion that "inspired by their knowledge of Atlantic world uprisings and the 'advantages of liberty'" the maroons became "among the staunchest opponents of the new order spreading across the land" (*New Order*, p. 125).

11. My quotation comes from Whitaker, *Mississippi Question*, p. 167. I have been following Whitaker's account, modified only a little as a result of scanning original documents including those cited by him in his excellent bibliography on Bowles. The other compendium of useful leads for further research is to be found in the bibliography in J. L. Wright, *Bowles*.

12. Bowles on Jamaica, ibid., p. 167.

13. Bowles's inventory, Whitaker, *Mississippi Question*, p. 168.

14. There are meticulous—and intriguing—accounts of these proceedings in Cox, *West Florida*, and in Bemis, *Pinckney's Treaty*, with a map of the neutral state on p. 118.

15. Bowles to Ellicott, quoted in Abernethy, *Mississippi*, p. 244.

16. Ibid.

17. Ibid. and J. L. Wright, *Bowles*.

18. The order of execution against him is quoted from Whitaker, *Mississippi Question*, p. 169.

19. Hawkins on Florida and Bowles, quoted ibid., p. 172.

20. Dearborn to Hawkins, quoted ibid., pp. 172–73.

21. Ibid.; Abernethy on the kidnaping of Bowles, *South*, p. 245: "Though thus arrested on American soil and under the authority of the United States, the prisoner was immediately turned over to a party of Indians who took him to Pensacola, delivered him into the hands of Folch, and collected the reward."

22. John Forbes quoted in *John Forbes' Description*, ed. Coker, p. 5.

Chapter 11

1. McKee's assurance, quoted in Cotterill, "A Chapter," p. 276. His meeting with Forbes is in Coker and Watson, *Indian Traders*, pp. 226-29.

2. Hamilton to King, quoted in Schachner, *Hamilton*, p. 384. Whitaker on McKee, *Mississippi Question*, pp. 125-26. Rowland, *Seventh Annual Report*, p. 29; Ellicott's suspicions, letters to the Secretary of State, Sept. 12, 1797, and March 14, 1798, *Ellicott Papers*, Library of Congress, Vol. 1, pp. 104-7, and RG 76, Entry 391, Vol. 2, pp. 273-74. I am grateful to Jack Jackson and Jack Elliott for these references.

3. Panton quoted in Coker and Watson, *Indian Traders*, pp. 200-201 and 302. Panton's reassurance from Gayoso de Lemos, Cotterill, "A Chapter," p. 277. McKee had to negotiate a difficult passage, by way of being a Blountian, then a Federalist, Jeffersonian, Burrite, and ultimately a Jacksonian.

4. Jack Elliott supplies these citations: RG 217, Entry 366, Vol. 6 (Journal F), p. 2972. McKee's spending the winter and spring of 1798 in the Natchez area: Ellicott to the Secretary of State, March 14, 1798, RG 76, Entry 391, Vol. 2, pp. 273-74; and deeds dated March 26 and May 28, 1798, involving McKee as either grantee or witness. May Wilson McBee, *The Natchez Court Records, 1767-1805: Abstracts of Early Records* (Baltimore, 1979, originally published in 1953), pp. 159 and 500.

5. Panton quoted in Coker and Watson, *Indian Traders*, pp. 200-201 and 302.

6. For the interactions of McKee, Jefferson, and Aaron Burr, see my *Burr, Hamilton, and Jefferson*, especially p. 325 ff. Jack Elliott fills in, in private correspondence of April 2000, that McKee "redeemed himself—in spades—during the Creek War."

7. Pickering to Sargent, in 1799, quoted in Usner, "Cotton Frontier," p. 299.

8. Dearborn to Dinsmoor, in 1803, ibid. TJ to Benjamin Hawkins, quoted in Clark and Guice, *Old Southwest*, p. 34. These two modern scholars described Jefferson's statement as "remarkably tactful," a quality they themselves merit in choosing to overlook that passage in Jefferson's letter in which he referred to "the wisdom of the animal which amputates and abandons to the hunter the parts for which he is pursued should be theirs, with this difference, that the former sacrifices what is useful, the latter what is not."

9. Letter, James McHenry to John McKee, May 20, 1800, Library of Congress, John McKee Papers, Box 3, #9.

10. This information, too, comes from Jack Elliott, who provided the following citations: Letter, Samuel Mitchell to Winthrop Sargent, March 31, 1799, Sargent Papers, Roll 5, Frames 37-39. Cf. Letter, Samuel Dexter to John McKee, Aug.? 1800, McKee Papers, Box 1, #227. Letter, John McKee to Winthrop Sargent, March 21, 1801, Sargent Papers, Roll 5, Frames 794-95.

11. The following citations come from Jack Elliott: Jesse D. Jennings, ed., "Nutt's Trip to the Chickasaw Country," *Journal of Mississippi History* 9 (1947), p. 44. "Excerpt of a letter from Silas Dinsmoor dated Chaktaw Agency 11 Septr. 1811," National Archives, RG 75 (Records of the Bureau of Indian Affairs), T500 (Records of the Choctaw Trading House, 1803–1824), Roll 2, Frame 45. James H. Stone, "Surveying the Gaines Trace, 1807–1808," *Alabama Historical Quarterly* 33 (1971). Claudio Saunt comments that the "Creeks involved in shipping cotton to markets on the Gulf Coast were usually men who owned plantations" and, by implication, owned slaves, and that the "market for homespun . . . was only local," thus distinguishing between shipping for others to mill and making one's own clothing. I am indebted to Saunt, in his *New Order* at p. 158, for bringing the Creeks into the story, and for the quotation.

12. TJ to the Cherokees, ibid., p. 561.

13. Captain Amos Ogden, a veteran of the Seven Years' War, applied for a royal grant of twenty-five thousand acres to be filled by his troops from New Jersey. Samuel Sweesy, a clergyman much influenced by Burr's father and by Jonathan Edwards, his grandfather, brought other colonists from New Jersey to his twenty-three-thousand-acre grant. Colonel Israel Putnam of Connecticut, later Burr's commander during the Revolutionary War, settled twenty-three thousand acres nearby with his Company of Military Adventurers.

14. Rohrbough, *Trans-Appalachian Frontier*, p. 107 ff.

15. I am grateful to Theda Perdue for a conversation in May 2002 leading me to these suggestions.

16. Dobyns, *Number Became Thinned*, p. 41 ff.

17. Hudson, *Southeastern Indians*, p. 159.

Chapter 12

1. TJ to Dickinson, Aug. 9, 1803, *Writings*, Ford, Vol. 8, p. 263. This letter is to be found neither in the Library of America selection nor in Padover's *Complete Jefferson*, but seems to me to show Jefferson at his most imaginative if not his most admirable. I found it quoted in Keller, "Philanthropy Betrayed," p. 60, following Keller's suggestion that "it is even possible that Jefferson intended to pay for the Louisiana territory by selling off the newly-vacated Eastern Indian lands to white settlers" (p. 59). It is difficult to conceive of any other meaning—the amounts required to pay off the indebtedness of the Indians to The Firm and thus to acquire the vast cessions of land on the eastern side of the Mississippi did not, so far as I can detect, require a specific debt issue by Mr. Jefferson's government. If rolled into that government's other domestic debt they would not constitute a single large discrete sum that would be described as a "whole debt contracted" to become "due" at a specific date. I am not an expert in Secretary Gallatin's management of domestic debt, but the context of Jefferson's letter to Dickinson was the consequences of the Louisiana Purchase—so I think Keller's suggestion is correct.

2. TJ to Claiborne, May 24, 1803, *Writings*, Memorial Ed., Vol. 10, pp. 390–91. TJ to Chickasaws, March 1805, quoted in Keller, "Philanthropy Betrayed," p. 61.

3. TJ to Dickinson, ibid.; Wilkinson to Dearborn, Sept. 22, 1805, quoted in Wallace, *Jefferson and the Indians*, p. 259.

4. Jefferson to Harrison, Aug. 9, 1803, quoted in Keller, "Philanthropy Betrayed," p. 60.

5. I have written of Wilkinson and Dinsmoor in *Burr, Hamilton, and Jefferson*, and of other aspects of Wilkinson's career in *Hidden Cities*. Wilkinson to Dinsmoor, Cotterill, "A Chapter," p. 281. Mssrs. Guice and Clark tell us admiringly: "[Jefferson] lectured Congress as well as his own Administrators on the need for 'the establishment of a strong front on our western boundary.' Although [his Indian Agents were] instructed to deal with problems [*sic*] related to Indian debts to traders, their main objective was procurement of lands along the river" (*Old Southwest*, pp. 34, 36, 38).

6. For Dinsmoor and slavery, see *Burr, Hamilton, and Jefferson*. Recent explanations of Jefferson's affinity for Wilkinson have ranged from David Chandler's suggestion in his *Jefferson Conspiracies* that Wilkinson had a hand in the death of Meriwether Lewis, and Jefferson covered up for him—but why?—to Anthony F. C. Lewis's considerably more credible thesis that Wilkinson was Jefferson's chosen general "to defend the independence" of whatever separatist state might emerge in the West against a Federalist army if the Federalists attempted a coup in the East. See Wallace, *Jefferson and the Indians*, pp. 263–64.

7. Wilkinson to Dinsmoor, Cotterill, "A Chapter," p. 281.

8. Ibid.

9. Wilkinson to Miro, July 20, 1790, quoted in Coker and Watson, *Indian Traders*, p. 147.

10. Fanny Kemble's *Journal* of 1838–39, pp. 96–97.

11. Wilkinson to Simpson, quoted in Cotterill, "A Chapter," p. 281; to Forbes, p. 283.

12. Forbes taking less than 100 cents, see Cotterill, p. 282.

13. Ibid. See also Whitaker, *Mississippi Question*, p. 70.

14. Usner, "Cotton Frontier," p. 314.

15. Anderson's *Kinsmen of Another Kind* established the concept of fictive kinship in 1984. My quotations from him come from private correspondence in August 2000.

16. Dearborn to Wilkinson, Feb. 21, 1803, and Wilkinson to Dearborn, Oct. 1, 1803. Cotterill ("A Chapter") makes allusion to the former on p. 280, and the latter is quoted in Coker, *Indian Traders*, pp. 245–46.

17. Wilkinson to Hamilton, quoted in Coker, *John Forbes' Description*, p. 6.

18. This portion of Hamilton's letter does not appear in Coker but does in Whitaker, *Mississippi Question*, pp. 264–65.

19. Ibid.

20. Monroe and Forbes, see Coker, "John Forbes and Company," p. 66. Wilkinson and Dauphin Island, *American State Papers, Public Lands*, Vol. 5, pp. 498–99l. This little treasure was found by William Coker.

21. Captain Wilkinson and The Firm in Mobile, Coker, "John Forbes and Company," pp. 66–67.

22. Ibid.

23. Ibid.

24. Wilkinson to Simpson, quoted in Cotterill, "A Chapter," p. 281; to Forbes, p. 283. Jefferson quoted in Usner, "Cotton Frontier," p. 301, and in a similar statement by Cotterill, "A Chapter," p. 279, fn.

25. Jefferson, in Usner, "Cotton Frontier," p. 279. For Granger and Wilkinson in concert, see *Burr, Hamilton, and Jefferson*.

26. Riley to Meigs, Nov. 29, 1806, from the Classified Files of the Interior Department Indian Office, quoted in Cotterill, "A Chapter," p. 279, fn. Clark and Guice offer an extended argument that "entrapment of the Indians by the factory system" was not "a high priority of Jefferson's" and that, in any case, he was "primarily discussing defense needs." Harrison, however, was not on the Mississippi frontier, nor were the Cherokee charges of Mr. Hocker. See Clark and Guice, *Old Southwest*, pp. 36–39.

27. "Certain mercantile characters," ibid., p. 38; Wilkinson, etc., Cotterill, "A Chapter," pp. 279–82.

28. For Dinsmoor and Burr, see *Burr, Hamilton, and Jefferson*, pp. 320–25.

29. Dinsmoor quoted in Cotterill, "A Chapter," p. 286. Neither McKee nor Dinsmoor admired Jefferson's other primary agent in the Southwest, W. C. C. Claiborne. McKee wrote of him: "I am not going to solicit favors from men who can listen to such puppies as Gov. Claiborne. I have labored painfully for the character of an honest public servant and should be mortified to see it tarnished by such poltroons." Letter, JM to Winthrop Sargent, Oct. 9, 1802, Sargent Papers, Reel 6, Frame 268; cf. letter, JM to James Wilkinson, Oct. 19, 1805, *American State Papers, Miscellaneous*, Vol. 1, 594–95. (These references came to me from Jack Elliott.)

McKee was reappointed as Choctaw agent in 1814. In this capacity he also served as treaty commissioner in 1816, 1818, and 1819. Following the failure of the last conference to produce a treaty, Andrew Jackson—who was infuriated by Dinsmoor's solicitude for the Indians (see my *Burr, Hamilton, and Jefferson*)—was apparently disturbed by McKee's deference to Choctaw interests, so that McKee was not appointed to be a commissioner in 1820 at Doak's Stand.

30. Dearborn quoted in Cotterill, "A Chapter," p. 286.

31. Innerarity to Forbes on Englishmen, Coker, "John Forbes and Company," p. 75.

32. The Firm sued the admirals. Pinckney's Treaty of 1795 had terminated the policy of the Kings of Spain that blacks or Indians who escaped the British or American plantation systems could have their freedom if they reached Florida or Texas. If the British courts in the 1820s took the posture Pinckney had taken, slaves claimed by Spanish subjects, such as the members of The Firm, should be returned, or the British Crown should compensate them for their loss.

In the *Amistad* case, in the 1840s, the lawyers for President Martin Van Buren urged the Supreme Court of the United States to take the same view of Pinckney's Treaty. The *Amistad* slaves, and their counsel, John Quincy Adams, won their case. The British courts had already decided the question. In 1825, the Court of King's Bench reversed a lower court decision and held that the slaves who found their way to the admirals, between 1812 and 1815, were free because British law did not recognize the legitimacy of slavery in *any* British possession. A British ship was such a possession, and so was an island under British military occupation.

Part Four Introduction

1. R. Blackburn, *New World Slavery*, pp. 6 and 11.

Chapter 13

1. Seward quoted in Richards, *Slave Power*, p. 8.

2. A review of William Freehling's *Road to Disunion* by Bertram Wyatt-Brown, in the *New York Review of Books* for Oct. 10, 1991, led me to this point.

3. My quotations about Kentucky are from Aron, *West Was Lost*, p. 92.

4. Dupuy, *Haiti in the World Economy*, pp. 55 and 62. This is not the place to debate the relationship of Toussaint and his generals to this set of aspirations. Dupuy is correct in positing a reluctance on their part to abandon world markets and the enforced labor system of plantation life even after the formal abolition of slavery.

5. Knight, "The Haitian Revolution," *American Historical Review* 105 (Feb. 2000), p. 103 ff.

6. Ibid., p. 120.

7. Long after the last Tory baronet among his Randolph kin departed for Britain, Jefferson was willing to honor the tradition of calling his kinswoman the wife of the baronet "Lady Skipwith."

8. My quotation comes from Gray, *Agriculture*, Vol. 1, pp. 446–47.

9. The house and estate passed from the 7th Bart. to his son Sir Gray, 8th Bart., who returned to England, where the family lived in rural obscurity until a new Sir Gray married another heiress, and acquired a fine Caroline mansion at Honington in 1905. Sir Peyton Skipwith only moved from Petersburg to remote Mecklenburg after his second marriage in 1788, and the house was not completed, woodwork and all, until 1795. Contra: Professor Waterman, *Mansions*, p. 195.

10. "Family exists," Langhorne, Lay, and Rieley, *Virginia Family*, p. 67.

11. Rebecca Coles Skipwith on dining, ibid., pp. 66–67. Perhaps beneath all this crockery there lurked some sign of anxiety; the Coles were rising, and the Skipwiths setting, and good marriages might stabilize things. (In Boston, the Cabots and Lodges were marrying Department Stores.) Selina Skipwith held out for a marriage for love, but her mother, Lady Jean, made her marry John Coles III, a bachelor of forty-eight, saying that the man Selina had previously in mind was too poor: "if a man wishes to keep a canary, he must have a cage to put her in" (ibid., p. 68).

12. Jefferson's introductory essay to his manual for Robert Skipwith, and the commentaries upon it of his biographers, are a little priggish, but the essay was written when Jefferson was barely twenty-eight, sequestered, and not yet the man who had known Maria Cosway. Nine years later, in 1780, James Monroe got his instruction manual from Jefferson. Monroe's biographer Harry Ammon suggests that his was "probably like the one he [Jefferson] sent to Fulwar Skipwith a decade earlier" (*Monroe*, p. 31). In a literal sense, Ammon was wrong, for Fulwar was only five years old in 1770: the instruction went to Robert.

13. FS to William Short, ibid., pp. 9, 13, 15. William Short was truly, as Marie Kimball said long ago, Thomas Jefferson's "only 'son,'" in the same affectionate sense

that John Quincy Adams was as much Jefferson's "boy" as John Adams's. Short was also the cousin of Jefferson, and both were cousins of Fulwar Skipwith—Short was the son of a daughter of Sir William Skipwith. It is through Short that we know as much as we do of Skipwith's early years. "Fiddling and dancing," from FS to William Short, July 18, 1786, Skipwith Family Papers, Library of Congress, quoted in H. B. Cox, *Parisian American*, p. 7.

14. Ibid., pp. 23, 24.

15. FS to TJ, ibid., pp. 25–26.

16. For Hamilton, Stevens, and Toussaint, please see my *Orders from France*.

17. We must not, throughout this account, fail to emphasize the importance of another impulse felt by many Americans. Some have called it "ideology" and others "conscience." Increasingly after 1800, many Yankee captains and crews, and their families at home, recognized that it was one thing to profit from supporting revolutionaries who were also trading partners, with the endorsement of one's own government, and quite another to act against the express desires of a new administration in resisting Napoleon's attempt after 1800 to restore slavery to the islands.

18. The consul-generalship in Paris was not an unalloyed gift, as it turned out, for on the night of February 22, 1795, three silver ingots to be used to repay a loan to the United States from its Dutch bankers were removed by thieves from "a spot only five yards from Skipwith's bed" in the consulate. Henry Bartholomew Cox, Skipwith's biographer, tells us:

> How they were taken away without Skipwith hearing a noise is indeed a mystery. . . . The robbers must have passed high gates, a courtyard, and a night watchman before they broke the door of communication between the courtyards of the adjoining house and forced a strong lock on the cabinet housing the ingots. . . . Skipwith, to scotch any rumors [that it was an inside job], advanced the sum to make up the loss from his own pocket, and Monroe approved the action on the spot. (Robbery, Cox, *Parisian American*, p. 53.)

The ingots were estimated to have a value of as much as $120,000 by Madison's biographer Irving Brant (*Madison*, p. 443). Though not disputing Brant in his own footnote on p. 54, Cox gives the exact sum in another footnote, on p. 127. Cox tells us that Skipwith "had been cleverly making money as a claims agent, as were the other American Consuls" (p. 54).

So nervous were all parties at this juncture that the Republican press asserted that the ingot theft was a political act, ever so subtly French, like the "cold and severe deportment" of the Committee on Public Safety a protest against Jay's intimacies with the British. The Federalist press responded that Monroe or Skipwith had faked the robbery to permit hired pens like Bache to discredit Jay. For the journalistic interchange, see ibid. pp. 53–54. After Monroe's departure and replacement first by Charles Cotesworth Pinckney and then by John Marshall, Skipwith became Virginia's mole in the American ministry. Using Skipwith as messenger, Monroe conveyed the impression to their French friends that Pinckney was a closet monarchist. Accordingly, the Directory, then in charge of the French government, refused to receive the new minister, and its subsidized press blossomed into adulation for the departing Monroe. When Marshall arrived, Skipwith wrote Jefferson indicating that he had shifted his antipathy from Pinckney to Marshall, who, he said, was "one of the declaiming apostles" of rapprochement with Britain. Marshall's colleague Elbridge Gerry may have been a Republican, but he was not a Virginian, and was dismissed by Skipwith as too weak to provide the balance lost by Monroe's departure. Skipwith on Marshall, Beveridge, *Marshall*, Vol. 2, p. 336.

The French did not, however, discover weakness in either Gerry or Marshall, as the XYZ Affair unfolded. Talleyrand, minister of foreign affairs, sent intermediaries given code names "X," "Y," and "Z" to suggest to the Americans that if bribed enough he, X, Y, and Z, could arrange relief for American shipping from the assaults by the French navy and privateers. The proposal, and Marshall's indignant rejection of it, were revealed by President John Adams to the Congress. Jefferson, who was Vice President, did not share in the popular enthusiasm for Marshall, nor did he join the cry "Millions for defense, but not one cent for tribute!" Instead, he wrote Madison and Monroe to decry the President's "insane message," expressing doubt as to the truth of Adams's charges against the French. When, two weeks later, Adams followed up his allegations with ample documentation received from Marshall, Jefferson reconsidered. Now, he said, it had become his "duty [as Vice President] to be silent." Jefferson on insane message and silence, Beveridge, ibid., pp. 336 and 339.

19. FS to Monroe, H. B. Cox, *Parisian American*, p. 45.

20. Monroe's speech, quoted in Ammon, *Monroe*, p. 120.

21. FS to Monroe, Cox, *Parisian American*, p. 45.

22. I am using James Madison's conversion tables from francs to dollars, as reported in Sprague, *So Vast*, at p. 304, Adams, *Jefferson Administrations*, pp. 333–34, and H. B. Cox, *Parisian American*, p. 44 ff., and the conversion tables in McCusker, *How Much*, pp. 343–34, brought up to date by the Consumer Price Index as reported on the website of the U.S. Commerce Department. There is no breakdown of who got exactly what, and I have been unable to find any evidence of what the Livingstons did with the money. I have reviewed the building records of their splendid houses along the Hudson, but all the key members of the family already had completed their major projects by 1802. Please see *Orders from France*. Henry Adams cites "View of Claims, etc. by a citizen of Baltimore, 1829," at p. 334 of his *Jefferson Administrations*. It doesn't help much from a banker's point of view.

The court of last resort for these claims by American merchants was "not the American, but the French Treasury." As George Dangerfield once commented, claims against the fund provided by the taxpayers of the United States had to work their way to an ultimately corruptible body, and, "considering the jobbery that flourished with such verdure among French official circles, this was a most improvident provision" made even more improvident after Americans of the means of the Livingstons engaged the services not only of relatively scrupulous agents such as Skipwith but of others, like James Swan, who made no pretense of avoiding bribery. The government of the United States was giving over the rights of its citizens to a large sum of its dollars to "the notorious corruption of Talleyrand and his band of confidential or secret agents." Dangerfield, in his *Livingston*, pp. 374–75. Henry Adams on Talleyrand's corruption, *Jefferson Administrations*, p. 333.

23. In his loyal service to his fellow Virginians, Skipwith was willing to send to them directly confidential documents the release of which might serve their Francophile interest, such as a message from Talleyrand to President John Adams that was published in the Francophile *Aurora* before it was sent to Congress by Adams, and probably before the President of the United States himself received it. The *Aurora* noted ibid., pp. 359–60. FS to J. H. Causton, June 30, 1828, quoted in H. B. Cox, *Parisian American*, p. 126.

24. FS to TJ, Oct. 30, 1801, *Jefferson Papers*, Library of Congress, quoted ibid., pp. 71–73.

25. Dunbar quoted in D. C. James, *Antebellum Natchez*, pp. 51–52.

26. Dunbar's correspondence with Green and Wainewright appears in Rowland, *Dunbar's Letters*, pp. 344, 356.

27. Dunbar quoted in D. C. James, *Antebellum Natchez*, pp. 51–52.

28. Custis quoted in Flores, *Southwest Exploration*, p. 112.

29. Livingston's Louisiana memorandum, Aug. 10, 1802, enclosed in a report to Madison, quoted in Dangerfield, *Livingston*, p. 331 ff., and quoted in Adams, *Jefferson Administrations*, p. 321.

30. Sumter's discovery of Parker and Livingston, Brant, *Madison*, p. 95. Skipwith's views of Livingston, restated by Henry Adams in *Jefferson Administrations*, p. 497. Skipwith and Sumter's account is supported by the fact that at the time Talleyrand also suggested that he, Parker, and Livingston go into another business with each other, moving Mexican silver from Vera Cruz to France in an alternative to the Great Silver Scheme—please see my *Orders from France*. See also "The Livingstons and West Florida" in the Appendix, p. 257.

31. Sumter and Parker, Brant, *Madison*, p. 95 ff. There were splendid architectural consequences of the Livingstons' acquaintance with things French, especially along the Mohawk and Hudson valleys—see my *Orders from France*, p. 35 ff.

32. Livingston on Virginia faction, Amman, *Monroe*, p. 222.

33. Skipwith tattling on Livingston to Monroe, quoted in Dangerfield, *Livingston*, p. 365.

34. Adams's account, in *Jefferson Administrations*, p. 329 ff. Though Adams failed his readers by passing with most uncharacteristic haste over the process by which Article Three entered the purchase contract, he warned against any willingness to believe the First Consul might have any enthusiasm for "the principles of the Federal Constitution. . . . He had two rooted hatreds," Adams tells us. "The deeper and fiercer of the two was directed against the republic . . . the organized democracy, and what he called ideology, which Americans knew in practice as Jeffersonian theories; the second and steadier was his hatred of England as the chief barrier to his military omnipotence."

35. "My colleague [Livingston]," Monroe wrote, "took Mr. Marbois's project with him, and brought me one very loosely drawn, founded on it." This cannot have been the final language of Article Three. Livingston was a meticulous lawyer, quite capable of precision. The final language was not "loosely drawn" but very precisely what the planters required. It is apparent that Monroe removed the looseness and conveyed a revised draft to Marbois on the twenty-ninth. That draft still exists, in Monroe's handwriting, containing the crucial slavery-protecting terms. On May 2,

1803, in a transaction essential to the spread of the plantation system, they "actually signed the treaty and convention." Adams, *Jefferson Administrations*, p. 329 ff.

36. Ibid., pp. 337–38.

37. Newspaper and Madison to Lafayette, Feb. 21, 1806, quoted in Pritchard, "Selecting a Governor," p. 303.

38. Rembert Patrick gives the details of Skipwith's remittances, his instructions from Madison, and a British source as to the transaction contemplated by Madison, *Fiasco*, on p. 28 and in fn. 47 on p. 308, citing archival sources.

39. Bartram on cotton in West Florida, *Travels*, p. 334. On growing conditions, see Julia Smith, *Slavery*, p. 15 ff.

40. Monroe and Skipwith, I. J. Cox, *West Florida*, pp. 123, 246–47.

41. Talleyrand to Skipwith, quoted ibid., pp. 258–59. For Madison's support of Girard, and other details, see Dangerfield, *Livingston*, pp. 323–34.

42. Skipwith wrote: "Keeping Armstrong in, on the other hand, would reward the conductor [of misinformation] to our good President, . . . [by providing him] popularity and perhaps [he may] participate in the emoluments anticipated." Ibid.

The means of forcing Skipwith into jail and out of Paris were not disclosed at the time and lay uncelebrated until the 1940s, when some leads to their rediscovery were discovered by Walter Pritchard. According to Pritchard, Skipwith "apparently purchased some of the claims which he was investigating for his government, hoping to profit from the transaction. These activities finally led to Skipwith's imprisonment in 1808, though the details of this episode have not yet been located." Pritchard seemed to suggest that "Skipwith's imprisonment" occurred in France, where Armstrong and Swan had powerful friends. That in turn would imply that the complainant was one Livingston or another, and invited the further conjecture that Talleyrand had to get him out again. (Dangerfield on Livingstons and Skipwith, and a bibliography, in fn 32 on p. 508 of his *Livingston*. Pritchard on Skipwith, "Selecting a Governor," pp. 305–6.)

Though Skipwith reached out to Monroe for support, he was losing his game as early as the end of 1806. Armstrong had intervened in the spoliation settlements to knock out a claim on which Skipwith was to receive a commission, advancing instead those from which his own associate, Swan, might profit. Armstrong dismissed Skipwith as a paltry fellow content with a "beggarly commission of 5 per cent." Skipwith disputed Armstrong's action in a complaint to the *French* authorities, asking for a hearing on a dispute between an American minister and an American commercial agent. The no doubt amused French offered a hearing, but "Skipwith declined to appear." Armstrong gloated that he had driven Skipwith to "sneak away from the trial and to cover . . . [himself] by alleging incompetency in the judges," having been unwilling to test the question as to what they might be willing to offer "out of mere deference to a commercial agent[.] Is he a kind of Pope?" Armstrong on Skipwith, H. B. Cox, *Parisian American*, pp. 104–10.

At the end of 1807, the American minister and the French Council of State directed Skipwith to remove himself from the scene. He did not go at once—and if he was sent to jail, this was the time for it. Still he would not go home. The French withheld their hand: the contest between Napoleon and Britain was aflame across the globe; the British had tightened their blockade and were boarding and sinking American ships who sought to smuggle through it, and the Jefferson administration had gone so far as to embargo shipping for Europe. Napoleon might well hope it could summon itself farther, and he had no reason to offend Jefferson by forcing his friend Skipwith to depart. Skipwith may have been imprisoned twice, once in France and again in England, but this seems doubtful in the absence of any corroboration of a French incarceration. The British imprisonment into which Armstrong entrapped Skipwith has its own puzzles, but this much seems sure: Fulwar Skipwith did go— briefly—to a British jail, and Armstrong had a hand in it. In 1808, after Skipwith broke with his private employers (who included one set of Livingston brothers and cousins) and with his superiors in the Paris ministry (another set), the French had no stake in his future. Napoleon was about to invade Spain and to set his brother Joseph upon a throne which the Bonaparte clan hoped might provide them with a New World Empire as well as a European peninsula. Livingston and Armstrong made no secret of their aversion to Skipwith, and the French lost little in accommodating their desire to get him out of town. As for Jefferson—he was going out of office, and with him Skipwith's ticket into the inner circles of power in France.

43. Ibid., pp. 114, 116, 117. Skipwith's ignominious departure from Paris was noted by Nicholas Biddle, the Philadelphia paragon and, later, the nation's banker. Biddle had been Skipwith's guest in Paris while he was briefed for a tour of ancient Greece. With Skipwith's advice in mind, and a copy of Pausanias in hand, he then went, alone, across the bandit-ridden Peloponnese, returning later to Philadelphia to become editor for the papers of Lewis and Clark. (See my *Orders from France*.) While engaged in that task, on November 18, 1808, he wrote Monroe about Skipwith's incarceration, to which Monroe responded on January 7, 1809: "Our friend Mr. S. has indeed experienced a severe destiny. His perfect integrity and patriotism have been ably requited. Had he been less honest, he might have been more wealthy, and perhaps enjoyed . . . better fame! Hard is the condition of the times when such is the lot of any individual. Strange indeed that such should have been his when his real merit and all other circumstances are taken into view" (Monroe to Biddle, ibid., p. 305).

Chapter 14

1. Randolph, in Wandell and Minnegerode, *Burr*, Vol. 2, p. 67.

2. TJ to Washington, quoted in Patrick, *Fiasco*, p. 50.

3. TJ to Gallatin, Oct. 29, 1803, quoted in Whitaker, *Mississippi Question*, p. 322, fn. 16.

4. For Clay, Jackson, McKee, and Dinsmoor, see my *Burr, Hamilton, and Jefferson*. For the secret statute, see D. H. Miller, *Secret Statutes*, p. 51. See also Adams, *Madison Administration*, p. 458.

5. Smith to Crawford, and Madison's satisfaction, quoted in Madison, *Presidential Papers*, Vol. 2, p. 310.

6. Holmes to Smith, ibid., p. 355; Madison to Smith, July 17, 1810, ibid., p. 313. The *Madison Presidential Papers* have these sequences neatly and concisely stated in the Editorial Note on pp. 305 ff. in Vol. 2. The other occasion on which two eminent men met privately in that room and period, and offered radically different accounts thereafter, was the meeting between Burr and Jefferson on March 22, 1806.

7. For Gallatin, Jefferson, and Toussaint, see my *Orders from France*.

8. Gallatin to Monroe and vice versa, Patrick, *Fiasco*, p. 257.

9. Infamous Spaniards, ibid., p. 110.

10. McIntosh's appeal quoted ibid., p. 155.

11. Mitchell quoted ibid., pp. 184 and 215.

12. I have taken this story, and its quotations, from Mr. Saunt's remarkable researches of the interactions of blacks and Indians in the Florida Borderlands, in his *New Order*, pp. 127–29. He and I may differ in our interpretation of the character of Alexander McGillivray, and we certainly do, but no one has shown diligence and intelligence such as his in seeking out the important sources and analyzing the results of such a search. His footnotes have now provided the necessary bibliography for many future researchers.

The primary curriculum of the national park is formed around the story of Fort George Island as a plantation by the African-born wife of Zephaniah Kingsley, who bought it from McIntosh.

13. McIntosh to Crawford, quoted Patrick, *Fiasco*, p. 301.

14. Monroe to Mathews, Senate Documents, Miscellaneous (Washington, 1860), No. 55, 36th Cong., 1st Sess., p. 113.

15. Smith's complaints, Patrick, *Fiasco*, p. 141. (Smith's General Orders, ibid., p. 231.) For Smith and Burr, see my *Burr, Hamilton, and Jefferson*, pp. 296–98.

16. Monroe and Jefferson, quoted, Patrick, *Fiasco*, p. 278.

17. McIntosh's appeal quoted ibid., p. 155; Monroe's piety quoted ibid., pp. 280 and 282.

18. Hunter quoted ibid., p. 251

19. Hunter, ibid. Tony's speech quoted in Saunt, *New Order*, p. 237.

20. Dunmore and Cochrane, quoted in Egerton, *Gabriel's Rebellion*, p. 5. Cochrane quoted in Patrick, *Fiasco*, p. 285.

21. I have written of MacGregor and his French associations in *Orders from France*. See also Owsley and Smith, *Filibusters*, p. 122 ff.

22. There is as yet no careful modern history of MacGregor. The account in T. Frederick Davis, *MacGregor's Invasion of Florida, 1817* (Jacksonville: Florida Historical Society, 1928), is lively. From it I gathered my information on the laird his grandfather, p. 11. My quotation comes from Owsley and Smith, *Filibusters*, p. 135. Owsley and Smith take their view of Aury from Frederick Davis, who pronounced MacGregor "sincere," Aury not so, and Savary's men "vicious mulattoes" (p. 33).

23. Quoted in Davis, *Invasion*, pp. 39 and 41.

24. Ibid., p.42.

25. Ibid., p. 62.

26. J. Q. Adams to George William Erving, Nov. 28, 1818, *Writings*, Vol. 6, pp. 477, 488. He had not yet been redeemed by the Amistad rebels.

Chapter 15

1. The sand-plain people became in the 1850s constituents of Jefferson Davis, under whose goading they rose against the cotton-growing magnates of Natchez and

New Orleans and, in 1861, took Mississippi into the Confederacy. In the 1950s, they were ready to follow the hard-bitten segregationist Senator Theodore Bilbo. Bilbo's people of the Florida Parishes were sociologically indistinguishable from those of the sand plain of upper Louisiana where Huey Long reigned, though geographically separated by the flooded canyon of the Mississippi.

2. Madison to Lafayette, Feb. 21, 1806, quoted in Pritchard, "Selecting a Governor," p. 303.

3. William C. C. Claiborne was born in Sussex County, Virginia, in 1775.

4. Berlin, *Many Thousands Gone*, pp. 199–201

5. I am using figures provided by Edward Austin Bradley, at p. 62 of his "Forgotten Filibusters."

6. My account is based upon that of Thomas Ingersoll, in *Mammon and Manon*, p. 221.

7. Gray gives a good account of French and Spanish encouragement of yeomen in *Agriculture*, Vol. 1, p. 337 ff.

8. Ibid., p. 340.

9. Knight, "The Haitian Revolution," p. 103 ff.

10. For Jefferson, Lafayette, and Monroe, see Pritchard, "Selecting a Governor," p. 290 ff.

11. The debate is set forth in the Brown edition of *Plumer's Memorandum of the Proceedings of the Senate*, p. 73 ff.

12. Ibid., p. 120 ff.

13. Ibid. p. 73 ff. Jackson is at 118, 120, 125–26.

14. Ibid., McClay is at p. 143.

15. Ibid., p. 118 ff.

16. Ibid., p. 130.

17. Ibid. Fehrenbacher, *Slavery*, p. 47. Plumer and juries, Brown ed., *Plumer's Memorandum*, p. 140.

18. Ibid., p. 132. Robert Wright must not be confused with his antislavery colleague of that state, Samuel White.

19. Fehrenbacher on Jefferson, *Slavery*, p. 46.

20. R. Blackburn, *Overthrow*, p. 285.

21. Peterson, *Jefferson*, p. 283; the resolution, in TJ, *Writings*, Ford, Vol. 1, p. 432.

22. Ibid.

23. Henry Clay quoted in Freehling, *Road*, p. 494.

24. Ibid. The verdict on Hillhouse's achievement is that of Fehrenbacher, *Slavery*, at p.47. In 1804, Hillhouse occupied a historic role like those of George Thacher of Massachusetts and David Wilmot of Pennsylvania. In 1798, Thacher attempted to force the admission of Mississippi Territory on the basis of the Northwest Ordinance, without slavery. In 1846, Wilmot proposed in his celebrated Proviso that the same inhibition cover all the territories to be carved out of the acquisitions of the Mexican War.

25. Florida's land prices and highway, see Julia Smith, *Slavery*, p. 15 ff.

26. The relationship of Unionism and diversification of planters' portfolios is the subject of several chapters in my *Architecture, Men, Women, and Money*.

27. I have taken the quotation of Elisha Mitchell from Helms's "Soil and Southern History," pp. 734–35, where it is used without reference to a limitation on slavery.

Chapter 16

1. For Monroe and Jefferson, see Pritchard, "Selecting a Governor," p. 297.

2. Ibid.

3. The ladies' patronymic has also been given variant spellings—van der Clooster, Vandenclooster, or Van den Kloster. An intriguing letter of recommendation for Skipwith from Talleyrand in the Louisiana State University Library in Baton Rouge raises another possibility as to the recovery of Skipwith's fortunes. The primary financial connections of the foreign minister were in Belgium, where Harris was said to have been a banker. Talleyrand frequently used Flemish bankers to finance his own speculations in American lands, using a variety of "fronts." Twenty years ago, there reposed among the Skipwith Plantation records in the Louisiana State University Library another letter, referring to the presence in Baton Rouge of Pierre Bellamy, of Bellamy and Ricci of Hamburg, Talleyrand's personal banker and the "Y" in the XYZ Affair.

It may be that Talleyrand and the Livingstons failed to reach an understanding in their discussions of West Florida real estate, and Talleyrand, backed by Bellamy, took the matter up again with Skipwith. In 1810, Skipwith's brother-in-law Harris went bankrupt, but for some reason, Skipwith's fortunes were now secure from his British creditors and did not collapse under the influence of Harris. (Though his marriage did; Harris made off with Skipwith's wife, after his own, her sister, died. Exactly when the transfer of affections occurred we do not know, though the record shows a remarkable willingness of Evelina Skipwith to accommodate John Armstrong with her husband's Registry Books.) (See annotations as to the Armstrong-Skipwith dispute, supra.)

4. Skipwith described in Arthur, *West Florida*, a compilation of newspaper articles published in the St. Francisville, La., *Democrat*, p. 91. This picture is confirmed by a portrait recently acquired for the collection at Prestwould (1997).

5. The Bryan Baptist Church was erected by William Bryan, who came of stock like the Kempers. His grandson, William Jennings Bryan, led many a populist struggle at the end of the century.

6. Pastor Craig preached without a license from the established church of Virginia and refused to heed warnings to cease. When he was hailed into court, Patrick Henry himself had to defend him. Thomas and his signs, in Arthur, *West Florida*, p. 92.

7. Pickett on the ears, *Alabama*, p. 507.

8. Reuben Kemper, described in *Louisiana Historical Quarterly* 21 (Jan.-Oct. 1938), p. 84. The names of New Valentia and its neighbor, St. Francisville, conjure up the whole history of multinational corporate speculation in Louisiana lands. Surely we can give such things a paragraph or two: names thought to have originated in the "Spanish Era," when tested, often turn out to have originated at later times. The spelling "Valentia" rather than "Valencia" gives this one away: Valentia is an islet off the coast of County Kerry; this town was named by an Irishman, not a Spaniard, in all likelihood that old Etonian son of Erin, Daniel Clark, wearer and distributor of black cockades, one of the circle of Reuben Kemper and at one time on good terms with Smith.

Valentia was one of three villages, a fort, and a monastery along the Bayou Sara. Only St. Francisville remains today. The first of these was founded by the Company of the Indies, under the direction of M. de Sainte Reine, when Louisiana was a corporate colony. Next door there was a royal installation, Fort St. Reine, abandoned about 1736 and reported to be in ruins in 1765. Not far from the fort there had been a Capuchin monastery named for St. Francis of Assisi—hence St. Francisville—but burnt shortly after 1785. The little town carrying a name we suppose nostalgic to Clark was established about 1800 and went to Smith by a grant in 1804 from Armand Duplantier. And finally, it is well to take note that the great Civil War battle of Port Hudson was fought on a nearby bluff where the free blacks of Louisiana gained their greatest renown.

9. Reuben Kemper in New Orleans, Whitaker, *Mississippi Question*, p. 250.

10. Abernethy on Morales, etc., *South*, p. 334. There is some doubt as to Mr. Randolph's first name. Some authorities give it as "Edmond."

11. Randolph's Declaration, quoted in Arthur, *West Florida*, p. 45.

12. Ashley and McIntosh's proclamation, quoted in Joseph Burkholder Smith, *Plot*, pp. 177–78.

13. Grand Pré and the Kempers, Pickett, *Alabama*, p. 485.

14. I am following the account of these events in Abernethy, *South*, p. 333 ff. J.F.H. Claiborne, characteristically, omits any events prior to the attack on the Kempers by the Spanish party.

15. Smith to Jefferson, quoted in Lomask, *Burr*, Vol. 2, p. 66. Smith also reported back to Burr, urging quick action to take advantage of the propitious moment. Burr took that bad advice. It comported with what he was hearing from Wilkinson. And so bemused, he fell into Jefferson's trap. See my *Burr, Hamilton, and Jefferson*.

16. The Hapsburgs had presided over the creation of the Spanish New World Empire, and now Napoleon's amiable brother Joseph, the family claimant to the throne of Spain, had acquired as his new sister-in-law a Hapsburg archduchess.

17. John Stagg has convincingly interpreted Madison's actions in 1810 as showing that he was "not so much thinking of overthrowing the colonial regime as he was trying to fill the vacuum he anticipated emerging as a result of the collapse of the Spanish Bourbon monarchy in both Spain and the Americas." Stagg may well be right. All we can know in hindsight was that a man so believing might well have taken the actions Madison did. Another person, so situated, might have been equally surprised that the Spanish regime, when pushed, did not collapse, and also that some of the agents at his disposal not only exceeded their instructions but did so coincidentally. Thus any President in like circumstances might be unjustly accused of having issued secret orders that these coincidences be simulated, leaving the impression that these obstreperousnesses were planned and instructed.

18. "Like Claiborne," we are told by the editors of the Madison *Presidential Papers* (Vol. 2, p. 313), Holmes "was a Virginian whom JM [Madison] had long known."

19. Holmes to Madison, via Smith, July 31 and Aug. 8, 1810, quoted in Arthur, *West Florida*, p. 58. Madison to Smith and Holmes, I. J. Cox, *West Florida*, p. 332.

20. Skipwith to his constituents, April 11, 1811, quoted in Padgett, "West Florida," p. 171 ff. John Stagg takes the letter straight, and may be right in doing so: "This letter did not advocate a filibuster, and it specifically ruled out any notion that West Florida

should declare its independence. Wykoff was told to assemble a convention, which would issue an invitation to the U.S. to make good its claim to the province." Undeniably true; Wykoff was told, for the record: "You know, that under the Louisiana Convention, we claim as far eastwardly as the Perdido . . . [that meant West Florida] under present circumstances it would be more pleasing that taking possession of the country be preceded by a request from the inhabitants. Can no means be devised to *obtain such a request* [Claiborne's emphasis]? . . . I hope the good inhabitants, the honest cultivators of the soil, will unite . . . to form themselves an independent governments out of the question! . . . Nature has decreed the union of Florida with the United States, and the welfare of the inhabitants imperiously demands it . . . were it done through the medium of a convention of delegates, named by the people, it would be more satisfactory." The actual text of Claiborne's letter to Wykoff appears in Arthur, *West Florida*, pp. 35–36.

Stagg's views appear in the Madison *Presidential Papers*, Vol. 2, at p. 309, in an extended note, and were extended even farther with great kindness in a personal communication dated January 17, 2001.

Leaving aside the quibble that not one of the people to be summoned by Wykoff was accustomed to cultivating the soil—that was done by their slaves—it is manifest what Claiborne had in mind.

21. Skipwith's letter to Graham of Dec. 23, 1810, appears in Padgett, "West Florida," pp. 156–57. Skipwith to his constituents, April 11, 1811, quoted ibid., p. 171 ff. Those who have a special interest in the history of presidential disavowals and deniability may find it convenient to keep upon their desks a neat summary provided by John Graham in the form of a report to Madison, dated September 3, 1810. Graham assured Madison that as President he had no "delegated power" to enforce the Neutrality Act of 1794; one implication was that he had no powerful injunction under law to do so. Instead, "instructions have generally been sent to the governors of states and territories." Accompanying that assurance, Graham sent Madison a copy of his instructions to Holmes "that you may know exactly what has been said to him" with regard to his action against Spanish East Florida, "and also a copy of a letter from the War Department to Governor Greenup" of Kentucky in November 1806. Greenup had been told to rouse the militia against Burr's expedition against either Spanish Florida or Texas. To these two instances, the one a case of a sponsored filibuster, and the other, in my view, a disavowed one, Madison added a third. He instructed Monroe, who had assumed the functions of Graham, to instruct the governor of Tennessee—who was in the position of Greenup of Kentucky just four years earlier and facing many of the same people on the ground— to obstruct the recruiting going on in his state in support of Augustus Magee's filibuster into Texas. In all likelihood, John Adair, Burr's subordinate, was as busy stirring things up for Magee against "the Dons" in Tennessee in 1810 as he had been for Burr in Kentucky in 1806. Ibid., p. 522. I am grateful to John Stagg for pointing out (in private correspondence in December 2000) the difficulty raised by Madison's instruction to Monroe for those who wish to take it at face value. In my view, all these carefully recorded presidential expressions of piety are to be regarded skeptically, beginning with Jefferson's against Burr, who, I believe, acted for more than a year with the administration's assent, in much the same way that Genet and Michaux were acting with Jefferson's assent in 1794, until Washington put an end to their

capers. My interpretation of the background of the Neutrality Act, and of the complicity of the administration in the early phases of Burr's "conspiracy," is presented in *Burr, Hamilton, and Jefferson*. Madison might well have been concerned with what exactly Holmes had been told, in the light of the Neutrality Act and his own responsibility under his oath of office.

22. The second West Florida Declaration, ibid., p. 114.

23. Quoted in Patrick, *Fiasco*, p. 11.

24. The death of Grand Pré, as told by Henry Adams, *Madison Administration*, p. 214.

25. Stanley Arthur, the Thucydides of St. Francisville, Louisiana, tells us (at pp. 29–30 in his *West Florida*) that de Lassus was born in 1764 and was probably the Royalist "Delousiere" said by Michaux (the botanical explorer-spy) to have been exiled from France for complicity in an endeavor to deliver Le Havre to a British squadron carrying a Royalist force. He arrived in New Orleans in 1793, having served the Catholic cause of Spain, and is said to have rescued Carlos III from an assassination attempt. He served as commandant at New Madrid, at St. Louis, and became commander at Baton Rouge in 1807. See also I. J. Cox, *West Florida*, p. 342. Skipwith's address, Arthur, *West Florida*, p. 129.

26. West Floridians seeking integration into the United States, quoted in Madison, *Presidential Papers*, Vol. 2, p. 317.

27. We learn from a manifestly hostile description of Kennedy by Gaines's dour commander at Fort Stoddert, Colonel Richard Sparks, that he had been "once the son-in-law of Abraham Baldwin, Sr. . . . and also brother-in-law to Joel Barlow. . . . He is a young man, educated in the Eastern States, ambitious, intriguing, and popular. . . . [A]lthough without real talents, yet in seditious intrigue, or for the low arts that secure popularity, he must be acknowledged eminent. He is a man of engaging address, popular manners, and daring" (quoted in I. J. Cox, *West Florida*, p. 445). A footnote to the *Papers* of Benjamin Henry Latrobe instructs us that the architect's friend Joel Barlow was the brother-in-law of Abraham Baldwin (1754–1807) and that "Clara Baldwin, Ruth Baldwin Barlow's younger half-sister, had been married and deserted before coming to live with the Barlows at Kalorama" (*Latrobe Papers*, p. 192 n.). Kennedy's country, quoted in I. J. Cox, *West Florida*, p. 464.

28. The Mobile expedition, in Pickett, *Alabama*, pp. 508–9.

29. Ibid.

30. Ibid., p. 416.

31. Claiborne to Smith, Arthur, *West Florida*, p. 133.

32. Slave revolts, see Holmes to Smith, Oct. 3, 1810, cited in note on p. 318 in Madison, *Presidential Papers*, Vol. 2.

33. Ibid.

34. Skipwith to his constituents, April 11, 1811, quoted in Padgett, "West Florida," p. 171 ff.

35. Skipwith and Holmes, ibid., pp. 134–39. I. J. Cox, *West Florida*, p. 573. The editors of the Madison *Presidential Papers* have provided a complete bibliographic note for these events on pp. 319–20 of Vol. 2.

36. My quotations, and the main thread of this part of my narrative, come from the masterly article on Skipwith by Augustus Ingram in the *Foreign Service Journal*.

37. Ibid. There is no record of Skipwith's ever having visited his second "seat," which he acquired sometime around 1804 in some obscure distress sale in Paris. It was a one-fourth interest in one of the yeoman colonies which the Baron de Carondelet had set out along the Ouachita. The seller was a wraithlike Parisian turned Louisianan who called himself "the Marquis de Maison Rouge." The Skipwith–Maison Rouge claim was situated just below that of "the Baron de Bastrop," where Aaron Burr sought to settle in 1806.

I have been unable to authenticate the claim of Maison Rouge to nobility among the swirl of creations of the Bonapartes and late Bourbons. Truth to tell, I hope he was no more authentic as a nobleman than Bastrop, for if both were bogus the Marquis and Baron may the more readily serve as prototypes for Mark Twain's Duke and Dauphin. Twain may have had them in mind. They were not unknown in the lower Mississippi Valley. In history, which is sometimes distinct from fiction, the Marquis was for Skipwith the equivalent to what Bastrop was for Burr: Skipwith bought his Ouachita claim from the heirs of the Marquis as Burr bought his from the creditors of the Baron.

Skipwith wrote John Graham of his troubles on August 14, 1811, at the same time he described his having purchased from Daniel Clark in 1804 that one fourth of the Marquis de Maison Rouge's claim along the Ouachita. Graham advised him to have the government take the property to clear its title. See Padgett, "The West Florida Revolution," pp. 166 and 170.

38. We may assume that Wade Hampton and Edward Livingston noted grimly that the outcome might have been quite different had Burr actually led the revolt rather than Skipwith: West Florida would, no doubt, have found itself annexed to the United States, and its imperialists would have "returned to the bosom of their native country," but those who had taken the major risks would not have been so willing as Skipwith to recede once more into the wallpaper of history.

Skipwith's blue ensign with a single white star went back up again in January 1811, when some unreconciled West Floridian hoisted it upon a sixty-foot staff above the little town of St. Francisville. Wade Hampton was in the vicinity, putting down a slave insurrection. Elbowing aside the civilian authorities, he ordered the flag taken down and gave it a formal military burial. Skipwith to his constituents, April 11, 1811, quoted in Padgett, "West Florida," p. 171 ff.

39. Ingram, "Skipwith," p. 356 ff.

40. Ibid.

41. Ibid.

42. Description of Skipwith by his nephew, Arthur, *West Florida*, pp. 142–43.

43. For Apalachee, see essays by John F. Scarry and John H. Hann, in Hudson and Tresser, eds., *Forgotten Centuries*.

44. C. Hudson in his *Knights of Spain* at p. 123.

Epilogue

1. Quotations from Hammond, etc., from James McPherson's wonderfully clear account of these currents and events in his *Battle Cry*, p. 383 ff.

2. TJ to Charles Pinckney, Sept. 30, 1820, *Writings*, Memorial Ed., Vol. 15, p. 263.

3. TJ to Thomas Pinckney, quoted in an admiring article by John Murrin and Gary Kornbluth entitled "The Jeffersonian Triumph and American Exceptionalism," p. 18. Murrin asserts that Jefferson succeeded in the "manipulation of Europe's detested balance of power to achieve hegemony for the United States," a conclusion with which I do not concur, for the reasons laid forth in this book.

Those who have read my *Burr, Hamilton, and Jefferson* will not be surprised to find me in disagreement with Dr. Murrin, whose view of the politics of the early republic differs in many ways from mine.

4. The "King Corn, King Cotton" line is McPherson's, in his *Battle Cry*, p. 383 ff.

5. Ibid.

6. *Works*, Lib. of Am. Ed., p. 289.

7. TJ to John Holmes, April 22, 1820, ibid., p. 1432.

8. Julian quoted in Griswold, *Farming*, p. 197.

9. In the North and West, as population increased, the minimum size of allotments from the public domain declined, and the price per acre declined with it. If the statistics demonstrating these trends were not so familiar they would astonish us:

	Population in millions	Size of allotment	Price–minimum per acre
1790	4	640 minimum	$2 (half in cash)
1800	5.3	320 minimum	$2 (1/4 in cash)
1820	9.6	80 minimum	$1.25
1830	12.9	160 maximum	$1.25
1841	18 est.	40 minimum, 160 maximum	$1.25
1862	33 est.	164 maximum	Zero with five years residence

10. Quoted in Griswold, *Farming*, p. 15.

11. Wickard quoted in ibid., p. 18.

12. I am quoting Lincoln, from *Works*, in the Nicolay and Hay edition, Vol. 6, p. 157.

Appendix

1. James Machor suggests in his *Pastoral Cities* (p. 84) that Condorcet's *Esquise d'un tableau historique des progrès de l'esprit humain* of 1790 contributed to the evolution of American thinking about cities vis-à-vis agrarian life, including, perhaps, Jefferson's. Adams, *Administrations*, pp. 91–95; TJ on seaport towns, quoted in Onuf, *Jefferson's Empire*, p. 20.

2. The pattern of dependence is found in Isaac, *Transformation*, p. 16.

3. Baltimore in 1780, quoted in *Maryland Guide*, p. 356.

4. Madison to Monroe, June 21, 1785, *Madison Papers*, Vol. 8, pp. 306–8.

5. My quotations are drawn from McCoy, *Elusive Republic*, pp. 19–20. McCoy provides an extensive bibliography for readers who wish to pursue these ideas in detail to their sources (pp. 39–40).

6. My quotation comes from an essay on Roman agrarian laws in the eleventh edition of the *Encyclopaedia Britannica*, Vol. 1, p. 383.

7. Peterson, *Jefferson*, p. 284. See also Finkelman, "Slavery and the Northwest Ordinance," in *New Perspectives*, p. 83, with extensive further bibliography on the point.

8. Peterson, *Jefferson*, p. 242.

9. TJ to Madison, *Writings*, Ford, Vol. 7, p. 118. Bowers, *Young Jefferson*, p. 342.

10. I am quoting Paul Finkelman's reading of Madison's proposal ("Slavery and the Northwest Ordinance," p. 97).

11. Madison in Fehrenbacher, *Slavery*, pp. 42–43. Peter Onuf provides a virtuosic demonstration both of empathy across time and of intellectual resourcefulness (no irony intended) in his discussion of the evolution of Jefferson's advocacy of a line between the slave and free territories of the West, in 1784, and his denunciation of any such lines, in 1819, in a section of his *Jefferson's Empire* after p. 113. *Writings*, Ford, Vol. 1, p. 432. TJ to Madison, ibid., p. 471.

12. Jefferson and Peterson in the latter's *Jefferson*, pp. 410–13.

13. Ellis, *Sphinx*, pp. 132–33.

14. TJ to Madison, Sept. 6, 1789, *Writings*, Lib. of Am. Ed., p. 959. There are complex questions to be avoided in this brief discourse, for debt had unpleasant consequences to debtors themselves in the eighteenth century. Madison and Jefferson did not walk away from their inheritances; they took assets from their fathers and mothers far exceeding the debts of which they complained.

15. Ibid. In 1995, Herbert E. Sloan published the definitive analysis of the origins of Jefferson's thinking on this matter, putting the emphasis on the problem of debt. That is surely where Jefferson's thinking began, but it is not where its implications ended. He did not content himself with wallowing in resentment.

16. Ellis, *Sphinx*, pp. 132–3; see also TJ to Madison, Oct. 28, 1785, p. 840 ff.

17. Ibid.

18. Bacon quoted in *Encyclopedia Britannica*, 11th ed., s.v. "plantation."

19. Curtis, *History of Ireland*, p. 227.

20. I am following Dobyns, *Their Number*.

21. My figures for surviving Florida Indians in the eighteenth century come from Milanich, *Florida Indians*, pp. 229–30.

22. See correspondence in the *Madison Presidential Papers*, Vol. 2, from Armstrong to Madison, May 6, 1810, and reports to Madison from Graham, on pp. 332–33, 498, and 502; Madison to Graham on p. 504. Armstrong's complaint appears ibid., on pp. 332–33.

23. Ibid.

24. I am quoting the summary of Morales's views in I. J. Cox, *West Florida*, pp. 211–12.

25. Armstrong quoted by John Graham, *Madison Presidential Papers*, p. 503.

26. See correspondence in the *Madison Presidential Papers*, Vol. 2, from Armstrong to Madison, May 6, 1810, and reports to Madison from Graham, on pp. 332–33, 498, and 502; Madison to Graham on p. 504. Madison's verdict is on p. 504.

27. My treatment of this phase of the proceedings is, I think, quite noncontroversial and is drawn from I. J. Cox, *West Florida*, p. 145 ff., and Abernethy, *South*. Claiborne was not a giant, but he was consistent. While a freshman congressman, he had opposed the Federalists' preparations for war with France in the West Indies on the ground that war with France would bring Spain in as a French ally, the closing of New Orleans would ensue, and "the commerce of the Southern States and the Western country would be immediately gone." Claiborne in Congress, quoted by Whitaker in footnote 31 on pp. 295–96 of his *Mississippi Question*.

28. Coles to Cabell, July 6, 1807, in a private collection quoted in Langhorne, Lay, and Rieley, *Family*, pp. 38–39.

29. Padgett, "Difficulties," p. 372 ff.

30. Jackson on Skipwith, letter to John McLean, March 22, 1824, quoted ibid.

31. Ibid.

Bibliographic Note

With regard to the spelling and punctuation of quotations to be found in this book: they have been translated in my text to the conventions of the 1990s (to the extent that I have caught up with them from the conventions of the 1940s), except when there is a point to be made by leaving them as they were when written. The risk in this method is that I may have misunderstood what was originally intended. The offsetting risk is that by leaving them in the original they may be unintelligible except to experts. If forewarned that there has been such an attempted updating, any expert can gain access to originals as general readers cannot. After sixty years of reading people quoting other people, I have always been grateful to get through the orthography to the meaning.

The same desire to increase the number of people who may become interested in this subject matter has determined my choice of sources. I am not attempting to produce a log of library hours or triumphs of invidious access. I am trying to make it as easy as possible for those who do not have access to a great university library or to the Library of Congress to check or extend a reference. It is sometimes useful to direct specialists or incipient specialists to bibliographers who have compiled extended lists of primary sources, and who have evaluated the secondary sources as well. Though I have often gone back to primary sources to do my own checking, I have chosen to direct readers to the most accessible source, unless the primary source says something significant that the secondary sources do not. Sometimes—though less often than in my earlier work—I have treated a work of architecture as a primary source. I have attempted to visit all the landscapes that have value as witnesses to the events described.

As to Jefferson's own work, I have cited whenever possible and with some paternal pride the edition of Jefferson's work by the Library of America, of which I was a founder. Otherwise I have on occasion cited Bernard Mayo's paperback anthology called *Jefferson Himself*, which is in print and relies most heavily upon the so-called Memorial Edition of Andrew Lipscomb and Albert

Ellery Bergh, in twenty volumes. On a few occasions I have used the earlier ten-volume edition of Jefferson's writing edited by Paul Leicester Ford. Merrill Peterson's bibliographic essay for the Library of America Edition clarifies the relationships among these various editions, which culminate in the grand, reliable, multivolume Princeton edition of Julian Boyd et al., commenced fifty years ago and still not complete. Thanks to John Stagg and his colleagues, I have made extensive use both of the Madison Presidential Papers and the Madison Secretary of State Papers. These supply useful references to any character whose life interdigitated with Madison's. In general, I have listed in my own bibliography only those books or papers from which I have taken quotations or which have led me through a sequence of events or ideas. When I have used a source only once, for a specific point, I list it in the endnotes at that point.

For full disclosure I should state that my previous studies of Jefferson and his times appear in *Architecture, Men, Women, and Money*; *Orders from France*; *Greek Revival America*; *Rediscovering America*; *Hidden Cities*; and in articles in publications ranging from the *Winterthur Portfolio* to *Architectural Digest*, from *Harper's* to *Law and Contemporary Problems*. The endeavor immediately before you was taking a more conventional course into political and economic history until my colleague at the National Museum of American History, Pete Daniel, provided me with a list of books to be read if one wished to situate Southern political history in Southern agricultural history. They were: Lewis Cecil Gray, *History of Agriculture in the Southern United States to 1860*, 2 vols. (Peter Smith reprint, 1958); *Soils and Men: Yearbook of Agriculture, 1938* (USDA); Albert E. Cowdrey, *This Land, This South: An Environmental History* (Lexington, 1983); James C. Bonner, *A History of Georgia Agriculture, 1732–1860* (Athens, 1964). I then commenced a journey into agricultural and environmental history, drawing upon the kindness of many scholars already acquainted with landscape to which I had until then been a stranger.

At the outset of any voyage toward the places and period before us one must pass Scylla and Charybdis, Henry Adams and Francis Parkman. Adams remains the most readable of historians of the early Republic. His gift for pungent synthesis has not yet been equaled by any later writer who may have come into possession of new information. But Adams can lead us into traps by his appearing to accept at face value a favorite falsity promulgated by those he held in contempt. It was his guile to make use of that deception to humiliate his opponents so subtly as to leave it doubtful that he bore them any animosity. There is, for example, this celebrated passage from his survey of the American scene in 1800: "The Virginian ideal was patriarchal, and an American continent of the Virginian type might reproduce the virtues of Cato, and perhaps the eloquence of Cicero, but was little likely to produce anything more practical in the way of modern progress" (Henry Adams, *Jefferson Administrations*, pp. 24–25).

Leaving aside the patronizing implication that Yankee merchants or Yankee writers were likely to be more lively and enterprising than Virginians, we can find in Adams a picture of Virginia reproduced in subsequent histories written as late as the 1940s: a classical patriarchy uncontaminated by trade and indifferent to the importunings of a mercantile life.

> [As for] the middle and lower classes . . . their character was stereotyped, and development impossible . . . intellectual activity was confined to hereditary commonplaces of politics, resting on the axiom that Virginia was the typical society of a future Arcadian America. To escape the tyranny of Caesar by perpetuating the simple and isolated lives of their fathers was the sum of their political philosophy; to fix upon the national government the stamp of their own idyllic conservatism was the height of their ambition. Debarred from manufactures, possessed of no shipping, and enjoying no domestic market, Virginian energies necessarily knew no other resource than agriculture. (Ibid., pp. 95–96.)

Small wonder that generations of readers have imagined Jefferson's Arcadia as a customer-indifferent Eden in which the patriarchy and their flocks—human and otherwise—lived "simple and isolated lives," where the beguilements of world markets, or the calls for collateral by bankers, would not be heeded amid the native woodnotes wild. An "idyllic conservatism, knowing no other resource than agriculture," sounds very much like an Appalachian subsistence farm. But it was not Jefferson's Virginia. Adams did not aid our understanding of Jefferson's dilemma by perpetuating two false notions. The first was that the Sage of Monticello wished Virginia or any other portion of the plantation South to abandon its customers and become an isolated Arcadia. The second was that Jefferson had any use for the myth that the gentlemen of Virginia were Cavaliers, free of any commercial taint and descended as a body from the troopers of Prince Rupert. Jefferson did not advocate subsistence farming and assaulted the patriarchate. When he was done, it was not true, as Adams asserted, that "the old Virginia society was still erect, priding itself on its resemblance to the society of England, which had produced Hampton and Chatham" (ibid.).

Nor was Parkman a better guide than Adams to understanding the demise of Jefferson's Lost Cause. He confused matters by throwing his weight behind the tradition that the Virginia gentry might "be described as English country squires transplanted to a warm climate and turned slave-masters." As shown in the main text, this is nonsense. (Parkman in his *Montcalm and Wolfe*, Library of America Edition, p. 865.)

My differences with other scholars are stated in modest bibliographic essays attached to the first extended references to the characters or events about which our opinions vary, not to attempt to score points but to warn readers that there are several points of view.

The classic history of the roles of tobacco and cotton in the American economy is that of Douglass North, in his *Economic Growth*, as amended and expanded by Ross Robertson, Gary Walton, Susan Previant Lee, Peter Passell, and two generations of "new economic historians."

In the case of Fulwar Skipwith, who occupies a prominent place in this tale because he saw much that is of interest to us, a little more bibliographic data may be of use. Only in the winter of 2000–2001 was I was able to secure a copy of the excellent doctoral dissertation on Skipwith by Henry Bartholomew Cox, of which a few copies were printed in 1964 by the Mount Vernon Publishing Company. Before that, I had been working for many years on primary documents about Skipwith in the Library of Congress, at Prestwould, at the University of Virginia, at George Washington University, at Louisiana State University, and at the College of William and Mary. Cox's bibliography is exceedingly useful, and for the period it covers more comprehensive than my own list of sources. Cox held some documents secured from the family, and—as I was when the staff at Prestwould came into the possession of portraits of Skipwith and his wife thirty years after Cox's work was published—Cox was a fortunate searcher. Those who wish to pursue his researches should obtain a copy of his book from George Washington University. Other sources are those cited throughout this text and in the Foreign Affairs Section of the National Archives, especially in a manila envelope filed under "Applications and Recommendations for Office, Jefferson Administration"; in the Causten-Pickett Papers, Fulwar Skipwith Collection, Vols. 5–14 in the Library of Congress; in the Fulwar Skipwith MSS at the Historical Society of Pennsylvania; and in the Peyton Skipwith material at the College of William and Mary.

Cox himself drew upon two earlier scholars, whose work is cited in my bibliography, Augustus E. Ingram and John S. Kendall, writing in 1934 and 1935. Cox remains the place to begin, though he gave almost no attention to Skipwith's career after leaving Paris and takes a sweetly loyal view of his subject—as we all tend to do, unless those subjects reveal themselves to be genuinely repulsive. I am grateful to Julian D. Hudson of the Prestwould Foundation for walking me slowly through the baffling progressions of Skipwiths. As Mr. Hudson points out, all printed sources except those in the hands of the family genealogists get at least parts of the story wrong. Some even say that Sir Peyton's son Humberton was the father of Fulwar. As a middle-aged man, Humberton married Fulwar's daughter, a beauty named Lelia. If, indeed, he had been her grandfather, that would have been improper even in Virginia.

As to slavery in Florida, Larry Eugene Rivers's book of that title (2000) brings up to date and adds many useful cross-disciplinary ideas to the works cited in the text and to Julia Smith's *Slavery and Plantation Growth in Antebellum Florida, 1821–1860* (1973).

The largest collection of Wilkinson papers is in the Chicago Historical Society. Other substantial holdings are in the Library of Congress and the

Historical Society of Pennsylvania. His *Memoirs of My Own Times* (3 vols., 1816) are essential but must be used with extreme caution. The most useful and scholarly biography is James Ripley Jacobs, *Tarnished Warrior: Major-General James Wilkinson* (1938). Other biographies are Thomas Robson Hay and M. R. Werner, *The Admirable Trumpeter: A Biography of General James Wilkinson* (1941), and Royal O. Shreve, *The Finished Scoundrel: General James Wilkinson* (1933). The politico-military setting in the Western lands is covered admirably by Richard H. Kohn, *Eagle and Sword: The Federalists and the Creation of the Military Establishment in America, 1783–1802* (1975).

Bibliographies ought from time to time to suggest books that need to be written to fill gaps. Here is my suggestion: there is a great book to be written about the contest between the Burrites and the Jeffersonians in the formation of American foreign policy toward Latin America, and the role of private parties such as Gregor MacGregor and Louis Aury in the process. The basis for it may be found in a memorandum from Eleanor V. Shodell to Milton Lomask, dated March 10, 1978, to be found in the Special Collections of the Library at Rutgers University. I wish to acknowledge the assistance of that library in finding that memorandum, with its documentation of the matters asserted in these two paragraphs. The citations are to other materials in libraries elsewhere. An interested scholar could pursue the matter through the many archives to which guidance is provided by Shodell. Burr and Samuel C. Reid, naval hero of the War of 1812, and harbormaster of the Port of New York, were jointly engaged in some enigmatic association with Aury and Aury's partner Pedro Gaul. They held letters of recommendation from—and presumably to—the rebels of Cartagena and Amelia. Burr acted as counsel to John Novion, who operated in the Caribbean under a privateer's charter from them, making use of at least one vessel provided by Gaul and captained by Aury. Burr's partner John Alderson operated along the waterways of Venezuela doing a little mercantile business but apparently much occupied in distributing copies of Rócios's *The Triumph of Liberty Against Despotism.*

Bibliography

Abel, Annie H. "Proposals for an Indian State." *Journal of the American Historical Association* 1 (1907), p. 89 ff.

Abernethy, Thomas P. *The South in the New Nation, 1789–1819*. Baton Rouge: Louisiana State University Press, 1976.

———. *Western Lands and the American Revolution*. New York: D. Appleton-Century, 1937.

Ackerman, James S. *The Villa: Form and Ideology of Country Houses*. Princeton: Princeton University Press, 1990.

Adams, Henry. *History of the United States of America During the Administrations of James Madison*. New York: Library of America, 1986.

———. *History of the United States of America During the Administrations of Thomas Jefferson*. Arr. Earl N. Harbert. New York: Library of America, 1986. [*Jefferson Administrations*]

———. *The Life of Albert Gallatin*. New York: Peter Smith, 1943.

Adams, John Quincy. "Argument of John Quincy Adams Before the Supreme Court of the United States in the Case of the United States, Appellants, vs. Cinque, and Others, Africans, Captured in the Schooner *Amistad*, by Lieut. Gedney, Delivered on the 24th of February and 1st of March, 1841." New York, 1841.

———. *Memoirs*. Ed. Charles Francis Adams. 12 vols. Philadelphia: Lippincott, 1874–77.

———. *Writings*. Ed. Worthington Chauncey Ford. New York: Greenwood, 1968.

Ahlstrom, Sydney E. *A Religious History of the American People*. New Haven: Yale University Press, 1973.

Allen, John Logan. *Passage Through the Garden*. Urbana: University of Illinois Press, 1975.

Ambler, Charles. *George Washington and the West*. Chapel Hill: University of North Carolina Press, 1936.

American Philosophical Society. *Documents Relating to the Purchase and Exploration of Louisiana* [2 reports, one by T. Jefferson and one by William Dunbar]. Boston: Houghton Mifflin, 1904.

Ammon, Harry. *James Monroe: The Quest for National Identity*. Charlottesville: University Press of Virginia, 1990.

Andrews, Kenneth. *Trade, Plunder, and Settlement: Maritime Enterprise and the Genesis of the British Empire, 1480–1630*. New York: Cambridge University Press, 1984.

Appleby, Joyce. "Commercial Farming and the 'Agrarian Myth' in the Early Republic." *Journal of American History* 68 (March 1982), p. 833 ff. Bloomington, Ind.: Organization of American Historians.

Aron, Stephen. *How the West Was Lost*. Baltimore: Johns Hopkins University Press, 1996.

Arthur, Stanley Clisby. *The Story of the West Florida Rebellion*. St. Francisville, La.: *St. Francisville Democrat*, 1935.

Ashworth, John. *"Agrarians" and "Aristocrats": Party Political Ideology in the United States, 1837–1846*. New York: Cambridge University Press, 1987.

Bacarisse, Charles A. "Baron de Bastrop." *Southwestern Historical Quarterly* 58, no. 3 (Jan. 1955).

Bailey, Kenneth P. *The Ohio Company of Virginia*. Glendale, Calif.: Arthur H. Clark, 1939.

Bailyn, Bernard. *Voyagers to the West: A Passage in the Peopling of America on the Eve of the Revolution*. New York: Vintage, 1988.

Bailyn, Bernard, with Philip D. Morgan, eds. *Strangers Within the Realm: Cultural Margins of the First British Empire*. Chapel Hill: University of North Carolina Press, 1991.

Bannon, John Francis. *The Spanish Borderlands Frontier, 1513–1821*. Albuquerque: University of New Mexico Press, 1988.

Barr, James T. *Whence We Came: The Family History Book: Bowles, Ray, Barr, Grinder, a Genealogical Record*. Lexington, S.C.: J. T. Barr, 1982.

Bartlett, Thomas, and Keith Jeffery, eds. *A Military History of Ireland*. Cambridge: Cambridge University Press, 1996.

Bartram, William. *The Travels of William Bartram*. Ed. Mark Van Doren. New York: Dover, 1955.

Baynton, Benjamin. *Authentic Memories of William Augustus Bowles*. New York: Arno Press, 1971.

Beard, Charles A. *An Economic Interpretation of the Constitution of the United States*. New York: Macmillan, 1957; first published in 1913.

———. *Economic Origins of Jeffersonian Democracy*. New York: Macmillan, 1949.

Beckett, J. V. *The Aristocracy in England, 1660–1914*. New York: Basil Blackwell, 1986; paperback ed., 1988.

Bedini, Silvio. *Thomas Jefferson: Statesman of Science*. New York: Macmillan, 1990.

Beeman, Richard, Stephen Botein, and Edward C. Carter II, eds. *Beyond Confederation: Origins of the Constitution and American National Identity*. Chapel Hill: University of North Carolina Press, 1987.

Bell, Malcolm, Jr. *Major Butler's Legacy: Five Generations of a Slaveholding Family*. Athens: University of Georgia Press, 1987.

Bemis, Samuel F. *Pinckney's Treaty*. Baltimore: Johns Hopkins University Press, 1960.

Ben-Atar, Doron, and Barbara B. Oberg. *Federalists Reconsidered*. Charlottesville: University Press of Virginia, 1998.

Bennett, Charles E. *Twelve on the River St. Johns*. Jacksonville: University of North Florida Press, 1989.

Berkeley, Edmund, and Dorothy Smith Berkeley. *The Life and Travels of John Bartram from Lake Ontario to the River St. John*. Tallahassee: University Presses of Florida, 1982.

Berlin, Ira. *Many Thousands Gone: The First Two Centuries of Slavery in North America*. Cambridge, Mass.: Belknap Press, 1998.

Berman, Eleanor. *Thomas Jefferson Among the Arts*. New York: New York Philosophical Library, 1947.

Berns, Walter. "The Constitution and the Migration of Slaves." *Yale Law Journal* 78 (Dec. 1968).

Bernstein, Peter L. *Against the Gods*. New York: John Wiley & Sons, 1996.

Berthoff, Rowland. *An Unsettled People: Social Order and Disorder in American History*. New York: Harper & Row, 1971.

Beveridge, Albert J. *The Life of John Marshall*, Vol. 4. New York: Houghton Mifflin, 1919.

Blackburn, Joyce. *James Edward Oglethorpe*. Marietta, Ga.: Mocking, 1994.

Blackburn, Robin. *The Making of New World Slavery*. London and New York: Verso paperback, 1998.

———. *The Overthrow of Colonial Slavery, 1776–1848*. London: Verso, 1988.

The Blackwell Encyclopedia of the American Revolution. Ed. Jack P. Greene and J. R. Pole. Cambridge, Mass.: Blackwell Ref., 1991.

Bodley, Temple, ed. *Reprints of Littell's Political Transactions in and Concerning Kentucky and Letter of George Nicholas to His Friend in Virgina; also General Wilkinson's Memorial*. Louisville, Ky.: John P. Morton, 1926.

Bolton, H. E. "Papers of Zebulon M. Pike, 1806–7." *American Historical Review* 13 (July 1908), pp. 801–2.

Bonner, James C. *A History of Georgia Agriculture, 1732–1860*. Athens: University of Georgia Press, 1964.

———. *Milledgeville: Georgia's Antebellum Capital*. Athens: University of Georgia Press, 1978.

Boorstin, Daniel J. *The Americans: The Colonial Experience*. New York: Random House, 1958.

———. *The Lost World of Thomas Jefferson*. Chicago: University of Chicago Press, 1993.

Bos, Harriet P. "Barthelemy Lafon." Master's thesis, Tulane University, 1977.

Bowers, Claude. *The Young Jefferson*. Boston: Houghton Mifflin, 1945.

Bowles, Charles A. *A Journey with the Bowles Family: Some Memories Along the Way*. Florida: C. A. Bowles, 1983.

Boyd, Julian P. *Number 7: Alexander Hamilton's Secret Attempts to Control American Foreign Policy*. Princeton: Princeton University Press, 1964.

Bradley, Edward Austin. "Forgotten Filibusters: Private Hostile Expeditions from the United States into Spanish Texas, 1812–21." Ph.D. dissertation, University of Illinois at Urbana-Champaign, 1999.

Brant, Irving. *James Madison: Secretary of State, 1800–1809*. Indianapolis: Bobbs-Merrill, 1953.

Brantley, William Henderson. *Banking in Alabama, 1816–1860*. Birmingham: Birmingham Printing, 1967.

Brewer, John. *The Sinews of Power: War, Money, and the English State, 1688–1783*. New York: Knopf, 1989.

Brock, William R. *Scotus Americanus: A Survey of the Sources for Links Between Scotland and America in the Eighteenth Century*. Edinburgh: Edinburgh University Press, 1982.

Brodie, Fawn. *Thomas Jefferson: An Intimate History*. New York: Bantam, 1981.

Brooks, Van Wyck. *The World of Washington Irving*. New York: Dutton, 1950.

Brown, C. Allan. "Poplar Forest: The Mathematics of an Ideal Villa." *Journal of Garden History* 10, no. 2 (1990).

Brown, Everett S. "The Senate Debate on the Breckinridge Bill for the Government of Louisiana, 1804." *American Historical Review* 22 (Oct. 1916 to July 1917), p. 340 ff.

———, ed. *William Plumer's Memorandum of the Proceedings in the United States Senate, 1803–1807*. New York: Macmillan, 1923.

Buck, Norman S. *The Development of the Organization of Anglo-American Trade, 1800–1850*. New Haven: Yale University Press, 1925.

Buley, R. Carlyle. *The Old Northwest*. 2 vols. Bloomington: Indiana University Press, 1950.

Burke, Harry R. "More About Moses Austin." *Missouri Historical Review* 33 (1938), pp. 154–56.

Burr, Aaron. *Correspondence of Aaron Burr and His Daughter Theodosia*. Ed. Mark Van Doren. New York: Covici-Friede, 1929.

———. *Political Correspondence and Public Papers*. Ed. Mary-Jo Kline. 2 vols. Princeton: Princeton University Press, 1983.

Burr-Powell, Ruth. *Burr-Bowles Genealogy*. Baltimore: Gateway Press, 1995.

Burrows, Edwin. "Notes on Settling America: Albert Gallatin, New England, and the American Revolution." *New England Quarterly* 58, no. 3 (1985).

Cain, P. J., and A. G. Hopkins. *British Imperialism: Innovation and Expansion, 1688–1914*. London: Longman, 1993.

Cannadine, David. *Aspects of Aristocracy: Grandeur and Decline in Modern Britain*. New Haven and London: Yale University Press, 1994.

Carney, Judith. *Black Rice: The African Origins of Rice Cultivation in the Americas*. Cambridge: Harvard University Press, 2001.

Cashin, Edward J. *Lachlan McGillivray, Indian Trader: The Shaping of the Southern Colonial Frontier*. Athens: University of Georgia Press, 1992.

Caughey, John W. *McGillivray of the Creeks*. Norman: University of Oklahoma Press, 1938.

Cayton, Andrew R. L. *The Frontier Republic: Ideology and Politics in the Ohio Country, 1780–1825*. Kent, Ohio: Kent State University Press, 1986.

Chaplin, Joyce E. *An Anxious Pursuit: Agricultural Innovation and Modernity in the Lower South, 1730–1815*. Chapel Hill: University of North Carolina Press, 1993.

Churchill, Winston S. *The Age of Revolution*. New York: Dodd, Mead, 1957.

———. *Maxims and Reflections*. Arr. Colin Coote. Boston: Houghton Mifflin, 1949.

Claiborne, J.F.H. *Mississippi as a Province, Territory, and State*, Vol. 1. Ann Arbor: Cushing-Malloy, 1964.

Claiborne, W.C.C. *Official Letter Books . . . , 1801-1816.* Ed. Dunbar Rowland. Jackson, Miss.: State Department of Archives and History, 1917.

Clark, Daniel. *Proofs of the Corruption of Gen. James Wilkinson, and of His Connexion with Aaron Burr.* Philadelphia: Wm. Hall, Jun. & Geo. W. Pierie, 1809.

Clark, Thomas D., and John D. W. Guice. *The Old Southwest, 1795-1830.* Norman and London: University of Oklahoma Press, 1996 paperback reissue.

Clarke, Mary Whatley. *Chief Bowles and the Cherokees.* Norman: University of Oklahoma Press, 1974.

Cleland, Hugh. *George Washington in the Ohio Valley.* Pittsburgh: University of Pittsburgh Press, 1955.

Clouse, Jerry A. *The Whiskey Rebellion.* Harrisburg: Bureau of Historic Preservation, Pennsylvania Historical and Museum Commission, 1994.

Coker, William S. "The Bruins and the Formulation of Spanish Immigration Policy in the Old Southwest, 1787-88." In John Francis McDermott, ed., *The Spanish in the Mississippi Valley, 1763-1804.* Urbana: University of Illinois Press, 1974.

———. "John Forbes and Company and the War of 1812 in the Spanish Boarderlands." In Coker, ed., *Hispanic-American Essays in Honor of Max Leon Moorhead.* Pensacola: Perdido Bay Press, 1979.

———, ed. *John Forbes' Description of the Spanish Floridas, 1804.* Pensacola: Perdido Bay Press, 1979.

Coker, William S., and Thomas D. Watson. *Indian Traders of the Southeastern Spanish Borderlands: Panton, Leslie & Company and John Forbes & Company, 1783-1847.* Gainesville: University Presses of Florida; Pensacola: University of West Florida Press, 1986.

Cole, Frank. "Thomas Worthington Of Ohio." *Old Northwest Genealogical Quarterly* (April 1902).

Coleman, Kenneth. *Colonial Georgia: A History.* New York: Charles Scribner's Sons, 1976.

Collot, Victor. *A Journey in North America.* 3 vols. New York: AMS reprint, 1974.

Coming, Alexander. "Travels." *Tennessee Historical Magazine* 5 (1919).

Cooper, Duff. *Talleyrand.* New York: Fromm, 1986.

Copeland, Pamela C., and Richard K. MacMaster. *The Five George Masons: Patriots and Planters of Virginia and Maryland.* Charlottesville: University Press of Virginia, 1975.

Corlew, Robert E. *Tennessee: A Short History.* Knoxville: University of Tennessee Press, 1981.

Cotterill, Robert S. "A Chapter of Panton, Leslie, and Company." *Journal of Southern History* 10 (Aug. 1944), pp. 275-92.

Coues, Elliot, ed. *The Expeditions of Zebulon Montgomery Pike.* 3 vols. New York, 1895.

Coulter, E. Merton. "Elijah Clarke's Foreign Intrigues." Mississippi Valley Historical Association, *Proceedings,* Vol. 10 (Pt. 2, 1919-21).

Cowdrey, Albert E. *This Land, This South: An Environmental History* (Lexington: University Press of Kentucky, 1983).

Cox, Henry Bartholomew. *The Parisian American: Fulwar Skipwith of Virginia.* Washington: Mt. Vernon Publishing, 1964.

Cox, I. J. "Hispanic-American Phases of the Burr Conspiracy." *Hispanic-American History Review* 12 (1932).

———. "The Louisiana-Texas Frontier." *Southwestern Historical Quarterly* 10 and 12 (1913).

———. "Monroe and Early Mexican Revolutionary Agents." *Annual Report of the American Historical Association, 1911*, Vol. 1, pp. 199–215.

———."The Opening of the Santa Fe Trail." *Missouri Historical Review* (Oct. 1930), p. 51 ff.

———. *The West Florida Controversy: A Study in American Diplomacy.* Gloucester, Mass.: Peter Smith, 1967.

Crane, Verner. *The Southern Frontier, 1670–1732.* New York: Norton, 1981.

Craven, Avery Odelle. *Soil Exhaustion as a Factor in the Agricultural History of Virginia and Maryland, 1606–1860.* 1926; Gloucester, Mass.: Peter Smith reprint, 1965.

Cunliffe, Marcus. *George Washington, Man and Monument.* New York: New American Library, 1982.

Curtis, Edmund. *A History of Ireland.* New York: Metheun, 1981.

Cusick, James Gregory. "Ethnic Groups and Class in an Emerging Market Economy: Spaniards and Minorcans in Late Colonial St. Augustine." Ph.D. dissertation, University of Florida, 1993.

Dangerfield, George. *The Awakening of American Nationalism.* New York: Harper Torchbooks, 1965.

———. *Chancellor Robert R. Livingston of New York, 1746–1813.* New York: Harcourt, Brace, 1960.

———. *The Era of Good Feeling.* New York: Harcourt, Brace, 1952.

Davis, D. B. *The Problem of Slavery in the Age of Revolution, 1770–1823.* Ithaca: Cornell University Press, 1975.

Davis, Matthew L., ed. *Memoirs of Aaron Burr.* 2 vols. New York: Harper & Brothers, 1836, 1837.

Davis, Ralph. *The Rise of the Atlantic Economies.* Ithaca: Cornell University Press, 1973.

Davis, T. Frederick. *MacGregor's Invasion of Florida, 1817; Together with an Account of His Successors.* Jacksonville: Florida Historical Society, 1928.

Day, Stacey B. *Edward Stevens.* Cincinnati: Cultural and Historical Publications, 1969.

Deagan, Kathleen, and Darcie MacMahon. *Fort Mose: Colonial America's Black Fortress of Freedom.* Gainesville: University Press of Florida, 1995.

DeConde, Alexander. *The Quasi-War: The Politics and Diplomacy of the Undeclared War with France, 1797–1801.* New York: Charles Scribner's Sons, 1966.

Denevan, Wm. M. "The Pristine Myth: The Landscape of the Americas in 1492." *Annals of the Association of American Geographers*, Vol. 82, pp. 369–85.

De Schweinitz, Karl, Jr. *The Rise and Fall of British India: Imperialism as Inequality.* London and New York: Methuen, 1983.

Devine, T. M. *Clanship to Crofter's War: The Social Transformation of the Scottish Highlands.* Manchester, Eng.: Manchester University Press, 1994.

DeVoto, Bernard. *The Course of Empire.* Cambridge, Mass.: Riverside, 1952.

DeWitt, John. "Journal of John Sevier." *Tennessee Historical Magazine* 5, no. 3 (1919).

Dobyns, Henry F. *Their Number Became Thinned: Native American Population Dynamics in Eastern North America.* Knoxville: University of Tennessee Press, 1991 ed.

Dodd, E. Merrill. *American Business Corporations Until 1860.* Cambridge: Harvard University Press, 1954.

Doolittle, William E. *Cultivated Landscapes of Native North America*. New York: Oxford University Press, 2002.

Dowd, Gregory Evans. *A Spirited Resistance*. Baltimore: Johns Hopkins University Press, 1992.

Doyle, David Noel. *Ireland, Irishmen, and Revolutionary America, 1760–1820*. Dublin: Mercier, 1981.

Drinnon, Richard. *Facing West: The Metaphysics of Indian-Hating and Empire Building*. New York: Meridian, 1980.

Dunn, J. P. *Indiana: A Redemption from Slavery*. Boston: Houghton Mifflin, 1905.

Dunn, Richard S. "Black Society in the Chesapeake, 1776–1810." In Ira Berlin and Ronald Hoffman, eds., *Slavery and Freedom in the Age of the American Revolution*. Urbana: University of Illinois Press, 1986.

Dupuy, Alex. *Haiti in the World Economy: Class, Race, and Underdevelopment Since 1700*. Boulder, Co.: Westview Press, 1988.

Edwards, Michael M. *The Growth of the British Cotton Trade, 1780–1815*. New York: Augustus M. Kelley, 1967.

Egerton, Douglas R. *Gabriel's Rebellion*. Chapel Hill: University of North Carolina Press, 1993.

Egnal, Marc. *A Mighty Empire: Origins of the American Revolution*. Ithaca: Cornell University Press, 1988.

Elkins, Stanley, and Eric McKitrick. *The Age of Federalism: The Early American Republic, 1788–1800*. New York: Oxford University Press, 1993.

Elliott, John Carroll, and Ellen Gale Hammett. *Charged with Treason, Jury Verdict: Not Guilty*. Parsons, W. Va.: McClain, 1986.

Ellis, Joseph J. *American Sphinx: The Character of Thomas Jefferson*. New York: Vintage, 1998.

Encyclopaedia Britannica. 11th ed. New York: Encyclopaedia Britannica Company, 1911.

Everett, Diane. *The Texas Cherokees*. Norman: University of Oklahoma Press, 1990.

Fabel, Robin F., and Robert Rea. *The Economy of British West Florida, 1763–1781*. Tuscaloosa: University of Alabama Press, 1988.

Fairbanks, Charles H. "The Kingsley Slave Cabins in Duval County, Florida." *Conference on Historical Archaeology Papers 1972*, no. 7 (1974).

Farquhar, Thomas M. *The History of the Bowles Family*. Manuscript available in the Library of Congress.

Fay, Bernard. *The Revolutionary Spirit in France and America*. New York: Cooper Square, 1966.

Faye, Stanley. "Privateersmen of the Gulf and Their Prizes." *Louisiana Historical Quarterly* 22, no. 4 (Oct. 1939).

Fehrenbacher, Don E. *Slavery, Law, and Politics: The Dred Scott Case in Historical Perspective*. New York: Oxford University Press, 1981.

Ferling, John. *John Adams: A Life*. Knoxville: University of Tennessee Press, 1992.

Filson, John. *The Discovery and Settlement of Kentucke*. Ann Arbor: University Microfilms, 1966.

Finkelman, Paul. "Jefferson and Slavery, Treason Against the Hopes of the World." In Peter S. Onuf, ed., *Jeffersonian Legacies*. Charlottesville: University Press of Virginia, 1993.

————. *Slavery and the Founders: Race and Liberty in the Age of Jefferson.* Armonk, N.Y.: Sharpe, 1996.

————. "Slavery and the Northwest Ordinance: A Study in Ambiguity." In Ralph D. Gray and Michael A. Morrison, eds., *New Perspectives on the Early Republic.* Urbana: University of Illinois Press, 1994.

Fischer, David H. *Albion's Seed: Four British Folkways in America.* New York: Oxford University Press, 1989.

Fitzpatrick, J. C., ed. *The Diaries of George Washington, 1748–1799.* Boston: Houghton Mifflin, 1925.

Fleming, John. *Robert Adam and His Circle: In Edinburgh and Rome.* London: John Murray, 1962.

Flexner, James T. *George Washington and the New Nation, 1783–1793.* Vol. 3. Boston: Little, Brown, 1970.

————. *George Washington: Anguish and Farewell, 1793–1799.* Vol. 4. Boston: Little, Brown, 1972.

————. *George Washington: The Forge of Experience, 1732–1775.* Vol. 1. Boston: Little, Brown, 1965.

————. *Washington: The Indispensable Man.* New York: Signet, 1984.

————. *The Young Hamilton: A Biography.* Boston: Little, Brown, 1978.

Fliegelman, Jay. *Prodigals and Pilgrims: The American Revolution Against Patriarchal Authority, 1750–1800.* Cambridge and New York: Cambridge University Press, 1982.

Flores, Dan, ed. *Jefferson and Southwestern Exploration: The Freeman and Custis Accounts of the Red River Expedition of 1806.* Norman: University of Oklahoma Press, 1984.

Flound, Roderick, and Donald McCloskey, eds. *The Economic History of Britain Since 1700,* Vol. 1, *1700–1860.* 2d ed. Cambridge: Cambridge University Press, 1994.

Fogel, Robert W. *Without Consent or Contract: The Rise and Fall of American Slavery.* New York: Norton, 1989.

Forbes, James Grant. *Sketches, Historical and Topographical, of the Floridas; More Particularly of East Florida.* New York: C. S. Van Winkle, 1821.

Forbes, John. "A Journal of John Forbes, May, 1803, the Seizure of William Augustus Bowles." *Florida Historical Quarterly* (April 1931).

Formwalt, Lee. "Benjamin Henry Latrobe and the Revival of the Gallatin Plan of 1808." *Pennsylvania History* 48, no. 2 (1981).

Fox, Dixon Ryan. *The Decline of Aristocracy in the Politics of New York.* New York: AMS, 1976.

Fox-Genovese, Elizabeth, and Eugene D. Genovese. *Fruits of Merchant Capital: Slavery and Bourgeois Property in the Rise and Expansion of Capitalism.* New York: Oxford University Press, 1983.

Freehling, William W. "The Founding Fathers and Slavery." *American Historical Review* 77 (1972), pp. 81–93. Rev. as "Founding Fathers, Conditional Antislavery, and the Nonradicalism of the American Revolution." In Freehling, *The Reintegration of American History.* New York: Oxford University Press, 1994.

————. *The Road to Disunion: Secessionists at Bay, 1776–1854.* New York: Oxford University Press, 1990.

Freeman, Joanne B. "Dueling as Politics: Reinterpreting the Burr-Hamilton Duel." *William and Mary Quarterly* 53 (April 1996).

Friedenberg, Daniel M. *Life, Liberty, and the Pursuit of Land*. Buffalo: Prometheus Books, 1992.

Gallatin, Albert. *Correspondence of Jean Badollet and Albert Gallatin*. Ed. Gayle Thornbrough. Indianapolis: Indiana University Press, 1963; Ind. Hist. Soc. Pubs., Vol. 22.

———. *The Papers of Albert Gallatin*. Ed. Carl E. Prince and Helene W. Fineman. Philadelphia: Historic Publications, 1969, 46 reels of microfilm, with *Guide* by Carl E. Prince, 1970.

———. *Selected Writings*. Ed. James E. Ferguson. Indianapolis: Bobbs-Merrill, 1967.

———. "Synopsis." *Proceedings of the American Antiquarian Society*, Vol. 2, 1838.

———. *The Works of Albert Gallatin*. Ed. Henry Adams. 3 vols. Philadelphia: Lippincott, 1879; rpt. New York: New York Antiquarian Society, 1960.

Gambill-Bowles, Mary Anna. *Bowles History and Related Families*. Ann Arbor: Edward Bros., 1959.

Gamble, Thomas. *Savannah Duels and Duellists, 1733–1877*. Savannah, Ga.: Review, 1923.

Garraty, John, ed. *Quarrels That Have Shaped the Constitution*. New York: Harper & Row, 1962.

Geinapp, William E. *The Origins of the Republican Party*. New York: Oxford University Press, 1987.

Gibson, Arrell M. *The Chickasaws*. Norman: University of Oklahoma Press, 1971.

Gilbert, Bill. *God Gave Us This Country: Tekamthi and the First American Civil War*. New York: Doubleday, 1989.

Girouard, Mark. *The Return to Camelot: Chivalry and the English Gentleman*. New Haven: Yale University Press, 1981.

Goetzmann, William H., and Glyndwr Williams. *The Atlas of North American Exploration: From the Norse Voyages to the Race to the Pole*. New York: Prentice-Hall, 1992.

Govan, Thomas Payne. *Nicholas Biddle: Nationalist and Public Banker, 1786–1844*. Chicago: University of Chicago Press, 1959.

Graff, Mary B. *Mandarin on the St. Johns*. Gainesville: University of Florida Press, 1953.

Grant, C. L., ed. *Letters, Journals, and Writings of Benjamin Hawkins*, Vol. 2, 1802–1816. Savannah, Ga.: Beehive, 1980.

Gray, Lewis Cecil. *History of Agriculture in the Southern United States to 1860*. 2 vols. Gloucester, Mass.: Peter Smith reprint, 1958.

Green, John C. *American Science in the Age of Jefferson*. Ames: Iowa State University Press, 1984.

Green, Michael D. *The Politics of Indian Removal: Creek Government and Society in Crisis*. Lincoln and London: University of Nebraska Press, 1982.

Green, Thomas M. *The Spanish Conspiracy*. Cincinnati, 1891.

Gregory, Jack, and Rennard Strickland. *Sam Houston with the Cherokees, 1829–1833*. Norman: University of Oklahoma Press, 1996.

Griffith, Benjamin W., Jr. *McIntosh and Weatherford, Creek Indian Leaders*. Tuscaloosa: University of Alabama Press, 1988.

Griswold, A. Whitney. *Farming and Democracy*. New York: Harcourt, Brace, 1948.

Griswold, Ralph E., and Frederick Doveton Nichols. *Thomas Jefferson: Landscape Architect*. Charlottesville: University Press of Virginia, 1978.

Gronet, Richard W. "The United States and the Invasion of Texas." *Americas* 25 (1969), pp. 281–306.

Gronowicz, Anthony. *Race and Class Politics in New York City Before the Civil War*. Boston: Northeastern University Press, 1998.

Hamilton, Alexander. *The Papers of Alexander Hamilton*, Vol. 25. Ed. Harold C. Syrett. New York: Columbia University Press, 1977. [*Hamilton Papers*]

Hamilton, Allan McLane. *The Intimate Life of Alexander Hamilton*. New York: Charles Scribner's Sons, 1910.

Hamlin, Talbot. *Benjamin Henry Latrobe*. New York: Oxford University Press, 1955.

Hartridge, Walter C., ed. *The Letters of Don Juan McQueen to His Family*. Columbia: Bostick & Thornley, 1943.

Hawes, Lilla M., ed. *Lachlan McIntosh Papers in the University of Georgia Libraries*. Athens: University of Georgia Press, 1968.

Hay, Robert. "The Pillorying of Albert Gallatin." *Western Pennsylvania Historical Magazine* 48, no. 3 (1982).

Hay, Thomas, and M. R. Werner. *The Admirable Trumpeter: A Biography of General James Wilkinson*. Garden City, N.Y.: Doubleday, Doran, 1941.

Helms, Douglas. "Soil and Southern History." *Agricultural History* 74 (Fall 2000), pp. 723–58.

Hirschfeld, Fritz. *George Washington and Slavery: A Documentary Portrayal*. Columbia: University of Missouri Press, 1997.

Holmes, Jack D. L. "The Abortive Slave Revolt at Pointe Coupée, Louisiana, 1795." *Louisiana History* 40 (1970).

———. *Gayoso: The Life of a Spanish Governor in the Mississippi Valley, 1789–1799*. Baton Rouge: Louisiana State University Press, 1965.

Holton, Woody. *Forced Founders: Indians, Debtors, Slaves, and the Making of the American Revolution in Virginia*. Chapel Hill: University of North Carolina Press, 1999.

———. "Rebel Against Rebel: Enslaved Virginians and the Coming of the American Revolution." *Virginia Magazine of History and Biography* 105 (1997), pp. 157–92.

Horgan, Paul. *Great River: The Rio Grande in North American History*. New York: Holt, Rinehart & Winston, 1954.

Hudson, Charles. *The Juan Pardo Expeditions: Explorations of the Carolinas and Tennessee, 1566–1568*. Washington: Smithsonian Institution, 1990.

———. *Knights of Spain, Warriors of the Sun: Hernando de Soto and the South's Ancient Chiefdoms*. Athens: University of Georgia Press, 1997.

———. *The Southeastern Indians*. Knoxville: University of Tennessee Press, 1976.

Hudson, Charles, and Carmen Chaves Tresser. *The Forgotten Centuries: Indians and Europeans in the American South, 1521–1704*. Athens: University of Georgia Press, 1994.

Hudson, Joyce Rockwood. *Looking for de Soto: A Search Through the South for the Spaniard's Trail*. Athens: University of Georgia Press, 1993.

Hunt, Alfred N. *Haiti's Influence on Antebellum America: Slumbering Volcano in the Caribbean*. Baton Rouge and London: Louisiana State University Press, 1988.

Hunter, George. *The Western Journals of Dr. George Hunter*. Ed. J. F. McDermott. *Transactions of the American Philosophical Society*, new series 53, pt. 4 (1963).

Huston, James L. "A Political Response to Industrialism: The Republican Embrace of Protectionist Labor Doctrines." *Journal of American History* 70 (Oct. 1983), pp. 35–57.

Imlay, Gilbert. *Topographical Description of the Western Territory of North America*. New York: Johnson Reprint, 1968.

Indian Papers, Vol. 1, 1835, Archives, Texas State Library.

Ingersoll, Thomas N. *Mammon and Manon in Early New Orleans: The First Slave Society in the Deep South, 1718–1819*. Knoxville: University of Tennessee Press, 1999.

Ingram, Augustus E. "Fulwar Skipwith." *American Foreign Service Journal* 12 (1935), pp. 320–21, 356–64.

Insh, G. P. *Scottish Colonial Schemes, 1620–1686*. Glasgow: Maclehose, Jackson, 1922.

Ireland, Robert M. *The Kentucky State Constitution: A Reference Guide*. Westport, Conn.: Greenwood Press, 1999.

Isaac, Rhys. *The Transformation of Virginia, 1740–1790*. Chapel Hill: University of North Carolina Press, 1982.

Jackson, Donald. *Thomas Jefferson and the Stony Mountains: Exploring the West from Monticello*. Urbana: University of Illinois Press, 1981.

———, ed. *Letters of the Lewis and Clark Expedition*. Urbana: University of Illinois Press, 1978.

Jackson, Harvey H. *Lachlan McIntosh and the Politics of Revolutionary Georgia*. Athens: University of Georgia Press, 1979.

Jacobs, James Ripley. *Tarnished Warrior: Major-General James Wilkinson*. New York: Macmillan, 1938.

Jacobs, Wilbur. *Dispossessing the American Indian*. Norman: University of Oklahoma Press, 1972.

James, D. Clayton. *Antebellum Natchez*. Baton Rouge: Louisiana State University Press, 1968.

James, James A. *The Life of George Rogers Clark*. New York: AMS reprint edition, 1970.

Jay, John. *The Correspondence and Public Papers of John Jay, 1763–1826*. Ed. Henry P. Johnston. New York: Da Capo, 1971.

Jefferson, Thomas. "Notes on the State of Virginia." In *The Complete Jefferson*. Ed. Saul K. Padover, New York: Duell, Sloan & Pearce, 1943.

———. *The Thomas Jefferson Papers*. Ed. Julian Boyd. Princeton: Princeton University Press, 1961.

———. *Thomas Jefferson, Writings*. New York: Library of America, 1984. [Lib. of Am. Ed.]

———. "Writings." *Literary Classics of the United States*. New York: Viking, 1984.

———. *Writings*. Ed. A. A. Lipscomb and A. E. Bergh. Washington: Thomas Jefferson Memorial Association, 1903–4. [Memorial Ed.]

———. *Writings of Thomas Jefferson*. Ed. Paul Leicester Ford. New York: Putnam's, 1892–99. [*Writings*, Ford]

———. *Writings of Thomas Jefferson.* Ed. Saul K. Padover. Norwalk, Conn.: Easton, 1967.

Jennings, Francis. *The Founders of America: From the Earliest Migration to the Present.* New York: Norton, 1993.

———. *The Invasion of America: Indians, Colonialism, and the Cant of Conquest.* New York: Norton, 1975.

Jennings, Jesse. "Nutt's Trip to the Chickasaw Country." *Journal of Mississippi History* 9 (1947).

———, ed. *Ancient North Americans.* New York: Freeman, 1983.

Jensen, Merrill. *The Articles of Confederation: An Interpretation of the Social-Constitutional History of the American Revolution, 1774–1781.* Madison: University of Wisconsin Press, 1940.

John, Elizabeth A. H. *Storms Brewed in Other Men's Worlds.* Lincoln: University of Nebraska Press, 1975.

Johnson, Phil Brian, and Robert Kim Stevens. "Impossible Job, Impossible Man!: Thomas Sumter, Jr., and Diplomatic Relations Between the United States and the Portuguese Court in Brazil, 1809–1821." In T. Ray Shurbutt, ed., *United States–Latin American Relations.* Tuscaloosa: University of Alabama Press, 1991.

Jones, Alfred E. "The Real Author of the Authentic Memoirs of W. A. Bowles." *Maryland Historical Magazine* (Dec. 1923).

Jones, Howard. *Mutiny on the Amistad.* Rev. ed. New York: Oxford University Press, 1987.

Jordan, Winthrop. *White over Black: American Attitudes Toward the Negro, 1550–1812.* Chapel Hill: University of North Carolina Press, 1968.

Josephy, Alvin M., Jr. *America in 1492: The World of the Indian Peoples Before the Arrival of Columbus.* New York: Vintage Books, 1993.

Kee, Robert. *The Most Distressful Country.* New York: Penguin, 1972.

Keller, Christian B. "Philanthropy Betrayed: Thomas Jefferson, the Louisiana Purchase, and the Origins of Federal Indian Removal Policy." *Proceedings of the American Philosophical Society* 144 (June 2000), p. 39 ff.

Keller, William. *The Nation's Advocate: Henry Marie Brackenridge and Young America.* Pittsburgh: University of Pittsburgh Press, 1956.

Kelsay, Isabel Thompson. *Joseph Brant, 1743–1807: Man of Two Worlds.* Syracuse: Syracuse University Press, 1984.

Kemble, Frances Anne. *Journal of a Residence on a Georgian Plantation in 1838–1839.* Athens: University of Georgia Press, 1984.

Kendall, John S. "Fulwar Skipwith." *Louisiana Historical Quarterly* 17 (Jan. 1935), pp. 88–90.

Kenin, Richard, and Justin Wintle, eds. *The Dictionary of Biographical Quotation.* New York: Knopf, 1978.

Kennedy, Roger G. *Architecture, Men, Women, and Money.* New York: Random House, 1985.

———. *Burr, Hamilton, and Jefferson: A Study in Character.* New York: Oxford University Press, 2000.

———. *Greek Revival America.* New York: Stewart, Tabori & Chang, 1989.

————. *Hidden Cities: The Discovery and Loss of Ancient American Civilization.* New York: Free Press, 1994.

————. "Jefferson and the Indians." *Winterthur Portfolio* 27, nos. 2/3 (Summer/Autumn 1992).

————. *Orders from France: The Americans and French in a Revolutionary World.* Philadelphia: University of Pennsylvania Press, 1990.

————. *Rediscovering America; Journeys Through Our Forgotten Past.* Boston: Houghton Mifflin, 1990.

Kerber, Linda K. *Federalists in Dissent: Imagery and Ideology in Jeffersonian America.* Ithaca: Cornell University Press, 1970.

Ketcham, Ralph. *James Madison: A Biography.* Charlottesville: University Press of Virginia, 1990.

Ketchum, Richard. *The World of George Washington.* New York: American Heritage, 1974.

Kimball, Fiske. "A Landscape Garden on the James in 1793." *Beginnings of Landscape Gardening* 7 (July 1917).

————. *Thomas Jefferson, Architect.* New York: Da Capo, 1968.

Kimball, Marie. *Jefferson: The Scene of Europe, 1784 to 1789.* New York: Coward-McCann, 1950.

————. *Jefferson: War and Peace, 1776 to 1784.* New York: Coward-McCann, 1947.

Kirk, Russell. *John Randolph of Roanoke.* Indianapolis: Liberty, 1951.

Knepper, George W. *Ohio and Its People.* Kent, Ohio: Kent State University Press, 1989.

Knight, Franklin. "The Haitian Revolution." *American Historical Review* 105 (Feb. 2000).

Kohn, Richard H. *Eagle and Sword: The Federalists and the Creation of the Military Establishment in America, 1783–1802.* New York: The Free Press, 1975.

Kolchin, Peter. *American Slavery, 1619–1877.* New York: Hill & Wang, 1993.

Kulikoff, Allan. "The American Revolution, Capitalism, and the Formation of the Yeoman Classes." In Alfred F. Young, ed., *Beyond the American Revolution: Explorations in the History of American Radicalism.* DeKalb: Northern Illinois University Press, 1993.

————. *From British Peasants to Colonial American Farmers.* Chapel Hill: University of North Carolia Press, 2000.

Lachicotte, Alberta Morrell. *Georgetown Rice Plantations.* Georgetown, S.C.: Georgetown County Historical Society, 1993.

Lancaster, Clay. *Vestiges of the Venerable City: A Chronicle of Lexington, Kentucky.* Lexington: Lexington–Fayette County Historic Commission, 1978.

Landers, Jane. "Black-Indian Interaction in Spanish Florida." *Colonial Latin American Historical Review* 2, no. 2 (Spring 1993).

————. *Fort Mose: Gracia Real de Santa Teresa de Mose, a Free Black Town in Spanish Colonial Florida.* St. Augustine: St. Augustine Historical Society, 1992.

Lane, Mills. *The People of Georgia.* Savannah: Beehive Press, 1975.

Langford, Paul. *A Polite and Commercial People.* New York and Oxford: Oxford University Press, 1989.

Langhorne, Elizabeth, K. E. Lay, and W. D. Rieley. *A Virginia Family and Its Plantation Houses.* Charlottesville: University Press of Virginia, 1987.

Latrobe, Benjamin Henry. *The Correspondence and Miscellaneous Papers of Benjamin Henry Latrobe.* 3 vols. New Haven: Yale University Press and Maryland Historical Society, 1984–88.

La Vere, David L. "Barr, Davenport, Murphy, and Smith: Traders on the Louisiana-Texas Border." Master's thesis, Northwestern State University of Louisiana, 1989.

———. *The Caddo Chiefdoms: Caddo Economics and Politics, 1700–1835.* Lincoln and London: University of Nebraska Press, 1998.

Leech, D.D.T. *History of the Post Office Department, 1789–1879.* Washington: Judd & Detweiler, 1879.

Leibiger, Stuart. "Thomas Jefferson and the Missouri Crisis: An Alternative Interpretation." *Journal of the Early Republic* 17 (1997), pp. 121–30.

Levy, Leonard W. *Jefferson and Civil Liberties: The Darker Side.* Chicago: Ivan R. Dee, 1989.

Lewis, Anthony Marc. "Jefferson and Virginia's Pioneers, 1774–1781." *Mississippi Valley Historical Review* 34, no. 4 (March 1948).

Lewis, James E., Jr. *American Union and the Problem of Neighborhood: The United States and the Collapse of the Spanish Empire, 1783–1829.* Chapel Hill: University of North Carolina Press, 1998.

Lewis, Jan. "Happiness." In Jack P. Greene and J. R. Pole, eds., *The Blackwell Encyclopedia of the American Revolution.* Cambridge, Mass.: Blackwell Reference, 1991.

Lewis, Thomas A. *For King and Country.* New York: HarperCollins, 1993.

Lincoln, Abraham. *Speeches and Writings, 1832–1858.* New York: Library of America, 1989.

Littlefield, Daniel C. "John Jay, the Revolutionary Generation, and Slavery." *New York History* 81 (April 2000), pp. 157–88.

Livermore, Shaw. *Early American Land Companies: Their Influence on Corporate Development.* New York: The Commonwealth Fund; London: H. Milford, Oxford University Press, 1939.

Lockridge, Kenneth A. *On the Sources of Patriarchal Rage.* New York: New York University Press, 1992.

Lodge, Henry Cabot. *Alexander Hamilton.* New York: Chelsea House, 1980.

Logan, Marie. *Mississippi-Louisiana Border Country: A History of Rodney, Miss., St. Joseph, La., and Environs.* Baton Rouge: Claitor's, 1970.

Lomask, Milton. *Aaron Burr: The Conspiracy and the Years of Exile.* New York: Farrar, Straus & Giroux, 1979, 1982.

———. *Aaron Burr: The Years from Princeton to Vice President.* New York: Farrar, Straus & Giroux, 1979.

Loomis, Noel M., and Abraham P. Nasatir. *Pedro Vial and the Roads to Santa Fe.* Norman: University of Oklahoma Press, 1967.

Lynch, William O. "The Westward Flow of Southern Colonists Before 1861." *Journal of Southern History* 9 (August 1943), p. 303 ff.

Lynd, Staughton. *Class Conflict, Slavery, and the United States Constitution.* Indianapolis: Bobbs-Merrill, 1968.

McCaleb, Walter Flavius. *The Aaron Burr Conspiracy* and *A New Light on Aaron Burr*. New York: Argosy-Antiquarian, 1966.

McCloughlin, William G. "Thomas Jefferson and the Beginning of Cherokee Nationalism, 1806 to 1809." *William and Mary Quarterly* 32 (1975), pp. 547–80.

McColley, Robert. *Slavery and Jeffersonian Virginia*. Urbana: University of Illinois Press, 1973.

McCoy, Drew R. *The Elusive Republic: Political Economy in Jeffersonian America*. Chapel Hill: University of North Carolina Press, 1980.

———. *The Last of the Fathers: James Madison and the Republican Legacy*. New York: Cambridge University Press, 1989.

McCusker, John J. *How Much Is That in Real Money?* Worcester, Mass.: American Antiquarian Society, 1991.

McCusker, John J., with Russell R. Menard. *Economy of British America, 1607–1789*. Chapel Hill: University of North Carolina Press, 1985.

McDermott, John Francis, ed. *The French in the Mississippi Valley*. Urbana: University of Illinois Press, 1965.

———. *The Spanish in the Mississippi Valley, 1762–1804*. Urbana: University of Illinois Press, 1974.

McDonald, Forrest, and Grady McWhiney. "The South from Self-Sufficiency to Peonage: An Interpretation." *American Historical Review* 85 (Dec. 1980), p. 1095 ff.

McFaul, John. "Expediency vs. Morality: Jacksonian Politics and Slavery." *Journal of American History* 62, no. 1 (June 1975).

Machor, James L. *Pastoral Cities: Urban Ideals and the Symbolic Landscape of America*. Madison: University of Wisconsin Press, 1987.

McIntosh, Lachlan. *The Papers of Lachlan McIntosh, 1774–1779*. Ed. Lilla M. Hawes. Collections of the Georgia Historical Society, Vol. 12 (1957).

McKay, A. G. *Houses, Villas, and Palaces in the Roman World*. Ithaca: Cornell University Press, 1975.

McLaughlin, Jack. *Jefferson and Monticello: The Biography of a Builder*. New York: Henry Holt, 1988.

McManus, Edgar J. *A History of Negro Slavery in New York*. Syracuse: Syracuse University Press, 1966.

McNeal, R. A., ed. *Nicholas Biddle in Greece: The Journals and Letters of 1806*. University Park: Pennsylvania State University Press, 1993.

McPherson, James M. *Abraham Lincoln and the Second American Revolution*. New York: Oxford University Press, 1990.

———. *Battle Cry of Freedom: The Civil War Era*. New York: Ballantine Books, 1988.

Madison, James. *Papers*. Chicago: University of Chicago Press, [1962]–1991. [*Madison Papers*]

———. *Presidential Papers*. Ed. John C. A. Stagg, Jeanne Kerr Cross, and Susan Holbrook Perdue. 4 vols. to date. Charlottesville: University Press of Virginia, 1984 onward.

Mahon, John K. *History of the Second Seminole War, 1835–1842*. Rev. ed. Gainesville: University Press of Florida, 1992.

Malone, Dumas. *Jefferson and the Ordeal of Liberty*. Vol. 3 of *Jefferson and His Time*. Boston: Little, Brown, 1962.

———. *Jefferson and the Rights of Man*. Vol. 2 of *Jefferson and His Time*. Boston: Little, Brown, 1951.

———. *Jefferson the President: First Term, 1801–1805*. Vol. 4 of *Jefferson and His Time*. Boston: Little, Brown 1970.

———. *Jefferson the President: Second Term, 1805–1809*. Vol. 5 of *Jefferson and His Time*. Boston: Little, Brown, 1974.

———. *Jefferson the Virginian*. Vol. 1 of *Jefferson and His Time*. Boston: Little, Brown, 1948.

———. *The Sage of Monticello*. Vol. 6 of *Jefferson and His Time*. Boston: Little, Brown, 1981.

Mannix, Richard. "Albert Gallatin and the Movement for Peace with Mexico." *Social Studies* 60, no. 7 (1969).

Marambaud, Pierre. *William Byrd of Westover, 1674–1744*. Charlottesville: University Press of Virginia, 1971.

Marsh, George Perkins. *Man and Nature*. Cambridge: Harvard University Press reprint, 2000.

Martin, Peter. *The Pleasure Gardens of Virginia: From Jamestown to Jefferson*. Princeton: Princeton University Press, 1991.

Marx, Leo. *The Machine in the Garden*. New York: Oxford University Press, 1964.

Masterson, William H. *William Blount*. Baton Rouge: Louisiana State University Press, 1954.

Matson, Cathy D., and Peter S. Onuf. *A Union of Interests: Political and Economic Thought in Revolutionary America*. Lawrence: University Press of Kansas, 1990.

Matthews, Richard K. *The Radical Politics of Thomas Jefferson: A Revisionist View*. Lawrence: University Press of Kansas, 1984.

Mayer, David N. *The Constitutional Thought of Thomas Jefferson*. Charlottesville: University Press of Virginia, 1994.

Mayo, Bernard, ed. *Jefferson Himself: The Personal Narrative of a Many-Sided American*. Charlottesville: University Press of Virginia, 1942.

Mayo, Robert. *Political Sketches of Eight Years in Washington*. Baltimore: Fielding Lucas, Jr., 1839.

Meinig, D. W. *The Shaping of America*, Vol. 2, *Continental America, 1800–1867*. New Haven: Yale University Press, 1993.

Merk, Frederick. *History of the Westward Movement*. New York: Knopf, 1980.

———. *Slavery and the Annexation of Texas*. New York: Knopf, 1972.

Meyer, Duane. *The Highland Scots of North Carolina, 1732–1776*. Chapel Hill: University of North Carolina Press, 1961.

Middleton, Arthur Pierce. *Tobacco Coast: A Maritime History of Chesapeake Bay in the Colonial Era*. Baltimore and London: Johns Hopkins University Press and Maryland State Archive, 1984.

Milanich, Jerald T. *Florida Indians and the Invasion from Europe*. Gainesville: University Press of Florida, 1995.

Miller, David H. *Secret Statutes of the United States*. Washington: GPO, 1918.

Miller, John Chester. *The Wolf by the Ears*. New York: Macmillan, 1977.

Miller, Kerby. *Emigrants and Exiles: Ireland and the Irish Exodus to North America*. New York: Oxford University Press, 1985.

Monette, John Wesley. *History of the Discovery and Settlement of the Misissippi Valley.* New York, 1846.

Moore, John Hebron. *Agriculture in Ante-bellum Mississippi.* New York: Octagon Books 1971, originally published 1958.

Morgan, Edmund S. *The Meaning of Independence: John Adams, Thomas Jefferson, and George Washington.* New York: Norton, 1978.

Morris, Richard B., ed. *Alexander Hamilton and the Founding of the Nation.* New York: Dial, 1957.

Moseley, Edward H. "The United States and Mexico, 1810–1850." In T. Ray Shurbutt, ed., *United States–Latin American Relations, 1800–1850.* Tuscaloosa: University of Alabama Press, 1991.

Murdoch, Richard K. *The Georgia-Florida Frontier, 1793–1796: Spanish Reaction to French Intrigue and American Designs.* Berkeley: University of California Press, 1951.

Murrin, John M., with Gary J. Kornbluth. "The Jeffersonian Triumph and American Exceptionalism," *Journal of the Early American Republic* 20, no. 1 (Spring 2000), p. 1 ff.

———. "The Making and Unmaking of an American Ruling Class." In Alfred F. Young, ed., *Beyond the American Revolution: Explorations in the History of American Radicalism.* DeKalb: Northern Illinois University Press, 1993.

Myers, Minor, Jr. *Liberty Without Anarchy: A History of the Society of the Cincinnati.* Charlottesville: University Press of Virginia, 1983.

Nash, Gary. *Red, White, and Black: The Peoples of Early America.* Englewood, N. J.: Prentice-Hall, 1974.

Nash, Gary B., and Jean R. Soderlund. *Freedom by Degrees: Emancipation in Pennsylvania and Its Aftermath.* New York: Oxford University Press, 1991.

National Museum of American History and the Foundation for Prussian Cultural Property, Berlin. *Steuben: Secret Aid for the Americans.* Washington: National Museum of American History, 1981–82.

Neuman, Robert. *An Introduction to Louisiana Archaeology.* Baton Rouge: Louisiana State University Press, 1984.

———. *Melanges: An Archaeological Assessment of Coastal Louisiana.* Baton Rouge: Louisiana State University Museum of Geoscience, March 21, 1977.

Nevins, Allan. *The Emergence of Lincoln.* New York: Scribner's, 1950.

The New Handbook of Texas. Austin: Texas State Historical Association, 1996.

Newcomb, Rexford. *Architecture in Old Kentucky.* Urbana: University of Illinois Press, 1953.

Nichols, Roy F. *Advance Agents of American Destiny.* Philadelphia: University of Pennsylvania Press, 1956.

Nolte, Vincent Otto. *Fifty Years in Both Hemispheres.* New York: Redfield, 1854.

North, Douglass C. *The Economic Growth of the United States, 1790–1860.* New York: Norton, 1966.

Oakes, James. *The Ruling Race: A History of American Slaveholders.* New York: Knopf, 1982.

———. *Slavery and Freedom: An Interpretation of the Old South.* New York: Vintage Books, 1991.

Onuf, Peter S. *Jefferson's Empire: The Language of American Nationhood.* Charlottesville and London: University Press of Virginia, 2000.

———, ed. *Jeffersonian Legacies*. Charlottesville: University Press of Virginia, 1993.

Orrmont, Arthur. *Diplomat in Warpaint: Chief Alexander McGillivray of the Creeks*. New York: Abelard-Schuman, 1968.

Osgood, E. S., ed. *The Field Notes of Captain William Clark*. New Haven: Yale University Press, 1964.

Owen, Thomas McAdory. *Annals of Alabama*. Spartanburg, S.C.: Reprint Co., 1988.

Owsley, Frank Lawrence, Jr. *Struggle for the Gulf Borderlands: The Creek War and the Battle of New Orleans, 1812–1815*. Gainesville: University Presses of Florida, 1981.

Owsley, Frank Lawrence, Jr., with Gene A. Smith. *Filibusters and Expansionists: Jeffersonian Manifest Destiny, 1800–1821*. Tuscaloosa: University of Alabama Press, 1997.

Padgett, James A. "The Difficulties of Andrew Jackson in New Orleans, etc." *Louisiana Historical Quarterly* 21, no. 2 (April 1938), p. 367 ff.

———. "The West Florida Revolution of 1810, as Told by the Letters of John Rhea, Fulwar Skipwith, Reuben Kemper, and Others." *Louisiana Historical Quarterly* 21 (Jan. 1938).

Pakenham, Thomas. *The Year of Liberty: The Story of the Great Irish Rebellion of 1798*. New York: Granada, 1982.

Parkman, Francis. *France and England in North America*, Vol. 2, *Count Frontenac and New France Under Louis XIV—A Half Century of Conflict—Montcalm and Wolfe*. New York: Library of America Press, 1983.

———. *LaSalle and the Discovery of the Great West*. New York: Modern Library, 1985.

Parton, James. *The Life and Times of Aaron Burr*, Vol. 2. New York: Chelsea House, 1983.

Patrick, Rembert W. *Florida Fiasco*. Athens: University of Georgia Press, 1954.

Patterson, Richard S., and Richardson Dougall. *The Eagle and the Shield*. Washington: Department of State, 1976.

Pearce, Roy. *The Savages of America: A Study of the Indian and the Idea of Civilization*. Baltimore: Johns Hopkins University Press, 1953.

Peet, Henry J. *Chaumiere Papers Containing Matters of Interest to the Descendants of David Meade, of Nansemond County, Va., Who Died in the Year 1757*. Chicago: Horace O'Donoghue, 1883.

Peter, S.W K. *Private Memoir of Thomas Worthington, Esq*. Cincinnati: Robert Clarke, 1882.

Peterson, Merrill D. *Thomas Jefferson and the New Nation: A Biography*. New York: Oxford University Press, 1970.

Phillips, L. L. "Cotton." In N. W. Simmons, ed., *The Evolution of Crop Plants*. London and New York: Longman, 1976.

Pickens, Buford. "Mr. Jefferson as Visionary Architect." *Journal of the Society of Architectural Historians* 34 (Dec. 1975), p. 257 ff.

Pickett, Albert James. *History of Alabama*. Spartanburg, S.C.: Reprint Co., 1988.

Pike, Zebulon M. *The Expeditions of Zebulon Montgomery Pike . . . During the Years 1805–6–7*. Ed. Elliott Coues. New York: Francis P. Harper, 1895

Pitt, Arthur. "Franklin and the Quaker Movement Against Slavery." *Friends Historical Association Bulletin* 32, no. 1 (Spring 1943).

Pope, John. *The Westward Movement*. Ed. Justin Winsor. Boston: Houghton Mifflin, 1897.

Porter, Kenneth Wiggins. "Negroes and the Seminole War." *Journal of Southern History* 30, no. 4 (Nov. 1964).

Posey, John Thornton. "Rascality Revisited: In Defense of General James Wilkinson." *Filson Club Historical Quarterly* 74 (Fall 2000), pp. 309–52.

Pound, Merritt B. *Benjamin Hawkins, Indian Agent.* Athens: University of Georgia Press, 1951.

Price, Jacob. "Economic Function and the Growth of American Port Towns in the Eighteenth Century." *Perspectives in American History* 8 (1974), pp. 123–88.

Pritchard, Walter. "Selecting a Governor for Louisiana." *Louisiana Historical Quarterly* 31, no. 2 (April 1948), p. 269 ff.

Prussing, Eugene. *The Estate of George Washington, Deceased.* Boston: Little, Brown, 1927.

Randall, E. O. "Washington's Ohio Lands." *Ohio Archaeological and Historical Quarterly* 19 (July 1990).

Randall, Henry S. *The Life of Thomas Jefferson.* Philadelphia: Lippincott, 1865.

Randolph, Sarah North. *The Domestic Life of Thomas Jefferson.* Charlottesville: University Press of Virginia, 1990.

Reeves, Carolyn Keller, ed. *The Choctaw Before Removal.* Jackson: University Press of Mississippi, 1985.

Reiter, Edith. *Marietta and the Northwest Territory.* 9th rpt. Marietta, Ohio: Hyde Bros., 1986.

Remini, Robert V. *Andrew Jackson and the Course of American Democracy, 1833–1845,* Vol. 3. New York: Harper & Row, 1984.

———. *Andrew Jackson and the Course of American Empire, 1767–1821,* Vol. 1. New York: Harper & Row, 1977.

Reps, John W. *The Making of Urban America: A History of City Planning in the United States.* Princeton: Princeton University Press, 1965.

Rice, Otis. *The Allegheny Frontier.* Lexington: University of Kentucky Press, 1970.

Richards, Leonard L. *The Slave Power.* Baton Rouge: Louisiana State University Press, 2000.

Riley, Carroll. *The Frontier People.* Albuquerque: University of New Mexico Press, 1987.

Rivers, Larry Eugene. *Slavery in Florida.* Gainesville: University Press of Florida, 2000.

Rodney, Thomas. "Arthur St. Clair." *Pennsylvania Magazine of History and Biography* 43 (1919).

———. "Cincinatti and Marietta." *Pennsylvania Magazine of History and Biography* 43 (1919).

———. "Natchez." *Pennsylvania Magazine of History and Biography* 44 (1920).

Rogers, George C., Jr. *The History of Georgetown County, South Carolina.* 5th printing. Spartanburg, S.C.: Georgetown County Historical Society, 1995.

Rogin, Paul. *Fathers and Children: Andrew Jackson and the Subjugation of the American Indian.* New York: Vintage, 1975.

Rogow, Arnold A. *A Fatal Friendship: Alexander Hamilton and Aaron Burr.* New York: Hill & Wang, 1998.

Rohrbough, Malcolm J. *The Trans-Appalachian Frontier: People, Societies, and Institutions, 1775–1850.* New York: Oxford University Press, 1978.

Roll, Eric. *A History of Economic Thought*. London and Boston: Faber and Faber, 1938; rev. ed., 1992.

Rorabaugh, W. J. *The Alcoholic Republic: An American Tradition*. New York: Oxford University Press, 1981.

Rowland, Dunbar. *Seventh Annual Report of the Director of the Department of Archives and History of the State of Mississippi*. Nashville, 1909.

Rowland, Dunbar (Mrs.). *Life, Letters, and Papers of William Dunbar*. Jackson: Press of the Mississippi Historical Society, 1930.

Rykwert, Joseph. *On Adam's House in Paradise*. Cambridge: MIT Press, 1981.

Sargent, Winthrop. *Memoirs of the American Academy of Arts and Sciences*, new series 5 (1853).

Sauer, Carl. *Sixteenth-Century North America*. Berkeley: University of California Press, 1971.

Saum, Lewis. *The Fur Trade and the Indian*. Seattle: University of Washington Press, 1965.

Saunt, Claudio. *A New Order of Things: Property, Power, and the Transformation of the Creek Indians, 1733–1816*. Cambridge and New York: Cambridge University Press, 1999.

Savelle, Max. *George Morgan: Colony Builder*. New York: Columbia University Press, 1932.

Scarborough, William K. "Heartland of the Cotton Kingdom." In R. A. McLemore, ed., *A History of Mississippi*, Vol. 1. Jackson: University and College Press of Mississippi, 1973.

Schachner, Nathan. *Aaron Burr: A Biography*. New York: Barnes, 1961.

———. *Alexander Hamilton*. New York: Appleton-Century, 1946.

Schelbert, Leo. "Albert Gallatin, 1761–1899." *Swiss American Historical Society Newsletter* 18, no. 1 (1982).

Schlesinger, Arthur, Jr. *The Age of Jackson*. Boston: Little, Brown, 1947.

Schultz, Christian. *Travels on an Inland Voyage . . . Made in 1807 and 1808*. New York: Isaac Riley, 1810.

Schwarz, Philip J. *Slave Laws in Virginia: Studies in the Legal History of the South*. Athens: University of Georgia Press, 1996.

Sears, Alfred. *Thomas Worthington: Father of Ohio Statehood*. Columbus: Ohio Historical Society, 1958.

Sheehan, Bernard W. *Seeds of Extinction: Jefferson Philanthropy and the American Indian*. New York: Norton, 1973.

Sheldon, Garrett Ward. *The Political Philosophy of Thomas Jefferson*. Baltimore: Johns Hopkins University Press, 1991.

Showalter, Joseph. "The Travels of George Washington." *National Geographic* 61, no. 1 (Jan. 1932).

Simmonds, N. W., ed. *The Evolution of Crop Plants*. London: Longman, 1976.

Simpson, Elizabeth M. *Bluegrass Houses and Their Traditions*. Lexington, Ky.: Transylvania, 1932.

Slaughter, Thomas. *The Whiskey Rebellion*. New York: Oxford University Press, 1986.

Sloan, Herbert E. "The Earth Belongs in Usufruct to the Living." In Peter S. Onuf, ed., *Jeffersonian Legacies*. Charlottesville: University Press of Virginia, 1993.

————. *Principle and Interest: Thomas Jefferson and the Problem of Debt*. New York: Oxford University Press, 1995.

Smith, Henry Nash. *Virgin Land: The American West as Symbol and Myth*. New York: Vintage Books, 1950.

Smith, Jean Edward. *John Marshall: Definer of a Nation*. New York: Holt, 1996.

Smith, Joseph Burkholder. *James Madison's Phony War: The Plot to Steal Florida*. New York: Arbor House, 1983.

Smith, Julia. *Slavery and Plantation Growth in Antebellum Florida, 1821–1860*. Gainesville: University Press of Florida, 1973.

Smith, Page. *John Adams*, Vol. 2, *1784–1826*. Garden City, N.Y.: Doubleday, 1962.

Smith, Richard N. *Patriarch: George Washington and the New American Nation*. Boston: Houghton Mifflin, 1993.

Smith, Thomas. *The Mapping of Ohio*. Kent, Ohio: Kent State University Press, 1977.

"Some Notes on British Intrigue in Kentucky." *Register of the Kentucky State Historical Society* 38 (1940).

Spalding, Phinizy. *Oglethorpe in America*. Athens: University of Georgia Press, 1984.

Sparks, William H. *The Memories of Fifty Years*. Philadelphia: Claxton, Remsen & Haffelinger, 1870.

Sprague, Marshall. *So Vast, So Beautiful a Land: Louisiana and the Purchase*. Boston: Little, Brown, 1974.

Squier, E. G., and E. H. Davis. "Ancient Monuments of the Mississippi Valley." *Smithsonian Contributions to Knowledge* 1 (1848).

Stagg, J. C. *Mr. Madison's War*. Princeton: Princeton University Press, 1983.

Stanley, Samuel. "The End of the Natchez Indians." *History Today* 28 (1978).

Starr, Emmet. *History of the Cherokee Indians and Their Legends and Folklore*. Tulsa: Oklahoma Yesterday, 1979.

Stevens, John A. *Albert Gallatin*. New York: Houghton Mifflin, 1972.

Stilgoe, John R. *Common Landscape of America, 1580 to 1845*. New Haven: Yale University Press, 1982.

Stoddard, Amos. *Sketches, Historical and Descriptive, of Louisiana*. Philadelphia: M. Carey, 1812.

Stone, Lawrence, and Jeanne C. Fawtier Stone. *An Open Elite? England, 1540–1880*. Oxford: Clarendon Press; New York: Oxford University Press, 1984.

Stuart, Reginald C. *The Half-way Pacifist: Thomas Jefferson's View of War*. Toronto: University of Toronto Press, 1978.

Sturdevant, Rick. *Quest for Eden: George Washington's Frontier Land Interests*. Ph.D. dissertation, University of California, Santa Barbara, 1982.

Sullivan, Buddy. *Early Days on the Georgia Tidewater: The Story of McIntosh County and Sapelo*. Darian, Ga.: McIntosh County Board of Commissioners, 1990.

Sword, Wiley. *President Washington's Indian War: The Struggle for the Old Northwest, 1790–1795*. Norman: University of Oklahoma Press, 1985.

Tanner, Helen. *Atlas of the Great Lakes Indian History*. Norman: University of Oklahoma Press, 1987.

Thwaites, Reuben. *Travels and Explorations of the Jesuit Missionaries in New France: The Voyages of Marquette*. Cleveland: Burrows Brothers, 1966.

Trevelyan, George Otto. *The American Revolution*. Ed. Richard P. Morris. New York: David McKay, 1965.

Truettner, William H., ed. *The West as America: Reinterpreting Images of the Frontier, 1820–1920*. Washington: Smithsonian Institution Press, 1991.

Tucker, Robert W., and David C. Hendrickson. *Empire of Liberty: The Statecraft of Thomas Jefferson*. New York: Oxford University Press, 1990.

Turner, Frederick Jackson. *The Frontier in American History*. Ed. Ray Billington. New York: Holt, Rinehart & Winston, 1962.

———. "Western State-Making in the Revolutionary Era II." *American Historical Review* 1, no. 2 (1896).

Tyler, Lyon G. "David Meade." *William and Mary Quarterly* 13 (1905).

U.S. Department of Agriculture. *Soils and Men: Yearbook of Agriculture, 1938*. Washington: Government Printing Office, 1938.

Usner, Daniel H., Jr. "American Indians on the Cotton Frontier: Changing Economic Relations with Citizens and Slaves in the Mississippi Territory." *Journal of American History* 72, no. 2 (Sept. 1985), p. 297 ff.

———. *Indians, Settlers, and Slaves in a Frontier Exchange Economy*. Chapel Hill: University of North Carolina Press, for Institute of Early American History and Culture, Williamsburg, Va., 1990.

Van Every, Dale. *Ark of the Empire: The American Frontier, 1784–1803*. New York: Quill, 1963.

———. *Forth to the Wilderness*. New York: Morrow, 1961.

Viola, Herman. *After Columbus: The Smithsonian Chronicle of North American Indians*. Washington: Smithsonian Institution Press, 1990.

Viola, Herman, and Carolyn Margolis. *Seeds of Change: Five Hundred Years Since Columbus*. Washington: Smithsonian Institution Press, 1991.

Virginia: A Guide to the Old Dominion. Compiled by the Workers of the Writers Program of the Works Project Administration. New York: Oxford University Press, 1941.

Volney, Constantin François de Chasseboeuf, comte de. *A View of the Soil and Climate of the United States of America*. Facsimile of Philadelphia 1804 ed. Ed. George W. White. New York: Hafner, 1968.

Von Hagen, Victor W. *Highway of the Sun*. London: Gollancz, 1956.

Wallace, Anthony F. C. *Jefferson and the Indians: The Tragic Fate of the First Americans*. Cambridge, Mass.: Belknap Press, 1999.

Walters, Raymond, Jr. *Albert Gallatin: Jefferson Financier and Diplomat*. Pittsburgh: University of Pittsburgh Press, 1957.

Wandell, Samuel H., and Meade Minnigerode. *Aaron Burr*. Vol. 2. New York: G. P. Putnam's Sons, 1925.

Ward, Christopher. *The Revolution*. 2 vols. New York: Macmillan, 1952.

Washington, George. *The Diaries of George Washington*. Ed. John Fitzpatrick. Boston: Houghton Mifflin, 1925.

———. *Writings*. Ed. John C. Fitzpatrick. 39 vols. Washington: U.S. Government Printing Office, 1931–65.

Waterman, Thomas T. *The Mansions of Virginia*. Chapel Hill: University of North Carolina Press, 1946.

Webb, Clarence, and Gregory Hiram. *The Caddo Indians of Louisiana*. Baton Rouge: Louisiana Archaeological Survey, Anthropological Study, no. 2, 1986.

Wellman, Paul. *The Indian Wars of the West*. Garden City, N.Y.: Doubleday, 1956.

Wells, Samuel J. "The Evolution of Jeffersonian Indian Policy with the Choctaws of Mississippi, 1800–1830." Master's thesis, University of Southern Mississippi, 1981.

Welty, Eudora. "Place in Fiction." In Welty, *Stories, Essays, and Memoir*. New York: Library of America, 1998.

Weston, Rob N. "Alexander Hamilton and the Abolition of Slavery in New York." *Afro-Americans in New York Life and History* 18 (1994).

Whitaker, Arthur Preston. *The Mississippi Question, 1795–1803*. New York: Appleton-Century, 1934.

White, Shane. *Somewhat More Independent: The End of Slavery in New York City, 1770–1810*. Athens: University of Georgia Press, 1991.

Williams, Eric. *Capitalism and Slavery*. New York: Capricorn Books, 1966.

Williams, Stephen. "Aboriginal Location of the Kadohadacho and Related Tribes." In Ward Goodenough, ed., *Explorations in Cultural Anthropology* (New York: McGraw-Hill, 1965).

———. "19th-Century Perceptions of Cahokia and its Meaning." Paper read at the Cahokia Symposium, Society of American Archaeology Meetings, April 26, 1991.

Wills, Garry. *Cincinnatus: George Washington and the Enlightenment; Images of Power in Early America*. Garden City, N.Y.: Doubleday, 1984.

Wilson, Douglas L. "The American Agricola: Jefferson's Agrarianism and the Classical Tradition." *South Atlantic Quarterly* 80 (1981), pp. 339–54.

Wilson, Ruth Danehower. "The Bulow Plantation, 1821–1835." *Florida Historical Quarterly* 23 (April 1945), pp. 227–40.

Wittkower, Rudolf. "English Neoclassicism and Palladio's 'Quatro Libri.'" In *Palladio and English Palladianism*. London: Thames & Hudson, 1974.

Wolf, Eric R. *Europe and the People Without History*. Berkeley: University of California Press, 1982; rev. ed., 1997.

Wood, Gordon S. *The Creation of the American Republic, 1776–1787*. Chapel Hill: University of North Carolina Press, 1969; New York: Norton, 1972.

———. *The Radicalism of the American Revolution*. New York: Knopf, 1992.

———. "The Trials and Tribulations of Thomas Jefferson." In Peter S. Onuf, ed., *Jeffersonian Legacies*. Charlottesville: University Press of Virginia, 1993.

Wood, Peter, Gregory Waselkov, and M. Thomas Hatley, eds. *Powhatan's Mantle: Indians in the Colonial Southeast*. Lincoln: University of Nebraska Press, 1989.

Wright, Gavin. *Old South, New South: Revolutions in the Southern Economy Since the Civil War*. New York: Basic Books, 1982.

———. *The Political Economy of the Cotton South: Households, Markets, and Wealth in the Nineteenth Century*. New York: Norton, 1978.

Wright, James Leitch. *Creeks and Seminoles*. Lincoln: University of Nebraska Press, 1986.

———. *William Augustus Bowles, Director General of the Creek Nation*. Athens: University of Georgia Press, 1977.

Wright, Louis B. *The Atlantic Frontier: Colonial American Civilization, 1607–1763.* Ithaca: Cornell University Press, 1959.

Young, Alfred F., ed. *Beyond the American Revolution: Explorations in the History of American Radicalism.* DeKalb: Northern Illinois University Press, 1993.

Young, Tommy R. "The United States Army and the Institution of Slavery in Louisiana, 1803–1815." *Louisiana Studies* (1974).

Zelinsky, Wilbur. "The Greek Revival House in Georgia." *Journal of the Society of Architectural Historians* 13, no. 2 (May 1954).

Zuckerman, Michael. "The Power of Blackness: Thomas Jefferson and the Revolution in St. Dominique." In Zuckerman, ed., *Almost Chosen People: Oblique Biographies in the American Grain.* Berkeley: University of California Press, 1993.

Index